The Gender Gap in Psychotherapy

Social Realities and Psychological Processes

The Gender Gap in Psychotherapy

Social Realities and Psychological Processes

EDITED BY

Patricia Perri Rieker

Harvard Medical School and
Dana Farber Cancer Institute
Boston, Massachusetts

AND

Elaine (Hilberman) Carmen

University of North Carolina School of Medicine
Chapel Hill, North Carolina

PLENUM PRESS • NEW YORK AND LONDON

Library of Congress Cataloging in Publication Data

Main entry under title:

The Gender gap in psychotherapy.

Includes bibliographical references and index.
   1. Women—Mental health. 2. Men—Mental health. 3. Sex role. 4. Feminist therapy. 5. Social psychology. I. Rieker, Patricia Perri. II. Carmen, Elaine (Hilberman), date–   . [DNLM: 1. Identification (Psychology). 2. Psychology, Social. 3. Psychotherapy. WM 420 G3255]
RC451.4.W6G46 1984   362.2   84-11511
ISBN 0-306-41657-3

©1984 Plenum Press, New York
A Division of Plenum Publishing Corporation
233 Spring Street, New York, N.Y. 10013

Printed in the United States of America

For Pasquale and Mollie
who taught us to see the world from odd angles

For there is no creature whose
inward being is so strong
that it is not greatly determined
by what lies outside it.

George Eliot
Middlemarch

Contributors

JANET R. ALLISON, PH.D. · Bitterroot Psychological Services, Missoula, Montana 59801

MICHAEL BERGER, PH.D. · Department of Psychology and Family Study Center, Georgia State University, Atlanta, Georgia 30303, and Intramural Training, Atlanta Institute for Family Studies, Atlanta, Georgia 30309

MARLENE (BOSKIND-LODAHL) BOSKIND-WHITE, PH.D. · Gannet Mental Health Section, University Medical Services, Cornell University, Ithaca, New York 14853

ELAINE (HILBERMAN) CARMEN, M.D. · Department of Psychiatry, University of North Carolina School of Medicine, Chapel Hill, North Carolina 27514

VIRGINIA DAVIDSON, M.D. · Department of Psychiatry, Baylor College of Medicine, Houston, Texas 77030. Present address: 4101 Greenbriar, Houston, Texas 77098

NANETTE GARTRELL, M.D. · Department of Psychiatry, Harvard Medical School and Beth Israel Hospital, Boston, Massachusetts 02215

SEYMOUR L. HALLECK, M.D. · Department of Psychiatry, University of North Carolina School of Medicine, Chapel Hill, North Carolina 27514

RACHEL T. HARE-MUSTIN, PH.D. · Counseling and Consulting Psychology, Harvard University, Cambridge, Massachusetts 02138

JUDITH HERMAN, M.D. · Department of Psychiatry, Harvard Medical School, Boston, Massachusetts 02215

LISA HIRSCHMAN, ED.D. · University of California Medical School, San Diego, California 92037

ROSABETH MOSS KANTER, PH.D. · Yale University, New Haven, Connecticut 06500, Harvard Law School, Cambridge, Massachusetts 02138, and Goodmeasure, Inc., Cambridge, Massachusetts 02138

ALEXANDRA G. KAPLAN, PH.D. · Stone Center for Developmental Services and Studies, Wellesley College, Wellesley, Massachusetts 02181

HARRIET E. LERNER, PH.D. · The Menninger Foundation, Topeka, Kansas 66601

ROBERT A. LEWIS, PH.D. · Child Development and Family Studies, Purdue University, West Lafayette, Indiana 47907

SHARON S. MAYES, PH.D. · Divorce Counseling Research Project, Children's Hospital of San Francisco, Department of Psychiatry, San Francisco, California 94118

JEAN BAKER MILLER, M.D. · Department of Psychiatry, Boston University School of Medicine, Boston, Massachusetts 02215

TRUDY MILLS, PH.D. · Department of Sociology, University of Arizona, Tucson, Arizona 85721

JOSEPH H. PLECK, PH.D. · The Wellesley College Center for Research on Women, Wellesley, Massachusetts 02181

PATRICIA PERRI RIEKER, PH.D. · Dana–Farber Cancer Institute and Harvard Medical School, Boston, Massachusetts 02115

NANCY FELIPE RUSSO, PH.D. · Women's Programs, American Psychological Association, Washington, D.C. 20036

ALAN A. STONE, M.D. · Faculty of Law and Faculty of Medicine, Harvard University, Cambridge, Massachusetts 02138

ELIZABETH A. WAITES, PH.D. · 206 South Main St., Ann Arbor, Michigan 48107

Preface

This collection of readings is designed to clarify the relationship between social structures and psychological processes. Our awareness of the need for such a book derives from our extensive experiences in teaching a formal course for mental health professionals on gender and psychotherapy. The material in this anthology emphasizes the clinical implications of the new research and knowledge that has changed our understanding of the psychological development of women and men. Throughout the book, we present ideas that challenge conventional explanations of psychological distress in women and men and suggest alternative conceptualizations of these processes.

As will be evident, our work is informed by and contributes to the growing field of knowledge produced by feminist scholars over the last decade. That this book on gender has more to say about women reflects the existence of a substantial body of research that reconceptualizes women's psychology. The corresponding research on men is still in its formative stages, due in part to the later development of a men's movement. Although many of the chapters focus on women, we have attempted in our discussion to consider the implications for men. We believe that the fundamental processes explored in this book are relevant to the understanding of both women and men.

We recognize that neither men nor women can be seen as a homogeneous group. Categorizing people by gender alone serves to highlight certain common experiences while masking important differences. We know that psychological development and social identities are differentially affected by race, ethnicity, social class, sexual preference, and similar factors. While we have chosen not to focus on the confounding effects of gender with, for example, age, race, ethnicity, or income, we encourage the reader to take account of the way in which these and other factors interact with gender in our daily lives.

It was not our intent to make this a comprehensive book. Rather, we selected articles to illustrate how structures of inequality set into motion psychological processes that affect women and men differently. The material in this book is presented within a framework that integrates sociological and psychological explanations of behavior. Although the articles are sequenced to form a coherent curriculum, each section can be read separately. Thus, the book can be used as a text either for teaching or for self-education. Each section of readings is introduced by a narrative that analyzes how subjective experiences are determined by a wider social reality and discusses the implications of this perspective for psychotherapy.

The perspective implicit in the organization of this book views psychological distress as an emergent process embedded in a cultural context. It provides a framework that identifies and organizes certain sociological concepts—disembeds them from the cultural context, so to speak—concepts that can help mental health professionals understand the nature of social change and its ramifications for individuals. For example, concepts such as socialization, social roles, tokenism, and power are used to explain how social factors shape the development, and sometimes the destruction, of an individual's social identity and psychological well-being.

The sociological imagination that we are advocating enables the therapist to focus on the matrix of social roles and power relationships that affect how people think, feel, and behave, and to disentangle the external realities from the subjective experience of those realities. By asking therapists to acquire a sociological imagination, we are asking them to try another way of gaining insight—another way of interpreting data. The therapist is encouraged to step outside his or her own frame of reference and to see things as *categories* of people see them (e.g., dominants, subordinates, victims, aggressors, privileged, low status, tokens). Making the connection between individual psychological states and social contexts in which identities develop provides the therapist with alternatives for understanding the content and process of therapeutic interactions.

Consider, for example, the therapeutic relationship, which practitioners believe has a major impact on the efficacy of clinical interventions. A psychological interpretation of this relationship focuses on the personality dynamics of the therapist and the patient. This intrapsychic view explains the patient's reactions to the therapist as instances of positive or negative *transference*, the patient's reaction to the psychotherapy process as *regression*, and the therapist's reactions to the patient as *countertransference*. A social interpretation of these same phenomena might center on the relative social positions occupied by the therapist and the patient and their impact on the therapeutic relationship. Defining the therapist–patient relationship as an example of authority relations produces a discussion of the interaction based on the differential distribution of power.

As a psychiatrist/sociologist team, we are convinced that mental health professionals and sociologists have much to say to one another. This is a book about just that—about the relationship of inner life to outer reality in terms of a rapprochement between two fields that, until now, have been "scientifically" studying human behavior by focusing on just one of these aspects. Nonetheless, we continue to be impressed with the power of some psychological theories to exclude the social context altogether. Such explanations have dominated the training of psychiatrists as well as other mental health professionals. But even more problematic, trainees are not taught that there *are* alternative explanations of behavior or that all intellectual perspectives contain implicit value assumptions that affect the therapeutic process. Since the professional identity of most clinicians rests, in part, on the intellectual perspectives acquired during training, there is often considerable resistance to changing them. This book attempts to provide some insight into the disquieting process of change while demonstrating the potential clinical advantages of examining one's own gender values.

Since we have been asking clinicians to examine the values concealed in their theories and practices, we think it is appropriate to make some of our most basic assumptions more explicit:

1. Intrapsychic explanations alone are insufficient for understanding psychological distress.
2. The elimination of sexism from the psychotherapies can only improve outcomes.
3. It is especially important to identify those taken-for-granted gender norms (for example, sex-role stereotypes, homophobia, and patriarchal ideologies) shared by patients and therapists that, if left unexamined, will negatively affect outcomes.
4. All modes of psychotherapy are limited in their ability to change the gender inequality that contributes to psychological distress; inevitably, change of that magnitude requires political action.
5. The myth of value-free psychotherapy is no less pervasive than the myth of value-free sociology—both positions derive from the more general myth of value-free science.
6. The continuous self-monitoring of personal and professional values as they influence clinical performance is hard work; mental health training programs must teach value clarification methods in addition to new knowledge and skills.
7. Although there are differences between male and female therapists that need to be explored further, neither sex nor ideology guarantees one's skill as a clinician.

Finally, as we have said elsewhere, a competent therapist has the ability to stand outside the self, to observe the cognitive–value interaction, and to question her or his values and intellectual framework without paralyzing fear of personal or professional annihilation.

Elaine (Hilberman) Carmen
Patricia Perri Rieker

Chapel Hill, North Carolina and Boston, Massachusetts

Acknowledgments

This book is a natural outcome of our 10-year friendship and collaboration. As is the case with all of our joint efforts, we have contributed equally to this work. Much of what we have come to understand about the interplay between the social and the psychological we have learned from each other. Much of what we have come to understand about the social psychology of women and men we have learned from our patients, our students, and, most of all, from our colleagues whose articles are part of this book. The intellectual risks taken by the contributing authors in applying their innovative thinking to psychological theory, research, and practice influenced our vision of this book.

Our appreciation of the importance of the cultural context is part of the legacy of our ethnic heritage. We grew up in the ghettos of Pittsburgh and New York City, one of us in an Italian-American family and the other in an east European Jewish-American family. Both of our mothers encouraged us to become self-sufficient and to pursue our own interests. As a result, we could not avoid the inevitable conflicts and confrontations that shaped our feminist perspectives.

There are many other people to thank for their help. Among them are Psychiatrists for ERA, for their initial interest in a project to educate psychiatrists about women; Susan Edbril, Donna Frick, Matt Hamabata, and Richard Rieker, for their critical review and editorial comments; Elissa Benedek, Robert Burnham, Anita and Leonard Cottrell, Paul Pedrazas, Bradford H. Patterson, and Martin Tannenbaum, for their encouragement, food, and humor; Hilary Evans, our discerning editor at Plenum; Elaine Carmen's son, Joshua Hilberman, for being our constant male companion and comic relief; Elizabeth Walsh and Mary-Alice Howard, for manuscript preparation; and especially, Debbie Vinson, for her valuable assistance in coordinating this project.

Finally, we want to acknowledge some important elements of the social context that contributed to our psychological well-being while writing this book. These include the Department of Psychiatry at the University of North Carolina School of Medicine and the Cancer Control Division of the Dana-Farber Cancer Institute; the gourmet take-out food businesses in Chapel Hill and Boston; and the endless opportunities for depression-spending in University Mall in Chapel Hill and the Chestnut Hill Shopping Mall in Newton.

Elaine (Hilberman) Carmen
Patricia Perri Rieker

Contents

III. Some Clinical Consequences of Inequality

A. *Suppression of Autonomy and Denial of Dependency*

B. *Restricted Sex Roles and Covert Conflicts*

C. *Violence and Psychiatric Disorders*

IV. Implications for Treatment and Training

A. Doing Psychotherapy

B. Gender and Psychiatric Education

Values, Inequality, and Mental Health

I

We have chosen to open this book with Alan A. Stone's 1980 presidential address to the American Psychiatric Association because the address was a direct response to the value conflicts that were profoundly disrupting personal and professional relationships within the organization. In 1979 a massive organizational crisis developed around ratification of the Equal Rights Amendment (ERA) and how far psychiatrists were willing to extend themselves in support of the ERA. In addition, many women and men psychiatrists joined together in asking for equal representation for women in organizational decision making and in the elimination of sex bias in psychiatric training, research, and practice.

In his address, "Conceptual Ambiguity and Morality in Modern Psychiatry," Stone reflects on the state of modern psychiatry. He analyzes the moral and intellectual dimensions of a condition that we would describe as an identity crisis for the psychiatric profession. The crisis arises from the tension created not only in having to choose from among competing intellectual perspectives, but also from having to recognize that there are moral assumptions concealed in each of these perspectives. Stone describes the variety of ways that psychiatry has avoided taking responsibility for its hidden value assumptions by either denying the crisis condition altogether or ignoring one of its dimensions. Those who would deny the crisis, he argues, do so when they mistakenly claim that psychiatry can be practiced in a neutral fashion; that is, they believe that psychiatric judgments can transcend all values. One form that this denial takes is for clinicians to acknowledge that social problems such as sexism, racism, and homophobia are important, but not really the proper subject matter of a "scientific" enterprise like psychiatry.

The idea of a value-free psychotherapy derives in part from a confusing message about how clinicians should practice. On the one hand, they are taught to avoid making value judgments. In our teaching experiences, we have been impressed that trainees in the mental health professions generally think of themselves as "neutral" in their clinical roles. As a result, they rarely appreciate the extent to which their values and beliefs affect their work with patients. The reality, however, is that value judgments are implicit whenever clinicians assess an individual's thoughts, feelings, and behaviors as "normal," "abnormal," "appropriate," or "inappropriate." In fact, Stone's article serves as a vivid illustration of the influence and destructiveness of hidden values about race, gender, and homosexuality that permeate psychiatric theories and practices.

As Stone argues, "perhaps the most penetrating and convincing attack on the hidden and destructive values in psychiatry has related to the subject of women." He points out that the questions raised in connection with both women and men are so pervasive that they mandate not only "a new conception of all our human values" but also changes in the theoretical structures of our paradigms. He cautions that the moral debate over concealed value positions about women cannot be ignored or bypassed by retreating to a narrower paradigm that is defined as more "scientific." Unfortunately, the attractiveness of this kind of pragmatic solution is reinforced by psychiatry's identification as a medical subspecialty. From this perspective, resolution of the identity crisis involves nothing more than selecting from among the appropriate medical or biological paradigms that will then bring conceptual clarity to the field. One clinical implication of this resolution is that psychiatrists come to believe that behavior can be understood in isolation from the social context.

In rejecting this scenario, Stone maintains that, even though difficult, it is the very debate over value conflicts and competing paradigms that will compel us "to reexamine not only our theories and therapy but also our own lives and relationships." Exploring these hidden values is disruptive and painful because it calls into question our most fundamental personal and professional beliefs, and in the process, we are forced to confront the moral uncertainties and conceptual ambiguities that are implicit to psychiatry. Stone's article, then, sets the stage for the clarification of gender values to which this book is addressed.

In his brief editorial, "Morality in Medicine," Seymour L. Halleck asserts that society's response to illness per se is itself conditioned by concealed moral assumptions. He illustrates this with a discussion of those illnesses in which it is believed that patients can voluntarily regulate their own behaviors; that is, "morality is an issue in the treatment of any disease which is associated with satisfaction of bodily pleasures." In discussing the inadequate medical responses to herpes and acquired immune deficiency syndrome (AIDS), Halleck comments that "pain experienced by people in the pursuit of pleasure is no less dreadful than pain which is inflicted for no apparent reason." With these examples he reminds us all of the ramifications of hidden values on social policy and approaches to research and treatment.

Elaine (Hilberman) Carmen, Nancy Felipe Russo, and Jean Baker

Miller, in "Inequality and Women's Mental Health: An Overview," demonstrate that neither psychiatric illness nor treatment takes place in a moral or historical vacuum. On the contrary, they show that the mental health of women must be considered within the context of the sex discrimination that still persists despite dramatic changes in women's roles and in attitudes toward women. The authors discuss, in some detail, the consequences of gender inequality for female psychological development and for mental health services. "Inequality," they state, "has obvious implications for the daily lives of women in the areas of economic status, power and prestige, and freedom of self-determination."

Going beyond these obvious consequences, the authors describe the less obvious consequences of the structures of inequality, "in which women's sense of identity is developed within a framework that defines women as a devalued group." In attempting to respond to their subordinate condition, women find themselves in a double bind. If they conform to dominant cultural expectations, they are left with a sense of self defined by others. If they rebel, they may remain in a perpetual state of conflict with and alienation from those in power. The clinical consequences of this no-win situation for the mental health of women are well documented by the authors.

Carmen et al. underscore Stone's concerns about psychiatry's failure to come to terms with value assumptions about women. They show how complex processes of sex bias and sex-role stereotyping also detract from the quality of mental health services to women (and men). The authors conclude that mental health professionals have an ethical mandate to eliminate sex bias from their theories and therapies. They further state that promoting mental health and preventing mental illness will require that mental health professionals confront the institutional structures of inequality that are so destructive to women's mental health.

Presidential Address

1

Conceptual Ambiguity and Morality in Modern Psychiatry

ALAN A. STONE

Last year in my response to the Presidential Address I rather presumptuously associated myself with the wisdom of the owl of Minerva—the owl that Hegel said only spreads its wings at dusk. From that lofty position I described a new era in psychiatry that I called pragmatic eclecticism, an era in which the four competing models in psychiatry had learned peaceful coexistence. These models—the biological, the psychodynamic, the behavioral, and the social—I suggested were held together by the medical model, which provided clinical coherence if not conceptual clarity. As I present the Presidential Address I must confess that the wings of the owl of Minerva were not fully extended last year. I recant nothing, but I now believe I glided too easily over that qualifying phrase about the absence of conceptual clarity. I intend today therefore to speak about the ambiguity of our eclectic medical model and my concern that having overcome the tyranny of narrow orthodoxy we are now in danger of retreating behind new walls. I shall touch briefly on subjects familiar to you all: racism, homosexuality, and the situation of women. I shall not attempt to deal in a deep way with the substance of these matters; rather, my intention is to examine how American psychiatry has grappled with them. These are all issues which have confronted us in our practice, challenged the moral assumptions that lie concealed in our theories, and confounded us with disputes and acrimony in our Association. It is as we attempt to deal with this kind of issue that the new walls are being built, and it is no accident that each invites psychiatry to take a stand on human values. Human values after all are a crucial link in the chain that binds the self to society. To take a stand on them reveals something about our own selves, our own relation to society, and our own vision of what it means to love and to work.

Many psychiatrists believe that our Association should limit itself to

Reprinted from *American Journal of Psychiatry* 137(8):887–891, 1980. Copyright © 1980 by the American Psychiatric Association. Reprinted by permission. Presented at the 133rd annual meeting of the American Psychiatric Association, San Francisco, California, May 3–9, 1980. Dr. Stone was the 108th president of the American Psychiatric Association.

issues that are clearly psychiatric, and they look back at some of the strong positions we have taken on what they consider social issues with regret. Many other psychiatrists believe these social issues are clearly psychiatric; they are proud of what we have done and urge us to do more. I shall claim that what separates these two groups can be understood only as part of the deeper theoretical dilemma in which American psychiatry finds itself, its lack of conceptual clarity. I know I shall be addressing a subject in public that most of us prefer to talk about in private, but my temerity is sustained by three considerations. First, our professional training obliges us to understand conflict rather than repress or deny it, and I believe that in view of recent events the time has come to confront this conflict openly. Second, I have become convinced that the basic limitation of pragmatic eclecticism is that it creates and sustains a mood of caution and expediency in all things, including matters that require moral ambition. Thus, perhaps without thinking it through, we are losing the courage of conscience. Finally, I do not intend to suggest an ultimate solution. I mean only to describe the problem as I encounter it in my own heart and mind.

THE PARABLE OF THE BLACK SERGEANT

I turn to what I have called the parable of the black sergeant. It is a parable about racism, about guilt and forgiveness, and about psychiatric theory and practice. The identifying information in this parable–case history has been disguised for reasons of confidentiality, but the value conflicts it presents are real enough. The patient, a black man, was a supply sergeant. He was caught by the military police stealing a deodorant stick from the post exchange. The Army, which had reason to suspect the sergeant of other thefts and was undeterred by Constitutional restraints on search and seizure, went to his home and reclaimed every piece of Army property that the sergeant could not account for. The pile of supplies— uniforms, blankets, picks and shovels, cartons of canned goods, mess kits, etc.—could have filled a trailer truck. It had all been photographed on the sergeant's front lawn, and that picture became part of his Army medical file.

The Army was determined to court-martial the sergeant, but he had been examined by a civilian psychiatrist who decided that much of what was stolen was of no use to the sergeant and, based on his understanding of the sergeant's psychodynamics, had diagnosed him as a kleptomaniac. This civilian psychiatrist was prepared to testify at court-martial that the stealing was due to unconscious and irresistible impulses. Unhappy with the civilian psychiatrist's report, the Army sent the sergeant to be evaluated at an Army hospital. There he was told repeatedly that anything he said could be used against him at the court-martial. The sergeant took the warning rather impassively, and his Army psychiatrist set to work to construct a very detailed anamnesis over the course of three weeks.

The sergeant, who was a very intelligent man, got caught up in telling the story of his life. He had grown up in a Southern city during the days of racial segregation. A good and serious student from a deeply religious family, he had done well in school and had gone to a small college where he studied literature. After graduation, despite his hopes and dreams, he had found no appropriate work and eventually was drafted into the Korean War. After the war, seeing no alternatives, he remained in the Army to serve his 20 years. As the years passed he became increasingly bitter. He was convinced that life had cheated him because he was black and that the Army, in the work and position it gave him, continued to discriminate against him. Out of this sense of being cheated there grew a sense of entitlement, and he came to feel that he was justified in taking whatever he could whenever he could. He had no sense of being impulsively driven to steal Army property; instead, he stole with a sense of entitlement and reparation in protest of the racist world that had deprived him of his hopes.

It is not clear why this black supply sergeant, despite being warned, told all this to the Army psychiatrist. At any rate he did, and the Army psychiatrist, after puzzling over the diagnostic possibilities (which included paranoid personality and depression), concluded that the sergeant did not have kleptomania or any other mental disorder that should excuse him from responsibility. Subsequently the Army psychiatrist testified at the court-martial. He told the story I have told you while trying to avoid the sergeant's eyes. The sergeant sat there in his dress uniform with his medals, his wife, and their small children. He was sentenced to five years at hard labor. As you may have guessed, I was the Army psychiatrist, and I felt something terrible happened that day. Each time my mind takes me back to that occasion I have a sense of dismay that will not be dissipated.

The Influence of Morality and History

It is tempting when one reflects on this parable of the black sergeant to conclude that it demonstrates no more than the abyss between the moral concerns of the law and the therapeutic concerns of psychiatry. But none of us, I trust, would claim that if a man like the sergeant came voluntarily seeking treatment his psychiatrist would at no point consider moral issues. And how could one treat such a man with no moral perspective and revealing no opinion about racism? Surely a psychiatrist treating the sergeant in 1980 would approach his problems differently than our predecessors would have done in 1940. Psychiatry does not stand outside history or morality, but how do we decide which history and which morality to accept? Is it all a matter of individual choice? Certainly one cannot find the rules controlling what history or morality to accept clearly delineated in the major theories of our biological, psychodynamic, and behavioral paradigms. Psychiatrists are taught to avoid value judgments in their dealings with patients, but I do not believe I make a radical claim when I assert that history and morality are a presence in the therapist's office. The only question is how do they get there.

Let me turn to a narrower question: What role does our practice and our theory play in the courtroom drama of guilt and forgiveness? The legal system, even the Army's legal system, was hesitant to assess guilt in the face of a diagnosis of kleptomania. That diagnosis and the account of human behavior that goes with it invoke the unconscious and the symbolic meaning of the theft. Those who sit in judgment are not asked to consider the sergeant's race and social identity. His behavior is presented in isolation from its historical and cultural context. His kleptomania is understood in the confines of a personality development that repeats a timeless sequence outside culture and history. The psychiatrist applying this kind of theory comprehends the sergeant's motives as nonutilitarian and not intended to offend the system. Such a man can be forgiven; his quarrel is not with us but with his introjects.

On the other hand, the account I gave takes the man as he experiences his life within a particular culture and history. His stealing is understood as part of his response to his predicament. It is his revenge against an unjust system. Such a man cannot be forgiven by our law, but if his judges are willing to condemn the racism of their society they can lighten his sentence. And if the psychiatrist is willing to lend his authority to the condemnation of a racist society he might even help the judges to reach that lighter sentence. But the moral and historical perspective that might have led me in that direction was not a presence in my office when I examined the sergeant. If in some sense I betrayed the sergeant, and I believe I did, it was because of the historical and moral perspective I brought to the subject of racism.

Psychodynamic versus Social Considerations

I have carefully distinguished the psychodynamic and the social account of the sergeant's behavior, not only because that is how the two psychiatrists presented them but also to emphasize the radically different moral implications and consequences of the two accounts. There is an irony here that should be underscored. The theory that excludes history and morality has the power to exculpate without disturbing the status quo. Thus the psychiatrist's choice of theory becomes crucial. I shall return to this question of choice. Many of you must be impatient with what seems an artificial distinction because as eclectics we are all accustomed to invoking both accounts. Indeed, the word "psychosocial" seems to have been invented to make this point. Most of us are prepared to believe that there was probably some truth in both accounts of the sergeant's behavior and to insist that anyone who hopes to understand the sergeant must give weight to both, not to mention biological and behavioral factors that are missing from this 20-year-old parable.

Here we touch on the greatest strength of eclecticism and its greatest weakness. Its strength lies in its openness to consider the complexity of the forces that touch our lives. The eclectic psychiatrist sees biological man, moved by dynamic passions and ideals, shaped by culture and shaping culture. The eclectic has the most comprehensive view of what Sartre called the "critical mirror which alone offers man his image." But still that image is only a reflection; even less than a reflection, it is a composite sketch pieced together from the accounts of different witnesses whose vision depends on different theoretical perspectives. It is not just the problem of getting a biological, a psychodynamic, a behavioral, and a social psychiatrist to agree among themselves. How does the individual eclectic psychiatrist who conscientiously considers all of these factors reach a judgment about their relative significance?

This is our greatest weakness. We do not know what weight to give each perspective's account. We can diligently catalogue the different accounts. We can artfully construct Venn diagrams to suggest the possible relationships of these accounts. We can in rare instances assert with confidence the primacy of a particular account. But most often we are condemned to the ultimate ambiguity that is the inevitable consequence of our eclecticism. This is not a problem to be resolved by mere numbers; we do not have a formula or a way of deciding how much something should count. We psychiatrists often say that behavior is overdetermined, but might it be that this concept of overdetermination conceals our very deepest confusion, our inability to order the different considerations? As clinicians each of us treats the whole person, and each day we try to piece together the composite sketch. But we also have a pressing responsibility to ease human suffering. Compassion draws us inevitably to expedient remedies. As pragmatic eclectics uncertain that we have put the pieces of the picture together correctly, we can never be confident that we can distinguish between the sick patient and the sick society.

Lacking that ability and given that it is easier to apply expedient remedies to sick patients than to sick societies, will we not inevitably be led by our clinical responsibilities to distort the composite sketch of the human condition? At the very least we should understand that we might seem to the outside world to be doing just that.

Sensibility at the Cost of Ambiguity*

Here is a second irony to be underscored: it was only when our generation of psychiatrists had the courage to overcome the walls of narrow orthodoxy that we confronted our greatest weakness. Only within the narrow paradigms could we construct if not a causal account at least something close to it. When we ventured outside we purchased sensibility at the cost of ambiguity. This theoretical ambiguity is at the very core of the conflicts that confound us. When we testify in court, when we formulate our diagnostic nosology, when we issue position papers, indeed, whenever we attempt to act, we confront this ambiguity. It is no wonder, then, that many psychiatrists are now eager to go back to their narrow paradigms, where they hope to capture the rigor of conceptual clarity that comforts the scientist and to escape from the complexity of human values that accompany a greater sensibility.

Biologists, psychoanalysts, and behaviorists can at least imagine this alternative, but social psychiatrists have no place to hide, no way to narrow their sensibilities. They have always stood outside the walls, urging their colleagues to broaden their horizons. It might even be possible to describe social psychiatry as the fractious adolescent member of the psychiatric family, disrupting the serenity of the household by arguing about values, morality, and social justice, the way all adolescents do. Shall we now expel them? Even if we could, I think it is too late. The broad sensibility they brought to psychiatry has opened eyes that will not be closed.

What I have described thus far is an honest picture of my own perplexity, if not of yours. First, I know that I do not abandon history, morality, and human values when I enter my office, but I do not know how I decide what to take in with me. I believe that most of you are in the same position, and for reasons I shall come to shortly I am deeply suspicious of anyone who makes the contrary claim that history, morality, and human values are all irrelevant to psychiatry. Second, I know that I at least am aware of no rules of ordering the different paradigms and their interactions. When I sat in judgment of the black sergeant, I believed that the hard truth of the matter was to be decided by choosing the particular paradigm which best fit the facts of the case. Having chosen the correct

*I wish to acknowledge my colleague Roberto Mangabeira Unger, whose ideas were helpful in the formulation of this section.

paradigm, I applied the explanatory theory of that paradigm and thus never experienced a lack of conceptual clarity. In a sense the four paradigms provided me a framework of differential diagnosis within which I proceeded rigorously, with the skill and objectivity of a scientist. My recognition that the goal of enlightened eclectics like Adolf Meyer was not to choose but to reconcile came when I began to examine the scientific problem of prediction in psychiatry and the moral consequences of my professional activity. Is it possible that our inability to reconcile our paradigms stands in the way of both our scientific and our moral progress?

Thus far I have drawn a picture in which most of psychiatry might seem to stand to one side on the crucial questions of morality and human values, with only social psychiatry on the other side demanding that we get involved in the real world. But during this century all of science has learned painfully and tragically that science is not remote. Every thinking person knows that the physicist's equations play a crucial role in the destiny of humanity. Psychiatry's role is also crucial, although its influence is much more subtle. One of the most remarkable developments in this century is the speed with which the psychiatrist's theories of human nature move from the arcane jargon of our journals through the mass media and into the consciousness of our culture. Psychiatry has played no small part in the transformation of the mind of modern man. This transformation takes place outside our control; theories are bowdlerized and sensationalized. Our drugs are prescribed and self-prescribed everywhere. Other treatment methods have also been coopted and arrayed in the struggles of interpersonal politics. Young people make love after they make therapy. There is in all the affairs of daily living, public and private, the pervasive if subtle influence of our profession.

The most powerful aspect of psychiatry is its contribution to what it means to be a person. This is not under our control, nor can it be in a free society. But we do bear a certain responsibility, and one of the themes in that responsibility is the hidden values in the theories and therapies that originated with us and contribute to the shaping of contemporary consciousness.

The thrust of this analysis is to claim that even without social psychiatry we are not on the other side. We have been engaged in an enterprise that involves concealed positions on human values, moral postures, and even politics. This claim comes not just from unfriendly critics, it comes from responsible colleagues. This is the indictment that confronts those psychiatrists who assert that their psychiatry has nothing to do with these things; although the indictment can be overdrawn and viciously expressed, the fundamental truth in it cannot be gainsaid. Therefore, given the power of our enterprise, whether we like it or not we are in some measure responsible for the influence of these hidden values. It is also important to remember that many of us have wanted to use psychiatry to influence the public to confront and even to treat the sick society through the media. It is not just a matter of aloof scientists being victimized by the vulgarity of the mass media.

HOMOSEXUALITY

One of the first great battlefields in the attack on psychiatry's hidden values was homosexuality. Psychiatrists had long assumed that as part of their humanistic tradition they had brought their scientific perspective to things that were once considered evil. Homosexuality became sickness rather than sin, and this perspective in this century was accepted not only by the secular masses but even by most religious authorities. However, gay liberation brought a different perspective. Their argument was that our judgments about homosexuality as sickness contained hidden values, a limited vision of human sensuality and intimacy, the old morality under a new guise, and perhaps even our own phobic limitations. A campaign was undertaken to remove the diagnosis of homosexuality from the nomenclature. Our Association, after considerable deliberation and not a little acrimony, accepted that perspective. Our Association went even further—it called for an end to legal discrimination against homosexuality. Here I come to the heart of the matter—the relationship of our lack of conceptual clarity to the actions we take. Recall the analysis I have developed here. Each of the four paradigms in psychiatry inevitably had its own theories about homosexuality.

Biological explanations can be sought in the endocrine system, psychodynamic explanations in childhood experiences and the Oedipus complex. Behaviorists can find answers in the sexual gratification reinforcement schedule. The social psychiatrist has the only paradigm that directly addresses the basic issues raised by gay liberation. Imagine if you will the eclectic psychiatrist who accepts all four paradigms but does not know how to reconcile them. Imagine such a psychiatrist who uses the four paradigms as a kind of differential diagnosis. Might that psychiatrist not conclude that there were four different kinds of homosexuality and that only the kind described by social psychiatry had been removed from our diagnostic manual?

This analysis may seem far-fetched and bizarre to you, but let me emphasize the structure of my argument. If we have no overarching theory that organizes the theories of the four basic paradigms, those paradigms cannot be changed from the top down, at least not by the logic of a controlling theory. Thus it is possible to argue that for many psychiatrists no fundamental change in their basic approach had occurred. They could go on as before. Therefore, the struggle for those concerned about gay liberation had to continue at a second level, which has two directions.

First, would psychiatry invest more in the effort to influence the public perception of homosexuality? Second, would each of the paradigms undertake the necessary theoretical reformulations essential to a fundamental change? My analysis in no way is meant to demean the decisions our Association reached. Nor do I minimize the importance of what we did. It was not an empty gesture. But I believe the real significance of our actions once again was moral. We changed the moral element in our composite sketch of homosexuality. I understand it as an act of moral compassion producing a small change in public perception. That small change in the long run can have a powerful effect on the most insular theory.

WOMEN'S ISSUES

Perhaps the most penetrating and convincing attack on the hidden and destructive values in psychiatry has related to the subject of women. Indeed, when one has the occasion to read the standard works in psychiatry written before 1970 it no longer seems appropriate to talk about hidden values. It is no wonder, then, that psychiatrists who are concerned about the quality of the composite sketch of women promulgated by their profession and assimilated into our culture should turn to this Association to rectify it. There was obviously a great deal to be rectified, but they confronted an enormous obstacle. There was no diagnosis of female that could be expunged from the diagnostic manual; thus there could be no obvious battlefield. The struggle had to begin at the second level. How far would our Association go in its efforts to rectify the public's perception of women, and how thoroughgoing would be the necessary changes in the theoretical structure of each of the paradigms?

Here I come to the last piece in the structure of my analysis of how American psychiatry deals with these issues, that is, the effect of our own psychology and our own historical situation. As far as I can see, the case against psychiatry as regards women is far more damaging, requires far more than a minor adjustment of our composite sketch, indeed compels each of us to reexamine not only our theories and therapy but also our own lives and relationships. One might even say that psychiatry has only recently discovered that the maxim to love and to work applies to women.

Is it possible that the issues raised concerning women cut deeper in American psychiatry than even racism and homosexuality? That the questions raised in connection with women touch our personal as well as our professional identity? There can be no new psychology of women that does not require a new psychology of men. That makes necessary a new conception of all our human values and all the paradigms of psychiatry. This challenge comes at a time when our profession is struggling—when we have trimmed our sails and yearn for the safety of calmer waters. It comes at a time when many would like to retreat to their narrow paradigm. It comes at a time when the spirit of pragmatic expedience dominates our profession, narrows our horizons, and saps our moral courage.

Most psychiatrists are not by temperament polemical or adversarial. We do not seek out moral controversy. Most of us spend our lives listening compassionately to people who are suffering, whose lives are disrupted by the uncontrolled demands of passion and by the pains of helplessness. We try to be nonjudgmental while we help them weave together the delicate fabric of personal strength that sustains love and intimacy. And we sustain ourselves by small triumphs and acts of private altruism. Our successes often go unnoticed and our failures loom large. Ours is a vulnerable profession, easy to attack and to belittle, but it is a noble profession because it is both a moral and a scientific enterprise.

When we move from the safety of our office to take action in the real world we usually are motivated by the same moral enterprise that guides us in our office: a mixture of compassion, understanding, art, and science. The world outside our office may seem increasingly treacherous. But that treacherous world is already inside our office, if only in microcosm, and our work can never be carried on in a moral and historical vacuum. If like Hercules we were to succeed in lifting our giant of a science from its earthly connections, if we were to cut away all the links that hold self to society, then psychiatry would become a corpse. We will make mistakes if we go forward, but doing nothing can be the worst mistake. What is required of us is moral ambition. Until our composite sketch becomes a true portrait of humanity we must live with our uncertainty; we will grope, we will struggle, and our compassion may be our only guide and comfort.

Editorial

2

Morality in Medicine

SEYMOUR L. HALLECK

About a decade ago I wrote a newspaper column in which I argued that almost everything that is pleasurable to people turns out to be bad for them. In support of this half serious thesis, I cited data that smoking is always harmful and that even moderately excessive eating or drinking was also unhealthy. The commonest rejoinder to my cynicism was that I was forgetting that there was one pleasure that could be indulged in with impunity, sex. In an era when effective and presumably safe contraceptive devices were available and venereal diseases seemed to be conquered, this was an effective argument.

Recently, however, sex, for at least a sizable number of people, has once again become risky. Herpes is now a highly prevalent venereal disease among those who are active with multiple partners and those who prefer homosexual sex are in special danger of contacting the very serious acquired immune deficiency syndrome (AIDS). It is impossible not to be aware that the likelihood of contacting these diseases is greatest among those who engage in activities which a major segment of society has always viewed as immoral. We should not be surprised, therefore, that society's ambivalence toward sex with multiple partners or with persons of the same sex would influence its response to diseases resulting from these activities. Those especially vulnerable to these diseases and particularly homosexuals who are at risk of a lethal disease are raising questions as to whether society's moral condemnation of their activities is compromising society's efforts to combat herpes and AIDS.

If those who feel society is "dragging its feet" are right (and I suspect they are) it will not be the first time in which moral issues have influenced society's response to illness. Psychiatrists should know this well. Morality is an issue in the treatment of any disease which is associated with satisfaction of bodily pleasures. In the case of herpes and AIDS the disease is, of course, incidental to appetitive functions. But psychiatrists have had plenty of experience with diseases related to an excess of appe-

Reprinted from *Contemporary Psychiatry* 2(2):86, 1983. Copyright © 1983 by Plenum Publishing Corporation. Reprinted by permission.

titive functions such as alcoholism, addiction, obesity, and anorexia. We have learned to anticipate a reluctance on the part of many to study or treat these disorders with an attitude of unambivalent compassion. Society has not invested a great deal of its medical resources in treating drug abuse or eating disorders. This is partly because we do not like the consequences of indulgence and partly because we believe that those who indulge could control their behavior if they wanted to.

The most important issue, here, is will or volition. As long as a substantial segment of society disapproves of a certain kind of behavior and as long as we believe that individuals have capacity to regulate that behavior on their own, the consequences of such behavior will be unlikely to be greeted with the most compassionate response. For that matter, the issue of volition probably accounts for society's reluctance to take mental illness as seriously as other illnesses. As long as we believe that psychiatric patients have considerable control over their behavior, their suffering tends not to receive the same attention as those of patients with physical disorders.

While the suffering of those who are plagued with the new sexually related disease calls for drastic action rather than mere philosophizing about the nature of morality and illness, there is still some value in expanding our awareness of the relationship of morality to medicine. If we are aware of moral prejudices in ourselves and others, we can do a better job of combating them. If we can find a better way of integrating the concept of volition into the disease model, we would probably do a better job in treating all of our patients. In the meantime, it is well to remind ourselves that pain experienced by people in the pursuit of pleasure is no less dreadful than pain which is inflicted for no apparent reason.

Inequality and Women's Mental Health

3

An Overview

ELAINE (HILBERMAN) CARMEN,
NANCY FELIPE RUSSO, AND JEAN BAKER MILLER

Over the last decade far-reaching changes have taken place in our beliefs and expectations about women's roles and identities in the contexts of work, family, and community. These changes have been accompanied by an unprecedented expansion of knowledge and literature that attempts to understand and to convey the female experience.[1-19] This new scholarship has identified sex bias in psychological theories and methods, documented the pervasive and destructive effects of gender inequality, and examined the stresses that differentially affect women by virtue of their subordinate social status, especially in their family roles. Every basic formulation about women's psychology has been questioned and, in many instances, reconceptualized.

There now exists a knowledge base of more relevant data concerning women and men from which we believe new theories and practices will emerge. Thus, the implications of a new psychology of women are extraordinary; they were eloquently expressed by Alan Stone in his 1980 presidential address to the American Psychiatric Association[20]:

> As far as I can see, the case against psychiatry as regards women . . . requires far more than a minor adjustment of our composite sketch, indeed compels each of us to reexamine not only our theories and therapy but also our own lives and relationships. . . . Is it possible that . . . the questions raised in connection with women touch our personal as well as our professional identity? There can be no new psychology of women that does not require a new psychology of men. That makes necessary a new conception of all our human values and all the paradigms of psychiatry.

Since these contemporary views often contradict established beliefs, the new scholarship presents a special challenge to mental health professionals. Traditional psychological theories have relied largely on intra-

Reprinted from *American Journal of Psychiatry* 138(10):1319–1330, 1981. Copyright © 1981 by the American Psychiatric Association. Reprinted by permission. The authors thank Patricia P. Rieker, Ph.D., for her contributions to this manuscript.

psychic explanations of how people think, feel, and behave. However, mental health educators and practitioners have not always recognized the extent to which an individual's identity, psyche, and sense of self derive from the social context. The link between women's disadvantaged status and their mental health creates an obligation for mental health professionals to understand how the social context contributes to the origin and persistence of the problems of their patients. We must go beyond symptomatic and adjustment forms of treatment to integrate intrapsychic theories with sociological explanations of identity and behavior and to explore the ways in which clinicians' attitudes and values alter diagnostic and treatment processes (P. P. Rieker, unpublished paper, 1979, and reference 21). This article summarizes some of the new knowledge about women's psychology and underscores the association between subordinate group status and mental health.

WOMEN'S DISADVANTAGED STATUS

In discussions of sex discrimination the term "equality" is often misunderstood. A common misconception is the equation of equality with sameness, i.e., the notion that a disadvantaged group desires to be "the same as" or "just like" members of the advantaged group. Such a view likely reflects the common trend for "superior" group members to assume that everyone's goal would be to be like them or to have what they have. "Equality" is used here, however, to refer to the equal right to participate in all areas of the life of society and to pursue one's unique psychological potential in all of its aspects. This would include the right to define oneself differently from the expected or historically derived definitions of proper femininity and woman's place.

American society is one of structured social inequality, in which there is an unequal distribution of rewards based on gender, race, and class differences, among others. Consider some highlights of the dramatic changes in women's work and family status that have occurred despite unchanging sex-based economic discrimination[22,23]:

1. In less than a generation the size of the paid female work force has more than doubled, largely due to change in work force participation by married women. In 1979, 60% of all women aged 18–64 were in the work force, compared with 88% of such men.[24]

2. The presence of children in a household only slightly inhibits work force participation. Fifty-five percent of all mothers with children under 18 years were in the work force in 1979, as were 45% of all married women with children under age 6.[24] Many employed women have young

children, but there are few social supports for child care outside the family. It is estimated that, in addition to the hours devoted to paid employment, married women spend another 27 hours per week on housework.[25]

3. These women work because of economic need: two-thirds are single, widowed, divorced, or separated or have husbands who earn less than $10,000. In husband–wife families, 14.8% were poor when the wife did not work; 3.8% were poor when she was in the work force.[24]

4. Women continue to be clustered in "female" jobs that are characterized by low pay; within the same occupation, women often earn less than men. In 1979 the median annual income of women who worked full time was 60% of that of men. The earnings gap is greatest for minority women.[24]

5. Sexual harassment has been a recent focus of attention for working women. There are estimates that 7 out of 10 women will experience sexual harassment on the job.[26,27] In the long history of this "tradition," many women are now providing anecdotal accounts of both psychological stress and loss of income as they leave jobs because they believe no relief or recourse is possible.

6. The average female worker is as well educated as the average male worker, with 12.6 years of schooling. In 1978 women with 4 years of college had less income than men with an eighth-grade education—$12,347 versus $12,965, respectively.[24]

7. In 1979 one out of seven families was headed by a woman; 40% of all black families were headed by women. Of all women workers, one out of six was a family head; one out of four black working women was a family head. Although women head one-seventh of all families in the United States, they head one-half of all families living in poverty. About three-fourths of black families living in poverty are headed by women. In the past 10 years the increase in the number of families living in poverty has been due almost entirely to the increase in the number of families headed by women.[28]

8. Women can expect to live many years after their children have left home and can expect to be widowed for a substantial length of time. In 1976 white women surviving to age 20 had a life expectancy of 78.7 years; black women, 71.6 years. The comparable figures for white and black men were 71.6 and 66.8 years, respectively.[26] Because of this difference in life expectancy, women constitute 80% of the population of individuals living in poverty who are over 65 years of age.[29]

9. The legal system provides little economic support for divorced mothers; less than 21% regularly collect child support.[24] One carefully documented report on middle-income women showed that their average family income dropped precipitously from $23,000 to $8500 after divorce;

in all cases this included total support for the children (D. Burlage, unpublished report prepared for the Office of the Assistant Secretary for Planning and Evaluation, HEW, 1976).

10. The ability to plan and to limit family size has a powerful impact on the health and economic well-being of women and their families. Despite advances in reproductive technology, women have high rates of unwanted pregnancy. In 1977, 28% of all pregnant women chose to terminate their pregnancies, and an estimated 1 in 12 children who were born were reported as unplanned or unwanted by 1 or both parents.[30]

11. The participation of women in the health professions follows the same pattern as women's participation in the larger society. Women health professionals are also clustered in "women's fields" where they earn less than men, even when they are in the same field. For example, in 1976 women constituted 11.9% of the psychiatrists, 28.3% of the psychologists, 56.2% of the social workers, and 94.1% of the nurses in community mental health centers. Men, in contrast, are overrepresented in administrative and leadership positions in mental health agencies, institutions, and professional organizations as well as on mental health governing boards, health systems agency boards, and the boards of directors of federally funded projects.[26]

THE EFFECTS OF INEQUALITY ON PSYCHOLOGICAL DEVELOPMENT

Inequality has obvious implications for the daily lives of women in the areas of economic status, power and prestige, and freedom of self-determination. In addition, there are many complex and less obvious psychological consequences of this system of stratification, in which woman's sense of identity is developed within a framework that defines women as a devalued group. Boys are taught that success as a man is contingent on the assertive use of individual talents and skills to ensure autonomy and achievement. Girls, however, are taught that the adult women's success will be acquired only indirectly through the status of the male alliance she makes. This knowledge is transmitted through patterns of sex-role socialization in which boys are encouraged to develop patterns of self-worth based on personal achievements in the real world while girls' self-esteem remains dependent on acceptance by others.[10,18,31]

Since men hold the power and authority, women are rewarded for developing a set of psychological characteristics that accommodate to and please men. Such traits—submissiveness, compliance, passivity, helplessness, weakness—have been encouraged in women and incorporated into some prevalent psychological theories in which they are defined as innate or inevitable characteristics of women. However, they are more accurately conceptualized as learned behaviors by which all subordinate group members attempt to ensure their survival.[10,32]

These survival skills exact a costly penalty because they are antithetical to the use of *active* psychic mechanisms for coping and resolving the conflicts inherent in healthy psychological development. Processes that mental health professionals consider desirable—for example, the individual's direct attempts to use all available psychological powers and resources toward establishing a grounded, self-determined, inner sense of self—are not encouraged for women. If women demonstrate these active processes, they are likely to experience negative and confusing responses during childhood and adult life.

Instead, girls and women have been encouraged to develop passive and indirect psychological strategies—a much more complex task. Behaviors such as inhibition, passivity, and submissiveness do not lead to favorable outcomes and play a role in the development of psychological problems. On a more superficial level, they contribute to a view of women as seductive, manipulative, and covertly controlling. Indeed, some women may resort to these behaviors as the only available strategies for affecting their own destinies in the absence of direct access to power and self-determination.

Finally, many women identify with and internalize the dominant cultural values and attitudes, denigrating themselves and other women, especially women whom they see as competitors for male attention. Bardwick and Douvan commented, "Ambivalence is clearly seen in the simultaneous enjoyment of one's feminine identity, qualities, goals, and achievements and the perception of them as less important, meaningful, or satisfying than those of men."[31]

MENTAL HEALTH CONSEQUENCES OF WOMEN'S DISADVANTAGED STATUS

The Subpanel on the Mental Health of Women of the President's Commission on Mental Health reported that circumstances and conditions which society accepts as normal or ordinary often lead to despair, anguish, and mental illness in women.[22,23] The subpanel documented the ways in which inequality creates dilemmas and conflicts for women in the contexts of marriage, family relationships, reproduction, child rearing, divorce, aging, education, and work. These same conditions of subordination also set the stage for extraordinary events that may heighten vulnerability to mental illness; the frequency with which incest, rape, and marital violence occur suggests that such events might well be considered normative developmental crises for women. Finally, mental health professionals are undoubtedly familiar with the epidemiological data that link mental illness with alienation, powerlessness, and poverty, conditions that accurately describe the status of many women. The specific forms of psychological distress suffered by women seem closely related to the convergence of these factors.

Given these circumstances, it is not surprising that both the frequency and the patterns of illness presented to mental health professionals are vastly different for women and men. What is surprising is the continued tolerance of misconceptions of how these differences are created and maintained and how they can be most effectively addressed. Our purpose here is to profile the problems of women that result in mental health consultation, identify the greatest gaps in understanding and knowledge, and highlight those areas where there is an urgent need for professionals to incorporate the new knowledge into training, research, and practice. We will discuss some, but not all, of the most prevalent manifestations of psychological distress in women and, in doing so, will suggest some of the factors that may play a significant role in all forms of psychological distress.

Women, Stress, and Depression

Psychiatrists often state that depression is *the* most common problem they encounter. One of the most consistent findings across institutional settings is that depression is closely associated with being female. There is now substantial documentation that more women than men are depressed; the ratio is about two to one.[7,23,33,34] Sex differences for utilization rates are most prominent in outpatient services, where rates for women are triple those for men in the 25–44 age group.[35] Evidence for the preponderance of depression among women comes from clinical sources as well as from population surveys of people not in treatment. Klerman and Weissman estimated that 20%–30% of all women experience depressive episodes, often of moderate severity, at some point during their lives.[36] In contrast to past beliefs about "the menopausal woman," it appears that young poor women have shown the greatest rise in the rate of both treated and untreated depression.[7,33-35]

These statistics invariably raise the possibility that the reported differences are artifacts based on response biases or the greater frequency with which women go to doctors. Weissman and Klerman commented, however, that researchers have found no significant sex differences in willingness to acknowledge symptoms of a psychological nature. In addition, since results of surveys of nonpatient populations are similar to those of patient populations, differences in health-care seeking behavior do not account for the sex differences. Thus, Weissman and Klerman asserted that reported differences in symptoms reflect real differences;

also found that men had higher admission rates than women for all marital status categories except that of married, in which there was a dramatic reversal. The degree of this reversal was greatest for minority group members. Looking at the age-adjusted admission rates per 100,000 population (14 years and older) for *all* marital status categories, we find that the rates are 1212 for white men, 1396 for white women, 1865 for minority-race men, and 1773 for minority-race women. In contrast, for *married* people the comparable rates are 657 for white men, 1051 for white women, 832 for minority-race men, and 1631 for minority-race women.[46]

Since married people have lower rates of illness than do people in other marital status categories, it has generally been assumed that marriage confers a "protective status" that makes married people less vulnerable to mental illness. The protective value associated with marriage, however, differs considerably depending on one's gender and race. Developing an index based on the proportional difference between the rates of the married and the never married, we find a 71% reduction in illness rates for minority-race men, 63% for white men, 28% for white women, and 8% for minority-race women. These differentials underscore the need to better understand how social forces, especially the family structure and context, affect mental health.

The landmark work of Brown and colleagues[47] explored the relationship between psychosocial stresses and affective disorders in a community survey in London. They found that working-class women with young children living at home were five times more likely to become depressed than middle-income women. Four factors were identified that contributed to the class difference: loss of a mother in childhood, three or more children under age 14 living at home, absence of an intimate/supportive relationship with her marital partner (not simply the presence of a marital partner), and lack of employment outside the home. The researchers concluded that employment had a protective effect by improving economic status, increasing self-esteem and social contacts, and alleviating boredom. Weissman's research suggests that marital discord is the most common event in the previous 6 months reported by depressed women in treatment.[48] Cooperstock[49] cited a study of women who were hospitalized for depression and matched for age and marital status; those employed outside the home recovered more quickly than did their housewife counterparts.

The data also demonstrate that young poor women who head single-parent families and young married women who work at dead-end jobs have shown the greatest rise in the rate of both treated and untreated depression.[7,33-35] They also refute the myth that the black female has an "invulnerability" to depression—a myth perhaps created by reliance on statistics from state and county mental hospitals. In 1975 an estimated 36% of the 3800 minority-race patients who were in those institutions and were diagnosed as having depressive disorders were women, compared with 53% for white patients. In contrast, the comparable figure for the 25,974 minority-race patients treated in outpatient facilities was 89%, while the comparable figure for white women was 69%.[46]

Women, Family Roles, and Relationships

How do we explain the differential effects of marriage on the well-being of husbands and wives? The epidemiological data suggest that the excess of psychological symptoms in women is not intrinsic to femaleness but to the conditions of subordination that characterize traditional female roles.

Gove and colleagues[42-45] concluded that women's higher rates of mental illness are a function of their limited roles. They noted that women are more often restricted to the single major role of housewife while men usually have both head of household and worker roles. Thus, if a woman finds her family role unsatisfactory, she may have no alternative sources of gratification. This single role is one of frustration and low status and is incompatible with the needs, aspirations, and capacities of many women. However, employment per se is not an easy solution. The wife/mother who works is likely to be further stressed by a low-status job combined with full responsibility for home and children so that her total work load is overwhelming. Finally, woman's family role is defined in terms of the needs of others, with her own needs considered to be secondary.

Families are usually viewed as providing the primary support networks for individuals, yet the data seem to indicate that it is in the context of marriage, as traditionally constructed, that the subjugation of women is most apparent and most destructive. Thus, it is in rigidly traditional families that female adults and children are at highest risk for violence and sexual abuse.[23,50-55] Violence is said to occur in 50% of American families.[50-52] It is estimated that 10% of all girls have had a sexual encounter with a relative and that 1% of all girls have been sexually abused by their fathers.[23,53,54] As Herman noted, "Incest occurs in families where the mothers have been subjugated and rendered powerless.[54] Therapists who routinely explore these issues report that a majority of their female clients have a history of some form of sexual abuse. As with incest, women do not reveal these events unless the therapist is able to encourage discussion of these issues, and many therapists have not been able to do so.

If women's entry into marriage and family membership is motivated in part by the need to define themselves through their alliance with powerful men, Dobash and Dobash[55] have made it clear that women pay an extraordinary price: "It is still true that for a woman to be brutally or systematically assaulted she must usually enter our most sacred institution, the family. It is within marriage that a woman is most likely to be slapped and shoved about, severely assaulted, killed, or raped."

There are many historical data to suggest that the subordination of wives and the right (if not obligation) of husbands to beat or at least control their wives is one legacy of patriarchal ideology and family structure. Dobash and Dobash asserted that our views of "normal" responsibility, control, and authority in marriage are transmitted in large part through sex-role socialization. In the usual transition from woman to wife, the wife gives up her name as well as most of her aspirations and activities. She experiences increasing isolation and segregation as her husband's possessiveness grows and the demands for her services by husband and children increase. The husband as worker and provider comes to expect her obedience and perceives challenges to his authority as affronts to the moral order. It is against the backdrop of these traditional marital roles and expectations that physical coercion can be viewed not as a deviant act but, rather, as a purposeful act to maintain the moral order of male dominance.[55]

To come full circle, these attitudes about family roles and relationships are maintained by pervasive patterns of sex discrimination. Women who leave unhappy marriages or violent homes are denied equal educational, vocational, and economic opportunities, excellent and supportive child care facilities, and a legitimate self-supporting role in society. The alternative to chronic depression in an unhappy marriage is often poverty, a dead-end job, and severe difficulties in attempting to care for children in either case.

SEX BIAS IN THERAPY: ISSUES OF APPROPRIATENESS

It would be surprising if the pervasive cultural biases that denigrate women were not found in the training of mental health professionals and the delivery of mental health services for women.[2,13,17,22,23,26] The new knowledge about women, men, and sex roles has not generally been incorporated into mental health training. Clinical theories of personality specify woman's innate nature as passive, dependent, masochistic, and childlike, and psychological treatment has often aimed at reducing her complaints about the quality of her life and promoting adjustment to the existing order.

There has been a double standard for mental health based on sex-role stereotyping and adjustment to one's environment. The classic Broverman and associates' study[56] of clinicians' attitudes suggested that clinicians believe healthy women differ from men and adults with gender unspecified in being more submissive, less independent, less adventurous, more suggestible, less competitive, more excitable in minor crises, more likely to have their feelings easily hurt, more emotional, more conceited about appearance, less objective, and more illogical. The researchers concluded that

> for a woman to be healthy, from an adjustment viewpoint, she must adjust to and accept the behavioral norms of her sex, even though these behaviors are generally less socially desirable and considered to be less healthy than the generalized competent mature adult.... Acceptance of an adjustment notion of health, then, places women in a conflictual position of having to decide whether to exhibit those positive characteristics considered desirable for men and adults, and thus have their femininity questioned ... or to behave in the prescribed second-class adult status....[56]

The complex issue of therapist attitudes and sex-role stereotyping has been the subject of considerable discussion and research in the 11 years that have elapsed since the original Broverman and associates' study and has been critically reviewed by Sherman.[57] Research design problems, the use of variables that are not clearly relevant to stereotyping—for example, confusing misogyny with stereotyping—and the likelihood of subjects misrepresenting their views in a liberal rather than conservative direction have all contributed to a wide variation in results. Sherman concluded, however, that "therapists' sex-role values are operative during therapy and counseling. Data indicate there is sex-role stereotyping in mental health standards and that sex-role-discrepant behaviors are judged more maladjusted."[57] There is also evidence that therapists' knowledge about issues affecting the lives of women is inadequate.[2,57]

The experiences of many women in therapy support these findings. Most psychiatrists are men and most of their patients are women. The traditional psychotherapy model is that of a man in authority and a woman in need, a dyad that replicates and reinforces the inequitable power distribution most women have had in their relationships with men as fathers, husbands, employers, and health professionals. Expressions of sex bias in the therapeutic process have been well documented.[2,15,23] These biases are especially prominent in the treatment of women who reject traditional role constructs of woman's place. For example, therapists are limited in their understanding of lesbians and the ways that they are both similar to and different from gay men. Lesbians, by creating an alternative cultural pattern, constitute a direct challenge to therapists' values about both sexuality and traditional roles.

Adjustment to traditional roles is stressed and anger in women is often labeled as pathological rather than understood as a consequence of a devalued position. In general, our culture and our psychological theories have viewed women's anger as inappropriate except when it is used in the service of others, as in a "lioness defending her cubs." Thus, most women experience considerable psychic conflict about anger. Women develop within a milieu that stimulates anger repeatedly. Simultaneously, their attempts to express or act on their anger are met with negative and condemning reactions from the environment. Most women do not aspire to the forms of anger seen in men. Well-intentioned therapists have sometimes mistakenly encouraged women toward this imitation of men and then not understood their lack of therapeutic effectiveness. More commonly, however, therapists are unaware of the ubiquitous sources of the anger, and they share the dominant cultural fear of anger in women. Thus, they are unable to tolerate or encourage the expression of anger in women as an important step toward health.[10,58,59]

Similarly, clinicians continue to use inaccurate and demeaning labels; for example, *he* is assertive while *she* is "castrating." Therapists are sometimes inattentive and disbelieving of real sources of anguish for women, so that the history of incest or rape is interpreted as a fantasied wish. This is generally a reflection of the therapist's own denial of the psychological forces involved in these situations. The problem, however, is that the therapist's inattention is consonant with the general cultural denial, and the woman remains in a state of confusion and self-doubt. Finally, there is the sexual abuse of women patients; some studies have indicated that as many as 10% of men psychiatrists and psychologists in practice report sexual contact with women patients.[23,60]

One of the most tangible measures of the adjustment model of treatment for women comes through world-wide reports of psychotropic drug-prescribing patterns. When drugs are obtained illicitly, patterns of use do not significantly differ by gender.[61] Sex differences in drug use are substantial, however, when the source of drugs is a physician—thus suggesting that sex-role stereotyping contributes to the relatively high prescription rate of psychotropic drugs for women.[62] In the United States more than two-thirds of all prescriptions for psychotropic drugs written each year are for women (*FDA Drug Bulletin*, February 1980), and it is estimated that at least half of the adult female population have been prescribed psychotropic drugs at some time (data from a national survey by the Program for Women's Concerns, National Institute on Drug Abuse, 1977). In 1977, 63% of the 51 million Americans who used tranquilizers were women; 71% of the 17 million who used stimulants were women (National Institute on Drug Abuse Capsules, April 1978). Women also received 71% of the prescriptions for antidepressants.[63] U.S. studies have identified nonworking housewives over the age of 35 as the largest single group of tranquilizer users.[49]

In a study of all prescriptions written in the Province of Ontario in 1970–1971 and 1973–1974, Cooperstock[49] reported that twice as many women as men received prescriptions for psychotropic drugs and that a higher proportion of women than men received multiple prescriptions. Further, once a woman receives a prescription, she has a better than even chance of receiving another prescription within the next 3 years. This overprescribing could not be explained on the basis of more visits to physicians by women. Women made 54% of the physician visits, and most of this excess occurred during the younger, reproductive years.

A recent report of the National Ambulatory Medical Care Survey,[64] which contains data obtained from a national sample of office-based physicians in the United States, found that drugs were ordered or provided during physician visits more than any other form of therapy (54% of all visits). Men psychiatrists prescribe drugs proportionately more often than women psychiatrists (33% versus 17% of office visits). For men psychiatrists, this tendency to prescribe drugs was more pronounced with women patients than with men patients (37% for women compared with 28% for men). Estimates of visits to women psychiatrists were too small to determine if the tendency to prescribe more drugs for women was significant for that group.

Clinicians alone do not pose these dilemmas for women, but clinicians' attitudes reflect the prevailing societal attitudes. By accepting the stereotypes of femininity, clinicians perpetuate them under the guise of "expert" opinion. As we shall see, these expert opinions exert a powerful influence not only in individual treatment settings but in the larger realm of state and national planning for mental health policy and service delivery.

SEX BIAS IN MENTAL HEALTH SERVICE DELIVERY: ISSUES OF ACCESS

Inadequacy of the Data

A comparison of patterns of illness and service utilization by gender is crucial in assessing the mental health needs of women and providing access to the appropriate services. Unfortunately, this task is enormously complicated by inadequate and incomplete data collection, widely varying definitions of illness, differing utilization measures (for example, admissions, additions, and discharges) for different kinds of institutions, and the absence of data from the private practice sector. Thus, conclusions about etiology, incidence, and prevalence will differ with the ori-

entation of the researcher, the type of facility, and the measuring instruments and will hamper comparability across facilities.[26,46,65,66]

Although a large amount of demographic and epidemiological data
is collected on alcohol, drug, and mental health problems and services,
the data are widely scattered and not reported in ways useful for improving treatment of women. *The Alcohol, Drug Abuse, and Mental Health
National Data Book*[67] does provide an overview of the national data related
to the incidence and prevalence of disorders, treatment facilities, service
utilization, clinical personnel, and the costs and financing of services. But
its use of global summaries masks the characteristics of sub-groups in the
patient populations.[46] When data are aggregated in ways that mask
important differences in subgroups of the patient population, service
approaches all too often are built on models based on expectations associated with male roles, as in alcohol programs geared toward treating
alcoholics and their *wives*.[26]

One particularly disturbing gap in our knowledge is with regard to
how differences in sex-role stereotypes and sex-role expectations among
racial and ethnic groups relate to different patterns of mental health
problems. Women are not a homogeneous group. The problems of
minority women, lesbians, handicapped women, young women, and
aged women differ. Bias due to race and age compounds the difficulties
of responding to women as individuals. Multiracial/multicultural
models for understanding the impact of sex bias and sex-role stereotyping on the creation, diagnosis, and treatment of mental disorders are virtually nonexistent.[46,68]

Sex differences in the duration of treatment raise issues concerning
both appropriateness of and access to mental health services. For example, it has been suggested that treatment for women may be unduly prolonged due to therapist stereotypes about women's dependency.[69] Since
these stereotypes are more applicable to white women than to women of
other races, analyses of the data by sex *and* race/ethnicity are needed to
explore the possible sources of bias in treatment. White women would
be expected to have longer durations of treatment than either males or
minority females, and indeed, this is the case.

Whether one looks at state and county mental hospitals, private
mental hospitals, or nonfederal general hospitals (public and nonpublic),
white women have a greater median number of days of stay than do
white men. This finding is particularly true for state and county mental
hospitals, where the difference is 13.1 days. In contrast, when minority-
race women and men are compared, men in state and county mental hospitals and in public general hospitals have longer median stays.[46]

Unfortunately, data by sex, race, age, and type of disorder across
institutions are not available. The *National Data Book*[67] does provide some

information about variations in median lengths of stay in state and county mental hospitals by sex *or* race for some disorders. Thus, we are tantalized with the knowledge that the median length of stay in those facilities for women compared to men is higher for drug disorders (30 versus 11 days) and neurotic disorders (60 versus 29 days) and lower for transient situational disturbances (23 versus 75 days) and personality disorders (12 versus 25 days). For depressive disorders the median length of stay is 55 days for minority-race patients compared with 26 days for whites. The difference for women and men with depressive disorders is not reported. We do learn that beyond age 25 depressed women had longer lengths of stay than did men, this difference reaching 3.4 times that of men by age 65. These data starkly remind us that conclusions drawn from data presented by race *or* sex may not be the same as conclusions drawn from data presented by race *and* sex.

Representation of Women as Patients in Mental Health Facilities

How do women differ from men in their utilization of mental health services? Although the data have limitations, it is possible to provide a partial answer to that question. One of the most striking characteristics of the data on patient populations is the diversity of sex differences in the profiles of the populations depending on the institution being studied. In 1975 a larger proportion of patients was estimated to be female in community mental health centers (52%), outpatient facilities (55%), private mental health centers (57%), and general hospital units (63%). For state and county mental hospitals and public general hospitals, the proportions were 35% and 49%, respectively. One percent of the patient populations of the VA hospital psychiatric inpatient units was estimated to be female.[46]

These figures include all patients. The proportions across facilities differ by age and race, and the interpretation of sex differences in utilization statistics is limited unless the age and race of the patient population is specified. Differences by sex in the proportion of patients served in outpatient facilities and community mental health centers become greater when patients under 18 years of age are eliminated from the statistics. Thus, an estimated 55% of patients served by outpatient facilities were female; however, 60% of white adult patients and 66% of adult patients of other races who were served in such facilities were female.

These utilization statistics do not adequately convey the extent to which sex bias permeates mental health services. Sex bias and sex-role stereotyping affect the delivery of mental health services in paradoxical ways, and detract from both appropriateness of and access to treatment.[26]

Women can be considered *both* overserved and underserved by mental health delivery systems. For disorders congruent with sex-role stereotypes, such as depression, conversion hysteria, and phobias, women show higher rates of service utilization than do men. As we have described earlier, issues of appropriateness of services are paramount in such cases. In contrast, problems of women that are congruent with societal views of male authority and female devaluation, such as rape, incest, and wife beating, have been ignored. Thus, services for female victims of male aggression have been provided largely through the coordinated efforts of women themselves at a time when mental health professionals were often either blaming the victims or not noticing them. Similarly, for disorders that are incongruent with society's idealized view of women, such as alcoholism and illicit drug abuse, women's service needs have usually been hidden and ignored. Issues of access to service are central in these latter categories.[26]

Identification and treatment of disorders associated with a special stigma for women require a high level of knowledge and sensitivity. For example, in discussing the stigma of alcoholism for women, Sandmaier[70] describes how persons around them contribute to their own tendency to deny that they have a problem with alcohol. Physicians reinforce these denial processes by avoiding confrontations with their clients. A physician may listen to the alcohol-related symptoms of a woman patient and then prescribe tranquilizers rather than refer her to an alcoholism treatment program. This may also contribute to the greater incidence of polydrug abuse for women compared with men.[70]

Substantial numbers of women with drinking problems are found in every age bracket, socioeconomic class, racial and ethnic group, region of the country, and employment situation. The alcoholic woman, however, is alternately viewed as a lower-class promiscuous woman or as a middle-class housewife. The few available programs have reflected these stereotypes in their restriction of outreach and treatment efforts to limited groups of women. If a woman happens to be very young, single, nonwhite, poor, or not pregnant, her needs are likely to be neglected. She does not fit the stereotypes.[26,70]

Women drug addicts face similar barriers to access. Although women's use of illicit drugs does not significantly differ from that of men, utilization statistics show marked sex differences in rates of entry into both drug abuse and emergency treatment programs.[61] Drug abuse treatment programs are generally oriented toward the needs of men addicts who abuse illicit drugs and tend to neglect prescription drug abusers, who are largely women. As a result, the dropout rate of women in such programs is twice that of men, and women addicts seek treatment less often than men (reference 26, and N. Naierman, ABT Associates, unpublished report submitted to HEW, Office of Civil Rights, Division of Planning, Budget, and Research, 1979).

The needs of institutionalized women are also neglected. Compounding the problems of chronically mentally ill women is the tendency to consider them as genderless persons. Test and Berlin described the rationale for this view: The problems related to the illness are so massive that there just isn't time or energy to think much about them as women or men.[71] Yet chronically mentally ill women are more likely to be sexually active than men. In one study 59% of such women versus 38% of their male counterparts reported sexual intercourse in the previous month.[71] Although a substantial number of chronically mentally ill women have children, little is known about them as mothers.[71]

The relative inaccessibility of birth control information and contraception combined with the vulnerability of these women to rape and exploitive sexual relationships suggests that the frequency of unwanted pregnancies among chronically mentally ill women may be substantial. Due to restrictions on Medicaid funding, legal abortion is a less likely option for them than for women in general. Thus self-induced abortions are not uncommon among chronically mentally ill women, and many also experience the stress of unwanted childbearing, child rearing, and the trauma of adoption.[71]

Finally, rehabilitative efforts are important in establishing self-esteem, providing a more stable economic base, and preventing mental illness. But institutionalized women are likely to be assigned to the kitchen or laundry to perform tasks they know only too well, while their male peers participate in business education courses, computer programming, construction work, and carpentry. For example, local jails make up 75% of all correctional facilities, and they are uniformly designed to house men. Since women prisoners represent less than 10% of the inmate population, it has been considered economically impractical to develop separate treatment and rehabilitative services in local facilities. Consequently, women inmates have almost no access to psychological, educational, or rehabilitative services.[26]

ANCILLARY SERVICES FOR WOMEN

The provision of ancillary services is particularly important for women, as their poverty and lack of control over resources in the family limit their ability to provide such services for themselves.

Child care facilities are a crucial service for women with responsibility for children. As a consequence of traditional views of the role of mother, women who have problems that impair their ability to care for their children also must bear the guilt such impairment produces. When the problem has a stigma for women, as alcohol or drug abuse, women are particularly self-blaming. Since treatment facilities for such problems are oriented toward men—and it is assumed that such men are not responsible for their children—child care facilities are not provided. Because of the lack of access to child care facilities, the woman is trapped in a system that gives her the responsibility for the care of children when she is unable to provide such care—and compounds her problem by reinforcing her view of herself as a "bad mother" for leaving them to seek help.[26]

The difference that child care can make in women's service utilization rates underscores this need. For example, in one residential drug treatment project, the ratio of men to women clients was 3 to 2. After residential services were offered for both mothers and children, there was an increase of 33% in utilization by women clients. In another case, a satellite clinic in a multiservice outpatient alcohol project began providing babysitting services. Utilization by women increased from 30% to over 50% (N. Naierman, ABT Associates, unpublished report to HEW, 1979).

Another essential service needed for women is housing. It cannot be assumed that women will have someone at home who will care for them, as is often assumed to be the case for men. Marital disruption may be more of a problem for women who need treatment. For example, men are more likely to leave their alcoholic spouses than are women, perhaps because women are socialized to care for those who depend on them.[70] Separation and divorce rates for chronically mentally ill women show a similar pattern.[71] Marital problems also contribute to the need for shelter facilities for battered women, displaced homemakers, and aged women. These services as well as transportation may be prerequisite for the access of many women to treatment.[26]

The lack of coordination and cooperation among health, mental health, and social service delivery systems creates further barriers to women who need mental health care. Alternative services such as feminist counseling collectives, childbirth centers, health clinics, home health care, rape crisis centers, and shelters for battered women must be considered in coordination efforts.

A recent evaluation of health and human development programs pointed to several specific gaps between services needed and services offered in various types of delivery systems (N. Naierman, ABT Associates, unpublished report to HEW, 1979). For drug and alcohol projects, five basic services especially important for female substance abusers were identified: treatment for prescription drug abuse, counseling for incest victims, counseling for battered women, medical and nutritional care for pregnant women, and women's support groups. For mental health centers, services identified as particularly important for women included therapy for bereavement, treatment for postpartum depression, sex-fair counseling with respect to changes in sex roles within the family and society, treatment for abused wives, and comprehensive services for rape victims. These are only a few of the growing number of services recently identified as essential components of mental health care for women.[2,13,17]

Thus, the provision of appropriate mental health services that women will use is contingent on full recognition of their multiple gender-based roles and needs and awareness that their resources are likely to be limited. In this light, the term "ancillary" may be a misnomer because these services are a necessary condition for access to treatment and an integral part of any service delivery system.

CONCLUSIONS

In summary, complex processes of sex bias and sex-role stereotyping continue to detract from the quality of mental health services to both sexes, but particularly to women because of their disadvantaged status. Understanding how such processes can simultaneously create barriers to service access and facilitate inappropriate treatment is essential to ensuring quality mental health services. Ameliorating the problems of women as providers and consumers in the mental health delivery system will require a sophisticated understanding of the nature of those problems and a firm commitment to creative solutions.

We have an ethical obligation to go further, however. Societal instiutions and norms maintain and reinforce the powerlessness and devaluation of women that are so destructive to their mental health. Thus, any carefully conceived strategy for the promotion of mental health and the prevention of mental illness must have as one of its basic goals eradication of sexism and racism in the larger society. The ethical mandate to address the institutional structures of inequality extends to all persons who are part of the mental health delivery system.

REFERENCES

1. Brickley, L. T., Garfunkel, G., Hulsizer, D. (eds): Women and Education, 1, 2. *Harvard Educational Review* 49(4), 1979;50(1), 1980
2. Brodsky, A. M., Hare-Mustin, R. (eds): *Women and Psychotherapy: An Assessment of Research and Practice.* New York, Guilford Press, 1980

3. Carter, L. A., Scott, A. F. (eds): *Women and Men: Changing Roles, Relationships, and Perceptions.* New York, Aspen Institute, 1976

4. Ehrenreich, B., English, D: *For Her Own Good: 150 Years of the Experts' Advice to Women.* Garden City, NY, Anchor/Doubleday, 1978

5. Franks, V., Burtle, V. (eds): *Women in Therapy: New Psychotherapies for a Changing Society.* New York, Brunner/Mazel, 1974

6. Gomberg, E. S., Franks, V. (eds): *Gender and Disordered Behavior: Sex Differences in Psychopathology.* New York, Brunner/Mazel, 1979

7. Guttentag, M., Salasin, S., Belle, D. (eds): *The Mental Health of Women.* New York, Academic Press, 1980

8. Kaplan, A. G. (ed): Psychological Androgyny: Further Considerations. *Psychology of Women Quarterly* 3(3), 1979

9. Miller, J. B.: *Psychoanalysis and Women.* Baltimore, Penguin, 1973

10. Miller, J. B.: *Toward a New Psychology of Women.* Boston, Beacon Press, 1976

11. Notman, M. T., Nadelson, C. C. (eds): *The Woman Patient: Medical and Psychological Interfaces,* vol 1: *Sexual and Reproductive Aspects of Women's Health Care.* New York, Plenum Publishing Corp, 1978

12. O'Leary V. E.: *Toward Understanding Women.* Monterey, Calif, Brooks/Cole, 1977

13. Rawlings, E. I., Carter, D. K. (eds): *Psychotherapy for Women: Treatment Toward Equality.* Springfield, Ill, Charles C. Thomas, 1977

14. Russo, N. F. (ed): The Motherhood Mandate. *Psychology of Women Quarterly* 4(1), 1979

15. Seiden, A. M.: Overview: research on the psychology of women, I, II. *Am J Psychiatry* 133:995–1007, 1111–1123, 1976

16. Sherman, J. A., Denmark, F. L. (eds): *The Psychology of Women: Future Directions in Research.* New York, Psychological Dimensions, 1978

17. Sobel, S. B, Russo, N. F. (eds): Sex Roles, Equality, and Mental Health. *Professional Psychology* 12(1), 1981

18. Tavris, C., Offir, C.: *The Longest War—Sex Differences in Perspective.* New York, Harcourt Brace Jovanovich, 1977

19. Williams, J.: *Psychology of Women: Behavior in a Biosocial Context.* New York, W. W. Norton & Co, 1977

20. Stone, A. A.: Presidential address: conceptual ambiguity and morality in modern psychiatry. *Am J Psychiatry* 137:887–891, 1980

21. Carmen, E., Driver, F.: Teaching women's studies: values in conflict. *Psychology of Women Quarterly* 7(1):81–95, 1982

22. Hilberman, E., Russo, N. F.: Mental health and equal rights: the ethical challenge for psychiatry. *Psychiatric Opinion* 15(8):11–19, 1978

23. President's Commission on Mental Health: Subpanel on the Mental Health of Women, in *Report to the President,* vol III. Washington, D.C., U.S. Government Printing Office, 1978, pp 1022–1116.

24. U.S. Department of Labor: *Twenty Facts on Women Workers.* Washington, D. C., Office of the Secretary, Women's Bureau, 1980

25. Hofferth, S. L., Moore, K. A.: Women's employment and marriage, in *The Subtle Revolution: Women at Work.* Edited by Smith R. E., Washington, D. C., Urban Institute, 1979

26. Russo, N. F., VandenBos, G. R.: Women in the mental health delivery system, in *A Community Mental Health Sourcebook for Board and Professional Action.* Edited by Silverman, W. H., New York, Praeger, 1980

27. Gordon, S. Y.: Occupational hazards include sexual harassment. *Jobs Watch* 1(2):12–13, 1980

28. Gordon, N. M.: Institutional response: the federal income tax system, in *The Subtle Revolution: Women at Work.* Edited by Smith, R. E., Washington, D.C., Urban Institute, 1979

29. U.S. Bureau of the Census: *Current Population Reports: Characteristics of the Population Below the Poverty Level, 1975* Washington, D.C., U.S. Government Printing Office, 1977

30. Russo, N. F.: Overview: sex roles, fertility, and the motherhood mandate. *Psychology of Women Quarterly* 4(1):7–15, 1979

31. Bardwick, J. M., Douvan, E.: Ambivalence: the socialization of women, in *Woman in Sexist Society.* Edited by Gornick, V., Moran, B. K., New York, New American Library, 1971

32. Rawlings, E. I., Carter, D. K.: Values and value change in psychotherapy, in *Psychotherapy for Women: Treatment Toward Equality.* Edited by Rawlings, E. I., Carter, D. K., Springfield, Ill, Charles C. Thomas, 1977

33. Guttentag, M., Salasin, S.: Women, men, and mental health, in *Women and Men: Changing Roles, Relationships, and Perceptions.* Edited by Carter, L. A., Scott, A. F., New York, Aspen Institute, 1976

34. Weissman, M. M., Klerman, G. L.: Sex differences and the epidemiology of depression. *Arch Gen Psychiatry* 34:98–111, 1977

35. Belle, D.: Who uses mental health facilities? in *The Mental Health of Women.* Edited by Guttentag, M., Salasin, S., Belle, D., New York, Academic Press, 1980

36. Klerman, G. L. Weissman, M. M.: Depressions among women: their nature and causes. Ibid

37. Makosky, V. P.: Stress and the mental health of women: a discussion of research and issues. Ibid

38. Dohrenwend, B. S.: Social status and stressful life events. *J Pers Soc Psychol* 28:225–235, 1973

39. Gilligan, C.: Woman's place in man's life cycle. *Harvard Educational Review* 49:431–446, 1979

40. Greywolf, E. S., Reese, M. F., Belle, D.: Stressed mothers syndrome: how to short-circuit the stress depression cycle. *Behavioral Medicine* 7(11):12–18, 1980

41. Radloff, L. S.: Risk factors for depression: what do we learn from them? in *The Mental Health of Women.* Edited by Guttentag, M., Salasin, S., Belle, D., New York, Academic Press, 1980

42. Gove, W. R.: The relationship between sex roles, marital status, and mental illness. *Social Forces* 51:34–44, 1972

43. Gove, W. R., Tudor, J. F.: Adult sex roles and mental illness. *Am J Sociol* 78(4):50–73, 1973

44. Gove, W. R., Geerken, M. D.: The effects of children and employment on the mental health of married men and women. *Social Forces* 56:66–76, 1977

45. Gove, W. R.: Sex differences in the epidemiology of mental illness: evidence and explanations, in *Gender and Disordered Behavior.* Edited by Gomberg, E. S., Franks, V., New York, Brunner/Mazel, 1979

46. Russo, N. F., Sobel, S. B.: Sex differences in the utilization of mental health facilities. *Professional Psychology* 12(1):7–19, 1981

47. Brown, G., Bhrolchain, M., Harris, T.: Social class and psychiatric disturbance among women in an urban population. *Sociology* 9:225–254, 1975

48. Weissman, M. M., Klerman, G. L.: Sex differences and the epidemiology of depression, in *Gender and Disordered Behavior.* Edited by Gomberg, E. S., Franks, V., New York, Brunner/Mazel, 1979

49. Cooperstock, R.: Sex differences in psychotropic drug use. *Soc Sci Med* 12B:179–186, 1978

50. Straus, M. A.: Sexual inequality, cultural norms, and wife-beating. *Victimology* 1:54–76, 1976

51. Straus, M. A.: A sociological perspective on the prevention and treatment of wife-

beating, in *Battered Women*. Edited by Roy, M., New York, Van Nostrand Reinhold Co, 1977

52. Hilberman, E.: Overview: the "wife-beater's wife" reconsidered. *Am J Psychiatry* 137:1336–1347, 1980
53. Herman, J., Hirschman, L.: Father–daughter incest. *Signs* 2:735–756, 1977
54. Herman, J.: Father–daughter incest. *Professional Psychology* 12(1):76–80, 1981
55. Dobash, R. E., Dobash, R.: *Violence Against Wives: A Case Against the Patriarchy*. New York, Free Press, 1979
56. Broverman, I. K., Broverman, D. M., Clarkson, F. E.: Sex-role stereotypes and clinical judgments of mental health. *J Consult Clin Psychol* 34:1–7, 1970
57. Sherman, J. A.: Therapist attitudes and sex-role stereotyping, in *Women and Psychotherapy*. Edited by Brodsky, A. M., Hare-Mustin, R., New York, Guilford Press, 1980
58. Bernardez-Bonesatti, T.: Unconscious beliefs about women affecting psychotherapy. *North Carolina Journal of Mental Health* 7(5):63–66, 1976
59. Lerner, H. E.: The taboo against female anger. *Menninger Perspective*, Winter 1977, pp 5–11
60. Davidson, V.: Psychiatry's problem with no name: therapist–patient sex. *Am J Psychoanal* 37:43–50, 1977
61. Burt, M. R., Gynn, T. S., Sowder, B. J.: *Psychosocial Characteristics of Drug-Abusing Women*. Washington, D. C., U.S. DHEW, 1979
62. Fidell, L. S.: Sex differentials in psychotropic drug use. *Professional Psychology* 12(1):156–162, 1981
63. Hughes, R., Brewin, R.: *The Tranquilizing of America: Pill Popping and the American Way of Life*. New York, Harcourt Brace Jovanovich, 1979
64. Cypress, B. K.: *Characteristics of Visits to Female and Male Physicians: The National Ambulatory Medical Care Survey, United States, 1977*. Hyattsville, Md. National Center for Health Statistics, 1980
65. Sobel, S. B., Russo, N. F.: Equality, public policy, and professional psychology. *Professional Psychology* 12(1):180–189, 1981
66. Gomberg, E. S.: Women, sex roles, and alcohol problems. *Professional Psychology* 12(1):146–155, 1981
67. Vischi, T. R., Jones, K. R., Shank, E. L., et al: *The Alcohol, Drug Abuse, and Mental Health National Data Book*. Washington, D. C., U.S. DHEW, 1980
68. Olmedo, E. L., Parron, D. L.: Mental health and minority women: some special issues. *Professional Psychology* 12(1):103–111, 1981
69. Fabrikant, B.: The psychotherapist and the female patient: perceptions and change, in *Women in Therapy: New Psychotherapies for a Changing Society*. Edited by Franks, V., Burtle, V., New York, Brunner/Mazel, 1974
70. Sandmaier, M.: *The Invisible Alcoholics: Women and Alcoholic Abuse in America*. New York, McGraw-Hill Book Co, 1980
71. Test, M. A., Berlin, S. B.: Issues of special concern to chronically mentally ill women. *Professional Psychology* 12(1):136–145, 1981

Social Structures and Psychological Processes

II

Most clinicians would acknowledge that existing social arrangements affect social identities and psychological states. What they fail to appreciate is the extent to which social structures, with their unequal distributions of power and status, influence how women and men think, feel and behave. The chapters in this section provide examples of how various structures of inequality set into motion psychological processes that affect women and men differently. This way of understanding how subjective experiences are determined by a wider social reality contrasts with psychological explanations that view individual behaviors in isolation from social forces other than the family. Even with explanations that take family dynamics into account, patriarchal structures within families are usually ignored.

Jean Baker Miller's article, "The Effects of Inequality on Psychology," analyzes the psychological characteristics that men and women develop because of dominant or subordinate group membership. When we view women and men from these categories that evolve from structures of gender inequality, the vast differences in developmental experiences can no longer be overlooked. The most damaging consequence of permanent subordinate status is that subordinates cannot maintain a valid or reliable sense of their own worth apart from the acceptable roles that have been defined for them by dominants. The most destructive psychological effect for dominants is that they miss the opportunity for self-knowledge that comes from understanding the impact of their own actions on others, and subordinates cannot risk telling them the truth.

Rosabeth Moss Kanter, in "Some Effects of Proportions on Group Life: Skewed Sex Ratios and Responses to Token Women," provides another example of how the structure of groups—in this case, the relative numbers of socially and culturally different people—determines the nature of social relations and individual experiences. Specifically, she describes the situation of women who are tokens in a peer group of men to illustrate the general effects on anyone who occupies token status. Tokens refer to persons who are a numerical minority and who are "often treated as representatives of their category, as symbols rather than individuals." Understanding the dynamics of tokenism is important because of the increasing numbers of women entering male-dominated professions and occupations and the unavoidable handicaps under which tokens must perform their work. Recognizing that tokens experience more personal stress (for example, social isolation, self-distortion, and work inhibition) than majority group members will help clinicians to appreciate the need for detailed information about the work settings of their clients. Further, these dynamics apply to all forms of group life in which there is a skewed numerical distribution, such as therapy groups, faculty meetings, or academic departments.

The last two chapters in this section explain how difficult it is for men to give up power and authority and what happens when women try to exercise power and authority. Power relations among men and women may be the most consequential aspect of social structures characterized by gender inequality. In "Men's Power with Women, Other Men, and Society: A Men's Movement Analysis," Joseph H. Pleck reasons that men's need for power over women derives from economic and pragmatic self-interests and from men's psychological needs. By defining the male role as unemotional, inexpressive, and heterosexual, men have found it necessary to keep their distance from other men and, hence, have come to depend on women to express their emotions and to validate their masculinity. These are the traditional functions that female subordinates generally provide for male dominants, and it is this dependency that may generate such intense male fear of and resistance to relinquishing control over women. Pleck believes that men's sexism cannot be understood without also analyzing men's power relationships with other men and, paradoxically, men's powerlessness in the larger political economy.

Sharon S. Mayes's article, "Women in Positions of Authority: A Case Study of Changing Sex Roles," gives us a vivid portrait of the responses of women and men to female-led small and large groups. Of particular note was the threat that female leadership posed to males and the lengths to which males went in their attempts to undermine, if not annihilate, women leaders. The male response was characterized by hostility, dependency, lack of cooperation, and self-reported fears of having lost control. Conversely, women tended to be more outspoken, assertive, and dominant in female-led groups. As the author concludes, "Male confusion in response to the female authority stemmed not from her authority per se but from the *male* way in which she exercised her authority; namely, with formal, objective, nonnurturant, asexual adherence to rules and boundaries."

Mayes further argues that the status of women in the family is still the source of imagery for female power and authority; thus, women leaders will be "interpreted through the universal experience of the family and placed in some aspect of the mother role." We have found this article to be particularly useful for understanding the frequently chaotic processes that emerge in work relationships when women exercise "male" kinds of authority, as, for example, female psychotherapy supervisor, committee chair, research project director, or professor. This was demonstrated some years ago when one of us, in her role as individual psychotherapy supervisor, was accused by two male supervisees on the same day of being "just like my mother." Needless to say, the composite portrait of mother was nothing short of fantastic; one trainee was a black southerner from a poor rural background, and the other a wealthy white northerner from a highly educated, urbane, middle-European family. The humor of this example notwithstanding, a woman in authority has a double burden of responsibility. It is not sufficient that she is competent in performing her various roles; she must also manage the complex and often angry responses that are generated simply by the appropriate uses of her authority.

The Effects of Inequality on Psychology

4

Jean Baker Miller

Why should psychiatrists be concerned with equality? We are not accustomed to including inequality as a determinant of psychic well- or ill-being. We tend to think on other levels, e.g., the intrapsychic or the biological, and in so doing, assume that we are dealing with universal factors.

It is possible, however, that we are unwittingly dealing with psychological events which some forms of actual inequality have set in motion? In the hope of approaching that question, we may set out some basic observations for examination.

There are several types of inequality. One form may be termed "permanent inequality." In these relationships, a group of people is defined as unequal by birth, or by ascription in sociological terminology. The inequality is based on race, sex, nationality, or other characteristics. In these relationships a series of regularly occurring tendencies are set in motion. A few of these may be mentioned on a very gross and superficial level. It will probably become apparent that they actually operate on a much more intense and profound psychic level. For the sake of brevity most of these tendencies will be asserted without attempts at full documentation here.

DOMINANTS

Once a group is defined as inferior, the "superiors" tend to label it as defective or substandard along various dimensions. Such labels accrete rapidly. Thus, blacks are less intelligent than whites, women are ruled by emotion, and the like.

The actions of the superior group tend to be destructive to the subordinate group. All historical evidence confirms this tendency.[1,2] There are also destructive effects on the dominants, though these are much less obvious. The latter are of a different order and are more difficult to recognize. They will be discussed further below.

Reprinted from *Psychiatric Opinion* 15(8):29–32, 1978. Copyright © 1978 by the Opinions Publication, Inc. Reprinted by permission. The ideas expressed in this paper are elaborated in J. B. Miller, *Toward a New Psychology of Women* (Boston: Beacon Press, 1976).

Dominant groups usually provide one or more acceptable roles for the subordinate group. These acceptable roles often include the performance of services that obviously no dominant group would prefer to perform for itself. Many of these involve the provision of bodily comforts and servicing, e.g., cleaning up for and after dominants, providing comfortable surroundings, feeding, and the like. The functions that a dominant group prefers to perform become closely guarded and inaccessible to the subordinates. In general, out of the total range of human possibilities, those which are most valued in any particular culture become associated with and enclosed within the domain of the dominant group. Those aspects which are less valued are delegated to the subordinates. It is usually said that subordinates are incapable of performing the more preferred roles. Such incapabilities are ascribed to innate defects or deficiencies of mind or body. They are, then, considered immutable, impossible of change or development. It becomes difficult for the dominants even to imagine that subordinates are capable of performing the preferred roles. This myth is often challenged only if something fairly drastic disrupts the usual arrangements. Such disruptions sometimes arise from outside—as, for example, in the emergency situation of World War II, when inexperienced blacks and incompetent women suddenly "manned" the factories with great skill.

It usually follows that subordinates tend to be described in terms of, and encouraged to develop, those personal psychological characteristics which any dominant group would obviously prefer in subordinates who are performing less valued roles. These psychological characteristics all seem to revolve around a certain cluster, and they tend to sound familiar: submissiveness; passivity; docility; dependency; lack of initiative; inability to act, to decide, to think, and the like. Indeed, if the subordinates adopt this set of characteristics, they are likely to be considered well-adjusted.[3]

If the subordinates somehow have the potential or even demonstrate other characteristics—let us say intelligence, initiative, assertiveness—there is usually little room available within the dominant framework for acknowledgment or expression of these characteristics. They are considered at least unusual if not definitely abnormal. There is also little opportunity for their application by subordinates within the existing social arrangements.

Dominant groups usually impede the development of subordinates, and the subordinates' freedom of expression and action. Again, historical evidence records this tendency.[1,2] Dominant groups tend also to prevent stirrings of greater rationality or greater humanity in any of their own members. It was not too long ago that "nigger lover" was a common appellation, and men who "allow their women" to have more than the usual scope are still subject to ridicule in many circles.

A dominant group inevitably has the greatest influence in determining a culture's overall outlook, its philosophy, morality, social theory, and, even, its science. The dominant group, then, legitimizes the unequal relationship and incorporates it into all of society's guiding concepts.

The dominant group's philosophical and social outlook is one that tends to obscure the true nature of this relationship and the very fact of the existence of inequality itself. Having done so, dominant culture has to go to other premises to explain the events which occur. Such premises are, of necessity, always false, such as racial or sexual inferiority. Although in recent years many such distortions have been elucidated on the larger social level, this point has particular application in psychological theory. Despite overwhelming evidence to the contrary, the theory was still rooted in the notion that women are inherently passive, submissive, and docile. From this premise the outcome of therapy has often been determined.

The dominant group becomes the model for "normal human relationships." It is, then, "normal" to subscribe to all the tendencies suggested so far—that is, to treat others destructively and derogate them, to obscure the truth of what one is doing, to create rationalizations, and to oppose actions toward equality.

Thus, if one is a member of a dominant group it becomes part of being normal to participate in these activities, often without full awareness. For example, it is easy to allow oneself to exist in an unequal relationship; to label falsely and demean the others as unequals; and to impede their attempts to move toward greater action and expression. Most of us hardly like to think of ourselves as either believing in or engaging in such behaviors. But it is difficult for a dominant group to do otherwise, since such behavior is "normal" for dominant group members.

Dominant groups generally do not like to be reminded about the existence of inequality. "Normally" they can avoid awareness because the explanation of the situation tends to become well integrated in other terms. Members of a dominant group tend to believe that both they and the subordinate groups share the same interests and even, to some extent share a common experience. Rationalizations become masked in other terms, such as those about "the poor black who doesn't have the white man's responsibilities" or "women's natural place."

Dominant groups prefer to avoid conflict that might call into question the entire situation. This is sometimes particularly and tragically true when the dominant group itself is in difficulty. It seems inevitable, however, that there would exist a situation generating profound conflict. In other words, the stage is set for conflict, but dominant groups have a major tendency to seek to suppress conflict. They tend to see any questioning of the "normal" situation as "abnormal" and any actions as more

so. Further, they usually are convinced that the way things are is right
and good, not only for them but especially for the subordinates. All
morality confirms this view and all social structures and social power
sustain it.

SUBORDINATES

What of the subordinates' part in this?

Since dominants determine what is "normal" and their outlook pre-
vails, we are not ever as familiar with how subordinates deal with their
part of the relationship.

The first direct expressions and actions by subordinates always come
as a surprise, and they usually are rejected as strangely atypical. After all,
dominants knew that blacks were always happy and cheerful or that all
women needed and wanted was a man around whom to organize their
lives. Members of the dominant group find it difficult to understand why
the first subordinates to speak out are so upset and angry.

A subordinate group has to be concerned primarily with survival.
Accordingly, direct and honest reaction to the destructive treatment it is
receiving often has to be avoided. Open, self-initiated action in its own
interest is likewise dangerous. Such actions can and still do result literally in death in some places. For women in our society, such direct kinds
of action have meant economic hardship, social ostracism, psychological
isolation, and even the possibility of a diagnosis of a psychological disorder.

A subordinate group, then, often resorts to disguised and indirect
ways of acting and reacting. These actions generally are designed to
accommodate and please the dominants. Often this mode can contain
hidden defiance and even a "put-on" of the dominants. Folktales, black
jokes, and women's stories of the wily peasant or sharecropper who out-
witted the rich landowner, boss, or husband are examples. The essence
of the story rests on the overlord's ignorance that he is the butt of the
joke.[4]

The dominant group is thus denied an essential part of life, that is,
direct "feedback" or the opportunity for knowledge about itself and its
actions. It is deprived of a large segment of consensual validation or the
opportunity for correction of its actions and expressions. Put simply, subordinates "won't tell." For the same reason, the dominant group is not
in possession of valid knowledge about the subordinates. (It is particularly ironic that those considered "experts" in knowledge about subordinates were usually members of the dominant group.)

Subordinates, then, may know much more about the dominants than
vice versa, from having to look to the sources of safety or rewards. Sub-

ordinates tend to become more attuned to dominants, and tend to be able to predict their reactions of pleasure and displeasure, and the like. Many black writers have now pointed out, for example, that in the old South blacks knew infinitely more about whites than whites knew about blacks. One might consider here, too, the place of "feminine intuition and feminine wiles." These are not mysterious gifts or biological derivatives but can be seen as skills developed through long practice in reading many small signals, both verbal and nonverbal.

Subordinates often have felt that they had to concentrate their interests and energies on knowing the dominants rather than on knowing themselves, since knowing the dominants determines a major part of a subordinate's fate. This tendency is reinforced by another factor. One comes to know oneself fully only as one is engaged in action and interaction. To the extent that this range is limited, one cannot truly know about his/her capabilities and about the problems he/she might have in using them.

Deeper confusion arises because subordinates absorb many of the untruths created by the dominants, so that there are blacks who feel inferior and women who believe they are less important then men. This internalization of dominant beliefs is more likely to occur if there are few or no alternative concepts available.

On the other hand, members of the subordinate group also have some experiences and perceptions that more accurately reflect the truth about themselves. These are bound to come into conflict with the mythology they have absorbed from the dominant group. An inner tension between these two sets of concepts and their multitudinous derivatives is almost inevitable.

Despite the obstacles, subordinate groups historically have tended to move toward greater freedom of expression and action, although this has varied greatly in different circumstances. There were always some slaves who revolted; there were some women who sought greater self-determination. Most records of these actions have not been preserved by the dominant culture, thus making it difficult for the subordinate group to find a supporting tradition and history.

Within each subordinate group, some members will imitate the dominants and internalize their concepts. This imitation can take various forms. Some may try to treat their fellow subordinates just as destructively as the dominants do, or perceive fellow subordinates as deficient. Many women have been encouraged to demean other women. A few subordinates may develop enough of the qualities possessed by the dominants to gain partial acceptance into the fellowship of the dominants or to "pass" as one of them. Usually such acceptance is incomplete and, in any case, forces the subordinates to forsake their identification with their fellow subordinates. "Uncle Toms" among blacks and professional women striving toward "masculine goals" often have been caught in this position. Thereby, for example, a few women have won the praise presumably embodied in such phrases as "she thinks like a man." Some subordinates may attempt to reverse the roles of oppressor and oppressed, that is, to seek to treat dominants as they have been treated by them by identifying with the aggressor. Also, being the subordinate in one relationship does not necessarily guarantee a benign effect upon one's performance as a dominant in another relationship. For example, women may put down blacks and vice versa.

CONFLICT

What is immediately apparent from the characteristics of dominant and subordinate groups is that mutually enhancing interaction is not probable. Instead, conflict and deprivation are inevitable. But this conflict and deprivation can remain obscure and misunderstood so long as subordinates "stay in their place."

While the factors suggested above may apply to all conditions of inequality, there are particular features which operate in each specific type.

In the female–male situation these features are infinitely compounded. As we all know, the female–male interaction affects the most intimate and personal experience and female and male definitions of self influence the total self-concept from the very beginnings of life.

To merely suggest some of these complexities, women, as subordinates, have been led readily to believe that their attempts to know, to express, and to act on their own needs or to enlarge their lives beyond the prescribed bounds are equivalent to attempts to either attack men or to be like men. Indeed, any attempt by women to enlarge their lives, even to enlarge them in the direction of their own specifically feminine concerns, was readily misinterpreted as an attempt to diminish men or to imitate them. It has been very difficult for women to perceive efforts at self-expression or self-development in any other terms.[5,6]

To concentrate on self-development is difficult for everyone. But, as has been recently demonstrated in many areas, it has been even more difficult for women. Women have not been encouraged to know and to act on their own needs, to use their resources openly, to develop as far as possible, to experience all the anguish, anxiety, and pain that self-knowledge can entail. Instead, they have been encouraged to concentrate on finding and holding a relationship and making themselves subordinate to another person. In fact, women are encouraged to believe that if they go through the anxiety and anguish of self-development, the end result will be only the forfeiture of the possibility of any close relationships—a penalty, a threat of isolation intolerable for anyone to contemplate.

All of the factors cited barely hint at the obstacles which have stood in the path of women's ability to explore and act on their most basic life needs. Today, however, many women have begun this difficult, but exhilarating attempt. In doing so, they find that their requirements and desires are quite different from those conceptualized for them by the dominant group.[7] This discovery can lead to surprise, discomfort, anxiety, and numbers of other pleasant and unpleasant reactions for all parties. The hope, however, is that this entire effort eventually can place the development of both sexes on a sound psychological path.

A change in the social system, alone, will not, of course, automatically solve all problems. There are many complex steps between external conditions and the intense psychological forces generated by these conditions. External conditions, however, do provide the total surrounding milieu which becomes incorporated in more complex psychological terms—especially a milieu which creates such basic definitions as the definitions of femaleness and maleness. Without a change in such definitions, an enhancement of psychological functioning is extremely difficult to attain.

As we have begun to seriously examine this milieu, it has become apparent that it has constricted and distorted the psychological potentialities available to members of both sexes. On the other hand, this examination has allowed a glimpse of the possibilities for a vast enlargement of the development of all individuals.

REFERENCES

1. Myrdal, G. *An American Dilemma.* Harper, New York, 1944.
2. Hacker, H. M. "Women as a Minority Group," *Soc. Forces,* Vol. 30, 1951, pp. 60–69.
3. Broverman, I., et al. "Sex-role Stereotypes and Clinical Judgements of Mental Health," *J. Consult. Clin. Psychol.,* Vol. 34, 1970, pp. 1–7.
4. Shainess, N. "Images of Woman: Past and Present, Overt and Obscured," *Amer. J. Psychother.,* Vol. 23, 1969, pp. 77–97.
5. Strouse, J. *Women and Psychoanalysis.* Grossman, New York, 1974.
6. Miller, J. B. *Psychoanalysis and Women.* Brunner/Mazel and Penguin Books, New York, 1973.
7. Gilligan, C., "In a Different Voice: Women's Conception of the Self and of Morality," *Harvard Educ. Rev.,* Vol. 47, 1977, pp. 481–517.

Some Effects of Proportions on Group Life

5

Skewed Sex Ratios and Responses to Token Women

Rosabeth Moss Kanter

In his classic analysis of the significance of numbers in social life, Georg Simmel (1950) argued persuasively that numerical modifications effect qualitative transformations in group interaction. Simmel dealt almost exclusively with the impact of absolute numbers, however, with group size as a determinant of form and process. The matter of relative numbers, of proportion of interacting social types, was left unexamined. But this feature of collectivities has an impact on behavior. Its neglect has sometimes led to inappropriate or misleading conclusions.

This paper defines the issues that need to be explored. It addresses itself to proportion as a significant aspect of social life, particularly important for understanding interactions in groups composed of people of different cultural categories or statuses. It argues that groups with varying proportions of people of different social types differ qualitatively in dynamics and process. This difference is not merely a function of cultural diversity or "status incongruence" (Zaleznick, Christensen, and Roethlisberger 1958, pp. 56–68); it reflects the effects of contact across categories as a function of their proportional representation in the system.

Four group types can be identified on the basis of various proportional representations of kinds of people. *Uniform* groups have only one kind of person, one significant social type. The group may develop its

Reprinted from *American Journal of Sociology* 82(5):965–990, 1977. Copyright © 1977 by The University of Chicago Press. Reprinted by permission. Thanks are due to the staff of "Industrial Supply Corporation," the pseudonymous corporation which invited and provided support for this research along with permission for use of the data in this paper. The research was part of a larger project on social structural factors in organizational behavior reported in Kanter (1977). An early version of this article was prepared for the Center for Research on Women in Higher Education and the Professions, Wellesley College, which provided some additional financial support. Barry Stein's colleagueship was especially valuable. This article was completed while the author held a Guggenheim fellowship.

own differentiations, of course, but groups considered uniform are homogeneous with respect to salient external master statuses such as sex, race, or ethnicity. Uniform groups have a "typological ratio" of 100:0. *Skewed* groups are those in which there is a large preponderance of one type over another, up to a ratio of perhaps 85:15. The numerically dominant types also control the group and its culture in enough ways to be labeled "dominants." The few of another type in a skewed group can appropriately be called "tokens," because they are often treated as representatives of their category, as symbols rather than individuals. If the absolute size of the skewed group is small, tokens can also be solitary individuals or "solos," the only one of their kind present. But even if there are two tokens in a skewed group, it is difficult for them to generate an alliance that can become powerful in the group. Next, *tilted* groups begin to move toward less extreme distributions and less exaggerated effects. In this situation, with a ratio of perhaps 65:35, dominants are just a majority and tokens a minority. Minority members are potentially allies, can form coalitions, and can affect the culture of the group. They begin to become individuals differentiated from each other as well as a type differentiated from the majority. Finally, at a typological ratio of about 60:40 down to 50:50, the group becomes *balanced.* Culture and interaction reflect this balance. Majority and minority turn into potential subgroups which may or may not generate actual type-based identifications. Outcomes for individuals in such a balanced peer group, regardless of type, will depend on other structural and personal factors, including formation of subgroups or differentiated roles and abilities. Figure 1 schematizes the four group types.

The characteristics of the second type, the skewed group, provide a

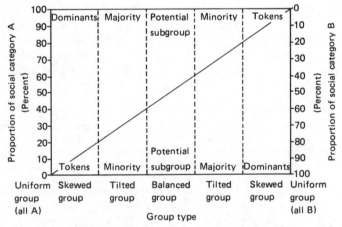

FIGURE 1. Group types as defined by proportional representation of two social categories in a membership.

relevant starting point for this examination of the effects of proportion, for although this group represents an extreme instance of the phenomenon, it is one encountered by large numbers of women in groups and organizations in which numerical distributions have traditionally favored men.

At the same time, this paper is oriented toward enlarging our understanding of male–female interaction and the situations facing women in organizations by introducing structural and contextual effects. Most analyses to date locate male–female interaction issues either in broad cultural traditions and the sexual division of labor in society or in the psychology of men and women whether based on biology or socialization (Kanter, 1976c). In both macroscopic and microscopic analysis, sex and gender components are sometimes confounded by situational and structural effects. For example, successful women executives are almost always numerically rare in their organizations, whereas working women are disproportionately concentrated in low-opportunity occupations. Conclusions about "women's behavior" or "male attitudes" drawn from such situations may sometimes confuse the effect of situation with the effect of sex roles; indeed such variables as position in opportunity and power structures account for a large number of phenomena related to work behavior that have been labeled "sex differences" (Kanter, 1975, 1976a, 1976d, 1976e). Therefore this paper focuses on an intermediate-level analysis: how group structures shape interaction contexts and influence particular patterns of male–female interaction. One advantage of such an approach is that it is then possible to generalize beyond male–female relations to persons-of-one-kind and person-of-another-kind interaction in various contexts, also making possible the untangling of what exactly *is* unique about the male–female case.

The study of particular proportions of women in predominantly male groups is thus relevant to a concern with social organization and group process as well as with male–female interaction. The analysis presented here deals with interaction in face-to-face groups with highly skewed sex ratios. More specifically, the focus is upon what happens to women who occupy token statuses and are alone or nearly alone in a peer group of men. This problem is commonly faced by women in management and the professions, and it is increasingly faced by women entering formerly all-male fields at every level of organizations. But proportional scarcity is not unique to women. Men can also find themselves alone among women, blacks among whites, very old people among the young, straight people among gays, the blind among the sighted. The dynamics of interaction (the process) is likely to be very similar in all such cases, even though the content of interaction may reflect the special culture and traditional roles of both token and members of the numerically dominant category.

Use of the term "token" for the minority member rather than "solo," "solitary," or "lone" highlights some special characteristics associated with that position. Tokens are not merely deviants or people who differ from other group members along any one dimension. They are people identified by ascribed characteristics (master statuses such as sex, race, religion, ethnic group, age, etc.) or other characteristics that carry with them a set of assumptions about culture, status, and behavior highly salient for majority category members. They bring these "auxiliary traits," in Hughes's (1944) term, into situations in which they differ from other people not in ability to do a task or in acceptance of work norms but only in terms of these secondary and informal assumptions. The importance of these auxiliary traits is heightened if members of the majority group have a history of interacting with the token's category in ways that are quite different from the demands of task accomplishment in the present situation—as is true of men with women. Furthermore, because tokens are by definition alone or virtually alone, they are in the position of representing their ascribed category to the group, whether they choose to do so or not. They can never be just another member while their category is so rare; they will always be a hyphenated member, as in "woman-engineer" or "male-nurse" or "black-physican."

People can thus be in the token position even if they have not been placed there deliberately for display by officials of an organization. It is sufficient to be in a place where others of that category are not usually found, to be the first of one's kind to enter a new group, or to represent a very different culture and set of interactional capacities to members of the numerically dominant category. The term "token" reflects one's status as a symbol of one's kind. However, lone people of one type among members of another are not necessarily tokens if their presence is taken for granted in the group or organization and incorporated into the dominant culture, so that their loneness is merely the accidental result of random distributions rather than a reflection of the rarity of their type in that system.*

While the dynamics of tokenism are likely to operate in some form whenever proportional representation in a collectivity is highly skewed, even if the dominant group does not intend to put the token at a disadvantage, two conditions can heighten and dramatize the effects, making

---

*As an anonymous reviewer pointed out, newness is more easily distinguished from rarity conceptually than it may be empirically, and further research should make this distinction. It should also specify the conditions under which "accidental loneness" (or small relative numbers) does not have the extreme effects noted here: when the difference is noted but not considered very important, as in the case of baseball teams that may have only one or two black members but lack token dynamics because of the large number of teams with many black members.

them more visible to the analyst: (1) the token's social category (master status) is physically obvious, as in the case of sex, and (2) the token's social type is not only rare but also new to the setting of the dominants. The latter situation may or may not be conceptually distinct from rarity, although it allows us to see the develoment of patterns of adjustment as well as the perception of and response to tokens. Subsequent tokens have less surprise value and may be thrust into token roles with less disruption to the system.

With only a few exceptions, the effects of differences in proportional representation within collectives have received little previous attention. Hughes (1944, 1946, 1958) described the dynamics of white work groups entered by a few blacks, pointing out the dilemmas posed by status contradictions and illuminating the sources of group discomfort as they put pressure on the rare blacks. There are a few studies of other kinds of tokens such as Segal's (1962) observations of male nurses in a largely female colleague group. Reports of professional women in male-dominated fields (e.g., Epstein, 1970; Hennig, 1970; Lynch, 1973; Cussler, 1958) mention some special issues raised by numerical rarity. More recently, Laws (1975) has developed a framework for defining the induction of a woman into token status through interaction with a sponsor representing the numerically dominant group. Wolman and Frank (1975) reported observations of solo women in professional-training groups; Taylor and Fiske (1975) have developed experimental data on the perception of token blacks in a white male group. The material in all of these studies still needs a theoretical framework.

With the exceptions noted, research has generally failed to take into account the effects of relative numbers on interaction. Yet such effects could critically change the interpretation of familiar findings. The research of Strodtbeck and his colleagues (Strodtbeck and Mann, 1956; Strodtbeck, James and Hawkins, 1957) on mock jury deliberations is often cited as evidence that men tend to play initiating, task-oriented roles in small groups, whereas women tend to play reactive, socioemotional roles. Yet a reexamination of these investigations indicates that men far outnumbered women as research subjects. There were more than twice as many men as women (86 to 41) in the 12 small groups in which women were found to play stereotypical expressive roles.* The actual sex composition of each of the small groups is not reported, although it could have important implications for the results. Perhaps it was women's scarcity in skewed groups that pushed them into classical positions and

---

*The 17 least active subjects (out of a total of 144) were dropped from the analysis; their sex is not mentioned in published reports. Those 17 might have skewed the sex distribution even further.

men's numerical superiority that gave them an edge in task performance. Similarly, in the early kibbutzim, collective villages in Israel that theoretically espoused equality of the sexes but were unable fully to implement it, women could be pushed into traditional service positions (see Tiger and Shepher, 1975) because there were often *more than twice as many men as women* in a kibbutz. Again, relative numbers interfered with a fair test of what men or women can "naturally" do (Kanter, 1976b).

Thus systematic analysis of the dynamics of systems with skewed distributions of social types—tokens in the midst of numerical dominants—is overdue. This paper begins to define a framework for understanding the dynamics of tokenism, illustrated by field observations of female tokens among male dominants.

THE FIELD STUDY

The forms of interaction in the presence of token women were identified in a field study of a large industrial corporation, one of the *Fortune 500* firms (see Kanter, 1976e, for a description of the setting). The sales force of one division was investigated in detail because women were entering it for the first time. The first saleswoman was hired in 1972; by the end of 1974, there had been about 20 in training or on assignment (several had left the company) out of a sales force of over 300 men. The geographically decentralized nature of sales meant, however, that in training programs or in field offices women were likely to be one of 10 or 12 sales workers; in a few cases, two women were together in a group of a dozen sales personnel. Studying women who were selling industrial goods had particular advantages: (1) sales is a field with strong cultural traditions and folklore and one in which interpersonal skills rather than expertise count heavily, thus making informal and cultural aspects of group interaction salient and visible even for members themselves; and (2) sales workers have to manage relations not only with work peers but with customers as well, thus giving the women two sets of majority groups with which to interact. Sixteen women in sales and distribution were interviewed in depth. Over 40 male peers and managers were also interviewed. Sales-training groups were observed both in session and at informal social gatherings for approximately 100 hours. Additional units of the organization were studied for other research purposes.

THEORETICAL FRAMEWORK

The framework set forth here proceeds from the Simmelian assumption that form determines process, narrowing the universe of interaction possibilities. The form of a group with a skewed distribution of social types generates certain perceptions of the tokens by the dominants. These perceptions determine the interaction dynamics between tokens and dominants and create the pressures dominants impose on tokens. In turn, there are typical token responses to these pressures.

The proportional rarity of tokens is associated with three perceptual phenomena: visibility, polarization, and assimilation. First, tokens, one by one, have higher visibility than dominants looked at alone: they capture a larger awareness share. A group member's awareness share, averaged over shares of other individuals of the same social type, declines as the proportion of total membership occupied by the category increases, because each individual becomes less and less surprising, unique, or noteworthy; in Gestalt terms, they more easily become "ground" rather than "figure." But for tokens there is a "law of increasing returns": as individuals of their type come to represent a *smaller* numerical proportion of the group, they potentially capture a *larger* share of the group members awareness.

Polarization or exaggeration of differences is the second perceptual tendency. The presence of a person bearing a different set of social characteristics makes members of a numerically dominant group more aware both of their commonalities with and their differences from the token. There is a tendency to exaggerate the extent of the differences, especially because tokens are by definition too few in number to prevent the application of familiar generalizations or stereotypes. It is thus easier for the commonalities of dominants to be defined in contrast to the token than it would be in a more numerically equal situation. One person can also be perceptually isolated and seen as cut off from the group more easily than many, who begin to represent a significant proportion of the group itself.

Assimilation, the third perceptual tendency, involves the use of stereotypes or familiar generalizations about a person's social type. The characteristics of a token tend to be distorted to fit the generalization. If there are enough people of the token's type to let discrepant examples occur, it is possible that the generalization will change to accommodate the accumulated cases. But if individuals of that type are only a small proportion of the group, it is easier to retain the generalization and distort the perception of the token.

Taylor and Fiske's (1976; Taylor, 1975) laboratory experiments provide supportive evidence for these propositions. They played a tape of a group discussion to subjects while showing them pictures of the group and then asked them for their impressions of group members on a number of dimensions. The tape was the same for all subjects, but the purported composition of the group varied. The pictures illustrated either an otherwise all-white male group with one black man (the token condition) or a mixed black–white male group. In the token condition, the subjects paid disproportionate attention to the token, overemphasized his prominence in the group, and exaggerated his attributes. Similarly, the token was perceived as playing special roles in the group, often highly stereotypical ones. By contrast, in the integrated condition, subjects recalled no more about blacks than whites and evaluated their attributes in about the same way.

Visibility, polarization, and assimilation are each associated with particular interaction dynamics that in turn generate typical token responses. These dynamics are similar regardless of the category from which the token comes, although the token's social type and history of relationships with dominants shape the content of specific interactions. Visiblity creates performance pressures on the token. Polarization leads to group boundary heightening and isolation of the token. And assimilation results in the token's role entrapment.

PERFORMANCE PRESSURES

The women in the sales force I studied were highly visible, much more so than their male peers. Managers commonly reported that they were the subject of conversation, questioning, gossip, and careful scrutiny. Their placements were known and observed throughout the sales unit, while those of men typically were not. Such visibility created a set of performance pressures: characteristics and standards true for tokens alone. Tokens typically perform under conditions different from those of dominants.

Public Performance

It was difficult for the women to do anything in training programs or in the field that did not attract public notice. The women found that they did not have to go out of their way to be noticed or to get the attention of management at sales meetings. One woman reported, "I've been at sales meetings where all the trainees were going up to the managers— 'Hi, Mr. So-and-So'—trying to make that impression, wearing a strawberry tie, whatever, something that they could be remembered by. Whereas there were three of us [women] in a group of 50, and all we had to do was walk in, and everyone recognized us."

Automatic notice meant that women could not remain anonymous or hide in the crowd; all their actions were public. Their mistakes and their relationships were known as readily as any other information. It was impossible for them to have any privacy within the company. The women were always viewed by an audience, leading several to complain of "overobservation."

Extension of Consequences

The women were visible as category members, and as such their acts tended to have added symbolic consequences. Some women were told that their performance could affect the prospects for other women in the company. They were thus not acting for themselves alone but carrying the burden of representing their category. In informal conversations, they were often measured by two yardsticks: how *as women* they carried out the sales role and how *as sales workers* they lived up to images of womanhood. In short, every act tended to be evaluated beyond its meaning for the organization and taken as a sign of "how women do in sales." The women were aware of the extra symbolic consequences attached to their acts.

Attention to a Token's Discrepant Characteristics

A token's visibility stems from characteristics—attributes of a master status—that threaten to blot out other aspects of the token's performance. While the token captures attention, it is often for discrepant characteristics, for the auxiliary traits that provide token status. No token in the study had to work hard to have her presence noticed, but she did have to work hard to have her achievements noticed. In the sales force, the women found that their technical abilities were likely to be eclipsed by their physical appearance, and thus an additional performance pressure was created. The women had to put in extra effort to make their technical skills known, to work twice as hard to prove their competence. Both male peers and customers would tend to forget information women provided about their experiences and credentials, while noticing and remembering such secondary attributes as style of dress.

Fear of Retaliation

The women were also aware of another performance pressure: to avoid making the dominants look bad. Tokenism sets up a dynamic that makes tokens afraid of outstanding performance in group events and tasks. When a token does well enough to show up a dominant, it cannot be kept a secret, because all eyes are on the token. Therefore it is difficult in such a situation to avoid the public humiliation of a dominant. Thus, paradoxically, while the token women felt they had to do better than anyone else in order to be seen as competent and allowed to continue, they also felt in some cases that their successes would not be rewarded and should be kept secret. One woman had trouble understanding this and complained of her treatment by managers. They had fired another woman for not being aggressive enough, she reported; yet she, who succeeded in doing all they asked and had brought in the largest amount of new business during the past year, was criticized for being too aggressive, too much of a hustler.

Responses of Tokens to Performance Pressures

There are two typical ways tokens respond to these performance pressures. The first involves overachievement. Aware of the performance pressures, several of the saleswomen put in extra effort, promoted themselves and their work at every opportunity, and let those around them know how well they were doing. These women evoked threats of retaliation. On the gossip circuit, they were known to be doing well but aspiring too high too fast; a common prediction was that they would be cut down to size soon.

The second response is more common and is typical of findings of other investigators. It involves attempts to limit visibility, to become socially invisible. This strategy characterizes women who try to minimize their sexual attributes so as to blend unnoticeably into the predominant male culture, perhaps by adopting "mannish dress" (Hennig, 1970, chap. 6). Or it can include avoidance of public events and occasions for performance—staying away from meetings, working at home rather than in the office, keeping silent at meetings. Several of the saleswomen deliberately kept such a low profile, unlike male peers who tended to seize every opportunity to make themselves noticed. They avoided conflict, risks, and controversial situations. Those women preferring social invisibility also made little attempt to make their achievements publicly known or to get credit for their own contributions to problem solving or other organizational tasks. They are like other women in the research literature who have let others assume visible leadership (Megaree, 1969) or take credit for their accomplishments (Lynch, 1973; Cussler, 1958). These women did blend into the background, but they also limited recognition of their competence.

This analysis suggests a reexamination of the "fear of success in women" hypothesis. Perhaps what has been called fear of success is really the token woman's fear of visibility. The original research identifying this concept created a hypothetical situation in which a woman was at the top of her class in medical school—a token woman in a male peer group. Such a situation puts pressure on a woman to make herself and her achievements invisible, to deny success. Attempts to replicate the initial findings using settings in which women were not so clearly tokens produced very different results. And in other studies (e.g., Levine and Crumrine, 1975), the hypothesis that fear of success is a female-linked trait has not been confirmed. (See Sarason, 1973, for a discussion of fear of visibility among minorities.)

Boundary Heightening

Polarization or exaggeration of the token's attributes in contrast to those of the dominants sets a second set of dynamics in motion. The presence of a token makes dominants more aware of what they have in common at the same time that it threatens that commonality. Indeed it is often at those moments when a collectivity is threatened with change that its culture and bonds become evident to it; only when an obvious outsider appears do group members suddenly realize their common bond as insiders. Dominants thus tend to exaggerate both their commonality and the token's difference, moving to heighten boundaries of which previously they might not even have been aware.*

Exaggeration of Dominants' Culture

Majority members assert or reclaim group solidarity and reaffirm shared in-group understandings by emphasizing and exaggerating those cultural elements which they share in contrast to the token. The token becomes both occasion and audience for the highlighting and dramatization of those themes that differentiate the token as outsider from the insider. Ironically, tokens (unlike people of their type represented in greater proportion) are thus instruments for under*lining* rather than under*mining* majority culture. In the sales force case, this phenomenon was most clearly in operation in training programs and at dinner and cocktail parties during meetings. Here the camaraderie of men, as in other work and social settings (Tiger, 1969), was based in part on tales of

---

*This awareness often seemed to be resented by the men interviewed in this study, who expressed a preference for less self-consciousness and less attention to taken-for-granted operating assumptions. They wanted to "get on with business," and questioning definitions of what is "normal" and "appropriate" was seen as a deflection from the task at hand. The culture in the managerial/technical ranks of this large corporation, like that in many others, devalued introspection and emphasized rapid communication and ease of interaction. Thus, although group solidarity is often based on the development of strong in-group boundaries (Kanter, 1972), the stranger or outsider who makes it necessary for the group to pay attention to its boundaries may be resented not only for being different but also for giving the group extra work.

sexual adventures, ability with respect to "hunting" and capturing women, and off-color jokes. Secondary themes involved work prowess and sports. The capacity for and enjoyment of drinking provided the context for displays of these themes. According to male informants' reports, they were dramatized more fervently in the presence of token women than when only men were present. When the men introduced these themes in much milder form and were just as likely to share company gossip or talk of domestic matters (such as a house being built), as to discuss any of the themes mentioned above, this was also in contrast to the situation in more equally mixed male-female groups, in which there were a sufficient number of women to influence and change group culture in such a way that a new hybrid based on shared male-female concerns was introduced. (See Aries, 1973, for supportive laboratory evidence.)

In the presence of token women, then, men exaggerated displays of aggression and potency: instances of sexual innuendo, aggressive sexual teasing, and prowess-oriented "war stories." When one or two women were present, the men's behavior involved showing off, telling stories in which masculine prowess accounted for personal, sexual, or business success. The men highlighted what they could do, as men, in contrast to women. In a set of training situations, these themes were even acted out overtly in role plays in which participants were asked to prepare and perform demonstrations of sales situations. In every case involving a woman, men played the primary, effective roles, and women were objects of sexual attention. In one, a woman was introduced as president of a company selling robots; she turned out to be one of the female robots, run by the male company sales manager.

The women themselves reported other examples of testing to see how they would respond to the "male" culture. They said that many sexual innuendos or displays of locker-room humor were put on for their benefit, especially by the younger men. (The older men tended to parade their business successes.) One woman was a team leader and the only woman at a workshop when her team, looking at her for a reaction, decided to use as its slogan "The [obscenity] of the week." By raising the issue and forcing the woman to choose not to participate in the workshop, the men in the group created an occasion for uniting against the outsider and asserting dominant-group solidarity.

Interruptions as Reminders of "Difference"

Members of the numerically dominant category underscore and reinforce differences between tokens and themselves, insuring that the former recognize their outsider status by making the token the occasion for interruptions in the flow of group events. Dominants preface acts with apologies or questions about appropriateness directed at the token; they then invariably go ahead with the act, having placed the token in the position of interrupter or interloper. This happened often in the presence of the saleswomen. Men's questions or apologies were a way of asking whether the old or expected cultural rules were still operative— the words and expressions permitted, the pleasures and forms of release indulged in. (Can we still swear? Toss a football? Use technical jargon? Go drinking? Tell in jokes? See Greenbaum, 1971, p. 65, for other examples.) By posing these questions overtly, dominants make their culture clear to tokens and state the terms under which tokens interact with the group.

The answers almost invariably affirm the understandings of the dominants, first because of the power of sheer numbers. An individual rarely feels comfortable preventing a larger number of peers from engaging in an activity they consider normal. Second, the tokens have been put on notice that interaction will not be "natural," that dominants will be holding back unless the tokens agree to acknowledge, permit, and even encourage majority cultural expressions in their presence. (It is important that this be stated, of course, for one never knows that another is holding back unless the other lets a piece of the suppressed material slip out.) At the same time, tokens have also been given the implicit message that majority members do *not* expect those forms of expression to be natural to the tokens' home culture; otherwise majority members would not need to raise the question. (This is a function of what Laws, 1975, calls the "double deviance" of tokens: deviant first because they are women in a man's world and second because they aspire inappropriately to the privileges of the dominants.) Thus the saleswomen were often in the odd position of reassuring peers and customers that they could go ahead and do something in the women's presence, such as swearing, that they themselves would not be permitted to do. They listened to dirty jokes, for example, but reported that they would not dare tell one themselves. Via difference-reminding interruptions, then, dominants both affirm their own shared understandings and draw the cultural boundary between themselves and tokens. The tokens learned that they caused interruptions in "normal" communication and that their appropriate position was more like that of audience than full participant.

Overt Inhibition: Informal Isolation

In some cases, dominants do not wish to carry out certain activities in the presence of a token; they have secrets to preserve. They thus move the locus of some activities and expressions away from public settings to which tokens have access to more private settings from which they can be excluded. When information potentially embarrassing or damaging to dominants is being exchanged, an outsider audience is not desirable because dominants do not know how far they can trust tokens. As Hughes (1944, 1958) pointed out, colleagues who rely on unspoken understandings may feel uncomfortable in the presence of "odd kinds of fellows" who cannot be trusted to interpret information in just the same way or to engage in the same relationships of trust and reciprocity (see also Lorber, 1975). The result is often quarantine—keeping tokens away from some occasions. Thus some topics of discussion were never raised by men in the presence of many of the saleswomen, even though they discussed these topics among themselves: admissions of low commitment to the company or concerns about job performance, ways of getting around formal rules, political plotting for mutual advantage, strategies for impressing certain corporate executives. As researchers have also found in other settings, women did not tend to be included in the networks by which informal socialization occurred and politics behind the formal system were exposed (Wolman and Frank, 1975; O'Farrell, 1973; Hennig, 1970; Epstein, 1970). In a few cases, managers even avoided giving women information about their performance as trainees, so that they did not know they were the subject of criticism in the company until they were told to find jobs outside the sales force; those women were simply not part of the informal occasions on which the men discussed their performances with each other. (Several male managers also reported their "fear" of criticizing a woman because of uncertainty about how she would receive it.)

Loyalty Tests

At the same time that tokens are often kept on the periphery of colleague interaction, they may also be expected to demonstrate loyalty to the dominant group. Failure to do so results in further isolation; signs of loyalty permit the token to come closer and be included in more activities. Through loyalty tests, the group seeks reassurance that tokens will not turn against them or use any of the information gained through their viewing of the dominants' world to do harm to the group. They get this assurance by asking a token to join or identify with the majority against those others who represent competing membership or reference groups; in short, dominants pressure tokens to turn against members of the latter's own category. If tokens collude, they make themselves psychological hostages of the majority group. For token women, the price of being "one of the boys" is a willingness to turn occasionally against "the girls."

There are two ways by which tokens can demonstrate loyalty and qualify for closer relationships with dominants. First, they can let slide or even participate in statements prejudicial to other members of their category. They can allow themselves to be viewed as exceptions to the general rule that others of their category have a variety of undersirable or unsuitable characteristics. Hughes (1944) recognized this as one of the deals token blacks might make for membership in white groups. Saleswomen who did well were told they were exceptions and were not typical women. At meetings and training sessions, women were often the subjects of ridicule or joking remarks about their incompetence. Some women who were insulted by such innuendos found it easier to appear to agree than to start an argument. A few accepted the dominant view fully. One of the first saleswomen denied in interviews having any special problems because she was a woman, calling herself skilled at coping with a man's world, and said the company was right not to hire more women. Women, she said, were unreliable and likely to quit; furthermore, young women might marry men who would not allow them to work. In this case, a token woman was taking over "gate-keeping" functions for dominants (Laws, 1975), letting them preserve their illusion of lack of prejudice while she acted to exclude other women.

Tokens can also demonstrate loyalty by allowing themselves and their category to provide a source of humor for the group. Laughing with others, as Coser (1960) indicated, is a sign of a common definition of the situation; to allow onself or one's kind to be the object of laughter signals a further willingness to accept others' culture on their terms. Just as Hughes (1946, p. 115) found that the initiation of blacks into white groups might involve accepting the role of comic inferior, the saleswomen faced constant pressures to allow jokes at women's expense, to accept kidding from the men around them. When a woman objected, men denied any hostility or unfriendly intention, instead accusing the woman by inference of lacking a sense of humor. In order to cope, one woman reported, "you learn to laugh when they try to insult you with jokes, to let it roll off your back." Tokens thus find themselves colluding with dominants through shared laughter.

RESPONSES OF TOKENS TO BOUNDARY HEIGHTENING

Numerical skewing and polarized perceptions leave tokens with little choice about whether to accept the culture of dominants. There are too few other people of the token's kind to generate a counterculture or to develop a shared intergroup culture. Tokens have two general response possibilities. They can accept isolation, remaining an audience for certain expressive acts of dominants, in which case they risk exclusion from occasions on which informal socialization and political activity take place. Or they can try to become insiders, proving their loyalty by defining themselves as exceptions and turning against their own social category.

The occurrence of the second response on the part of tokens suggests a reexamination of the popularized "women-prejudiced-against-women" hypothesis or the "queen bee syndrome" for possible structural (numerical) rather than sexual origins. Not only has this hypothesis not been confirmed in a variety of settings (e.g., Ferber and Huber, 1975), but the analysis offered here of the social psychological pressures on tokens to side with the majority also provides a compelling explanation for the kinds of situations most likely to produce this effect, when it does occur.

ROLE ENTRAPMENT

The third set of interaction dynamics centering around tokens stems from the perceptual tendency toward assimilation: the distortion of the characteristics of tokens to fit preexisting generalizations about their category. Stereotypical assumptions and mistaken attributions made about tokens tend to force them into playing limited and caricatured roles in the system.

Status Leveling

Tokens are often misperceived initially as a result of their statistical rarity: "statistical discrimination" (U.S. Council of Economic Advisers, 1973, p. 106) as distinguished from prejudice. That is, an unusual woman may be treated as though she resembles women on the average. People make judgments about the role played by others on the basis of probabilistic reasoning about the likelihood of what a particular kind of person does. Thus the saleswomen like other tokens encountered many instances of mistaken identity. In the office, they were often taken for secretaries; on the road, especially when they traveled with male colleagues, they were often taken for wives or mistresses; with customers, they were usually assumed to be substituting for men or, when with a male peer, to be assistants; when entertaining customers, they were assumed to be wives or dates.

Such mistaken first impressions can be corrected. They require tokens to spend time untangling awkward exchanges and establishing accurate and appropriate role relations, but they do permit status leveling to occur. Status leveling involves making adjustments in perception of the token's professional role to fit the expected position of the token's category—that is, bringing situational status in line with master status, the token's social type. Even when others knew that the token saleswomen were not secretaries, for example, there was still a tendency to treat them like secretaries or to make demands of them appropriate to secretaries. In the most blatant case, a woman was a sales trainee along with three men; all four were to be given positions as summer replacements. The men were all assigned to replace salesmen; the woman was asked to replace a secretary—and only after a long, heated discussion with the manager was she given a more professional assignment. Similarly, when having professional contacts with customers and managers, the women felt themselves to be treated in more wifelike or datelike ways than a man would be treated by another man, even though the situation was clearly professional. It was easier for others to make their perception of the token women fit their preexisting generalizations about women than to change the category; numerical rarity provided too few examples to contradict the generalization. Instances of status leveling have also been noted with regard to other kinds of tokens such as male nurses (Segal, 1962); in the case of tokens whose master status is higher than their situational status leveling can work to their advantage, as when male nurses are called "Dr."

Stereotyped Role Induction

The dominant group can incorporate tokens and still preserve their generalizations about the tokens' kind by inducting them into stereotypical roles; these roles preserve the familiar form of interaction between the kinds of people represented by the token and the dominants. In the case of token women in the sales force, four role traps were observed, all of which encapsulated the women in a category the men could respond to and understand. Each centered on one behavioral tendency of the token, building upon this tendency an image of her place in the group and forcing her to continue to live up to the image; each defined for dominants a single response to her sexuality. Two of the roles are classics in Freudian theory: the mother and the seductress. Freud wrote of the need of men to handle women's sexuality by envisioning them as either madonnas or whores—as either asexual mothers or overly sexual, debased seductresses. (This was perhaps a function of Victorian family patterns, which encouraged separation of idealistic adoration of the mother and animalistic eroticism—Rieff, 1963; Strong, 1973.) The other roles, termed the pet and the iron maiden, also have family counterparts in the kid sister and the virgin aunt.

Mother. A token woman sometimes finds that she has become a mother to a group of men. They bring her their troubles, and she comforts them. The assumption that women are sympathetic, good listeners, and can be talked to about one's problems is common in male-dominated organizations. One saleswoman was constantly approached by her all-male peers to listen to their domestic problems. In a variety of residential-sales-training groups, token women were observed acting out other parts of the traditional nurturant-maternal role: cooking for men, doing their laundry, sewing on buttons.

The mother role is a comparatively safe one. She is not necessarily vulnerable to sexual pursuit (for Freud it was the very idealization of the madonna that was in part responsible for men's ambivalence toward women), nor do men need to compete for her favors, because these are available to everyone. However, the typecasting of women as nurturers has three negative consequences for a woman's task performance: (1) The mother is rewarded by her male colleagues primarily for service to them and not for independent action. (2) The mother is expected to keep her place as a noncritical, accepting, good mother or lose her rewards because the dominant, powerful aspects of the maternal image may be feared by men. Since the ability to differentiate and be critical is often an indicator of competence in work groups, the mother is prohibited from exhibiting this skill. (3) The mother becomes an emotional specialist. This provides her with a place in the life of the group and its members. Yet at the same time, one of the traditionally feminine characteristics men in positions of authority in industry most often criticize in women (see Lynch, 1973) is excess emotionality. Although the mother herself might not ever indulge in emotional outbursts in the group, she remains identified with emotional matters. As long as she is in the minority, it is unlikely that nurturance, support, and expressivity will be valued or that a mother can demonstrate and be rewarded for critical, independent, task-oriented behaviors.

Seductress. The role of seductress or sexual object is fraught with more tension than the maternal role, for it introduces an element of sexual competition and jealousy. The mother can have many sons; it is more difficult for a sex object to have many lovers. Should a woman cast as sex object, that is, seen as sexually desirable and potentially available ("seductress" is a perception, and the woman herself may not be consciously behaving seductively), share her attention widely, she risks the debasement of the whore. Yet should she form a close alliance with any man in particular, she arouses resentment, particularly because she represents a scarce resource; there are just not enough women to go around.

In several situations observed, a high-status male allied himself with a seductress and acted as her "protector," not only because of his promise to rescue her from the sex-charged overtures of the rest of the men but also because of his high status per se. The powerful male (staff member, manager, sponsor, etc.) can easily become the protector of the still "virgin" seductress, gaining through masking his own sexual interest what other men could not gain by declaring theirs. However, the removal of the seductress from the sexual marketplace contains its own problems. Other men may resent a high-status male for winning the prize and resent the woman for her ability to get an in with the high-status male that they themselves could not obtain as men. While the seductress is rewarded for her femaleness and insured attention from the group, then, she is also the source of considerable tension; and needless to say, her perceived sexuality blots out all other characteristics.

Men may adopt the role of protector toward an attractive woman, regardless of her collusion, and by implication cast her as sex object, reminding her and the rest of the group of her sexual status. In the guise of helping her, protectors may actually put up further barriers to a solitary woman's full acceptance by inserting themselves, figuratively speaking, between the woman and the rest of a group. A male sales trainer typically offered token women in training groups extra help and sympathetically attended to the problems their male peers might cause, taking them out alone for drinks at the end of daily sessions.

Pet. The pet is adopted by the male group as a cute, amusing little thing and taken along on group events as symbolic mascot—a cheerleader for the shows of male prowess that follow. Humor is often a characteristic of the pet. She is expected to admire the male displays but not to enter into them; she cheers from the sidelines. Shows of competence on her part are treated as extraordinary and complimented just because they are unexpected (and the compliments themselves can be seen as reminders of the expected rarity of such behavior). One woman reported that, when she was alone in a group of men and spoke at length on an issue, comments to her by men after the meeting often referred to her speech-making ability rather than to what she said (e.g., "You talk so fluently"), whereas comments the men made to one another were almost invariably content or issue oriented. Competent acts that were taken for granted when performed by males were often unduly fussed over when performed by saleswomen, who were considered precocious or precious at such times. Such attitudes on the part of men in a group encourage self-effacing, girlish responses on the part of solitary women (who after all may be genuinely relieved to be included) and prevent them from realizing or demonstrating their own power and competence.

Iron Maiden. The iron maiden is a contemporary variation of the stereotypical roles into which strong women are placed. Women who fail to fall into any of the first three roles and in fact resist overtures that would trap them in such roles (like flirtation) might consequently be responded to as though tough or dangerous. (One saleswoman developed just such a reputation in company branches throughout the country.) If a token insisted on full rights in the group, if she displayed competence in a forthright manner, or if she cut off sexual innuendos, she was typically asked, "You're not one of those women's libbers, are you?" Regardless of the answer, she was henceforth viewed with suspicion, treated with undue and exaggerated politeness (by references to women inserted into conversations, by elaborate rituals of *not* opening doors), and kept at a distance; for she was demanding treatment as an equal in a setting in which no person of her kind had previously been an equal. Women inducted into the iron maiden role are stereotyped as tougher than they are (hence the name) and trapped in a more militant stance than they might otherwise take.

Responses of Tokens to Role Entrapment

The dynamics of role entrapment tend to lead to a variety of conservative and low-risk responses on the part of tokens. The time and awkwardness involved in correcting mistaken impressions often lead them to a preference for already-established relationships, for minimizing change and stranger contact in the work situation. It is also often easier to accept stereotyped roles than to fight them, even if their acceptance means limiting a token's range of expressions or demonstrations of task competence, because acceptance offers a comfortable and certain position. The personal consequence for tokens, of course, is a certain degree of self-distortion. Athanassiades (1974), though not taking into account the effects of numerical representation, found that women, especially those with low risk-taking propensity, tended to distort upward communication more than men and argued that many observed work behaviors of women may be the result of such distortion and acceptance of organizational images. Submissiveness, frivolity, or other attributes may be feigned by people who feel these are prescribed for them by the dominant organizational culture. This suggests that accurate conclusions about work attitudes and behavior cannot be reached by studying people in the token position, since there may always be an element of compensation or distortion involved. Thus many studies of professional and managerial women should be reexamined in order to remove the effects of numbers from the effects of sex roles.

Implications

This paper has developed a framework for understanding the social perceptions and interaction dynamics that center on tokens, using the example of women in an industrial sales force dominated numerically by men. Visiblity generates performance pressures, polarization generates group-boundary heightening, and assimilation generates role entrapment. All of the phenomena associated with tokens are exaggerated ones: the token stands out vividly, group culture is dramatized, boundaries become highlighted, and token roles are larger-than-life caricatures.

The concepts identified here are also applicable to other kinds of tokens who face similar interaction contexts. Hughes's (1944, 1946, 1958) discussions of the problems encountered by blacks in white male work groups are highly congruent with the framework presented here. Taylor and Fiske's (1976) laboratory research demonstrates the perceptual phenomena mentioned above in the black—white context. Segal (1962) also provides confirming evidence that, when men are tokens in a group of women, the same concepts apply. He studied a hospital in which 22 out of 101 nurses were men. He found that male nurses were isolates in the hospital social structure, not because the men disassociated themselves from their women peers but because the women felt the men were out of place and should not be nurses. Male and female nurses had the same objective rank, but people of both sexes felt that the men's subjective status was a lower one. The women placed the men in stereotypical positions, expecting them to do the jobs the women found distasteful or considered men's work. During a personal interview, a male nursing student reported that he thought he would enjoy being the only man in a group of women until he found that he engendered a great deal of hostility and that he was teased every time he failed to live up to the manly image, for example, if he was vague or subjective in speech. And "token men" working in child-care centers were found to play minor roles, become social isolates, and bear special burdens in interaction, which they handled like the saleswomen, by defining themselves as "exceptional" men (Seifert, 1974). Similarly, a blind informant indicated to me that, when he was the only blind person among sighted people, he often felt conspicuous and more attended to than he liked. This in turn created pressure for him to work harder in order to prove himself. In the solo situation, he was never sure that he was getting the same treatment as other members of the group (first, fellow students; later, fellow members of an academic institution), and he suspected that people tended to protect him. When he was the only one of his kind, as opposed to situations in which other blind people were present, sighted people felt free to grab his arm and pull him along and were more likely to apologize for references to visual matters, reinforcing his sense of being different and cast in the role of someone more helpless than he in fact perceived himself to be.

If the token's master status is higher than that of the situational dominants, some of the content of the interaction may change while the dynamics remain the same. A high-status token, for example, might find that the difference-reminding interruptions involve deference and opinion-seeking rather than patronizing apology; a high-status token might be allowed to dominate formal colleague discussion while still being excluded from informal, expressive occasions. Such a token might be trapped in roles that distort competence in a favorable rather than an unfavorable direction; but distortion is involved nonetheless. Further research can uncover appropriate modifications of the framework which will allow its complete extension to cases in the category just discussed.

The analysis undertaken here also suggests the importance of intermediate-level structural and social psychological variables in affecting male—female interaction and the roles of women in work groups and organizations. Some phenomena that have been labeled sex related but have not been replicated under all circumstances might be responses to tokenism, that is, reflections of responses to situational pressures rather than to sex differences. "Fear of success" might be more fruitfully viewed as the fear of visibility of members of minority groups in token statuses. The modesty and lack of self-aggrandizement characteristic of some professional and managerial women might be accounted for in similar ways, as situational responses rather than sex-linked traits. The prejudice of some women against others might be placed in the context of majority-culture loyalty tests. The unwillingness of some professional and managerial women to take certain risks involving a change in relationships might be explained as a reasonable response to the length of time it may take a token to establish competence-based working relationships and to the ever-present threat of mistaken identity in new relationships.

The examination of numerical effects leads to the additional question of tipping points: how many of a category are enough to change a person's status from token to full group member? When does a group move from skewed to tilted to balanced? Quantitative analyses are called for in order to provide precise documentation of the points at which interaction shifts because enough people of the "other kind" have become members of a group. This is especially relevant to research on school desegregation and its effects or changing neighborhood composition as well as occupational segregation by sex. Howe and Widick (1949, pp. 211–12) found that industrial plants with a small proportion of blacks in their work force had racial clashes, whereas those plants in which blacks constituted a large proportion had good race relations.

Exact tipping points should be investigated. Observations from the present study make it clear that even in small groups two of a kind are *not* enough. Data were collected in several situations in which two women rather than one were found among male peers but still constituted less than 20% of the group. Despite Asch's (1960) laboratory finding that one potential ally is enough to reduce the power of the majority to secure conformity, in the two-token situation in organizations dominants were nearly always able to defeat an alliance between two women by setting up invidious comparisons. By the exaggeration of traits in both cases, one woman was identified as a success, the other as a failure. The one given the positive label felt relieved to be accepted and praised. She recognized that alliance with the identified failure would jeopardize her acceptance. The consequence in one sales office was that the identified success stayed away from the other woman, did not give her any help with her performance, and withheld criticism she had heard that might have been useful. The second woman soon left the organization. In another case, dominants defeated an alliance, paradoxically by trying to promote it. Two women in a training group of 12 were treated as though they were an automatic pair, and other group members felt that they were relieved of responsibility for interacting with or supporting the women. The women reacted to this forced pairing by trying to create differences between themselves and becoming extremely competitive. Thus structural circumstances and pressures from the majority can produce what appear to be prejudicial responses of women to each other. Yet these responses are best seen as the effects of limited numbers. Two (or less than 20% in any particular situation) is not always a large enough number to overcome the problems of tokenism and develop supportive alliances, unless the tokens are highly identified with their own social category.

Tokens appear to operate under a number of handicaps in work settings. Their possible social isolation may exclude them from situations in which important learning about a task is taking place and may also prevent them from being in a position to look good in the organization. Performance pressures make it more dangerous for tokens to fumble and thus give them less room for error. Responding to their position, they often either underachieve or overachieve, and they are likely to accept distorting roles which permit them to disclose only limited parts of themselves. For all these reasons, in situations like industrial sales in which informal interaction provides a key to success tokens are not very likely to do well compared with members of the majority category, at least while in the token position.

These consequences of token status also indicate that tokens may undergo a great deal of personal stress and may need to expend extra energy to maintain a satisfactory relationship in the work situation. This fact is reflected in their common statements that they must work twice as hard as dominants or spend more time resolving problematic interactions. They face partially conflicting and often completely contradictory expectations. Such a situation has been found to be a source of mental stress for people with inconsistent statuses and in some cases to reinforce punitive self-images. In addition, turning against others of one's kind may be intimately connected with self-hatred. Finally, tokens must inhibit some forms of self-expression and often are unable to join the group in its characteristic form of tension release. They may be asked to side with the group in its assaults-through-humor but often cannot easily join the group in its play. They potentially face the stresses of social isolation and self-distortion.*

Thus social-policy formulations might consider the effects of proportions in understanding the sources of behavior, causes of stress, and possibilities for change. The analysis of tokenism suggests, for example, that merely adding a few women at a time to an organization is likely to give rise to the consequences of token status. Despite the contemporary controversy over affirmative action quotas (Glazer, 1976), numbers do appear to be important in shaping outcomes for disadvantaged individuals. Women (or members of any other underrepresented category) need to be added to total group or organization membership in sufficient proportion to counteract the effects of tokenism. Even if tokens do well, they do so at a cost, overcoming social handicaps, expending extra effort, and facing stresses not present for members of the numerically dominant group. The dynamics of tokenism also operate in such a way as to perpetuate the system that keeps members of the token's category in short supply; the presence of a few tokens does not necessarily pave the way for others—in many cases, it has the opposite effect.

Investigation of the effects of proportions on group life and social interaction appears to be fruitful both for social psychological theory and for understanding male–female interaction. It is a step toward identifying the structural and situational variables that intervene between global cultural definitions of social type and individual responses—that shape the context for face-to-face interactions among different kinds of people. Relative as well as absolute numbers can be important for social life and social relations.

---

*The argument that tokens face more personal stress than majority group members can be supported by studies of the psychosocial difficulties confronting people with inconsistent statuses. Among the stresses identified in the literature on class and race are unsatisfactory social relationships, unstable self-images, frustration over rewards, and social ambiguity (Hughes, 1944, 1958; Lenski, 1956; Fenchel, Monderer, and Hartley, 1951; Jackson, 1962). Token women must also inhibit self-expression and self-disclosure, as the examples in this paper and the discussion below indicate; yet Jourard (1964) considers the ability to self-disclose a requisite for psychological well-being.

References

Aries, Elizabeth. 1973. "Interaction Patterns and Themes of Male, Female, and Mixed Groups." Ph.D. dissertation, Harvard University.

Asch, Solomon E. 1960. "Effects of Group Pressure upon the Modification and Distortion of Judgments." Pp. 189–200 in *Group Dynamics*, edited by Dorwin Cartwright and Alvin Zander, 2d ed. Evanston, Ill.: Row, Peterson.

Athanassiades, John C. 1974. "An Investigation of Some Communication Patterns of Female Subordinates in Hierarchical Organizations." *Human Relations* 27 (March): 195–209.

Coser, Rose Laub. 1960. "Laughter among Colleagues: A Study of the Social Functions of Humor among the Staff of a Mental Hospital." *Psychiatry* 23 (February): 81–95.

Cussler, Margaret. 1958. *The Woman Executive.* New York: Harcourt Brace.

Epstein, Cynthia Fuchs. 1970. *Woman's Place: Options and Limits on Professional Careers.* Berkeley: University of California Press.

Fenchel, G. H., J. H. Monderer, and E.L. Hartley. 1951. "Subjective Status and the Equilibrium Hypothesis." *Journal of Abnormal and Social Psychology* 46 (October): 476–79.

Ferber, Marianne Abeles, and Joan Althaus Huber. 1975. "Sex of Student and Instructor: A Study of Student Bias." *American Journal of Sociology* 80 (January): 949–63.

Glazer, Nathan. 1976. *Affirmative Discrimination.* New York: Basic.

Greenbaum, Marcia. 1971. "Adding 'Kenntnis' to 'Kirche, Kuche, und Kinder.'" *Issues in Industrial Society* 2(2):61–68.

Hennig, Margaret. 1970. "Career Development for Women Executives." Ph.D. dissertation, Harvard Univeristy.

Howe, Irving, and B. J. Widick. 1949. *The UAW and Walter Reuther.* New York: Random House.

Hughes, Everett C. 1944. "Dilemmas and Contradictions of Status." *American Journal of Sociology* 50 (March): 3535–59.

Hughes, Everett C. 1946. "Race Relations in Industry." Pp. 107–22 in *Industry and Society,* edited by W. F. Whyte, New York: McGraw-Hill.

Hughes, Everett C. 1958. *Men and Their Work.* Glencoe, Ill.: Free Press.

Jackson, Elton F. 1962. "Status Inconsistency and Symptoms of Stress." *American Sociological Review* 27 (August): 469–80.

Jourard, Sidney M. 1964. *The Transparent Self: Self-Disclosure and Well-Being.* Princeton, N.J.: Van Nostrand.

Kanter, Rosabeth Moss. 1972. *Commitment and Community.* Cambridge, Mass.: Harvard University Press.

Kanter, Rosabeth Moss. 1975. "Women and the Structure of Organizations: Explorations in Theory and Behavior." Pp. 34–74 in *Another Voice: Feminist Perspectives on Social Life and Social Science,* edited by M. Millman and R. M. Kanter. New York: Doubleday Anchor.

Kanter, Rosabeth Moss. 1976a. "The Impact of Hierarchical Structures on the Work Behavior of Women and Men." *Social Problems* 23 (April): 415–30.

Kanter, Rosabeth Moss. 1976b. "Interpreting the Results of a Social Experiment." *Science* 192 (May 14): 662–63.

Kanter, Rosabeth Moss. 1976c. "The Policy Issues: Presentation VI." *Signs: Journal of Women in Culture and Society* 1 (Spring, part 2): 282–91.

Kanter, Rosabeth Moss. 1976d. "Women and Organizations: Sex Roles, Group Dynamics, and Change Strategies." In *Beyond Sex Roles,* edited by A. Sargent. St. Paul: West.

Kanter, Rosabeth Moss. 1976e. *Men and Women of the Corporation*. New York: Basic.

Laws, Judith Long. 1975. "The Psychology of Tokenism: An Analysis." *Sex Roles* 1 (March): 51–67.

Lenski, Gerhard. 1956. "Social Participation and the Crystallization of Status." *American Sociological Review* 21 (August): 458–64.

Levine, Adeline, and Janice Crumrine. 1975."Women and the Fear of Success: A Problem in Replication." *American Journal of Sociology* 80 (January): 964–74.

Lorber, Judith. 1975. "Trust, Loyalty, and the Place of Women in the Informal Organization of Work." Paper presented at the annual meeting of the American Sociological Association, San Francisco.

Lynch, Edith M. 1973. *The Executive Suite: Feminine Style*. New York: AMACOM.

Megaree, Edwin I. 1969. "Influence of Sex Roles on the Manifestation of Leadership." *Journal of Applied Psychology* 53 (October): 377–82.

O'Farrell, Brigid. 1973. "Affirmative Action and Skilled Craft Work." Xeroxed. Center for Research on Women, Wellesley College.

Rieff, Philip, ed. 1963. *Freud: Sexuality and the Psychology of Love*. New York: Collier.

Sarason, Seymour B. 1973. "Jewishness, Blackness, and the Nature–Nurture Controversy." *American Psychologist* 28 (November): 961–71.

Segal, Bernard E. 1962. "Make Nurses: A Case Study in Status Contradiction and Prestige Loss." *Social Forces* 41 (October): 31–38.

Seifert, Kelvin. 1973. "Some Problems of Men in Child Care Center Work." Pp. 69–73 in *Men and Masculinity*, edited by Joseph H. Pleck and Jack Sawyer. Englewood Cliffs, N.J.: Prentice-Hall, 1974.

Simmel, Georg. 1950. *The Sociology of Georg Simmel*. Translated by Kurt H. Wolff. Glencoe, Ill.: Free Press.

Strodtbeck, Fred L., Rita M. James and Charles Hawkins, 1957. "Social Status in Jury Deliberations." *American Sociological Review* 22 (December): 713–19.

Strodtbeck, Fred L., Rita M. James and Charles Hawkins. 1957. "Social Status in Jury Deliberations." *American Sociological Review* 22 (December): 713–19.

Strong, Bryan. 1973."Toward a History of the Experiential Family: Sex and Incest in the Nineteenth Century Family." *Journal of Marriage and the Family* 35 (August): 457–66.

Taylor, Shelley E. 1975. "The Token in a Small Group." Xeroxed. Harvard University Department of Psychology.

Taylor, Shelley E., and Susan T. Fiske. 1976. "The Token in the Small Group: Research Findings and Theoretical Implications." In *Psychology and Politics: Collected Papers*, edited by J. Sweeney. New Haven, Conn.: Yale University Press.

Tiger, Lionel. 1969. *Men in Groups*. New York: Random House.

Tiger, Lionel, and Joseph Shepher. 1975. *Women in the Kibbutz*. New York: Harcourt Brace Jovanovich.

U.S. Council of Economic Advisers. 1973. *Annual Report of the Council of Economic Advisers*. Washington, D.C.: Government Printing Office.

Wolman, Carol, and Hal Frank. 1975. "The Solo Woman in a Professional Peer Group." *American Journal of Orthopsychiatry* 45 (January): 164–71.

Zaleznick, Abraham, C. R. Christensen, and F. J. Roethlisberger. 1958. *The Motivation, Productivity, and Satisfaction of Workers: A Prediction Study*. Boston: Harvard Business School Division of Research.

Men's Power with Women, Other Men, and Society

A Men's Movement Analysis

JOSEPH H. PLECK

My aim in this paper is to analyze men's power from the perspective afforded by the emerging antisexist men's movement. In the last several years, an antisexist men's movement has appeared in North America and in the Western European countries. While it is not so widely known as the women's movement, the men's movement has generated a variety of books, publications, and organizations* and is now an established presence. The present and future political relationship between the women's movement and the men's movement raises complex questions which I do not deal with here, though they are clearly important ones. Instead, here I present my own view of the contribution which the men's movement and men's analysis make to a feminist understanding of men and power, and of men's power over women, particularly in relation to the power that men often perceive women have over them. Then I will analyze two other power relationships men are implicated in—men's power with other men, and men's power in society generally—and suggest how these two other power relationships interact with men's power over women.

---

*See, for example, Deborah David and Robert Brannon, eds., *The Forty-Nine Percent Majority: Readings on the Male Role* (Reading, Mass.: Addison-Wesley, 1975); Warren Farrell, *The Liberated Man* (New York: Bantam Books, 1975); Marc Feigen Fasteau, *The Male Machine* (New York: McGraw-Hill, 1974); Jack Nichols, *Men's Liberation: A New Definition of Masculinity* (Baltimore: Penguin, 1975); John Petras, ed., *Sex: Male/Gender: Masculine* (Port Washington, N.J.: Alfred, 1975); Joseph H. Pleck and Jack Sawyer, eds., *Men and Masculinity* (Englewood Cliffs, N.J.: Prentice-Hall, 1974). See also the *Man's Awareness Network (MAN) Newsletter*, a regularly updated directory of men's movement activities, organizations, and publications, prepared by a rotating group of men's centers (c/o Knoxville, Tenn. 37916); the Men's Studies Collection, Charles Hayden Humanities Library, Massachusetts Institute of Technology, Cambridge, Mass. 02139.

MEN'S POWER OVER WOMEN, AND WOMEN'S POWER OVER MEN

It is becoming increasingly recognized that one of the most fundamental questions raised by the women's movement is not a question
about women at all, but rather a question about men. Why do men
oppress women? There are two general kinds of answers to this question.
The first is that men want power over women because it is in their rational self-interest to have it, to have the concrete benefits and privileges
that power over women provides them. Having power, it is rational to
want to keep it. The second kind of answer is that men want to have
power over women because of deep-lying psychological needs in male
personality. These two views are not mutually exclusive, and there is certainly ample evidence for both. The final analysis of men's oppression of
women will have to give attention equally to its rational and irrational
sources.

I will concentrate my attention here on the psychological sources of
men's needs for power over women. Let us consider first the most common and commonsense psychological analysis of men's need to dominate women, which takes as its starting point the male child's early experience with women. The male child, the argument goes, perceives his
mother and his predominantly female elementary school teachers as
dominating and controlling. These relationships *do* in reality contain elements of domination and control, probably exacerbated by the restriction
of women's opportunities to exercise power in most other areas. As a
result, men feel a lifelong psychological need to free themselves from or
prevent their being dominated by women. The argument is, in effect,
that men oppress women as adults because they experienced women as
oppressing them as children.

According to this analysis, the process operates in a vicious circle. In
each generation, adult men restrict women from having power in almost
all domains of social life except childrearing. As a result, male children
feel powerless and dominated, grow up needing to restrict women's
power, and thus the cycle repeats itself. It follows from this analysis that
the way to break the vicious circle is to make it possible for women to
exercise power outside of parenting and parent-like roles and to get men
to do their half share of parenting.

There may be a kernel of truth in this "mother domination" theory
of sexism for some men, and the social changes in the organization of
child care that this theory suggests are certainly desirable. As a general
explanation of men's needs to dominate women, however, this theory
has been quite overworked. This theory holds women themselves, rather
than men, ultimately responsible for the oppression of women—in Wil-

liam Ryan's phrase, "blaming the victim" of oppression for her own oppression.* The film *One Flew over the Cuckoo's Nest* presents an extreme example of how women's supposed domination of men is used to justify sexism. This film portrays the archetypal struggle between a female figure depicted as domineering and castrating and a rebellious male hero (played by Jack Nicholson) who refuses to be emasculated by her. This struggle escalates to a climactic scene in which Nicholson throws her on the floor and nearly strangles her to death—a scene that was accompanied by wild cheering from the audience when I saw the film. For this performance, Jack Nicholson won the Academy Award as the best actor of the year, an indication of how successful the film is in seducing its audience to accept this act of sexual violence as legitimate and even heroic. The hidden moral message of the film is that because women dominate men, the most extreme forms of sexual violence are not only permissible for men but, indeed, are morally obligatory.

To account for men's needs for power over women, it is ultimately more useful to examine some other ways that men feel women have power over them than fear of maternal domination.† There are two forms of power that men perceive women as holding over them which derive more directly from traditional definitions of adult male and female roles, and which have implications which are far more compatible with a feminist perspective.

The first power that men perceive women have over them is *expressive power*, the power to express emotions. It is well known that in traditional male–female relationships, women are supposed to express their needs for achievement only vicariously through the achievements of men. It is not so widely recognized, however, that this dependency of

*William Ryan, *Blaming the Victim* (New York: Pantheon, 1970).
†In addition to the mother domination theory, there are two other psychological theories relating aspects of the early mother–child relationship in men's sexism. The first can be called the "mother identification" theory, which holds that men develop a "feminine" psychological identification because of their early attachment to their mothers and that men fear this internal feminine part of themselves, seeking to control it by controlling those who actually are feminine, i.e., women. The second can be called the "mother socialization" theory, holding that since boys' fathers are relatively absent as sex-role models, the major route by which boys learn masculinity is through their mothers' rewarding masculine behavior, and especially through their mothers' punishing feminine behavior. Thus, males associate women with punishment and pressure to be masculine. Interestingly, these two theories are in direct contradiction, since the former holds that men fear women because women make men feminine, and the latter holds that men fear women because women make men masculine. These theories are discussed at greater length in Joseph H. Pleck, "Men's Traditional Attitudes toward Women: Conceptual Issues in Research," in *The Psychology of Women: New Directions in Research*, ed. Julia Sherman and Florence Denmark (New York: Psychological Dimensions, 1979).

women on men's achievement has a converse. In traditional male–female relationships, men experience their emotions vicariously through women. Many men have learned to depend on women to help them express their emotions, indeed, to express their emotions for them. At an ultimate level, many men are unable to feel emotionally alive except through relationships with women. A particularly dramatic example occurs in an earlier Jack Nicholson film, *Carnal Knowledge*. Art Garfunkel, at one point early in his romance with Candy Bergen, tells Nicholson that she makes him aware of thoughts he "never even knew he had." Although Nicholson is sleeping with Bergen and Garfunkel is not, Nicholson feels tremendously deprived in comparison when he hears this. In a dramatic scene, Nicholson then goes to her and angrily demands, "You tell him his thoughts, now you tell me *my* thoughts!" When women withhold and refuse to exercise this expressive power for men's benefit, many men, like Nicholson in the film, feel abject and try all the harder to get women to play their traditional expressive role.

A second form of power that men attribute to women is *masculinity-validating* power. In traditional masculinity, to experience oneself as masculine requires that women play their prescribed role of doing the things that make men feel masculine. Another scene from *Carnal Knowledge* provides a pointed illustration. In the closing scene of the movie, Nicholson has hired a call girl whom he has rehearsed and coached in a script telling him how strong and manly he is, in order to get him sexually aroused. Nicholson seems to be in control, but when the girl makes a mistake in her role, his desperate reprimands show just how dependent he is on her playing out the masculinity-validating script he has created. It is clear that what he is looking for in this encounter is not so much sexual gratification as it is validation of himself as a man—which only women can give him. As with women's expressive power, when women refuse to exercise their masculinity-validating power for men, many men feel lost and bereft and frantically attempt to force women back into their accustomed role.

As suggested before, men's need for power over women derives both from men's pragmatic self-interest and from men's psychological needs. It would be a mistake to overemphasize men's psychological needs as the sources of their needs to control women, in comparison with simple rational self-interest. However, if we are looking for the psychological sources of men's needs for power over women, their perception that women have expressive power and masculinity-validating power over them is critical to analyze. These powers are the two resources women possess which men fear women will withhold, and whose threatened or actual loss leads men to such frantic attempts to reassert power over women.

Men's dependence on women's power to express men's emotions and to validate men's masculinity has placed heavy burdens on women. By and large, these are not powers over men that women have wanted to hold. These are powers that men have themselves handed over to women by defining the male role as being emotionally cool and inexpressive and as being ultimately validated by heterosexual success.

There is reason to think that over the course of recent history—as male friendship has declined, and as dating and marriage have occurred more universally and at younger ages—the demands on men to be emotionally inexpressive and to prove masculinity through relating to women have become stronger. As a result, men have given women increasingly more expressive power and more masculinity-validating power over them, and they have become increasingly dependent on women for emotional and sex-role validation. In the context of this increased dependency on women's power, the emergence of the women's movement now, with women asserting their right not to play these roles for men, has hit men with a special force.

It is in this context that the men's movement and men's groups place so much emphasis on men learning to express and experience their emotions with each other, and on men learning how to validate themselves and each other as persons, instead of needing women to validate them emotionally and as men. When men realize that they can develop in themselves the power to experience themselves emotionally and to validate themselves as persons, they will not feel the dependency on women which has led in the past to so much male fear, resentment, and need to control women. Then men will be emotionally more free to negotiate the pragmatic realignment of power between the sexes that is under way in our society.

MEN'S POWER WITH OTHER MEN

After considering men's power over women in relation to the power men perceive women have over them, let us consider men's power over women in a second context: the context of men's power relationships with other men. In recent years, we have come to understand that relations between men and women are governed by a sexual politics that exists outside individual men's and women's needs and choices. It has taken us much longer to recognize that there is a systematic sexual politics of male–male relationships as well. Under patriarchy, men's relationships with other men cannot help but be shaped and patterned by patriarchal norms, though they are less obvious than the norms governing male–female relationships. A society could not have the kinds of power dynamics that exist between women and men in our society without certain kinds of systematic power dynamics operating among men as well.

One dramatic example illustrating this connection occurs in Marge Piercy's novel *Small Changes*. In a flashback scene, a male character goes along with several friends to gang-rape a woman. When his turn comes, he is impotent, whereupon the other men grab him, pulling down his pants to rape *him*. This scene powerfully conveys one form of the relationship between male–female and male–male sexual politics. The point is that men do not just happily bond together to oppress women. In addition to hierarchy over women, men create hierarchies and rankings among themselves according to criteria of "masculinity." Men at each rank of masculinity compete with each other, with whatever resources they have, for the differential payoffs that patriarchy allows men.

Men in different societies choose different grounds on which to rank each other. Many societies use the simple facts of age and physical strength to stratify men. The most bizarre and extreme form of patriarchal stratification occurs in those societies which have literally created a class of eunuchs. Our society, reflecting its own particular preoccupations, stratifies men according to physical strength and athletic ability in the early years; later in life it focuses on success with women and ability to make money.

In our society, one of the most critical rankings among men deriving from patriarchal sexual politics is the division between gay and straight men. This division has powerful negative consequences for gay men and gives straight men privilege. In addition, this division has a larger symbolic meaning: Our society uses the male heterosexual–homosexual dichotomy as a central symbol for *all* the rankings of masculinity, for the division on *any* grounds between males who are "real men" and have power and males who are not. Any kind of powerlessness or refusal to compete becomes imbued with the imagery of homosexuality. In the men's movement documentary film *Men's Lives*,* a high school male who studies modern dance says that others often think he is gay because he is a dancer. When asked why, he gives three reasons: because dancers are "free and loose," because they are "not big like football players," and because "you're not trying to kill anybody." The patriarchal connection: If you are not trying to kill other men, you must be gay.

Another dramatic example of men's use of homosexual derogations as weapons in their power struggle with each other comes from a document which provides one of the richest case studies of the politics of male–male relationships yet to appear: Woodward and Bernstein's *The Final Days*. Ehrlichman jokes that Kissinger is queer, Kissinger calls an

---

*Available from New Day Films, P.O. Box 615, Franklin Lakes, N.J. 07417.

unnamed colleague a psychopathic homosexual, and Haig jokes that Nixon and Rebozo are having a homosexual relationship. From the highest ranks of male power to the lowest, the gay–straight division is a central symbol of all the forms of ranking and power relationships which men put on each other.

The relationships between the patriarchal stratification and competition which men experience with each other and men's patriarchal domination of women are complex. Let us briefly consider several points of interconnection between them. First, women are used as *symbols of success* in men's competition with each other. It is sometimes thought that competition for women is the ultimate source of men's competition with each other. For example, in *Totem and Taboo* Freud presented a mythical reconstruction of the origin of society based on sons' sexual competition with fathers, leading to their murdering the fathers. In this view, if women did not exist, men would not have anything to compete for with each other. There is considerable reason, however, to see women not as the ultimate source of male–male competition but as symbols in a male contest whose real roots lie much deeper.

The film *Paper Chase* provides an interesting example. This film combines the story of a small group of male law students in their first year of law school with a heterosexual love story between one of the students (played by Timothy Bottoms) and the professor's daughter. As the film develops, it becomes clear that the real business is the struggle within the group of male law students for survival, success, and the professor's blessing—a patriarchal struggle in which several of the less successful are driven out of school and one even attempts suicide. When Timothy Bottoms gets the professor's daughter at the end, she is simply another one of the rewards he has won by doing better than the other males in her father's class. Indeed, she appears to be a direct part of the patriarchal blessing her father has bestowed on Bottoms.

Second, women often play a *mediating* role in the patriarchal struggle among men. Women get men together with each other and provide the social lubrication necessary to smooth over men's inability to relate to each other noncompetitively. This function has been expressed in many myths, as, for example, in the folk tales included in the Grimm brothers' collection about groups of brothers whose younger sister reunites and reconciles them with the king-father, who had previously banished and tried to kill them. A more modern myth, illustrated in James Dickey's *Deliverance*, is that when men get beyond the bounds of civilization, which really means beyond the bounds of the civilizing effects of women, men rape and murder each other.*

---

*Carolyn G. Heilbrun, "The Masculine Wilderness of the American Novel," *Saturday Review* 41 (January 29, 1972), 41–44.

A third function women play in male–male sexual politics is that relationships with women provide men a *refuge* from the dangers and stresses of relating to other males. Traditional relationships with women have provided men a safe place in which they can recuperate from the stresses they have absorbed in their daily struggle with other men, and in which they can express their needs without fearing that these needs will be used against them. If women begin to compete with men and have power in their own right, men are threatened by the loss of this refuge.

Finally, a fourth function of women in males' patriarchal competition with each other is to reduce the stress of competition by serving as an *underclass*. As Elizabeth Janeway has written in *Between Myth and Morning*,* under patriarchy women represent the lowest status, a status to which men can fall only under the most exceptional circumstances, if at all. Competition among men is serious, but its intensity is mitigated by the fact that there is a lowest possible level to which men cannot fall. One reason men fear women's liberation, writes Janeway, is that the liberation of women will take away this unique underclass status of women. Men will now risk falling lower than ever before, into a new underclass composed of the weak of both sexes. Thus, women's liberation means that the stakes of patriarchal failure for men are higher than they have been before, and that it is even more important for men not to lose.

Thus, men's patriarchal competition with each other makes use of women as symbols of success, as mediators, as refuges, and as an underclass. In each of these roles, women are dominated by men in ways that derive directly from men's struggle with each other. Men need to deal with the sexual politics of their relationships with each other if they are to deal fully with the sexual politics of their relationships with women.

Ultimately, we have to understand that patriarchy has two halves which are intimately related to each other. Patriarchy is a *dual* system, a system in which men oppress women, and in which men oppress themselves and each other. At one level, challenging one part of patriarchy inherently leads to challenging the other. This is one way to interpret why the idea of women's liberation so soon led to the idea of man's liberation, which in my view ultimately means freeing men from the patriarchal sexual dynamics they now experience with each other. Because the patriarchal sexual dynamics of male–male relationships are less obvious than those of male–female relationships, however, men face a real danger. While the patriarchal oppression of women may be lessened as a result of the women's movement, the patriarchal oppression of men may be untouched. The real danger for men posed by the attack that

*Elizabeth Janeway, *Between Myth and Morning* (Boston: Little, Brown, 1975); see also Elizabeth Janeway, "The Weak Are the Second Sex," *Atlantic Monthly* (December, 1973), 91–104.

the women's movement is making on patriarchy is not that this attack will go too far, but that it will not go far enough. Ultimately, men cannot go any further in relating to women as equals than they have been able to go in relating to other men as equals—an equality which has been so deeply disturbing, which has generated so many psychological as well as literal casualties, and which has left so many unresolved issues of competition and frustrated love.

MEN'S POWER IN SOCIETY

Let us now consider men's power over women in a third and final context, the context of men's power in the larger society. At one level, men's social identity is defined by the power they have over women and the power they can compete for against other men. At another level, most men have very little power over their own lives. How can we understand this paradox?

The major demand to which men must accede in contemporary society is that they play their required role in the economy. Howver, this role is not intrinsically satisfying. Social researcher Daniel Yankelovich* has suggested that about 80% of U.S. male workers experience their jobs as intrinsically meaningless and onerous. They experience their jobs and themselves as worthwhile only through priding themselves on the hard work and personal sacrifice they are making to be breadwinners for their families. Accepting these hardships reaffirms their role as family providers and therefore as true men.

Linking the breadwinner role to masculinity in this way has several consequences for men. Men can get psychological payoffs from their jobs which these jobs never provide in themselves. By training men to accept payment for their work in feelings of masculinity rather than in feelings of satisfaction, men will not demand that their jobs be made more meaningful, and as a result jobs can be designed for the more important goal of generating profits. Further, the connection between work and masculinity makes men accept unemployment as their personal failing as males, rather than analyze and change the profit-based economy whose inevitable dislocations make them unemployed or unemployable.

Most critical for our analysis here, men's role in the economy and the ways men are motivated to play it have at least two negative effects on women. First, the husband's job makes many direct and indirect demands on wives. In fact, it is often hard to distinguish whether the wife is dominated more by the husband or by the husband's job. Sociologist Ralph Turner writes: "Because the husband must adjust to the demands of his occupation and the family in turn must accommodate to

*Daniel Yankelovich, "The Meaning of Work," in *The Worker and the Job*, ed. Jerome Rosow (Englewood Cliffs, N.J.: Prentice-Hall, 1974).

his demands on behalf of his occupational obligations, the husband appears to dominate his wife and children. But as an agent of economic institutions, he perceives himself as controlled rather than as controlling."*

Second, linking the breadwinner role to masculinity in order to motivate men to work means that women must not be allowed to hold paid jobs. For the majority of men who accept dehumanizing jobs only because having a job validates their role as family breadwinner, their wives' taking paid jobs takes away from the major and often only way they have of experiencing themselves as having worth. Yankelovich suggests that the frustration and discontent of this group of men, whose wives are increasingly joining the paid labor force, is emerging as a major social problem. What these men do to sabotage women's paid jobs is deplorable, but I believe that it is quite within the bounds of a feminist analysis of contemporary society to see these men as victims as well as victimizers.

One long-range perspective on the historical evolution of the family is that from an earlier stage in which both wife and husband were directly economically productive in the household economic unit, the husband's economic role has evolved so that now it is under the control of forces entirely outside the family. In order to increase productivity, the goal in the design of this new male work role is to increase men's commitment and loyalty to work and to reduce those ties to the family that might compete with it. Men's jobs are increasingly structured as if men had no direct roles or responsiblities in the family—indeed, as if they did not have families at all. Paradoxically, at the same time that men's responsibilities in the family are reduced to facilitate more efficient performance of their work role, the increasing dehumanization of work means that the satisfaction which jobs give men is, to an increasing degree, *only* the satisfaction of fulfilling the family breadwinner role. That is, on the one hand, men's ties to the family have to be broken down to facilitate industrial work discipline; and on the other hand, men's sense of responsibility to the family has to be increased, but shaped into a purely economic form, to provide the motivation for men to work at all. Essential to this process is the transformation of the wife's economic role to providing supportive services, both physical and psychological, to keep him on the job, and to take over the family responsibilities which his expanded work role will no longer allow him to fulfill himself. The wife is then bound to her husband by her economic dependency on him, and the husband in turn is bound to his job by his family's economic dependence on him.

*Ralph Turner, *Family Interaction* (New York: John Wiley, 1968), p. 282.

A final example from the film *Men's Lives* illustrates some of these points. In one of the most powerful scenes in the film, a worker in a rubber plant resignedly describes how his bosses are concerned, in his words, with "pacifying" him to get the maximum output from him, not with satisfying his needs. He then takes back this analysis, saying that he is only a worker and therefore cannot really understand what is happening to him. Next, he is asked whether he wants his wife to take a paid job to reduce the pressure he feels in trying to support his family. In marked contrast to his earlier passive resignation, he proudly asserts that he will never allow her to work, and that in particular he will never scrub the floors after he comes home from his own job. (He correctly perceives that if his wife did take a paid job, he would be under pressure to do some housework.) In this scene, the man expresses and then denies an awareness of his exploitation as a worker. Central to his coping with and repressing his incipient awareness of his exploitation is his false consciousness of his superiority and privilege over women. Not scrubbing floors is a real privilege, and deciding whether or not his wife will have paid work is a real power, but the consciousness of power over his own life that such privilege and power give this man is false. The relative privilege that men get from sexism, and more importantly the false consciousness of privilege men get from sexism, plays a critical role in reconciling men to their subordination in the larger political economy. This analysis does not imply that men's sexism will go away if men gain control over their own lives, or that men do not have to deal with their sexism until they gain this control. I disagree with both. Rather, my point is that we cannot fully understand men's sexism or men's subordination in the larger society unless we understand how deeply they are related.

To summarize, a feminist understanding of men's power over women, why men have needed it, and what is involved in changing it, is enriched by examining men's power in a broader context. To understand men's power over women, we have to understand the ways in which men feel women have power over them, men's power relationships with other men, and the powerlessness of most men in the larger society. Rectifying men's power relationship with women will inevitably both stimulate and benefit from the rectification of these other power relationships.

Women in Positions of Authority

A Case Study of Changing Sex Roles

7

SHARON S. MAYES

This paper aims to contribute to the study of women in positions of authority. By examining the dynamics of patriarchal relations, sex roles, and sex-role behavior among the staff of an American university in a stressed situation, it attempts to go beyond traditional sociological explanations of the way men and women behave in small groups.

Most of the sociological literature on women in positions of authority focuses on the successful woman, all-female organizations, or women in traditional positions of authority.[1] Work on women in small groups, where it exists, tends to ignore women as leaders in groups where there are male subordinates and the respective interactions with subordinates by men and women in the same positions of authority.[2] Many researchers on women in male-led groups find traditional behavior such as deference to men, less commitment to work, preference for centralization, passive participation, and general pliability.[3] In addition, Jo Freeman has suggested that the preference for structurelessness and egalitarianism in leaderless female groups prevents them from task-oriented activity on their own behalf.[4] Traditional research explains, following Bales in *Interaction Process Analysis* and Bales and Parsons in *Family, Socialization, and Interaction Process*, that women's roles in groups mirror the sex-role behavior functional to the family.[5] Feminist criticism calls into question this paradigm's leap from description to explanation and its failure to take into account the long-time participation of women in the work force and women's more recent move into nontraditional positions of leadership. Although what follows is less far-ranging than the problem of women in nontraditional positions of authority demands, it nevertheless provides observations and analyses on which to build.

The suspicion of many sociologists that the events surrounding social research interact with, condition, and modify data collection was confirmed in this study.[6] The research data themselves proved to be a "microcosm" of the forces operating in the institution where they were

Reprinted from *Signs: Journal of Women in Culture and Society* 4(3):556–568, 1979. Copyright © 1979 by the University of Chicago. Reprinted by permission.

collected and, to a lesser extent, in the society.[7] In the university under study polarization between men in positions of power and authority and women seeking access to these positions was prominent. Prior to the fall of 1971 and continuing into the spring of 1973, the university underwent HEW investigations, the inclusion of women in the faculty, the resignation of the medical school dean over this issue, and the unrelenting demand that women be included in every level of university operations. Two years previously, the entire undergraduate class was male, and female graduate students were so scarce they were an oddity in the institution. Only the secretaries and domestics were female.

By late 1971 ambivalence and confusion about sex-role behavior could be observed in informal contacts between men and women. In one-to-one meetings, informal luncheons, and parties men were chivalrous, charming, and deferential toward university women. In formal meetings, classrooms, or decision-making situations women were ignored, patronized, or insulted. As women began to wield some power, during the HEW investigations, male behavior toward them began to change. The more power and authority a woman was perceived to have, the more respect and deference she was accorded. However, this respect was combined with cold formality and hostility in many instances. The more women in the institution had any authority, the more new attitudes toward women's roles were discussed. Within the context of this larger social climate sex-role cleavages in small group settings were expected to be volatile, and under these conditions I hoped to view the entire range of responses from both men and women to the emergence of women with demands for alternative role choices.

Method

The data for this research were collected by participant observation at four separate small-group conferences held at a private northeastern university from November 1971 to April 1973.[8] Two, the first and the last, were conferences that focused on the self-analytic small group; the second focused on intergroup dynamics; and the third was a self-analytic large group. In each instance women were one-fourth to one-third of the group leaders. The leaders were selected by the same male conference director and hence were the same group of women and men in each conference. The female leaders were regularly employed, as were the male leaders, in supervisory positions in nursing and psychiatry and as faculty members in the university. The ranking of the leaders in their regular occupational status shows that males were not at the time of the conferences in higher-status positions than the females.[9]

Each conference averaged between 50 and 60 participants organized into small groups of 11 or 12 members and one leader. The participants were psychiatric residents, nurses, some social science students, and mental health workers. Ranking among the participants in occupational status did not show sex-based differences.[10] Six female-led groups and 12 male-led groups form the core of small-group data. The intergroup and large-group exercises provided supportive material on the issues that arose in response to female leaders in the small groups. The duration of three conferences was two and one-half days beginning on a Friday night and ending Sunday evening. The large group met twice a week for two hours over a 12-week period. In looking at four conferences it is possible to prevent the suspicion that the differential male–female dynamics were the unique occurrence of one conference. The role conflict of participants and responses to the leaders were consistent in every conference.

The sex-role behavior of the leaders was unusually consistent because of the theoretical posturing they used in their leadership behavior. The Tavistock method of group consultation requires that each leader act in a specific authoritarian manner.[11] Male and female leaders have the same training and are, as far as possible, supposed to behave in the same way. This structure lent itself to observations of mixed-sex responses to male and female leadership and to the behavior of men and women leaders. The collapsed time periods of the groups and the intensity of the experience quickly broke down "proper" social fronts and "normal" image management and forced participants to deal with ordinarily unspoken feelings, fears, and reactions to others. The unconscious sex-role socialization of early life was opened up to observation.[12]

The authoritarian behavior of the Tavistock leaders parodies rather than represents the family and the bureaucratic structure of modern institutions.[13] Once within this structure, participants experience the demands of an unyielding, total authority with which there is no overt communication. Whether the sex of that type of authority determines behavior has never been investigated by those who have studied "real-life" total institutions, such as the father in the family, the SS guard in the concentration camp, the master on the slave plantation, and so on.[14] Equally important are the internal dynamics within the leadership groups in which a male was always the ultimate authority. Women were forced to lament: If you go all the way to the top there is still a man ahead of you. Under these conditions one is forced to explain why any role change at all occurred and what happened to this change over time.

The male response to female authority in the small groups was characterized by *hostility* and/or *dependency*. The majority of the males would not cooperate as subordinates with the goal of the leader. They were not task oriented. Although males outnumbered females in every group, in female-led groups they spoke less often, initiated conversation less frequently, and reacted less to female-initiated conversation than women members. The women tended, conversely, to be more outspoken, assertive, and dominant in the conversation. As each meeting began, a women spoke first, contrary to patterns observed in small-group studies of male-led or leaderless groups.[15] The assertiveness of the women, and the nature of the male reaction, was interpreted by a female leader: "The men in the group feel uncomfortable with the female activism. The last comment by a women is felt as a castrating remark."

Right or wrong in her interpretation, she provoked considerable male hostility. Most proceeded to reject all her remarks, and one man suggested that the group ignore her. She was described by the men as "manipulative," "devious," "inhuman," and "cruel." In the application groups where the participants could engage the leaders in conversation, several men were unable to talk to her. These men were sullen, withdrawn, and suspicious. One male in a female-led group said he was "choked up on betrayal." In the intergroup exercises that fell on the second day the same males reacted to the male leaders with quiet relief. After some time with male leaders erratic competitive behavior could be observed. Male responses were conspicuously more hostile to the female authorities and the assertive women participants than to the male leaders. Assertive women in the study groups were labeled by the men (perhaps, taking their cue from the female leaders) "castrating" and "power hungry."

Males in the female-led groups regularly expressed a fear of having lost control. Women were described as "plotting against" them. One male reported that he felt confused and uncomfortable in the female-led group: "I can't be myself in here," he said, whereas in the intergroup without the female leader he reported feeling comfortable because he was "in control of the situation"and "my relations with women are more normal in the intergroup." Other men expressed similar relief on leaving the female-led groups. They reportedly wished for "a more normal group" environment.

Fear of the female authorities and overt anger often preceded expressions of dependency on the female leaders. Men occasionally identified the leader as a "female-father" figure.[16] They expressed doubt about the "real"sex of the leader."If she's real woman why doesn't she act like one?" one male shouted at the rest of his group. A discussion ensued in which the men insisted that women were supposed to be "supportive," "expressive," "warm," and "loving"; not "cold and unfeeling"as the female leader was described. One man suggested that she "might be in drag," or "perhaps, she had an operation." On the other side, a few males coped with the femaleness of the leader by identifying her as mother, ignoring her "coldness," and trying to gain her approval by being "good boys." They said they could not help feeling dependent on the female leader, and they decided not to fight it. About one-third of the males in female-led groups were passive throughout the meetings. These men, when questioned, acknowledged their respect and liking for the assertive women participants and the female leaders. Resentful of what they considered a lack of female closeness, these men said they "let" the women be leaders. As time went by, these men expressed fears about their masculinity and became more uncomfortable with their dependent postures.

Sex-role confusion dominated behavior in the female-led group. It was the major, and in some cases, the only, topic of conversation. In the intergroups men were much more aggressive and relaxed with the women. Many topics were discussed other than sex or sex roles. As long as men were in control, sex-role behavior was what is considered "normal," hence, male feelings of discomfort, frustration, and impotency were related to their loss of control. When asked to explain their feelings men said that they experienced loss of control when every level of their ability to function *as males* came into question. This was particularly important in the area of sexuality. Loss of control was revealed to mean loss of sexual control. When questioned about his overt advances toward the female leader one male said, "The sexual component is present in every relationship I have with women; I AM a MAN, you know." When she failed to respond he said he felt "wounded."

Males adopted several strategies to gain control over the situation. Some openly advocated rebellion, although this was an admission that the female leader was actually powerful. Others suggested leaving the leader and moving the group to another location without informing her. Some men insisted that one or the other of them had to "seduce" the leader, assuming that male control would result. When these strategies failed with the leaders, the men turned to the female participants and claimed deprivation. They tried to persuade the women to "give up this nonsense" and "act natural." They pleaded that the female leader was trying to immobilize them. As one might expect, guilty feelings were kindled in most women. The women who could not be persuaded to give up their identification with the leader were severely rebuked. The men questioned their sexual adequacy in comparison with the women "who knew their proper place."

By the end of the second day of each conference the women were less assertive, identified less with the female leader, and sought to keep male attention in a traditional manner. This was more characteristic of single than married women in the small groups.

Initially the women in the female-led study groups behaved in ways contrary to sociological studies of women in groups. They were assertive, instrumental, and more task oriented than the men. Although the men perceived the women as not being warm and friendly, the women perceived each other in just that way. The female leaders noted several times that the women were more comfortable with their activism because they were identifying with their role. The female leader lessened fears of being rejected by the men and competition for male attention. Women did not report feelings of intellectual inadequacy. None of the women were openly rebellious toward the female leaders, but neither were they competitive. Divisions occurred between "female-oriented" women and "male-oriented" women participants.[17] If leadership was to change hands from the assigned leader, most of the women did not want another woman to become the leader. In discussions of the leader's competency, she was described as "special," "unique," and "unusually qualified" in comparison with other females. The more active women said they "did not want to give her up."[18]

As the conferences wore on the outspoken women became quieter and expressed feelings of confusion. They reported dreams of conflicting loyalties to men and to women. On the first evening of one conference, a woman who talked a lot was accused of being aggressive and intrusive by two men; the next day she remarked that she had thought it over and decided that she was talking too much. She was quiet for the remainder of the conference.

Fears of being rejected by the men outside of the small groups were reported by many women on the second day of each conference. When given time overnight, during the coffee breaks, and in the intergroups to interact with men in traditional sex roles, the women from the female-led groups expressed feelings of inadequacy and a desire to ask the men for support. Some women became hostile to the assertive women participants who did not "tone down" their behavior. In three of the female-led groups a man was asked to "take over and save" the group by a woman who appeared on the last day wearing a dress, high heels, and makeup for the first time. The behavior of this woman was repeated by different women in each conference. She said that in the intergroup exercises she had come to rely on male leadership and now wanted a man to take the lead in the small group. One particularly vehement woman turned to the most active woman participant and said, "I don't dislike you just in here; I don't think I would have liked you anywhere we met." She followed this with a plea to a male to lead the group.

Women participants who refused to give up their assertive roles received the brunt of male and female anger. The female leaders noted that the anger was being deflected off them as the "real" leaders and displaced to a manageable substitute. Feelings of inadequacy, anger, and discomfort in the women participants were blamed on each other rather than on the men or the female leader. The few women who blamed the men for the problems in the groups were harshly rebuked. It was hinted that these women were lesbians and were trying to "destroy the male world." The leaders interpreted these women as attempting to "pair" with her and thus form a stronger barrier to male takeover. There were strong efforts on the part of the men and some of the women to prevent any woman-to-woman pairs in the small groups. Women who did not conform were ostracized from informal activities. Assertions of heterosexuality were common if and when a particular woman openly allied herself with the female leader or another woman in the group.

The final small-group sessions saw initial resistance to traditional sex roles fade, particularly as the groups confronted the end of their conference. The women began to renounce their leadership roles in the small groups and act more dependent on the male participants for guidance than on the female leader. Assertive women knew they had to face their male fellows later in the intergroups without the female leader to "protect" them. The women who refused to give up their leadership roles and make peace with the men often left the conferences early. One woman said on leaving that she was "just plain disgusted with the rampant sexism." She also hurriedly added, "I'm afraid I'll be eaten alive."

The more traditional sex-role patterns of behavior were reported in groups with male leaders. The men reported feelings of competitiveness with the male leader.[19] Many men said they were jealous of the leader's superior status in relation to the women in their group. The leader was their role model, their boss, and their representative. Most men wanted to convince the women that they were as competent and attractive as the male leader. They were not hostile to him; rather, they conducted their competition with gentlemanly grace. The women participants were not part of this competition in an active sense, nor were they ever the dominant figures or initiators in these groups. Males said they felt protective toward "their" women and described them as less intellectual, less aggressive than the women in the female-led groups. (There was no reason why this would have occurred by chance. The women were randomly assigned to the study groups.)

During the unled intergroup exercises male-led men formed highly structured task groups in contrast to the men in the female-led groups who went into unstructured "Esalen" type groups. Esalen intergroups were established spontaneously at every conference and were so called by the participants. This name was descriptive of the activities they pursued—encounter exercises, sensitivity sessions, relaxation exercises, sitting on the floor, removing shoes, ties, and the like, and revealing personal feelings—and was taken from the Esalen Institute in California. The deprivation expressed by the men in the female-led groups was relieved through physical contact with the women in the Esalen-type intergroups. The extent of the choice was astounding: All of the men in female-led groups went into the Esalen intergroups, whereas none of the men in any of the male-led groups went into them.

Neither a lack of authority nor a need for female reassurance was described as important by men in male-led groups. When asked, the men said they aspired to be like their leader—they identified with his position and wanted to have that position themselves. They unanimously agreed that the male leader was competent and deserved to be in his position. The women were acknowledged to be the objects of sexual competition, and they were the rewards for male leadership. Some women, too, reported that the leader was more attractive than the participants.

Women in the male-led groups behaved primarily, but not entirely, in accordance with the dominant sex-role stereotypes. They competed with each other for the favors and attention of the leader, but they did not compete for leadership. Several said that the males were smarter and more competent in leading the group. The women reported feeling hostile to, suspicious and jealous of each other. They were less assertive but more sullen and angry than the women in the female-led groups. Some of the women insisted they resented being placed in a competitive situation with other women and expressed confusion with regard to their own behavior. Anger among male-led women was directed inward rather than toward the male members or the leaders. One woman was upset with herself for having "gotten into this situation in the first place." The loyalties expressed to the leader were ardent but uncomfortable and had a tone of resentment.

In the intergroups male-led women moved into the structured groups with participant male leaders. None stayed with the Esalen intergroups which were composed almost entirely of the men and women from the female-led groups. Conversely, some of the women from the female-led groups went into the highly structured male-led intergroups. The traditional posture the women in male-led groups had toward the leader allowed them to interact comfortably with the male-led intergroups. They were complimented, protected, and taken care of by the men in these groups. The women who visited female-led or unstructured groups expressed dislike for the women leaders, and only three ever chose to join in the groups' activities.

When asked about their feelings toward the males, conflict and contradiction emerged from the women in male-led groups. These women moved around most from group to group during the intergroup exercises. Several women said they felt as if they "didn't belong anywhere."

Some wanted to stay with the Esalen groups but eventually left because of loyalties to males from their small groups.

STAFF: IS GOD DEAD?

In the staff groups the confusion over sex roles was easily observable. When some task had not been completed, or there was disagreement on staff rules, the male leaders looked to the women as the culprits. The female leaders protested to the male director that confusion reigned in the staff over their own rules. The women were instructed by the director not to be "insubordinate." Awkward and only half-successful attempts were made by the director to exercise consistent authority and control over the staff leaders. Whenever the participants got out of hand there was a tendency to blame the male director for not being "potent" enough to keep his women leaders in line. One male leader said that the male participants were "pulling out their penises and taking over." Comments made by the female leaders in the staff meetings were often "unheard" or ignored. Many of the dynamics observed in the male-led staff group mirrored the dynamics in the male-led small groups; the female-led groups were characterized as "special" with their own peculiar dynamics. The female leaders were second-level shock troops between the masses of unruly children and the "real" authority—the conference director. The analogy of the mother role, mediator between children and father in the family, is obvious.

The confusion over authority, tasks, and roles was interpreted by the staff themselves as a reflection of the confusion in the medical school, the departments of psychiatry and psychology, and the university in general. Not daring to fully interpret their own dynamics, they blamed them on external factors. Indeed, symbolically the belief that male authority was breaking down and women were "taking over" plagued the well-trained staff. They, too, were victims of the confusion about the meaning of even a small-scale opposition to male dominance in the university. Female authority and resistance to male authority provoked fear, anger, and chaos.

CONCLUSION

Two themes are prominent in these data: First, women in nontraditional positions of authority over men and women subordinates evoke different reactions than men in equivalent positions. Second and more complicated, the resistance to changing sex-role behavior on the part of men and women involves the deeply embedded fear that change means chaos and collapse in the norms and behaviors that govern the most sacred areas of everyday life—the family and sexuality.

The ambivalence and contradiction that one finds in the reponses must be explained separately for men and women. Yet, both responses are predicated on the fact that power and authority are today the domains of men. Women in such positions have vacillated in their ability to cope with and modify their behavior to remove its cutting edge. Women often question their own sexuality as others question them.

To ease her own fears a woman may refuse authority-laden positions or remain silent in decision-making situations with male equivalents. This, in turn, creates the context for her competency to be questioned as it was observed in all the female-led groups. Anxiety about being labeled incompetent tends to provoke another reaction in female authorities: They may overidentify with male role behavior and become worse tyrants to subordinates than male authorities who are often considered benevolent regardless of their behavior. Women at the top may feel, as subordinates do, that they are somehow "special" and "unique," not like other women.[20] This response, however beneficial to the individual woman's short-run interest, does not aid her long-run interest in fundamental sex-role change.

Male ambivalence is seen in their desire for strong, nurturant, supportive females *and* their desire to retain control over the traditional male roles which require weak, passive, obedient, and sexually available females. Male confusion in response to the female authority stemmed not from her authority per se but from the *male* way in which she exercised her authority; namely, with formal, objective, nonnurturant, asexual adherence to rules and boundaries. If these leaders had shown any normative traits of female authority they might have been showered with affection or put on a pedestal and worshipped as Supermom. An example from the data is the discomfort the men felt about rebelling against the female leader. They did not want to grant her the social equality or even superiority that rebellion would imply. In order to rebel against her legitimately she had to be sexually transformed in their minds, hence the discussions as to the female leaders' "real" sex.

The fear that if traditional sex roles were destroyed all male love would be lost seems an unusual fear easily aroused in women training to be professionals. The oppositional nature of career to traditional female roles is revealed in women's role conflict. Traditional female roles were threatened by the female leader; the choice seemed to be either/or but not both. The female leader appeared in her role consistency to have resolved the career/family role conflict that many women at the conference were concerned with. Her posture, in turn, seemed to evoke additional conflict without resolution in the women who both wanted to be like her (career) and were afraid to be like her (loss of male approval, marriage). To retain the security of familiar roles and diminish the threat of male loss, many women chose to retreat. The power of fantasy life in making these decisions is enormous. Although women were making demands on the institution, the real gains in authority for women were infinitesimal. In 1976 the institution has less than 1% of its positions of authority filled by women.

An explanation of the women's fantasized power does not, unfortunately, lie in these data but in the generalized societal fear that patriarchy, riddled with contradiction on every level, can no longer provide the context for institutional or personal behavior. Opposition to male dominance in any area—the bedroom or the office—invokes panic because the structures that support it as a worldview are weakening. The data presented here confirm Mitchell's suggestion that a full-scale analysis of patriarchy is necessary before modification of sex roles alone will become a viable strategy for change. Much of the vitality of patriarchy lies in the unconscious and the structures of myth as they interact with a superimposed social rationality. The fantasy lives of women and men in alternative situations may well expose the weakest links in patriarchal culture *and* the reasons why individuals retreat to learned behavior.

Insofar as social attitudes are related to behavior, women in positions of male authority can be said to promote some sex-role change for both males and females. However, the experience of acting in a new role creates anxiety and resistance. In a limited context pressure for sex-role dynamics to return to normative patterns is strong. Women leaders are interpreted through the universal experience of the family and placed in some aspect of the mother role. The status of women in the family and the status of the family in society indicate that this is still the home base for images of female power and authority. If the family is not the *actual* context for interaction it will become the *fantasized* context, and female authority will be seen in this light. Replication of this research in another setting where women in male equivalent positions have mixed-sex subordinates on a daily basis will provide valuable information on the validity of these observations.

Notes

1. Margaret Cussler, *The Woman Executive* (New York: Harcourt Brace & Co., 1958); Cora Bagley Marrett, "Centralization in Female Organizations," *Social Problems* 19, no. 3 (Winter 1972): 348–57; Edmond Constantini and Kenneth Craik, "Women as Politicians: The Social Background, Personality and Political Careers of Female Party Leaders," *Journal of Social Issues* 28, no. 2 (1972): 217–35; Ruth Oltman, "Women in the

Professional Caucuses," *American Behavioral Scientist* 15, no. 2 (November/December 1971): 281–302; Alice Rossi and Ann Calderwood, eds., *Academic Women on the Move* (New York: Russell Sage Foundation, 1973).

2. Some exceptions are R. V. Exline, "Effects of Sex, Norms and Affiliation Motivation upon Accuracy of Perception of Interpersonal Preferences," *Journal of Personality* 28 (1960): 397–412a; T. L. Stroedbeck and R. D. Mann, "Sex Role Differentiations in Jury Deliberations," *Sociometry* 19 (1956): 3–11. O. Gusky, "A Case for the Theory of Familial Role Differentiation in Small Groups," *Social Forces* 35 (1957): 209–17; R. V. Exline and V. Ziller, "Influence Process in Relation to the Ratio of Sexes in Decision Making Groups," unpublished manuscript (Newark: University of Delaware, Fels Group Dynamic Center, n.d.); Eugen Lupri, "Social Correlates of Family Authority Patterns: The West German Case," *Sociologia Ruralis* 10, no. 2 (1970): 99–119; Rosabeth M. Kanter, *Men and Women of the Corporation* (New York: Basic Books, 1977).

3. Marrett, p. 351; George Brager and John Michael, "The Sex Distribution in Social Work: Causes and Consequences," *Social Casework* 50 (December 1969): 595–601; Robert Wyer, Donald Weatherly, and Glenn Terrall, "Social Role, Aggression, and Academic Achievement," *Journal of Personality and Social Psychology* 1 (June 1965): 645–49.

4. Jo Freeman, "The Tyranny of Structurelessness," *Berkeley Journal of Sociology* 17 (1972–73): 151–64.

5. Robert F. Bales, *Interaction Process Analysis* (Chicago: University of Chicago Press, 1951); Talcott Parsons et al., *Family, Socialization, and Interaction Process* (Glencoe, Ill.: Free Press, 1955). See the extensive bibliography on small-group research in R. E. L. Faris, ed., *The Handbook of Modern Sociology* (Chicago: Rand McNally & Co., 1964), pp. 257–64.

6. The arguments for and against specific methodologies and theoretical frameworks are too numerous to list; see Thomas Kuhn, *The Structure of Scientific Revolutions* (Chicago: University of Chicago Press, 1962); Larry T. Reynolds and Janice M. Reynolds, eds. *The Sociology of Sociology* (New York: David McKay Co., 1970); Leon Bramson, *The Political Context of Sociology* (Princeton, N.J.: Princeton University Press, 1961).

7. Philip Slater, *Microcosm* (New York: John Wiley & Sons, 1966); and Peter Berger and Thomas Luckmann, *The Social Construction of Reality* (New York: Doubleday & Co., 1966).

8. Data were collected by me and a research staff of 12 persons for each conference. They consisted of detailed case histories of each group, coded questionnaires given at the beginning and end of the conferences, and video- and audiotapes. When disagreement on coding occurred a third researcher was asked to code the behavior; this interpretation was compared with the others, and the one with the most agreement was used.

9. The occupational status of male leaders ranged from full professor of psychiatry to graduate student in psychology. The majority of males were professors without tenure. The female leaders ranged from the director of the School of Nursing to graduate student in psychology. There were status differentials among the leaders, but there were not always males in the higher-status positions.

10. Among the participants who were mental health workers more women were in supervisory capacities than men. However, among community participants more women identified themselves as faculty spouses than men. Except for the equal status of graduate-student participants and leaders, all leaders were of higher occupational status than the participants. All these individuals reflect a certain stratum of society. They were professionals or academics, highly educated, and attached to an elite university. They cannot be considered representative of other social classes, although the conferences tended to attract the less elite members of the community.

11. Tavistock theory is based on the work of W. R. Bion, *Experiences in Groups* (New York: Basic Books, 1959) and A. K. Rice, *Learning for Leadership* (London: Tavistock Publications, 1965).

12. See Erving Goffman's analysis of role disintegration among mental patients in a "total institution" in *Asylums* (Chicago: Aldine Publishing Co., 1961), pp. 7–125, and "Stigma and Social Identity," in *Woman in a Man-Made World*, ed. Nona Glazer-Malbin and Helen Youngelson Wachrer (New York: Rand McNally & Co., 1972); Claude Lévi-Strauss, *Structural Anthropology* (London: Penguin Press, 1968); and Juliet Mitchell, *Psychoanalysis and Feminism* (New York: Random House, 1972), pp. 371–98.

13. Max Horkheimer, "Authority and the Family," *Critical Theory: Selected Essays* (New York: Herder & Herder, 1972), pp. 47–129.

14. Goffman; Mitchell; Stanley Elkins, *Slavery* (New York: Universal Library, 1963). An exception is the graphic portrayal in the film *Seven Beauties* by Lina Wertmüller in which a brutal female concentration-camp mistress is pitifully seduced by an Italian prisoner attempting to gain his freedom and his life.

15. All of the studies cited in n. 2 were groups with male leaders or foremen.

16. Norman O. Brown, *Love's Body* (New York: Random House, 1966).

17. Douglas T. Hall, "A Model of Coping with Role Conflict: The Role Behavior of College Educated Women," *Administrative Science Quarterly*, vol. 17 (1972).

18. Mitchell, *Psychoanalysis and Feminism*, pp. 109–21.

19. R.D. Mann, *Interpersonal Styles and Group Development* (New York: John Wiley & Sons, 1967).

20. A. Leffler, D. L. Gillespie, and E. Lerner Ratner, "Academic Feminists and the Women's Movement," *Insurgent Sociologist* 4, no. 1 (Fall 1973): 45–56.

Some Clinical Consequences of Inequality

A. Suppression of Autonomy and Denial of Dependency

The two chapters in this section provide another way of understanding how sex-role stereotypes differentially influence expressions of autonomy and dependency in women and men. We have chosen to focus on the universal experiences of striving for autonomy and mastery of dependency because their integration is central to the development of an individual's psychological well-being. However, achieving this integration is immeasurably complicated by the structure of inequality, which encourages dependency in women and autonomy in men.

In the first article, "Early Origins of Envy and Devaluation of Women: Implications for Sex-Role Stereotypes," Harriet E. Lerner provides an intrapsychic explanation for the pervasive devaluation of women and feminine traits that occurs in most cultures. She argues that "the devaluation of women as well as the very definitions of appropriate 'masculine' and 'feminine' behavior stem in large part from a defensive handling of the powerful and persistent affects of the early infant–mother relationship. [These] profound affects (i.e. envy, fear, rage, shame) [are] aroused by the child's helpless dependency on an all-powerful maternal figure. . . ."

What men and women carry into adulthood, *if these childhood perceptions are left unexamined,* is a primitive imago of an omnipotent mother who possesses the power to be nurturant and comforting or to be dominating and destructive. Lerner maintains that the fear and envy of women's mythic powers are defensively managed by devaluing women, "for as long as an object is devalued it need not be envied."

In this schema, the envy–devaluation constellation is manifested in cultural definitions of "appropriate" sex-linked behaviors. Women are encouraged to retain their nurturant qualities while suppressing expressions of dominance, control, autonomy, anger, and aggression (which are defined as "masculine"). In contrast, men are expected to be independent and to exert power and control over women, thus achieving a reversal of the early childhood experience. Indeed, men are encouraged to suppress and deny their feelings of vulnerability and dependency, not only because they evoke irrational anxieties about female power and destructiveness, but also because they are defined as unmanly.

In her next article, "Female Dependency in Context: Some Theoretical and Technical Considerations," Lerner further explores the developmental and clinical implications of defining dependency as a "feminine" trait. One notable implication is that we tend to hear little about men's dependency needs, "the fulfilling of which has been women's assigned role." As Lerner states: "women are still encouraged to protect men by containing and expressing the very passivity and dependency that men fear in themselves and do not wish to be 'weakened' by. Because women do learn that being an autonomous self-directed person is hurtful to others, especially men, their dependent behaviors are often an unconscious 'gift' or sacrifice to those they love; it is the gift of giving up self so that the other may gain in self."

Therapists have generally failed to recognize that many women assume an "underfunctioning" role that serves a protective and systems-maintaining function within families. This underfunctioning and dependent stance, however, is incompatible with the normal internal push toward personal growth and autonomy. The inevitable conflicts that are generated by this situation are further confounded by the fact that all problem-solving options are accompanied by perceived and real threats of loss. Any moves toward autonomy and separateness are experienced by both the woman and her family as destructive and disloyal. Alternatively, her "choice" of retaining a dependent posture at the expense of her own growth leaves her with an unavoidable burden of rage, which often remains unidentified and unvalidated. This rage may surface in the guise of inappropriate or irrational affects and behaviors. When confronted with these initially inexplicable patterns, it is important for clinicians to explore the covert conflicts that underly these behaviors.

Consequently, therapists must examine women's resistance to change within the context of family systems and the cultural values that reinforce these gender roles. Therapists must also be aware that the same female underfunctioning can occur in the therapeutic relationship: "While unconsciously associating autonomy and separateness with disloyalty, betrayal, and potential loss, the female patient will repeatedly test out in the transference the degree to which the [male] therapist will choose to see her as dependent and dysfunctional and the degree to which the therapist is comfortable with her competence and autonomy" (Lerner).

These articles underscore the importance of clarifying certain hidden values that are likely to be shared by patients and therapists. These include taken-for-granted assumptions about female power and male vulnerability, about the "rightness" of sex-role stereotypes for women and men, and about the usefulness of individual psychotherapy as the treatment of choice for "excessively dependent" wives. In considering these assumptions, therapists must help men confront their illusions of invulnerability and excessive independence. Indeed, men's psychological well-being (and the well-being of women) will require that they reclaim the affective functions they have delegated to women and that they share responsibility for their own dependency needs as well as those of significant others. Although Lerner limits her discussion to heterosexual relationships, we believe that it will also be important to explore issues of autonomy and dependency as they occur in gay and lesbian relationships.

Early Origins of Envy and Devaluation of Women

Implications for Sex-Role Stereotypes

8

HARRIET E. LERNER

Psychoanalysts have long believed that penis envy is central to the understanding of women and have invoked this concept to explain everything from a woman's desire for a husband and child to her strivings to work and compete in traditionally masculine fields. Those outside psychoanalytic circles have shown less enthusiasm for such explanations—particularly members of the Women's Liberation Movement who angrily protest that women have cause to be envious of men's position in society for reasons other than their possession of the desired penis. Certain psychoanalysts have, in turn, insisted that the Women's Liberation Movement is itself a manifestation of penis envy and that discontent with the female role is a psychiatric problem.

Narrow and stereotyped notions concerning women's appropriate place in society are not confined to a mere handful of psychoanalysts. The most authoritative of psychoanalysts have concurred that the "true" nature of women is to find fulfillment in the traditional role of wife and mother (Chesler, 1972). Without sharing Freud's views of the oedipus complex and penis envy, Jung (1928) nevertheless stated, "that in taking up a masculine calling, studying, and working in a man's way, woman is doing something not wholly in agreement with, if not directly injurious to, her feminine nature" (p. 169). Bettelheim (1965) commented, "as much as women want to be good scientists or engineers, they want first and foremost to be womanly companions of men and to be mothers" (p. 15). Women who are not happy with this state of affairs, according to Freud (1925), have refused adaptively to come to grips with their sexual inferiority and still have the "hope of some day obtaining a penis in spite of everything . . ." (p. 191).

Reprinted from *Bulletin of the Menninger Clinic* 38(6):538–553, 1974. Copyright © 1974, The Menninger Foundation. Reprinted by permission. The author would like to express her gratitude to Dr. Otto Kernberg, Dr. Paul Pruyser, and Dr. Tobias Brocher for their helpful comments and criticisms.

While I am not in agreement with those who discredit the importance of penis envy, I do believe psychoanalysts who rationalize certain maladaptive aspects of femininity as unavoidable biological necessities court contempt by carrying the concept of penis envy to untenable extremes. As Chesler (1972) has commented, "The 'Freudian' vision beholds women as essentially 'breeders and bearers' as potentially warm-hearted creatures, but more often as cranky children with uteruses, forever mourning the loss of male organs and male identity" (p. 79).

It is unfortunate, however, that feminist anger and misunderstanding have led to a global damnation of all psychoanalytic thinking, as well as a somewhat more benign condemnation of other established modes of treatment. There have been numerous revisions of Freud's viewpoints on women with frequent references to the unfortunate "phallocentric" bias of his theorizing and open acknowledgment that femininity and female sexuality are insufficiently understood (David, 1970; Torok, 1970). Even Freud expressed reticence and insecurity in the face of that "dark continent" of femininity and never failed to stress the incomplete and tentative nature of his theorizing. Recent psychoanalytic writers have, in fact, shown considerable appreciation of feminist protests and of the intense cultural pressures that combine with intrapsychic factors to encourage "women [to] accept [a] . . . neurotically dependent, self-effacing solution in life" (Symonds, 1971–72, p. 224).

Long before the current feminist movement, however, there existed wide recognition that femininity in most cultures is much devalued and that frequent exaltation and idealization of women hardly mask the underlying contempt for them (Horney, 1932). Writers from many disciplines, psychoanalysts among them, have written about the quasi-racial discrimination that exists against women. David (1970), for example, has noted one primitive tribe that refers to women as "the race which is not entitled to speak" (p. 50); and anthropologists have observed that the devaluation of women in many cultures is no less intense than the oppression of racial or ethnic minority groups.

The oppression of women is unique, however, in one important respect: Women participate as vigorously in their own depreciation as do men. The "masochistic attitude" of many women can be easily recognized, and women's belittling of their own sex is observed daily in our consulting rooms, demonstrated in experimental research (Goldberg, 1968), and is inherent in cultural institutions around the world (Lederer, 1968).

The devaluation of women is readily documented, but the reasons behind the complicity of both sexes are less than clear. In addition to powerful cultural pressures on women to devalue themselves, there must be strong internal pressures as well, for institutionalized patterns are not so readily established and maintained unless there are advantages for all involved. For men as well, the reasons for complicity with a sexist solution are not obvious. Men have too frequently been described as having all the advantages and power of a "ruling class" when, in fact, the cost for their situation is no less dear. As one psychoanalyst has written:

> . . . on examining the question more closely, it is not obvious a priori that men should naturally want such a relationship of mastery. The falsity, the ambivalence, and the refusal of identification it conceals should appear to him as so many snags on which his own full and authentic achievement comes to grief. . . . What interest has he in giving in to his need to dominate the being through whom he could understand himself and who could understand him? To discover oneself through the other sex would be a genuine fulfillment of one's humanity, yet this is exactly what escapes most of us. (Torok, 1970, pp. 168–169)

For many psychoanalytic theorists, the devaluation of women is an irreducible problem that stems from the genital deficiency (real or imagined) of the female sex. Intense hatred directed toward the mother because of her penis-less state and the resulting contempt not only for her but for all women is the inescapable lot of girls (due to their castration complex) and of boys (due to their castration anxiety). As long as men have penises and women vaginas, institutionalized sexism is an inevitable symptom of our anatomical destinies, for which phylogenesis alone must bear the responsibility.

However, by overextending the concept of genital inferiority in explaining the devaluation of women, we have failed to appreciate other important determinants. My opinion is that the devaluation of women as well as the very definitions of appropriate "masculine" and "feminine" behavior stem in large part from a defensive handling of the powerful and persistent affects of the early infant–mother relationship. The profound affects (i.e., envy, fear, rage, shame) aroused by the child's helpless dependency on an all-powerful maternal figure have indeed received recognition, but their resulting impact on adult life has continually been underplayed and insufficiently elaborated. As Lederer (1968) commented, "of our fear and envy of women, we, the psychoanalytic-papers-writing-men, have managed to maintain a dignified fraternal silence " (p. 153).

ENVY OF WOMEN

If the concept of penis envy is familiar even to the layman, psychoanalytic speculations regarding breast envy require a more arduous search through the literature. This fact is surprising for society's intense idealization, devaluation, and literal obsession with breasts seems to point to the significance of such a phenomenon. Also of relevance is the critical importance of the mother's breast in early infancy. The breast is the earliest source of gratification and frustration, of love and hate, as well as the first vehicle of intimate social contact (Fairbairn, 1952). Klein (1957), for example, has highlighted the infant's early relationship to the mother's breast: "in the analysis of our patients . . . the breast in its good aspect is the prototype of maternal goodness, inexhaustible patience and generosity, as well as of creativeness" (pp. 5–6).

Although the idea of breast envy has no formal conceptual status in psychoanalytic theory, it is of central importance in Melanie Klein's theoretical work. Defining envy as "the angry feeling that another person possesses and enjoys something desirable—the envious impulse being to take it away or to spoil it" (1957, p. 6), she writes: "My work has taught me that the first object to be envied is the feeding breast, for the infant feels that it possesses everything he desires and that it has an unlimited flow of milk and love which the breast keeps for its own gratification" (1957, p. 10). To Klein, the desire to internalize and thus possess the breast, so all the power and magic that the infant attributes to it will be his own, is of central importance. She reports that in the analysis of female patients even penis envy can be traced back to envy of the mother's breast (or its symbolic representation, the bottle).

Freud (1909, 1918) also recognized that there is a counterpart to penis envy when he described pregnancy fantasies and the wish for a baby among men. In the analytic literature, one can find case studies describing pregnancy fantasies and enacted pregnancies both in grown men and young boys. Others such as Ruth Mack Brunswick (1940) have elaborated this theme, stating that in girls the wish for a child precedes the wish for a penis and that penis envy itself can be understood as the desire to possess the omnipotent mother and her attributes.

It is not my intention to popularize the notion of breast envy, but rather to suggest that male envy of female sex characteristics and reproductive capacity is a widespread and conspicuously ignored dynamic. Of greater importance is the fact that envy tends to be a larger phenomenon for both sexes, not typically confined to such part objects as penises and breasts. As Torok (1970) points out, it is not the absence of a thing (like the penis or breast) that produces such profound feelings of envy, despair, and self-hatred, but rather, such envy is a symptom of unconscious desires, wishes, or fears that may have little to do with objective anatomical realities. Penis envy, for example, frequently has its origin in the dyadic relationship between mother and daughter and may be a symptom reflecting difficulties in identifying with and achieving differentiation from a mother who is perceived as jealous, destructive, and intrusive (Chasseguet-Smirgel, 1970; Torok, 1970). For men, it is unlikely that envy of women is derived simply from the feeding breast and reproductive capacities, but rather from the varied impressions of infancy and early childhood in which the mother is experienced as an omnipotent object who possesses inexhaustible supplies as well as the power both to inflict and ward off all pain and evil.

ENVY AND DEVALUATION: REVERSING AN EARLY MATRIARCHY

Of central importance to the dynamic understanding of defensive sexism is the close relationship between envy and devaluation. Devaluation of an envied object is a typical defensive maneuver, for as long as an object is devalued it need not be envied. Klein has suggested that spoiling and devaluing are inherent aspects of envy and that the earliest and most important objects of envy and devaluation are the mother and her breast. Kernberg (1972) has also noted in his work with borderline and narcissistic patients that intense envy and hatred of women are conspicuous dynamics that impair the capacity to form love relationships. He finds that envy and hatred are defensively dealt with by depreciating and devaluating women.

The question arises whether envy and devaluation of women is confined to persons with serious psychopathology or whether it is a more pervasive if not universal dynamic. Although Kernberg implies that this constellation is a serious problem only for very disturbed patients, he also notes it is not a circumscribed clinical phenomenon: "One finds intense envy and hatred of women in many male patients. Indeed, from a clinical viewpoint, it seems the intensity of this dynamic constellation in men matches that of penis envy in women . . ." (1972, p. 14).

I agree with Kernberg's statement that devaluation of women is "in the final analysis, devaluation of mother as a primary object of dependency" (1972, p. 14). However, I would further suggest that this dynamic is a pervasive one which is expressed in the institutionalized values and mores regarding gender in cultures around the world. In this culture, for example, I believe that the envy–devaluation constellation is reflected in the selection of what traits, qualities, behaviors, and roles are deemed appropriate for each sex. Our current notions of "masculinity" and "femininity" are such that enormous pressures are put on females to "let the man win," to avoid direct expressions of aggression, self-assertion, competitiveness, and intellectual prowess, and to suppress wishes to be leader and initiator rather than follower and helpmate (Lerner, 1974; Lynn, 1972). I suspect these widely accepted gender definitions and sex-role stereotypes are themselves a reflection of a defensive devaluating of women, and thus of an early dependency relationship with mother.

Our gender definitions and sex-role stereotypes also reflect an attempt to reinstate and retain in adult relations all the nurturant qualities of the "good mother." Thus, according to most cultural stereotypes, the desirable, "feminine" woman is one who embodies all aspects of the good mother (e.g., cleaning, feeding, providing emotional understanding, comfort, softness, warmth), but who possesses no elements of power, dominance, and control that are also factors within the imago of the omnipotent, envied mother. To put it somewhat differently, in conventional adult relationships, males stereotypically experience a *defensive reversal* of an early matriarchy, yet retain the nurturant functions of the good mother. A psychic and social situation is created in which the adult male retains the good aspects of mother but is now dominant and in control of a female object on whom, as in the case of his mother, he was initially helpless and dependent; that is, his wife (or female peer) becomes his own child. As long as this defensive reversal of an early dependency situation continues, envy and devaluation of women is subdued or seemingly eliminated; the devaluation of women achieves expression in the reversal itself.

But how are we to understand women's active participation in this system? For although women reverse the helpless dependency of their own infantile situation through the role of mother, they often "choose" in peer relations with men to remain the dependent child. As Kernberg (1972) points out, envy and devaluation of the mother as a primal source of dependency is no less intense in women than in men. Thus, women's acceptance and perpetuation of feminine stereotypes (e.g., fragility, dependency, passivity) as well as idealization of men and the penis may also be an attempt to devalue the omnipotence and power of the maternal figure. This notion is compatible with Chasseguet-Smirgel's (1970) statement that images of women as castrated or deficient are a denial for both sexes of the imagos of the primitive mother (i.e., the good omnipotent mother is symbolized by the generous breast, fruitful womb, wholeness, abundance; the bad omnipotent mother is symbolized by frustration, invasion, intrusion, evil).*

Other theorists as well, while not focusing specifically on envy, have linked early maternal power to the depreciation of women. David (1970)

---

*Penis envy and castration concerns in women reflect a defensive need to devalue the imagos of the primitive mother. Yet, such symptoms may also reflect deep guilt and anxiety in identifying with this imago, especially when mother is experienced as a powerful, malevolent, and castrating figure in her relationship with father. Thus, women's self-experience of being "castrated" (and their idealization of men and the penis) is often a reaction against their own feared "castrating" and aggressive wishes. (See Chasseguet-Smirgel, 1970, for an excellent discussion of this issue.)

speculates that profound narcissistic injuries inflicted on the infant by the omnipotent mother lead to a powerful need for revenge. He suggests that our distorted concept of femininity and female sexuality, the discrimination that women suffer by men and women, and the masochistic attitude that characterizes women are all the result of "revenge" for the radical narcissistic wounds inflicted on both male and female infants at the breast. Horney (1932) relates both the idealization and depreciation of women to the violently aggressive desires for revenge that stem from the mother's dominance and power and the small child's related feelings of weakness, impotence, and humiliation. Brunswick (1940) notes the powerful character of the primitive maternal image and emphasizes the early narcissistic injuries resulting from the child's dependency on the omnipotent mother "who is capable of everything and who possesses every valuable attribute" (p. 304).

Chasseguet-Smirgel (1970) suggests another determinant of the need to reverse the infantile situation, namely, the fear and terror of women.

> I believe that a child, whether male or female, even with the best and kindest of mothers, will maintain a terrifying maternal image in his unconscious, the result of projected hostility deriving from his own impotence. . . . the child's primary powerlessness . . . and the inevitable frustrations of training are such that the imago of the good, omnipotent mother never covers over that of the terrifying, omnipotent, bad mother. (pp. 112–113)

Horney (1932) and Lederer (1968) each present an impressive amount of clinical, mythological, and anthropological evidence regarding man's terror of women. Although both authors comment on the remarkable lack of recognition and attention this topic has received, I suggest that perhaps it is not that the fear of women has gone unrecognized, but that the consequences of the fear for the patriarchal nature of societies have not been sufficiently appreciated. To what extent has our concept of femininity been distorted by a need to discourage women from the recognition and expression of self-seeking, aggressive, competitive, ambitious strivings, in order to assure that the primitive maternal imago can, in adult life, at last be controlled, dominated, and revenged? Similarly, if men were encouraged to experience and express so-called feminine qualities (e.g., dependency, passivity, fragility), would they then feel in danger of returning to that dreaded (although wished for) condition of early maternal omnipotence? In keeping with this theme, Chasseguet-Smirgel (1970) has related religious mythology to the difficulties that maternal dominance and omnipotence present to both sexes.

> Man and woman are born of woman: before all else we are our mother's child. Yet all our desires seem designed to deny this fact, so full of conflicts and reminiscent of our primitive dependence. The myth of Genesis seems to express this desire to free ourselves from our mother: man is born of God,

an idealized paternal figure.... Woman is born from man's body. If this
myth expresses the victory of man over his mother and over woman, who
thereby becomes his own child, it also provides a certain solution for woman
inasmuch as she also is her mother's daughter: she chooses to belong to man,
to be created *for* him, and not for herself, to be a part of him—Adam's rib—
rather than to prolong her "attachment" to her mother. (pp. 133–134)

SEX-ROLE STEREOTYPES

At the cost of oversimplifying, I believe it may be worthwhile to
examine how the values and mores of traditional male–female relationships in this country can be understood within the stated theoretical
framework.* The fact that the nurturant functions of the good mother
are retained by women in marriage (e.g., feeding, cleaning, providing
emotional comfort, support) hardly requires description or elaboration.
The following points are offered to support the notion that the cultural
stereotypes of adult gender interactions (apart from nurturant functions)
involve a reversal for males of their early helplessness and dependency
on a powerful female object.

1. Women are encouraged to be dependent and are frequently portrayed as lost and helpless without a male partner. "Little girl"qualities
typically make women more attractive, and it is of significance that
women are affectionately referred to as "girls," "chicks," "baby," and
"doll." Mother tends to foster dependency to a greater degree in female
children (Lynn, 1972); and research indicates that adult men and women
tend to equate assertive, independent strivings in girls and women with
a loss of femininity (Baumrind, 1972).

Expressions of dependency needs in men are considered unattractive, weak, or effeminate, and are more frequently denied than cultivated. For males, the notion of men's greater independence is a reversal
of the infant–mother paradigm, in which it is the child who is helplessly
dependent on the powerful maternal figure.

2. In male–female relationships, intellectual ability and competence
are frequently seen as the man's domain. A girl's sense of intellectual
mastery and skill is progressively discouraged as she is trained to be

---

*It is, of course, naive to assume that the devaluation of women and the establishment
and maintenance of traditional sex-role stereotypes can entirely be understood according to the stated theoretical framework which emphasizes the early oral dyadic relationship between mother and child without regard for the complexities inherent in the oed-
ipal triangle. Additional socioeconomic, biological, and psychodynamic factors are
relevant to the present discussion, and the narrow focus of this paper is due only to the
necessity for brevity. The speculations offered in this paper are to be considered partial
rather than exhaustive explanations of complicated phenomena.

"feminine"; she is encouraged to be smart enough to catch a man but never to outsmart him (Baumrind, 1972; Lerner, 1974). In the media, wives are often portrayed as silly, capricious, gossipy, illogical, and intellectually helpless; and mockery of a female's ability to think logically and critically is an extremely popular form of humor. Although women are acknowledged to have a type of wisdom which goes by the name of "feminine intuition," there is a persistent insinuation that for females organized and sustained logical thinking is not critically involved. Research findings indicate that both sexes regard intellectual achievement as "unfeminine" and that college women tend to equate academic success with detrimental social consequences (Baumrind, 1972).

Although many men do not value the "dumb blonde" stereotype, few seek love relationships with a female partner who is comfortably acknowledged to be an intellectual equal or superior. Similarly, a woman who assumes an intellectually aggressive, critical, or dominant stance is often labeled "masculine" or "castrating." Again, this social situation appears to be a reversal of the male's position as an infant in which the intellectually helpless child is slowly taught to master his environment by a maternal figure who is experienced as infinitely capable and wise. The role of early teacher (and frustrator) moves systematically from mother to a continuing series of figures (governesses, babysitters, elementary schoolteachers) who are predominantly female.

3. Physical strength and prowess, which are glorified and cultivated in men, are considered unattractive in women; the strong athletic female or gymnast is generally not thought to be the most attractive of mates. Although men may be encouraged to go to painful extremes in body building, women are taught to exaggerate and even feign weakness in the interest of "femininity." Men enjoy treating women as weak and delicate creatures who cannot open their own doors or carry their own packages. Similarly, it is typically important for men to be physically taller than their mates. Short or small men are devalued. Again, for men, this paradigm reverses the infant's experiences of the small and weak child who is carried about with ease in the arms of the powerful mother. Horney (1932) emphasized the small boy's feeling of distress and humiliation at being small and weak in comparison with mother.

4. In love relationships, men are typically older than their female partner. While there is nothing unusual about a match between a 35-year-old man and a 23-year-old woman, the reversed situation is evaluated as eccentric if not pathological. Similarly, when a man marries a woman "young enough to be his daughter," the match may be either criticized or condoned by society, but the desires of both parties are considered understandable. Were a woman to marry a man young enough to be her son, society tends to respond with scorn and shock. Again, for

males, this situation reverses the infant–mother relationship in which the "older woman" is the sole object of the young child's libidinal desires. One might further speculate that the intense pressures on women to look eternally like adolescent girls (rather than "mothers") stems in part from the matronly woman's capacity to arouse infantile envy of the inexhaustible feeding breast as well as to stimulate anxiety laden wishes for returning to a helpless state of dependency.

5. The perpetuation of personality characteristics and traits associated with infancy and childhood is encouraged in the female sex only. For example, crying, whining, seductively manipulative and petulant behavior are all acceptable ways for women to make their demands felt and are portrayed as typical feminine qualities in the media. Such behaviors are unacceptable in men, encouraged as they are to assert themselves in a more "manly" fashion. Similarly, females are most frequently portrayed as emotional and males as intellectual. The stereotype is of the "hysterical," overemotional wife who is kept in check by her husband who allegedly makes decisions by the laws of logic and cool reason. Again, males experience a reversal of the infant's situation in which it is the mother who supplies the intellectual controls to the child who has considerable affective lability and emotionality.

6. In courtship and sexual relations, women stereotypically assume a passive stance and men an overly active one. Men are taught actively to pursue what they want; women are taught to make themselves pretty enough to be sought after. Although females may learn "feminine wiles" to attract the men of their choice, they are discouraged from openly and directly pursuing a male figure. This state of affairs for males is again the reversal of the infant's situation in which the baby is unable actively to determine whether it will get the breast or the mother's affection. The baby may actively attempt to "court" her in a number of ways (e.g., by crying or being cute), but it is the active mother who initiates or fails to initiate contact with the child.

7. Stereotyped notions of feminine sexuality tend to glorify naiveté and "innocence," whereas for males, "experience" tends to enhance their sexual attractiveness. (One might consider the difference between an "experienced man" and a "loose woman.") Similarly, in regard to the expression of aggressive impulses, Symonds (1972) notes that what is called "strength of character" in boys is called "unfeminine" in girls. Stereotypes that have encouraged the stifling of sexual and aggressive expression in women and the frank expression of impulse life in males are also for men a reversal of the infant–mother paradigm: It is the mother who inhibits the expression of "unacceptable" impulses early in the child's life. Many psychoanalytic writers, including Horney, Klein, and Freud, have stressed that mothers are experienced as punitive because they are the first to forbid a child's instinctual activities.

THE SIGNIFICANCE OF SEX-ROLE STEREOTYPES

I anticipate the objection that the generalizations presented in this paper are oversimplified clichés that fail to account for the richness of individual differences in our culture. Clearly, both clinical knowledge and human experience reveal that there are varied bases for successful male–female relationships and that many stable and gratifying marriages involve variations if not thoroughgoing modifications of these general themes. Sydney Smith* points out that a common American cliché holds that the woman is the real decision maker in the family despite the man's belief that he is the boss. This understanding of power relationships between the sexes is familiar and is well illustrated by the European saying: "The man is the head of the family but the woman is the neck that carries the head and determines the direction." Underlying the notion that the woman gets her way despite the husband's stated authority as boss is the idea that the woman wields her power in subtle and manipulative ways that allow the husband to retain his fantasies of being in charge. Many families are indeed matriarchal in their power balance, but the cultural ideal is that the man be the "head" of the household rather than a relatively submissive, passive (and thus "effeminate") figure. When we say that the wife, "wears the pants" in the family, we imply that she has stepped into the role that rightfully belongs to the man.

That women surreptitiously wield power is further illustrated in movies, novels, and plays where one frequently runs across the theme of the egocentric, unrealistic male who meets his match in an eminently reasonable, practical woman. Smith also mentions A. J. Liebling's psychological and sociological studies of the American soap opera in which men are characteristically portrayed as weak, helpless, and impotent, or who become physically crippled and must be sustained by a good woman who alone maintains contact with the real world.

I do not purport to provide in this paper a factual description of all possible relationships between men and women, which are indeed infinitely variable and complex. Rather, what I present in an outline of widespread cultural values and ideal types—society's definition of the way relationships "should be" if both partners have fulfilled the criteria for appropriate masculine and feminine behavior. Thus, a frail, dependent, and intellectually inept man may indeed seek out a strong, assertive, and capable woman to protect and care for him; and the needs and dynamics of the two individuals might "fit" in a manner that results in a stable and rewarding marriage. However, such a man is hardly the prototype of the successful male, and he is likely to be considered a poor if not pathognomonic role model for his son. Similarly, the woman married to such a

*Personal communication.

man is perceived as having made a "bad catch," accompanied by the speculation that some neurotic problem kept her from "doing better." Men may indeed be passive, conforming, childlike, and unrealistically dependent but, as Chesler (1972) points out, they are hardly taught to romanticize these qualities as essential aspects of their masculinity.

Furthermore, the sex-role stereotypes I have described are not peripheral to the culture but are powerful and ubiquitous forces affecting even the most "liberated" persons. Some authors (Baumrind, 1972; Symonds, 1972) suggest that lifelong consequences exist for the growing girl whose concept of femininity is based on the model that to be more aggressive, assertive, or intellectually capable than one's male partner is to be unfeminine, unlovable, and even "castrating." Similarly, boys are deeply affected by current notions of masculine attractiveness that glorify such traits as power, dominance, and intellectual skill, and that do not allow for even realistic expressions of fear, dependency, childishness, and weakness. Although in intellectual circles there is a tendency to see such stereotypes as outdated and inapplicable to today's changing patterns of relationships, the psychic and social dynamics persist. Even if recent social changes were indeed substantial, there remains the important task of making sense of the intense subjugation and devaluation of women that has occurred throughout the world. The specifics of male–female sex role stereotypes may vary across time and place, but the ethos of male dominance and phallocentric prejudice is as old as humanity itself.

Concluding Remarks

Rather than applying psychoanalytic principles toward understanding how our distorted notions of masculinity and femininity have been established and maintained, we have instead tended to incorporate these stereotypes into our theorizing and language, thus allowing myth and anxiety to prevail over scientific thought. A review of psychoanalytic writings reveals how practitioners and theorists pervasively and glibly label active displays of competitiveness, aggression, and intellectual ambitiousness in women as "phallic" or "masculine," and similarly label manifestations of passivity, submissiveness, malleability, childishness, emotionality, and dependency in men as "effeminate" or "feminine" (Young, 1973).

For example, the character of the primitive maternal imago (and women's related fear of their castrating and destructive potential) may be such that the female sex has relatively greater difficulty acknowledging and directly expressing aggressive, competitive, and ambitious strivings. Labeling these qualities as "masculine," however, only serves to increase women's guilt and inhibitions and to reinforce a masochistic position. Similarly, anxiety about reenacting an early matriarchy with its related castration fears may make men more fearful of acknowledging their own passive, dependent, and regressive longings; but it does not follow that these longings are "feminine" ones. There are indeed different developmental tasks that the two sexes must master based on anatomical differences; however, I believe that our present gender definitions are less a reflection of anatomical realities and more an expression of a defensive reaction to the imagos of the primitive mother. It is imperative that we gain greater conceptual clarity regarding the treatment implications and underlying theoretical rationale for labeling specific traits and behaviors as "masculine" or "feminine."*

In order to defuse the character of the primitive maternal imago and to prevent excessive envy and fear of women, I suggest that shared parenting may be important. While the psychiatric literature is replete with the hazards of inadequate mothering, there has been only minimal concern with the infant–father relationship. The child's formula for mental health seems to involve spending the early years with a mother who "is always present, alert and responsive to the child's needs . . ." (Mandelbaum 1973, p. 6), the later relationship with father being secondary to and dependent on the quality of this first interaction. While many mental health professionals are protesting that we have held onto this model of mothering at a tremendous cost to women's growth and development, there has been less emphasis on its hazards for the growing infant and child. Is not defensive idealization and devaluation of women one pathological consequence of the child's world being a matriarchal one, where the powerful figures that gratify and frustrate the child's impulses and wishes are predominantly female? We have not as yet applied our sophisticated psychoanalytic principles to understanding the consequences of shared parenting or examined how such a system would effect the developmental tasks that each sex must master. Clearly, shared parenting would affect the maternal and paternal imagos that the child internalizes and may consequently lead to a capacity for adult men and

---

*Research findings demonstrating sex differences along some dimension (e.g., relatively greater activity and aggressiveness in male infants) are often used to argue that a particular characteristic is a masculine or feminine one. Apart from the fact that there is always considerable overlap between the sexes, such conclusions are arbitrary ones. For example, female children are more verbal and articulate than male children; however, we do not label verbal skills as "feminine" and proceed actively to encourage these skills in girls or call them "feminine" to discourage them in boys. Group sex differences in no way imply that a trait or quality is healthy for one sex and less adaptive or important for the other.

women to relate to each other from a position of greater equality, openness, and mutual respect.

REFERENCES

Baumrind, Diana: From Each According to Her Ability. *School Rev.* 80(2):161–97, 1972.

Bettelheim, Bruno: The Commitment Required of a Woman Entering a Scientific Profession in Present-Day American Society. In *Women and the Scientific Professions: The M.I.T. Symposium on American Women in Science and Engineering*, J. A. Mattfield and C. G. Van Aken, eds. Cambridge, Mass.: M.I.T. Press, 1965, pp. 3–19.

Brunswick, R. M.: The Preoedipal Phase of the Libido Development. *Psychoanal. Q.* 9:293–319, 1940.

Chasseguet-Smirgel, Janine: Feminine Guilt and the Oedipus Complex. In *Female Sexuality: New Psychoanalytic Views*, Janine Chasseguet-Smirgel et al. , Ann Arbor: University of Michigan Press, 1970, pp. 94–134.

Chesler, Phyllis: *Women and Madness*. Garden City, N. Y.: Doubleday & Co., 1972.

David, Christian: A Masculine Mythology of Femininity. In *Female Sexuality: New Psychoanalytic Views*, Janine Chasseguet-Smirgel et al. Ann Arbor: University of Michigan Press, 1970, pp. 47–67.

Fairbairn, W. R. D.: *An Object-Relations Theory of the Personality*. New York: Basic Books, 1952.

Freud, Sigmund (1909): Analysis of a Phobia in a Five-Year-Old Boy. *Standard Edition* 10:3–149, 1955.

Freud, Sigmund (1918): From the History of an Infantile Neurosis. *Standard Edition* 17:3–122, 1955.

Freud, Sigmund (1925): Some Psychological Consequences of the Anatomical Distinction Between the Sexes. In *Collected Papers*, Vol. 5, James Strachey, ed. London: Hogarth Press, 1950.

Goldberg, Philip: Are Women Prejudiced against Women? *Trans-action* 5(5):28–30, 1968.

Horney, Karen: The Dread of Women. *Int. J. Psychoanal.* 13:348–60, 1932.

Jung, C. G.: *Contributions to Analytical Psychology*, H. G. and C. F. Baynes, trans. London: Routledge & Kegan Paul Limited, 1928.

Kernberg, Otto: Barriers to Being in Love. Unpublished manuscript, The Menninger Foundation, 1972.

Klein, Melanie: *Envy and Gratitude*. New York: Basic Books, 1957.

Lederer, Wolfgang: *The Fear of Women*. New York: Grune & Stratton, 1968.

Lerner, Harriet: The Hysterical Personality: A "Women's Disease." *Compr. Psychiatry* 15(2):157–64, 1974.

Lynn, D. B.: Determinants of Intellectual Growth in Women. *School Rev.* 80(2):241–60, 1972.

Mandelbaum, Arthur: Separation. *Menninger Perspective* 4(5): 5–9, 27, 1973.

Symonds, Alexandria: Discussion (of Ruth Moulton's paper, "Psychoanalytic Reflections on Women's Liberation"). *Contemp. Psychoanal.* 8:224–28, 1971–72.

Torok, Maria: The Significance of Penis Envy in Women. In *Female Sexuality: New Psychoanalytic Views*, Janine Chasseguet-Smirgel et al. Ann Arbor: University of Michigan Press, 1970, pp. 135–70.

Young, Enid: A Review of Feminine Psychology. Unpublished manuscript, University of California at Berkeley, 1973.

Female Dependency in Context

9

Some Theoretical and Technical Considerations

Harriet E. Lerner

Dependency needs are a universal aspect of human experience. The struggle to achieve a healthy integration of passive-dependent longings and active autonomous strivings constitutes a lifelong developmental task for both men and women. Yet, despite such universality, the very word "dependency" is more frequently associated with the female sex. Indeed, dependency, like passivity, has been considered the very hallmark of femininity.[7]

It is true enough that women show dependent behaviors more openly than do men. On the adaptive side, women tend to be more affiliative and self-disclosing, and better able to acknowledge and express realistic fears, vulnerability, and wishes to be cared for.[15,16] On the maladaptive side, women more frequently display pathological dependency[15]; such women do not take action to solve their own problems, do not state clearly their opinions and preferences out of fear of conflict or disapproval, turn fearfully away from the challenges of the outside world, and avoid successful and autonomous functioning at all costs. While the ability to acknowledge and express realistic dependency is an essential aspect of healthy psychological functioning, it is the pathological aspects of dependency that have loomed largest in the literature on female psychology.

While certain psychoanalytic writings have invoked anatomy-is-destiny theories to account for the association of femininity with passive-dependent behavior, the more recent literature emphasizes familial and cultural determinants.[14] More than a decade of research by feminist

Reprinted from *American Journal of Orthopsychiatry* 53(4):697–705, 1983. Copyright © 1983 by the American Orthopsychiatric Association, Inc. Reprinted by permission. Based on a presentation to the 1982 annual meeting of the American Psychiatric Association, Toronto, Canada.

scholars and mental health professionals has indicated that females are often trained in pathological dependency from birth.[2,18] While etiological factors remain controversial, there nonetheless seems to be wide agreement that woman are, in fact, the more dependent sex. Certainly we hear a great deal more about the dependency needs of women than of men—as if women, by nature or nurture, were possessed of more of a bad thing. Much of the professional literature, as well as popular books such as *The Cinderella Complex*,[7] speaks clearly to the ubiquity of this belief.

Part of the reason for spurious generalizations about excessive female dependency is that the structural or contextual factors which evoke women's dependent behavior have not been taken seriously enough by mental health professionals. For example, the professional literature has noted that even active and self-reliant women often become excessively dependent, if not phobic, following marriage.[17] Little attention, however, has been given to the ways in which the structure of traditional marriage facilitates an increasing sense of economic and psychological dependence in women, their individual strengths notwithstanding. In addition, the popular and professional literature has tended to maintain a dignified fraternal silence regarding the obvious fact that men also have dependency needs, the fulfilling of which has been a role assigned to women.

Unlike men, who go from mother to mother again, in the form of wife, women often relinquish their mothers in order to do the mothering. By traditional standards, a "good wife" cleans, cooks, comforts, nurtures, soothes, admires, encourages, listens, sympathizes, and supports—although she is less frequently on the receiving end of such nurture and caretaking. Through the process of providing for the dependency needs of others (i.e., husband and children), a woman may consciously or unconsciously anticipate that her own needs will be met; when her needs are left unmet, she may manifest behavior that appears to be excessively dependent or demanding. Little attention, however, may be given to the fact that the woman's dependency needs are not being adequately met by important others, or that she is unable actively to pursue self-directed, self-seeking activities that would allow her to provide for her own wants. From this perspective, women are not the excessively dependent sex. A more accurate generalization might be to say that women are not dependent enough. Most women are far more expert in worrying about the needs of others than in identifying and assertively claiming their own needs.

Spurious generalizations about female dependency stem from an additional conceptual failure. Many theorists and practitioners fail to distinguish between the passive-dependent behavior that women so fre-

quently display, if not actively cultivate, and the actual level of autonomy or differentiation of self that women have, in fact, achieved. As a
group, women may behave in a more passive-dependent fashion than do
men, but women are not more dependent than men if we consider the
actual level of autonomy or differentiation of self that an individual
achieves. To understand the distinction between a woman's passive-
dependent behavior and her actual level of differentiation, it is important to appreciate that women's displays of passive-dependency
frequently have a protective and systems-maintaining function for significant others. This point will be examined in greater detail.

THE PROTECTIVE ASPECTS OF FEMALE DEPENDENCY

Research in marital systems has indicated that both partners tend to
be at the same level of psychological differentiation or independence.[5]
There is generally little difference between spouses in the actual level of
autonomous functioning or clarity of self that each has achieved in the
family of origin. Often it may appear dramatically otherwise, as when a
high-powered businessman brings his symptomatic, infantile-dependent
wife into a psychiatric hospital. The reason for this apparent discrepancy
is that the "underfunctioning" of one spouse allows for the "overfunc-
tioning" of the other. In Bowen's[5] terms, if one person "de-selfs" herself
or himself, the other gains in "pseudoself." Like a seesaw, the helpless-
dependent stance of one partner has an adaptive, ego-bolstering effect
on the other. When the "underfunctioner" moves in the direction of
more autonomous functioning, the "overfunctioner" starts to do worse
and will predictably make any number of "countermoves" to restore the
relationship to its prior equilibrium.

In my clinical work, I have noted how frequently the passive-dependent stance that characterizes so many women is inextricably interwoven
with the prescribed underfunctioning role that women assume to protect
and stabilize the systems in which they operate. Put somewhat differently, women's dysfunctional passive-dependent behavior is, in part,
derived from the unconscious "rules" that guide certain relational systems. Women are rarely as dependent as they learn to appear; rather,
women learn to display passive-dependent behavior in order to protect
others (including the therapist) and maintain the delicate homeostatic
balance of systems in which any move away from a dependent stance is
responded to by important others as a hurtful and aggressive act; it is
disloyalty, a betrayal. Maintaining a dependent self-experience in order
to protect and bolster others is a dynamic that has its roots in the family

of origin. It is also culturally prescribed and spelled out most clearly in women's adult relationships with men.

Protecting Men

Before the current wave of feminism, girls and women were explicitly encouraged to offer males narcissistic protection by cultivating passive-dependent behavior and by feigning weakness and incompetence if these did not come naturally. As one expert in female popularity advised in the mid-sixties[6]:

> If you smoke, don't carry matches. In a restaurant, let your mate or date do the ordering ... you may know more about vintage wine than the wine steward, but if you are smart, you'll let your man do the choosing and be ecstatic over his selection, even if it tastes like shampoo ... the successful female never lets her competence compete with her femininity. (p. 8)

This bit of advice is characteristic of the majority of guidebooks for women written before the seventies, which explicitly prescribed male dominance while implicitly warning women that men were weak. In one popular book, *Help Your Husband Stay Alive*,[9] the author went so far as to insist that men are physically incapable of surviving unless women assume a dependent and subordinate role. Underlying her prescription to underfunction, the author wrote:

> What is humiliating about being under a man—whether in business, in government, or any role of life ... if it is clear to you that he is only on top because you are holding him up? (p. 14)

The paradoxical notion that women must strengthen men by relinquishing their own strength is widespread even today. An explicit example of this philosophy can be found in *Fascinating Womanhood*, a bestselling book based on the same principles as Marabelle Morgan's *Total Woman*. In a 1980 edition,[1] the author provided the reader with detailed instructions on how to cultivate a childlike dependent stance, with the explicit goal of protecting the marital bond. One assignment, for example, instructed the reader to carefully observe and copy the behavior and mannerisms of little girls, while other chapters suggested ways to suppress tendencies to appear competent or self-reliant in "masculine" independent pursuits.

Our time-honored fairy tales also contain the paradoxical prescription that females should protect men by letting men protect women. These stories teach that passive-dependent behavior is the hallmark of successful femininity, as well as the vehicle that permits and encourages masculine independence and activity.[4] It is the damsel in distress who provides her brave rescuer with the opportunity to slay dragons, solve riddles, or otherwise be heroic. The male hunter could not have rescued Little Red Riding Hood were it not for the fact that she was utterly helpless in the teeth of the wolf and lacked even the intellectual resourcefulness to distinguish her grandmother from a wolf in a nightcap. Little Red Riding Hood is just one of many fairy tale heroines who does not solve her own problems, but rather provides men with the opportunity to act on her pathetic behalf.

It is tempting to view the dictates of popular culture as outdated clichés that have little relevance to current clinical practice or to the real life experience of contemporary women. Certainly, most women who enter our consulting rooms today do not willfully or effortfully practice childlike dependence in order to bolster the male ego and thus insure the predictable security of their relationships. Nonetheless, the behavior occurs unconsciously, without awareness or intent. Underlying the passive-dependent stance of many women is the unconscious motivation to bolster and protect another person as well as the unconscious conviction that one must remain in a position of relative weakness for one's most important relationships to survive. Even intellectually liberated women unconsciously feel frightened and guilty about "hurting" others, especially men, when fully exercising their capacity for independent thinking and action. In reality, women who do begin to define more clearly the terms of their own lives are frequently accused of diminishing men, hurting children, or in some way being destructive to others. These reactions, which occur in response to the anxiety that is stirred when a woman behaves more autonomously, represent a powerful counterforce to change.

Our gender arrangements as well as our very definitions of "femininity" contain an important metacommunication which remains an unconscious guiding rule for many women. The message is that *the weaker sex must protect the stronger sex from recognizing the strength of the weaker sex lest the stronger sex feel weakened by the strength of the weaker sex.* This message persists despite changing times and new egalitarian beliefs; women are still encouraged to protect men by containing and expressing the very passivity and dependency that men fear in themselves.[10,15] Because women do learn that being an autonomous, self-directed person is hurtful to others, especially men, their dependent behavior is often an unconscious "gift" or sacrifice to those they love; it is the gift of giving up self so that the other may gain in self.

Needless to say, not all women succumb to pressures to assume a dependent role with men, and not all heterosexual relationships are based on such complementarity. In couples that operate at a relatively high level of differentiation, there is less reliance on splitting and projective identification; each spouse is able to tolerate the complicated and conflictual experience of integrating bipolarities (e.g., activity–passivity, dependence–independence) within one's own self. Each partner is able to feel competent and to view the other as competent, with no need either to minimize or exaggerate dependency, vulnerability, or helplessness. Nonetheless, large numbers of women who appear in our consulting rooms do unconsciously protect men by cultivating a passive-dependent stance. This dysfunctional position reflects, in part, powerful cultural injunctions to underfunction which are fueled by irrational fantasies about female power and male vulnerability[10,11]; however, it also has its roots in the family of origin where separation-individuation issues are first negotiated. It is there that the growing girl may learn to inhibit her strivings toward more autonomous functioning in order to protect the family system or to solve some problem in her parent's relationship.

In families where the marital relationship is weak, and mother herself has been blocked from proceeding with her own growth, daughters frequently learn to cling to passive-dependent behavior as an unconscious "oath of fidelity" to remain mother's child, as if the daughter's own moves toward greater separateness and autonomy constitute disloyalty and betrayal. Later this drama is continued in adult heterosexual relationships and is reinforced by warnings to women that men must be protected from women's full strength and abilities. Although space does not permit discussion here, I believe that girls and women are especially vulnerable to anxiety and guilt in regard to making their own declaration of independence from their first family.[10,13] (As an old folk saying puts it, "A son is a son till he gets him a wife; a daughter's a daughter for the rest of her life.") Many psychotherapists fail to appreciate the degree to which female anxiety and guilt about autonomy and separateness reflect, in part, the patient's accurate perception that her most important relationships have little flexibility to tolerate her continuing growth and independence and that, further, her passive-dependent stance serves a protective function for other family members. Paradoxically, a patient may become free to relinquish a dependent position when her therapist can identify and respect the adaptive functions that are served by her maintaining a dependent stance, and appreciate with her the actual risks and potential losses that she and others face if she permits herself to behave in a more autonomous and self-directed fashion.

IMPLICATIONS FOR TREATMENT

In my supervisory work, I have noted that a woman's dependent self-experience and behavior frequently elicit negatively toned interpretations implying that her dependency needs are "weak," "childish," or "excessive." In addition to exacerbating the patient's feelings of guilt or inadequacy, such interventions seriously miss the point. A patient may, indeed, present herself as a needy child, motivated by the infantile wish to be passively nurtured by, or symbiotically fused with, an all-providing mother; however, this is less than half the story. All human beings, irrespective of sex and diagnostic category, strive for autonomy and competence. The internal press toward growth is always more powerful than the wish to remain a dysfunctional child; therapeutic interventions which imply that the patient does not want to grow up fail to recognize that the costs of growing up may be quite high, including the outbreak of symptomatology in other family members and the threat of dissolution of important relationships.

The "oral rage" that characterizes severely dependent women stems not from the fact that their excessive dependency needs are being frustrated; rather, their rage is associated with their unconscious conviction that they must continue to thwart their own growth for the sake of protecting family ties and fulfilling family loyalties and obligations. Family systems theory has elegantly demonstrated how a patient's resistance to change must be understood in the context of the powerful pressures against change exerted by the multigenerational, rule-governed family and cultural systems in which the patient operates.[8] This focus is especially crucial in regard to the therapeutic management of female dependency.

While the current feminist movement has helped therapists become more aware of their failure to confront passive-dependent behavior in women, the focus here will be on a therapeutic error of a different order. Therapists frequently encourage their women patients to be more assertive or independent without first analyzing the adaptive function being served, or the family problem being solved, by the patient's dependent stance. The nontherapeutic outcome is frequently a resistant impasse in which the patient feels caught between the therapist who is pushing for change, and family communications that press for homeostasis and sameness. At this point, the treatment may go from bad to worse, as the therapist begins to confer a strong negative connotation not only on the patient's dependency, but also on her resistance to change, as if this resistance is simply a countertherapeutic force or a negative transference reaction to be abolished through interpretation. The resistance impasse may be broken when the therapist is able to assess carefully the family system's tolerance for change and appreciate the function served by the patient's dependent stance in this context. This requires, among other things, the ability to track carefully the actual reactions of other family members when a situation of systems disequilibrium arises as a result of the patient's tentative moves toward greater independence. It also requires a phenomenological shift on the part of the therapist which allows for a truly neutral, respectful, and emotionally unreactive position regarding the patient's choice to change or not to change.

In regard to transference–countertransference issues, another point deserves attention. The same therapist who prematurely encourages female patients to be more assertive and independent in their family and work relationships may unwittingly foster dependency in the therapeutic relationship.[3,12] To quote one exasperated therapist in supervision, "No matter how much I interpret, or try to push her, she still won't be assertive with her husband!" This therapist failed to recognize the double-bind situation evoked by his injunction to the patient to assert herself outside the hour and the therapist's disqualifying message that she should be a "good patient" within the therapeutic relationship and dutifully value and follow his advice. He accurately interpreted the maladaptive aspects of the patient's refusal to make use of his help; yet he failed to appreciate the adaptive components of what the patient was trying to accomplish by asserting her wish to not assert herself. As a result of the therapist's interventions, the patient shifted from a defiant to a compliant stance in which she inhibited expressions of differences and unconsciously attempted to make the therapist feel useful and important. While the therapist saw this shift as an "improvement," the patient was actually placating him and protecting his narcissism, while she remained as stuck as ever in her own life. When the therapist was able to connote positively the patient's ability to disagree with him, and when he was able to relinquish his sense of responsibility for the patient's own decision regarding how dependently or independently she would behave in her marriage, the patient felt safer to assume a more differentiated stance with both her therapist and her husband.

It may be especially difficult for male therapists to appreciate the degree to which female patients, like our fairy tale heroines, underfunction in the therapeutic hour as an unconscious attempt to help the therapist feel bolstered and protected.[12] The patient may cultivate a needy, dependent stance for the therapist's sake, or otherwise pull for excessive worry and concern, because to do otherwise may feel like a violation of an unconscious allegiance, obligation, or contract to remain "close" through underfunctioning. While unconsciously associating autonomy and separateness with disloyalty, betrayal, and potential loss, the female patient will repeatedly test out in the transference the degree to which the therapist will choose to see her as dependent and dysfunctional and the degree to which the therapist is comfortable with the patient's competence and autonomy. The unconscious tests may take an infinite variety of forms. Sometimes they consist of the patient's requesting or demanding something that, in fact, she is quite capable of doing without. The "something" may be an additional hour, a telephone call at home, extra time at the end of the session, or a request to see another professional during the therapist's absence. It is easy for therapists to "fail" the tests by going along with the patient's requests and replicating a dysfunctional family picture of excessive protectiveness, overconcern, and overresponsibility, which translates to a prescription or injunction to underfunction for the identified patient. Therapists commonly encourage female patients to be assertive with their spouses, while covertly prescribing compliant behavior and discouraging a challenging, independent stance which includes the expression of anger and competitiveness within the patient–therapist dyad. The incongruent nature of such therapeutic interventions often goes unidentified by patient, therapist, and supervisor.

CONCLUSION

Rather than attempt a comprehensive overview of the multifaceted and complex subject of female dependency, this paper has focused on a point that can significantly alter the direction and tone of a particular treatment. Women who are "stuck" in a dysfunctional passive-dependent stance frequently elicit negatively toned interventions which only heighten the patient's resistance to change and lead to a negative therapeutic outcome. In the midst of such an impasse, it may be especially difficult for therapists to recognize that a woman's passive-dependent self-experience and behavior are essentially a sacrifice. This sacrifice of competence, clarity, and growth cannot be understood in terms of its "secondary gains" or "masochistic gratifications" (although these may be present), nor can it be analyzed successfully solely in light of the patient's projections, infantile wishes, irrational anxieties, early deprivations, and distorted internalized object representations. It is important that the patient's behavior be analyzed and understood in terms of the family systems pressure for homeostasis as well as its flexibility to tolerate change; a systemic conceptualization of the patient's dependent posture allows for an appreciation of the loyal and adaptive aspects of what the patient is trying to accomplish and the ways in which her dependent posture plays an important role in the self-regulatory needs of the family system as a whole. Appreciating the systemic meaning of the patient's ongoing sacrifice of personal growth is effective when it occurs in the context of a therapeutic relationship that encourages the patient's autonomy and that does not foster or collude with patient–therapist "closeness" based on the patient's underfunctioning position.

REFERENCES

1. Andelin, H. 1980. *Fascinating Womanhood*. Bantam Books, New York.
2. Bardwick, J. 1971. *Psychology of Women*. Harper & Row, New York.
3. Bernardez-Bonesatti, T. 1976. Unconscious beliefs about women affecting psychotherapy. *North Carolina J. Ment. Hlth* 7(5):63–66.
4. Bettelheim, B. 1976. *The Use of Enchantment*. Knopf, New York.
5. Bowen, M. 1978. *Family Therapy in Clinical Practice*. Aronson, New York.
6. Dahl, A. 1965. *Always Ask A Man*. Prentice-Hall, Engelwood Cliffs, N.J.
7. Dowling, C. 1981. *The Cinderella Complex*. Simon & Schuster, New York.
8. Keeney, B. 1979. Ecosystemic epistemology: an alternative paradigm for diagnosis. *Fam. Proc.* 18:117–119.
9. Lees, H. 1957. *Help Your Husband Stay Alive*. Appleton-Century-Crofts, New York.
10. Lerner, H. 1978. On The comfort of patriarchal solutions: some reflections on Brown's paper. *J. Pers. Soc. Systems* 1(3):47–50.
11. Lerner, H. 1974. Early origins of envy and devaluation of women: implications for sex role stereotypes. *Bull. Menninger Clin.* 38(6):538–553.
12. Lerner, H. 1982. Special issues for women in psychotherapy. In *The Woman Patient: Medical and Psychological Interfaces*, M. Notman and C. Nadelson, eds. Plenum Press, New York.
13. Lerner, H. 1980. Internal prohibitions against female anger. *Amer. J. Psychoanal.* 40(2):137–148.
14. Miller, H. 1973. *Psychoanalysis and Women*. Brunner/Mazel, New York.
15. Miller, J. 1976. *Toward A New Psychology of Women*. Beacon Press, Boston.
16. Pleck, J. and Sawyer, J. 1974. *Men and Masculinity*. Prentice-Hall, Englewood Cliffs, N.J.
17. Symonds, A. 1971. Phobias after marriage: women's declaration of dependence. *Amer. J. Psychoanal.* 31(2):144–152.
18. Women on Words and Images. 1972. *Dick and Jane as Victims*. Carolingian Press, Princeton, N.J.

B. Restricted Sex Roles and Covert Conflicts

The chapters in this section are about the constraints on behavior and choices that derive from restricted sex roles. They emphasize how cultural expectations for sex-role behaviors are incorporated into social identities as powerful intrapsychic prohibitions. As a result, life choices become restricted in different ways for women and men. Unfortunately, the psychological interpretations of the internal conflicts that result from these internalized values are often misguided because therapists fail to take sufficient account of the social origins of these conflicts.

Elizabeth A. Waites, in "Female Masochism and the Enforced Restriction of Choice," provides a cogent analysis of the inadequacy of theories of masochism for explaining why women "choose" or remain in destructive relationships. She maintains that the apparent acceptance of suffering does not imply that women enjoy pain or are driven to it by instinct. To substantiate this claim, she presents an alternative interpretation of these "masochistic" behaviors—namely, "in situations in which choice is externally restricted, the question of internal motivation approaches irrelevance as the restriction of choice becomes more extreme."

Waites asserts that clinicians focus on internal motivation as the sole explanation for destructive and maladaptive behaviors in a way that excludes external realities. She describes how external barriers can directly prevent adaptive behaviors: For example, poverty may make it impossible for a woman to leave an abusive relationship. Or in a more indirect way, external factors can produce internal barriers that prevent the learning of adaptive behaviors or foster the learning of maladaptive behaviors. These internal barriers are shaped by sex-role definitions, as for example, the woman who is unable to leave an abusive marriage, despite available resources, because her social identity, sense of femininity, and self-esteem are contingent on being a submissive ("good") wife. As Waites cautions therapists, "If a woman's reality testing, which often involves a clear and correct perception of the negative alternatives actually available to her, is devalued as incorrect or dismissed as a form of resistance, she can scarcely disentangle the rational from the irrational aspects of her own behavior."

Janet R. Allison applies the concept of restricted choice to the issue of infertility in "Roles and Role Conflict of Women in Infertile Couples." She argues that social roles always generate ambivalence; however, when a role is obligatory, as the role of wife and mother is usually perceived, negative feelings about it are likely to be unacceptable, and as a result, such affects often remain unacknowledged. The extent to which women feel they have a choice about adherence to or rejection of these obligatory roles determines whether any role conflicts that result will be acknowledged or covert. In her research, Allison found that the discrepancy between the traditional female role definitions adhered to by the infertile women and their high occupational achievements did not produce the overt role conflict one would expect. To explain this unexpected finding, the author postulates that, in the absence of structural organic pathology, the infertility may be an adaptive somatic solution that serves to reduce the unconscious role conflict.

Although there is a superficial resemblance between Allison's role-conflict interpretation of infertility and conventional psychoanalytic explanations, the difference is that Allison defines the woman's ambivalence as normal while psychoanalytic theory views the rejection of traditional feminine roles as psychopathological. Obviously, when considering any perspective on infertility, it is critical that the husband's motivation for having a child and his participation in the sex-role restrictions be evaluated.

Anorexia nervosa is one of the most perplexing and potentially fatal of the psychiatric disorders. Although there are numerous theories of the origins of anorexia and bulimia, there have been no adequate explanations of why these have been mostly female disorders. Marlene Boskind-Lodahl's article, "Cinderella's Stepsisters: A Feminist Perspective on Anorexia Nervosa and Bulimia," presents a new way of analyzing these disorders. While we recognize that her approach is not a fully developed theory, we include it as another interesting example of how sex-role restrictions and limited choices may be translated into maladaptive and destructive behaviors. In contrast to psychoanalytic interpretations of anorexia that emphasize rejection of femininity, the author suggests that the opposite may be the case. She maintains that women with these disorders have, in fact, internalized an even more rigid and restricted model of femininity, which they attempt to emulate through extreme behaviors.

Given that the stereotypic female sex role with its emphasis on passivity, dependency, and accommodation creates some identity confusion in most women, the severe distortions we see in anorectics seem to leave them even more devoid of identity and power. Perfect control over one's body may be one of the few choices that the anorectic perceives as available to her in her struggle for autonomy and identity. The all-consuming battle between starving and binge-ing becomes, as Boskind-Lodahl notes, "a struggle against a part of the self rather than a struggle toward a self." Before much can be said of the treatment implications of this approach based on a sex-role analysis, we will need to better understand the conditions (social and biological) that leave some women (and many fewer men) vulnerable to these disorders. For example, our clinical experiences suggest some association between these disorders and a history of physical and/or sexual victimization.

The last chapter in this section shows the significant behavioral restrictions that derive from stereotypic male sex-role norms; although not considered pathological, these norms have important consequences for all males. In "Emotional Intimacy among Men," Robert A. Lewis describes the barriers to intimacy and the ramifications for men's lives and relationships. Among all the obstacles to closeness among males, we want to emphasize the importance of homophobia (fear and/or intolerance of homosexuality) as a central dynamic in maintaining narrowly defined male sex roles in both gay and straight men.

Until recently, men have been largely unaware of their lack of intimacy with other men, and the emotional deprivation that results. For example, men have been deprived of intimate relationships with their fathers and with male peers. Thus, the empathic understanding from other males that would enhance self-knowledge and emotional development and validate maleness does not occur. Instead, men become increasingly dependent on women for these functions and, at the same time, increasingly resentful of the power they have delegated to women. As Lewis comments, "although males report more same-sex friendships that women do, most of these are not close, intimate, or characterized by self-disclosure." In our teaching and supervisory experiences, we have also been impressed with the vastly different meanings that men and women attach to the word "intimacy."

Female Masochism and the Enforced Restriction of Choice

10

Elizabeth A. Waites

Rationale for the Subjugation of Women

It is not recorded that Adam beat his wife; on the question of her subjugation to him, however, the Bible is explicit. It is also clear in the biblical account that this subjection, rather than being a consequence of Eve's natural inferiorty, was an imposed punishment. Eve, the first human being who chose to disobey authority, was brought low; from the day she disobeyed, her right to choose was severely restricted. Historically, the story of the Fall has prvided both a model and a rationale for the subjugation and scapegoating of women in Western culture. Until modern times, it was unnecessary to postulate that women are inherently masochistic in order to explain their suffering. The explanation that they are inherently bad sufficed. "Bad" furthermore seems to have been closely associated with the activity and aggression of women. Far from assuming that females are basically passive or that they naturally turn their aggression inward, our ancestors were careful to provide real and often insurmountable restraints. Although Westerners did not go so far as the Chinese who permanently restricted female locomotion by means of footbinding, the corsets and chastity belts they devised illustrate the degree of physical restraint that was acceptable. And West met East in the sanction accorded wife-beating as a form of physical and psychological control. The right of chastisement, as it was called, was recognized by law as well as custom not only in England, but in the United States as late as the 19th century (Eisenberg and Micklow, 1974). Even subsequent to technical repudiation of the legal right, wife-beating has continued to be tolerated by professionals and public alike to the extent that laws expressly forbidding it have been and continue to be inconsistently enforced.

Since about the 12th century, however, theological and social sanctions for the abuse of women have been modified by an attitude appar-

Reprinted from *Victimology: An International Journal* 2(3–4):535–544, 1977–1978. Copyright © 1978 by Visage Press Inc. All rights reserved. Reprinted by permission.

ently opposite to that which emphasized female subjection. With the development of this attitude, woman, the despised outcast, was elevated to the status of Woman, the revered Ideal. This romantic attitude did not supplant the old scapegoating, but flourished alongside it; and as feminists have noted (see Millett, 1971), the romantic attitude did not produce much change in the inferior social and economic position of women. It did, however, represent a more complex expression of ambivalence than simple scapegoating. As importantly, it had a profound effect on the fantasy life of Western civilization for the following eight centuries. The romantic attitude was characterized by a fantasied reversal of power relations between the sexes. Eve's subjection to Adam was replaced by the submissive adoration of the lord for his lady. This transformation, however confined to fantasy, seemed to mark a shift in attitude toward male aggression as well as toward those tendencies formerly scorned as "feminine." In this sense, the romantic attitude encouraged the development of what might be characterized as a masochistic, that is, internalized mode of expressing aggression. But these developments were intricately bound up with those tendencies toward idealization which are a hallmark of romanticism. The result was that suffering and death, formerly viewed as the stigmata of fault and positively valued only in the context of Christian asceticism, came to be idealized and eroticized as an aspect of relations between the sexes.

THE "MASOCHISM HYPOTHESIS"

The psychoanalytic concept of masochism, a product of the late 19th century, may be viewed as one consequence of the flowering of the romantic tradition. In psychoanalytic theory, the intimate tie between love and pain which had long been emphasized in the fantasies of the culture was finally postulated as an explanatory construct. Perhaps it was the romantic flavor of the concept itself which eventually made it so popular in explanations of female behavior. For, in spite of an increasing emphasis on empiricism in all the sciences, the study of real women continued to be confounded by that ideal vision of the Eternal Feminine which, along with the idealization of suffering, had characterized the romantic tradition. As an explanation of female behavior, the "masochism hypothesis" is basically simple though burdened with paradox. It suggests that suffering, for women, is inherently bound up with erotic pleasure and desired for that reason. The romantic notion that suffering is ennobling has particularly influenced those discussions of female sexuality which consider childbearing, rather than orgasm, the acme of pleasure for women. Creation through suffering is a favorite romantic theme, and the rationalization that the whole future of the human race is somehow contingent on woman's pain has long been a convenient dodge for avoiding hard social questions about the status of women.

There are, in fact, several theories of female masochism sharing the fundamental premise that women enjoy suffering, but differing in hypotheses about the specific developmental correlates of this presumed enjoyment. Most such theories derive from Sigmund Freud, who was intrigued by masochistic phenomena throughout his life. Freud's earliest speculations about masochism proposed that it represents a transformation of sadism. In "Instincts and Vicissitudes" (1905), he distinguished three stages in this transformation: (1) sadistic impulses are directed against another person; (2) the original object of these sadistic impulses is replaced by the ego as object; and (3) another person is found to take over the role of sadistic subject. It should be noted that this sequence describes the *passive aim* in masochism, but does not imply any connection between masochism and *passivity* as a state of reduced activity; the search for a sadistic partner might, theoretically, require considerable activity. In "A Child is Being Beaten" (1919), Freud emphasized the role of guilt in masochism. Although he acknowledged that such guilt may be a consequence of sadistic impulses per se, he especially emphasized the guilt presumed to be associated with the gratification of incestuous impulses. Beating fantasies in both males and females were interpreted as a conscious representation of the repressed wish to be loved by the father. The close association between masochism, passivity, and femininity, a basis for the emerging concept of feminine masochism, was also stressed. In later life, Freud (1924) revised his earlier theories to give more weight to the role of aggression in human behavior. He postulated a primary form of masochism, the death instinct, as the origin of seemingly self-destructive behavior. Even so, he retained his earlier classification of certain forms of masochism as "feminine." "Castration," a concept by means of which Freud linked together certain fantasies with theoretical assumptions about the actual biological inferiority of women, was emphasized as an important motivational determinant of masochistic behavior. Subsequent theories of female masochism retained this focus on "castration" as a biological variable necessarily limiting female activity and thus predisposing females toward masochism.

A number of psychoanalysts took issue with Freud's concept of primary masochism as well as with his interpretation of biology. Reich (1949), for example, stressed that it is not instinct, but repressive culture which results in masochistic behavior in both sexes. But among psychoanalysts particularly concerned with the psychology of women, the concept of a biologically based masochism, even if not specifically linked with the concept of a death instinct, continued to be influential. Helene

Deutsch (1930) implied that the substitution of passive aims associated with the vagina for active ones associated with the clitoris is the necessary condition for a successful female adaptation. She further suggested that woman's existence is dominated by a "masochistic triad": castration-rape-parturition. Jeanne Lampl De Groot (1933) also considered passivity, involving the turning inward of aggressive impulses, a basic feminine attribute. Marie Bonaparte (1951) contended, "The male must resist against passivity and masochism in general, which his biological constitution does not impose, whereas women must accept theirs." Other female psychoanalysts, however, viewed the relationship between social reality and masochism as potentially more variable. Melanie Klein, for example, emphasized the distinction between ego and internal representations of others, these internal "objects" being good or bad according to the experiences of gratification with which they are associated in both fact and fantasy (Klein, 1975). This theory implies that the ego may try to join with real partners, including sadistic ones, in an alliance against bad internalized objects. A woman seeking protection from a sadistic parent, for example, might choose a sadistic husband as a fantasied ally in her battle against the (internalized) parent. Melanie Klein accepted Freud's concept of the death instinct. The "badness" of internal objects, in other words, was not considered simply to be a function of reality but was assumed to be derived from the inherent aggression of the individual. Nevertheless, Klein acknowledged the importance of actual experience in confirming or denying internal fantasies.

The female psychoanalyst who most strongly and explicitly differed with Freud on the subject of female masochism was Karen Horney, who countered more orthodox psychoanalytic views with an appeal to empiricism:

> Let us ask again: What are the data [concerning female masochism]? As far as I can see, only the fact that there may exist in small children early sadistic fantasies.... There is no evidence for the ubiquity of these early sadistic fantasies, and I wonder, for instance, whether little American Indian girls or little Trobriand girls have them. (Horney, 1967, p. 217)

Taking the fantasies for granted for the sake of argument, Horney concluded that they are not sufficient in themselves to support the hypotheses of a biologically based feminine masochism. But, noting the restrictive social factors which might prove causative in the development of masochistic behavior in women, she considered the possibility that "certain fixed ideologies" concerning the "nature of woman" are correlated both with actual restrictions and with positive rewards for masochistic behavior. Horney (1967, p. 231) concluded:

> One sees that these cultural factors exert a powerful influence on women: so much so, in fact, that in our culture it is hard to see how any woman can escape being masochistic to some degree from the effect of culture alone.

ALTERNATIVE APPROACHES TO MALADAPTIVE CHOICE BEHAVIOR

Horney's analysis of the problem of female masochism exphasized the lack of empirical support for traditional psychoanalytic theories. But the concept may be as easily criticized on logical grounds as well. The observation that some women seem to accept or to seek out suffering, for example, does not imply that they enjoy it or are driven to it by instinct. Before such a conclusion can be reached, it is necessary to examine what choices are actually available to such women, what affects they experience in conjunction with their suffering, and how their actions contribute to those interactions interpreted as masochistic. Even the discovery that some individuals seem to find pleasure in miserable situations does not imply masochistic motivation; the study of how people make the best of bad but inescapable situations may be more relevant in interpreting such an observation than the masochism hypothesis. Upon examination, however, such rationalizations as "No woman has to put up with an abusive husband; she can always leave" or "Rape is an invited attack" prove to be more than excuses for avoiding the fact of victimization. These rationalizations are fundamentally related to the use of the concept of masochism. For, in situations in which choice is externally restricted, the question of internal motivation approaches irrelevance as the restriction of choice becomes more extreme.

Enforced restriction is potentially related to behavior often described as masochistic in two distinct ways:

1. As an *external barrier* preventing adaptive behavior. In such situations, labeling the phenomena in question masochistic is at best an evasion of determining factors and at worst a naive excuse for cruelty. For example, an abused wife who is denied all access to money or means of accommodation away from her husband, who is refused aid by police and not given any practical remedy against further abuse, is up against formidable external barriers. Assuming that she overcomes these to the extent of extricating herself physically from the abusive situation, she may confront a number of external barriers: a discriminatory job market; legal disadvantages, such as her disadvantage in child custody proceedings if she leaves her children, even temporarily; difficulty in finding (and paying) a lawyer sympathetic to her position; and the tendency of others, including mental health professionals, to assume that she does have control over her situation.

2. As an external factor *producing* or eliciting *internal barriers* to adaptive behavior.

    a. Restriction may effectively *prevent the learning of adaptive behavior* by excluding opportunities for learning. In addition to facing actual discrimination in job training, for example, women may fail to acquire needed job skills as a result of subtle psychological restrictions against competing with males or working outside the home. And apart from specific deficits in job skills, women in whom dependency has been fostered may find themselves lacking in a host of skills necessary to independent survival. These range from knowledge of how to handle money to how to accomplish practical tasks formerly assigned to a husband as part of his attributed sex role—how to maintain an automobile, acquire credit, talk to professionals as an equal, and, in general, how to project an image of oneself as a credible, competent citizen, aware of and willing to defend her rights. Another corollary of this dependency may be simply not knowing where to go for needed help in a crisis.

b. Restriction may also *foster the learning of maladaptive behavior.* One learned consequence of extreme restriction may be the immobilization of all assertive behavior and a general inhibition of affective responses—a kind of learned straitjacketing. This inhibition should be distinguished from the helplessness sometimes learned as a strategy in female coping. The immobilized victim neither acts in her own defense nor reacts emotionally to stimuli that an observer might consider quite painful. Therapists gain a practical appreciation of the straitjacketing effect when, during the course of therapy, extremely inhibited clients begin to experience the rage and pain they might have been expected to feel all along.

Several experimental studies suggest insights into phenomena clinically interpreted as masochistic. In a series of animal studies later extended to human subjects, Maier (1949) studied frustration by introducing into a forced choice situation a set of constraints which made adaptive solution impossible. Subjects forced to respond in such "no win" situations tended to develop stereotyped responses which were not only highly resistant to extinction, but tended to be associated with a decreased ability to learn adaptive responses. The only adaptive value of the learned fixated response was an incidental lowering of tension after the subject began responding in a stereotyped fashion. In subsequent experiments, Maier concluded that frustrated subjects do learn to differentiate which situations will lead to punishment, but are unable to practice more adaptive responses even when given the opportunity.

In contrast to clinical studies and learning experiments on frustration, a body of studies on risk taking have been evaluated from the standpoint of mathematical decision theory. Such studies have been primarily concerned with behavior, such as economic behavior in which we might expect rational choice to take precedence over affectively charged decisions. In a critique of expected utility theory as a model for explaining actual human judgment, Kahneman and Tversky (1977) point out that subjects tend to evaluate risky options not in terms of absolute outcomes, but in terms of gains and losses. In addition, they note, losses may have more of an effect than gains on choice behavior. The implications of this theory are that any outcome must be evaluated from the standpoint of whether it represents a gain or a loss for the individual choosing and that relative losses, as well as relative gains may be weighed against each other in a rational decision. The possibility that women who choose to put up with unpleasant situations may be behaving as rationally as men in risky situations has seldom been considered. Such an explanation not only runs counter to accepted clinical theory, but is inconsistent with the stereotyped view that women are inherently irrational and tend to act on the basis of emotion rather than intellect. Nevertheless, such an approach may be as relevant to so-called masochistic behavior as those theories concerned with inner dynamics.

THE CHOICE SPACE OF THE ABUSED SPOUSE

If we examine the options available to women confronted with occasional or chronic abuse from their husbands, it is by no means obvious that alternatives which would provide a clear escape from pain are available. Even if all attempts to change the undesirable behavior of the abusive spouse have failed and options have been narrowed to staying or leaving, the wife may characterize her situation as a "damned if I do–damned if I don't" one. The negative consequences of staying, a predictable repetition of abusive behavior, must be weighed against the negative consequences of leaving. The following sets of incentives may be particularly relevant to the wife's decision:

1. *Identity versus identity loss*. It has been noted that, while man achieves an identity, woman marries one. Whatever her other roles and goals, the role of wife is likely to remain a cornerstone of identity. This development is in part a function of the relation between "women's work" and self-esteem. As Laws (1976) has pointed out, the jobs available to women are the least motivating ones and, it may be inferred, the jobs least likely to raise a woman's self-esteem. The popular contrast between career woman and homemaker has never reflected the real options available to most women. In conseqence of existing sex-role stereotypes, many women are socialized to define the role of wife as a submissive one. And, to the extent that authoritarian attitudes are an expectable concomitant of a traditionally "feminine" identity, we might expect any autonomously assertive act to threaten the submissive wife with identity loss. Thus, even choosing to leave may be threatening.

2. *Social approval versus stigmatization.* Marriage is not only the traditional route to female identity—or, as Sheehy (1976) has suggested, the traditional substitute for female identity; it is also the surest route to social approval as far as many women are concerned. Singleness, particularly for women, has often been stigmatized in American Culture, the epithets "old maid" and "gay divorcee" being pervasive cultural stereotypes. A woman may view her ability to get or keep a man as the major dimension along which she is evaluated by others. And, in addition to feeling that she is a failure if she leaves her husband, she may share the social tendency to stigmatize the "broken home" as a cause of all sorts of social ills, ranging from the maladjustment of children to the downfall of Western civilization. The stigma attached to the "broken home" is especially likely to fall on women (Brandwin, Brown, and Fox, 1974). Since they typically obtain child custody following divorce, they often come under the scrutiny of sociologists, mental health professionals, and the courts who employ such pejorative labeling.

The abused woman who attempts to leave her husband is also subject to another type of stigmatization, the implicit or even explicit accusation that she must have done something to deserve the abuse she suffered. This assumption of deserved insult—the notion that those who suffer must be at fault—is associated with a number of primitive but perenially popular fantasies about suffering, including the fantasy that the fact of suffering is a sign of fault. Thus Job's "comforters" urged him to search his soul for his offense. Similarly the abused spouse is often encouraged to focus on what she did to provoke an assault. It is scarcely surprising that, given such attitudes, she often concludes that she is really guilty or that, at the very least, she might have done something to prevent the socially stigmatized event, the breakup of a family unit.

3. *Economic support versus economic deprivation and downward social mobility.* Although there is no real evidence that wife abuse is a lower class phenomenon or that the abused wife is economically disadvantaged while living with her husband, the economic deprivation of the separated or divorced woman has been clearly established. In 1969, single women between the ages of 25 and 44 who had children had a median income of $4000 a year (Brandwein, Brown, and Fox, 1974). A study of divorced mothers and their children in treatment at a psychiatric hospital (Tooley, 1976) reported a drastic reduction in family income as a major cause of stress in single-parent families.

The factors contributing to the economic deprivation of the woman who leaves her spouse include those which affect women generally: the low pay associated with women's jobs, lack of training, discriminatory hiring practices, etc. In addition to these, the woman with young children is faced with the prospect of supporting them should she leave her husband. Practically speaking, this often means providing child care for them while she works or seeking welfare assistance. Either way, it may be difficult to rise above the poverty level following a separation from her husband.

The assumption that fathers provide support following marital dissolution, particularly in cases where the father chooses to be recalcitrant, is largely unfounded. It is estimated that over 5.8 million nonwelfare families in the United States have problems of nonsupport, in addition to the 2.9 million families on assistance (U.S. Senate Committee on Finance, 1975). Lack of effort on the part of states to enforce support is judged a major factor in welfare dependency in this study. The abused wife or former wife may also be subject to further abuse if she attempts to enforce support.

Ironically, the no-fault divorce statutes enacted in many states to make divorce more humane by replacing adversary proceedings with an irretrievable breakdown standard have contributed to the economic disadvantages of women (Citizens' Advisory Council on the Status of Women, n. d.). The bargaining power which might formerly have been available to an abused woman in a divorce proceeding is lost when abuse is no longer grounds for divorce. Eisenberg and Micklow (1974) have pointed out, however, that women did not gain much economically under fault proceedings either. Legally, it has never been easy for a woman to obtain any economic remedy for a spouse's abuse: married, she cannot institute a civil suit against him and in a divorce action, she is likely to gain little more than the dissolution itself.

Downward social mobility as a consequence of marital separation is feared by some women as much or more than poverty itself. In this regard, the motivational significance of loss, as opposed to absolute level of income, is evident. Finally, the prospect of poverty interacts with fear of social stigmatization. Stigma accrues not only to poverty in our society, but to the individual judged to be illegitimately dependent on others for support. The image of the female divorcee who leeches her former husband for alimony is contradicted by real-life statistics (Citizens' Advisory Council on the Status of Women, n. d.). Nevertheless, the image persists, along with the socially devalued stereotype of the "welfare freeloader" to serve as a powerful deterrent to some women who are reluctant to accept even the economic aid to which they are entitled.

4. *Love versus loss of attachment.* The trauma of losing love is usually cited as a major support for the masochism hypothesis. There is, of course, an important logical distinction between loving a spouse in spite of his abusive behavior and loving him because of it. Even so, the statement that abused wives love their husbands need not be taken at face value. It may represent merely a denial of ambivalence or even unmiti-

gated hatred. It is also likely to be bound up with the wishes for identity and social approval typically associated with marriage itself. And it functions as a rationalization for remaining in an abusive situation.

Those spouses who do love their husbands in spite of abuse face the prospect of a formidable loss should they decide to leave. Not infrequently, the submissive wife has focused all her affection on her family, sacrificing ties to adults other than her husband. Under these circumstances, the loss of the husband may threaten to isolate the wife from any close interpersonal relationship.

The professed love of an abused spouse for her abuser may also, from a clinical standpoint, resemble addiction. To conclude that such love is masochistic is to beg the question; the concept of masochism explains no more about addictive love than it explains alcoholism. In this regard, it may be significant that a high proportion of the spouses interviewed by Eisenberg and Micklow (1974) reported that assault was associated with heavy drinking. This observation suggests that the interaction between some assaultive and assaulted partners may reflect a pattern of mutual symbiosis between addicts, each of whom looks to the partnership as a kind of security blanket but one of whom, the husband, is able to externalize feelings of rage when the sense of security is threatened. In order for an abused woman to extricate herself from such a situation, she would have to overcome her own addiction and find more reliable sources of security. Here, again, she is often confronted with few positive options.

IMPLICATIONS FOR INTERVENTION

A first step in any rational approach to clinical intervention in cases of abuse is a recognition of the actual external constraints the "masochistic" woman faces. While the clinician, as an individual, is seldom in a position to remove such constraints directly, she/he does have some power to bring the facts about wife abuse to greater public attention. The very popularity of the masochism hypothesis derives in no small part from the scientific sanction of the concept, a phenomenon which indicates the influence of clinical attitudes on public policy. At the very least, it behooves thoughtful professionals to refrain from reinforcing existing tendencies to rely on the concept of masochism as a facile explanation for abusive behavior toward women. Such behavior not only plays into a public apathy toward the problems of abuse; it tends to substantiate the individual client's negative concept of herself.

In a direct treatment situation, an awareness of external constraints can be helpful in raising the self-esteem of the client as well as in helping her sort out the extent to which her own actions do interact with circumstances to keep her in a destructive situation. If a woman's reality testing, which often involves a clear and correct perception of the negative alternatives actually available to her, is devalued as incorrect or dismissed as a form of resistance, she can scarcely disentangle the rational from the irrational aspects of her own behavior. Once reality is acknowledged, however, irrational behavior patterns can be examined both from the standpoint of how such patterns were originally acquired and how they may be changed.

SUMMARY

The lack of differentiation popularly attributed to women is, perhaps not surprisingly, matched by the lack of differentiation in scientific concepts explaining female behavior. The concept of *masochism* is a case in point, having traditionally been, along with stereotypes about female hysteria, a cornerstone of clinical theories about women. Although psychoanalysts, the most influential sources of this clinical tendency, disagreed about particular focal points in female development, the notion of a biologically determined disposition toward masochism has been widely accepted.

If facts, such as the social prevalence of such phenomena as wife abuse, are closely examined, however, the picture which emerges is neither undifferentiated nor simple. Female motivation, like motivation generally, must be studied in the context of external constraints such as the actual choices available and the consequences of particular choices. In this light, the masochistic woman often appears as an individual who has almost no choice, given the lack of social support for extricating herself from her situation or who is confronted with alternatives which are, for the most part, negatively valued. Only a realistic appraisal of these alternatives can lead to the kind of therapeutic intervention which facilitates self-esteem as well as behavioral change.

REFERENCES

Bonaparte, M. 1951. *Female Sexuality*. Paris: Presse Universitaire de France. Quoted in J. Chasseguet-Smirgel, *Female Sexuality*. Ann Arbor, Michigan: University of Michigan Press, 1970.

Brandwein, R. A., Brown, C. A., and Fox, E. M. 1974. Women and Children Last: The Social Situation of Divorced Mothers and Their Families. *Journal of Marriage and the Family*, August: 498–514.

Citizens' Advisory Council on the Status of Women. n. d. *Recognition of Economic Contribution of Homemakers and Protection of Children in Divorce Law and Practice.* Washington DC: Department of Labor.

Deutsch, H. 1930. The significance of Masochism in the Mental Life of Women. *International Journal of Psychoanalysis* 11: 48–60.

Eisenberg, S. E., and Micklow, P. L. 1974. *The Assaulted Wife: Catch 22 Revisited.* Ann Arbor, Michigan.

Freud, S. 1905. Instincts and their Vicissitudes. In *The Collected Papers of Sigmund Freud.* New York: Basic Books.

Freud, S. 1919. A Child is Being Beaten. In *The Collected Papers of Sigmund Freud.* New York: Basic Books.

Freud, S. 1924. The Economic Problem in Masochism. In *The Standard Edition of the Complete Psychological Works of Sigmund Freud,* edited by James Strachy. London: Hogarth Press.

Horney, K. 1967. *Feminine Psychology,* edited by Harold Kelman, New York: Norton.

Kahneman, D., and Tversky, A. 1977. Prospect Theory: An Analysis of Decision Making under Risk. Technical Report PTR, Decision Research.

Klein, M. 1975. *Envy and Gratitude and Other Works: 1946–1963.* New York: Delta.

Lampl de Groot, J. 1933. Contribution to the Problem of Femininity. *Psychoanalytic Quarterly* 2: 489–518.

Laws, J. L. 1976. Work Aspiration of Women: False Leads and New Starts. *Signs: Journal of Women in Culture and Society,* Vol. 1, Spring: 33–49.

Maier, N. R. F. 1949. *Frustration: The Study of Behavior without a Goal.* Ann Arbor: University of Michigan Press (paperback edition 1961).

Millett, K. 1971. *Sexual Politics.* New York: Avon.

Reich, W. 1949. *Character Analysis.* New York: Farrar, Straus and Giroux.

Schuyler, M. 1976. Battered Wives: An Emerging Social Problem. *Social Work,* November: 488–491.

Sheehy, G. 1976. *Passages.* New York: E. P. Dutton.

Tooley, K. M. 1976. Anti-Social Behavior and Social Alienation Post-Divorce: "The Man of the House" and His Mother. *Journal of Orthopsychiatry,* Vol. 46, 1, January.

U.S. Senate Committee on Finance. 1975. *Child Support Data and Materials: Background Information Prepared by the Staff.* Washington DC: U.S. Government Printing Office.

Roles and Role Conflict of Women in Infertile Couples

11

JANET R. ALLISON

Pregnancy is probably the most dramatic, strictly female biological event—one that has meaning not only biologically, but culturally, interpersonally, and intrapsychically as well. Fertility is closely tied to woman's identity and roles (Russo, 1976), and a psychology of women that is founded in women's own experience and values must address this area.

Infertility has become a particularly interesting problem in the current ecological and social contexts. There is real worldwide necessity to control and reduce fertility. With the aid of the women's movement, extrafamilial roles for women that offer rewards and status competing with those offered by motherhood are becoming increasingly legitimized. Despite these changes, the woman who fails to become pregnant still tends to see herself, and often is seen by others, as somehow unnatural, shameful, a failure as a woman. Substantial medical resources each year are devoted to research to alleviate infertility. Recent advances in reproductive medicine that make fertilization possible outside the body reflect the view that infertility is a "problem" requiring priority attention by society.

PSYCHOLOGICAL ASPECTS OF INFERTILITY

Literature on the motivation for and the meaning of motherhood ranges from the thinking of some Freudians who assume motivation for motherhood to be natural, inevitable, and biologically based (Benedek and Rubenstein, 1939; Deutsch, 1944; Freud, 1959a, 1959b) to that of some feminists who see motherhood as a cultural role trap for women (Jones, 1970; Mitchell, 1973). With the development of the women's movement and some new views on the psychology of women, some writers describe pregnancy as an almost inevitably ambivalent and ambiguous matter,

Reprinted from *Psychology of Women Quarterly* 4(1):97–113, 1979. Copyright © 1974 by the Human Sciences Press, Inc. Reprinted by permission. Based upon the author's doctoral dissertation, *Infertility and Role Conflict: A Phenomenological Study of Women.* Unpublished doctoral dissertation, California School of Professional Psychology, 1976.

given our present cultural context and role expectations (Bardwick, 1970; Bardwickand Douvan, 1971; Lott, 1973). Motivation for childbearing is a complex phenomenon, which involves biologically based factors and social roles and expectations, including some response to the perceived demands and consequences involved in having children within the woman's specific situation (Clifford, 1962; Greenberg, Loesch, and Lakin, 1959; Hatcher, 1973).

Much of the literature that speculates about the relationship of psychological factors to infertility has arisen out of a psychoanalytic framework (Noyes and Chapnick, 1964). Its focus has been on "psychogenic" infertility in women, that is, infertility presumed to be caused by psychological factors since no organic dysfunction can be found (Benedek, 1970; Deutsch, 1945; Ford, Forman, Wilson, Char, Mixson, and Scholz, 1953; Mandy and Mandy, 1958). Most of this work, which has supported the notion that infertility is related to rather severe psychopathology in the woman, was based on clinical impressions. More systematic studies using the Rorschach (Eisner, 1963) and the Minnesota Multiphasic Personality Inventory (Carr, 1963) also reported more psychopathology among infertile than fertile wives. Nonetheless, the findings of a number of subsequent studies have been inconsistent with the view that infertility is caused by severe psychopathology (Denber and Roland, 1969; Hampson, 1963; Mai, Munday, and Rump, 1972a; Mattson, 1963; Richardson, 1972; Seward, 1965).

In infertility research to date, sex-role identity generally has been viewed as an inherent personality characteristic of the woman rather than as a factor that may be environmentally affected. The lack of attention to social-psychological aspects of sex role and identity could partially explain the inconsistent findings in the infertility literature. Also, looking at sex-role identity as a stable intrapsychic trait fails to account adequately for cases of secondary infertility (i.e., those in which pregnancy has occurred in the past, but not recently). If role conceptions are influenced by the woman's life situation at any given time, and if they can in turn influence her fertility, then it is not difficult to imagine that she might become infertile, temporarily or permanently, due to changed role demands and conflicts.

The difficulty of differentially diagnosing organic versus psychogenic infertility has been addressed by Mai, Munday, and Rump (1972b) and Decker (1972). Sandler's (1968) approach dealt with these problems by defining emotionally based infertility as a somatic response to a state of stress rather than defining it in terms of the absence of demonstrable endocrine dysfunction or organic disease. McDonald (1968) has conceptualized the psychogenesis of obstetric complications in a similar fashion.

Beck (1972) has developed a model of psychophysiological disorders, positing the existence of an external situation that creates stress for the

individual because of the meaning attached to it. Once the anxiety-pro-
voking situation is established, the situational cues for anxiety, together
with the symptoms of the physiological disorder, evoke additional anxiety; consequently, a "cognition-anxiety-physiological disorder" spiral is
produced.

Role Theory and Women's Roles

Role theory in general is concerned with the social context, rather
than the individual in isolation, thus providing a clear contrast to those
approaches to the psychology of women that have assumed a strong biological determinism and ignored social-psychological factors.

The phenomenon of women's ambivalence toward their roles was
examined from a role theory perspective by Rossi (1972), who stated that
social roles always evoke ambivalence, but that when a role is optional,
negative feelings about it are admissible. Because traditional women's
roles (especially of wife and mother) have been required, ascribed roles,
women's ambivalence toward them has been unacceptable and heavily
sanctioned, creating guilt and other problems for women and their families. This ambivalence has physiological implications. There is evidence
that if an individual is unable to resolve a role conflict, role performance
is impaired and somatic disorders may result (Jackson, 1962; Sarbin and
Allen, 1968).

In the growing body of literature on "psychological androgyny,"
there is increasing evidence that the stereotypically sex-typed woman (or
man) has a narrower range of functioning than the androgynous individual. Moreover, sex-typed individuals have been found to rank lower
in self-esteem and higher in anxiety, and to be sick more often than their
androgynous counterparts (Bem, 1975; Bem, Martyna, and Watson, 1976;
Deaux, 1976).

Factors associated with differences in degree of role conflict include
marital status (Nevill and Damico, 1975) and husband's role expectations
for his wife (Stuckert, 1962; Arnott, 1972). Women who are employed,
especially in higher-level positions, face particular conflicts between traditional role expectations and the role of the working person (Bass, Krusell, and Alexander, 1971; Epstein, 1970; Gordon and Hall, 1974; Hall and
Gordon, 1973). This is more of a problem for married women with a more
traditional sex-based division of labor in the household (Markus, 1970).

Women's Roles as Related to Fertility/Infertility

Most researchers exploring the relationship of women's roles and
role conflict to fertility/infertility have been concerned only with consciously chosen fertility, with the exception of Safilios-Rothschild (1972).

In general, the research has revealed that high work commitment is correlated with low fertility (Beckman, 1974; Harmon, 1970; Hass, 1972; Safilios-Rothschild, 1972; Weller, 1968). A study by Vogel, Rosenkrantz, Broverman, Broverman, and Clarkson (1975) indicated that women with less stereotypic sex-role conceptions wish to have fewer children.

For women who hold a traditional view of women's roles, any expectations or needs that conflict with the traditional maternal role may be stressful, increasing the likelihood of a somatic response. But a somatic response to stress is not necessarily dysfunctional. In some situations a physiological response can be more adaptive than the lack of autonomic involvement (Kagan and Moss, 1962; Lacey, 1967; Schacter, Williams, Rowe, Schacter, and Jameson, 1965). More specifically, infertility may have behaviorally adaptive significance in the transactions of the individual with her/his environment.

For example, Mead (1958) found that Samoan girls normally are sexually promiscuous before marriage but rarely become pregnant. They manifest a kind of temporary, functional infertility that is in no way a disease entity within their phenomenological and social context. In their culture, girls are expected to be sexually active, but they are not considered ready for motherhood. Infertility obviously functions differently in the cultural context of married American women than it does for Samoan girls. Nonetheless, the Samoan example suggests the possibility that infertility could be functional in our society as well.

HYPOTHESES

This study was designed to explore the notion that infertility may be a somatic correlate to the stress of role conflict. More specifically, it was predicted that the lives of infertile women would display sources of role conflict, but that their perception of role conflict would be minimized. The following hypotheses were generated:

1. *Infertile women's views of themselves will include more traditional women's role conceptions than those of women in the comparison group.* Evidence from androgyny studies cited above suggests that traditionally sex-typed women are more restricted in their functioning, more anxious, and more illness-prone than women with less strictly traditional views of themselves.

2. *Infertile women will display greater discrepancy than comparison group women on the following measures: (a) "real self" role conceptions versus "ideal woman" role expectations; (b) "real self" role conceptions versus their perception of "man's ideal woman" role expectations; (c) "ideal woman" role expectations versus perceptions of "man's ideal woman" role expectations; (d) total internal role discrepancy.*

3. *Infertile couples will display more discrepancy than comparison group couples on the following: (a) wife's "real self" role conceptions versus husband's "ideal woman" role expectations; (b) wife's perception of "man's ideal woman" role expectations versus husband's actual "ideal woman" role expectations.* These discrepancies would demonstrate conflict of role expectations between wife and husband.

4. *Infertile women will report less perceived conflict than comparison group women in the following areas: (a) child care (for women with children only); (b) relations with husband; (c) household management; (d) roles as women overall.* In other words, an infertile woman would perceive herself to be relatively unconflicted if infertility is functional in reducing the woman's *experience* of role conflict (which she is unable to resolve in any other fashion).

5. *In the area of occupation: (a) more infertile women than comparison group women will be employed; (b) infertile women's occupational status will be higher than that of comparison group women; (c) more infertile women than comparison group women will have had mothers who were employed; (d) infertile women will have had mothers who had higher occupational status than comparison group women's mothers.* The first two parts are based directly on Safilios-Rothschild's (1972) findings. Predictions regarding mothers' work commitment were based on the rationale that the role model provided by a mother with a work commitment would be another source of role conflict with the traditional role conceptions predicted in the first hypothesis.

METHOD

Subjects

The infertile subjects in the study were 29 women between ages 21 and 40 who, with their husbands, were beginning an infertility program at a private medical clinic in Los Angeles. To begin the program, a couple must have engaged in intercourse, without using contraception and without conceiving a pregnancy, for at least 12 months.

Comparison group subjects consisted of 29 married women, in the same age range and from comparable socioeconomic areas, who had no history of inability to conceive pregnancy. Six of them were found through a dentist's office near the infertility clinic; married patients were approached, the nature of the study briefly explained, and their participation requested. The other control subjects were found through a "grapevine" procedure, in which each comparison subject was asked whether she could suggest other potential participants. All subjects signed voluntary consent forms for anonymous use of all relevant data for research. The two groups were comparable on demographic variables of age, family's income bracket, level of education, and religion, although there was a nonsignificant trend toward more Catholicism among the infertile group ($p < 0.10$).

Procedures

After cooperation was obtained, each subject was asked to complete three Maferr Inventories of Feminine Values (Steinmann and Fox, 1974), from which role conceptions and expectations were measured. Each husband was also asked to complete a fourth Maferr Inventory. Each Inventory contains 34 statements, to be rated on a 5-point Likert scale of agreement. Half of the statements delineate "family-oriented" or traditional women's role conceptions, and half are "self-achieving" or nontraditional. Form A measures the woman's "real self" role conceptions; Form B asks how her "ideal woman" would respond. The husband's form, BB, indicates his role expectations for his "ideal woman." Role discrepancy scores were obtained by computing discrepancies between various pairs of scores, so that A minus B, for example, measures the woman's discrepancy between her perceptions of "real" versus "ideal self" role conceptions. The woman's total internal role discrepancy score was obtained by summing the absolute values of the discrepancy scores involving only the wife's forms (A, B, and C).

A Life Style Questionnaire, measuring experienced role conflict in several areas (Nevill and Damico, 1974), and a medical history questionnaire, developed and used routinely by the clinic, were also completed by each woman. The latter contained demographic information and some medical history to follow up in the interview.

Finally, a semi-structured interview was conducted with each subject, which was designed to explore the woman's experience and view of herself, with particular emphasis on the meaning of pregnancy and parenthood, and role conceptions and conflicts. Areas of focus included demographic variables, attitudes, motivations and experience related to pregnancy and having children, the marriage, the woman's parents and childhood experience, her view of herself, and possible role conflict. Due to space limitations, discussion of the interview material is beyond the scope of this paper, however.

RESULTS

Data Analysis

Statistical findings supported the hypotheses dealing with the women's role conceptions, self-reported role conflict, and occupational data. Significant differences between the infertile and comparison groups were found in the opposite direction from those predicted with regard to the women's internal role discrepancies.

Women's Role Conceptions. With regard to the first hypothesis, as Table 1 indicates, the ranked scores for "woman's view of herself" for the infertile sample are significantly lower than those for the comparison group ($p < 0.005$). The infertile group's scores on "woman's ideal woman" are also significantly lower than those of the comparison group ($p < 0.005$). In other words, as predicted, infertile women see not only themselves, but also their ideal woman, as significantly more traditional than do control group women.

Role Discrepancies. Hypotheses 2 and 3 were tested by Mann-Whitney *U* comparisons of the absolute values of discrepancy scores. Absolute values were used because the discrepancies could emerge as either a positive or a negative value, with a score of zero representing no discrepancy. In Table 2, the findings are summarized, including non-absolute-value median scores to indicate the direction of the discrepancies.

Hypothesis 2, that infertile women would display more role discrepancy than comparison group women, was not supported. In fact, the findings were in the *opposite* direction from those predicted, with the infertile group displaying less discrepancy than the comparison group between their view of themselves and their perception of what men want from a woman ($p < 0.05$), and less discrepancy between their own role expectations for their ideal woman and those they perceive men to hold ($p < 0.05$). The infertile group also displayed less total internal role discrepancy than comparison group subjects ($p < 0.01$).

Self-Reported Role Conflict. In Hypothesis 4, it was predicted that

TABLE 1. Mann-Whitney *U*-Test Comparisons of Maferr Inventory Scores

| Inventory | Infertile group ($n = 29$) | | Comparison group ($n = 29$) | | |
	Median score	Mean *R*	Median score	Mean *R*	*U*
A: Woman's real self	2	22.41	14	36.59	10.21[a]
B: Woman's ideal woman	6	22.91	20	36.09	8.82[a]
C: Woman's perception of man's ideal woman	−4	29.41	−4	29.59	0.001
BB: Husband's ideal woman	10	28.71	10	30.29	0.13

[a] $p < 0.005$.

infertile women would report less perceived role conflict than comparison group women. All parts of this hypotheses were supported by Mann-Whitney U analysis of the data (see Table 3). (a) Infertile women with children reported significantly less ($p < 0.01$) perceived conflict in the area of child care than comparison group women with children. Infertile women also reported less perceived conflict than control women in (b) the area of relations with husband ($p < 0.05$), and in (c) the area of household management ($p < 0.05$). (d) The last part of this hypothesis was tested in two different ways. First, when a comparison of all women in both samples was made (excluding the "child care" conflict item, because of the number of subjects who had no children), infertile women showed less ($p < 0.05$) total reported role conflict than the control women. When a second comparison looked at only women with children (now including all of the self-reported role conflict items), the difference between infertile and control group women was even more significant ($p < 0.005$).

TABLE 2. Mann-Whitney U-Test Comparisons of Maferr Role Discrepancy Scores[a]

Role discrepancy variable	Infertile group ($n = 29$)		Comparison group ($n = 29$)		
	Median discrepancy	Mean R	Median discrepancy	Mean R	U
A − B: Real self vs. ideal woman	−3	25.72	−4	33.82	2.90
A − C: Real self vs. perception of man's ideal woman	7	24.57	16	34.43	4.95[b]
B − C: Ideal woman vs. perception of man's ideal woman	8	24.88	19	34.12	4.34[b]
|A − B| + |A − C| + | B − C| : Total internal role discrepancy	26	23.43	42	35.57	7.49[c]
A − BB: Real self vs. husband's ideal woman	−7	30.76	3	28.84	0.32
C − BB: Perception of man's ideal woman vs. husband's ideal woman	−23	28.00	−19	31.00	0.46

[a]Absolute values of discrepancy scores were used for statistical comparison.
[b]$p < 0.05$.
[c]$p < 0.01$.

TABLE 3. Mann-Whitney U-Test Comparisons of Life Style Questionnaire Scores on Role Conflict Areas[a]

| Conflict area | Infertile group ($n = 29$) | | Comparison group ($n = 29$) | | U |
	Median reported conflict	Mean R	Median reported conflict	Mean R	
Time management	3	24.12	5	34.88	5.89[e]
Relations with husband	1	23.50	2	35.50	7.32[e]
Household management	2	23.97	3	35.03	6.23[d]
Child care	2	13.93[b]	3.5	24.04[c]	6.81[e]
Financial	2	26.38	2	32.62	1.98
Expectations for self	3	25.95	5	33.05	2.57
Expectations from others	2	28.93	2	30.07	0.07
Guilt	2	26.79	3	32.21	1.49
Total reported role conflict, excluding child care item	18	24.34	23	34.66	5.41[d]
Total reported role conflict, including child care item	19	13.42[b]	27	24.29[c]	7.80[f]

[a]Scores are subjects' ratings from 1 (least conflict) to 7 (most conflict).
[b]$n = 14$.
[c]$n = 26$.
[d]$p < 0.05$.
[e]$p < 0.01$.
[f]$p < 0.005$.

Occupational Involvement. The fifth hypothesis was tested by comparing occupational data collected in the interview, with results summarized in Tables 4 and 5. Parts 5a and 5b were supported by the data, indicating that significantly more infertile women were employed ($p < 0.05$), and at significantly higher occupational statuses than comparison group women ($p < 0.05$). Parts 5c and 5d were not confirmed.

TABLE 4. Chi-Square Comparisons of Frequency of Employment

| Variable | Infertile group ($n = 29$) | | Comparison group ($n = 29$) | | χ^2 |
	Freq.	%	Freq.	%	
Employment of subject	18	62.07	8	27.59	5.65[a]
Employment of subject's mother	9	31.03	5	17.24	0.85

[a]$p < 0.05$.

TABLE 5. Mann-Whitney U-Test Comparisons of Occupational Status[a]

| Variable | Infertile group ($n = 29$) | | Comparison group ($n = 29$) | | |
	Median	Mean R	Median	Mean R	U
Occupational status of subject	4	24.09	8	34.91	5.96[b]
Occupational status of subject's mother	8	27.52	8	31.48	0.80

[a]Occupational status was coded according to the following adaptation of Hollingshead's (1957) scale:
   1 = Higher executives, proprietors of large concerns, major professionals
   2 = Business managers, proprietors of medium-sized businesses, lesser professionals
   3 = Administrative personnel, small independent businesses, minor professionals
   4 = Clerical and sales workers, technicians, owners of little businesses
   5 = Skilled manual workers
   6 = Machine operators and semi-skilled employees
   7 = Unskilled employees
   8 = No employment—housewives
[b]$p < 0.05$.

DISCUSSION

The findings indicate that the infertile women have significantly more traditional role conceptions than the comparison group, and that they consistently report less internally experienced role conflict than comparison group women. There is evidence, however, that the infertile women are and have been confronted with situations that could be expected to generate role conflict. Their levels of wife–husband role discrepancy are at least as high as those of the control group, and their higher levels of employment and occupational status seem to contradict their more traditional role conceptions.

One explanation for these findings is that the discrepancy between the traditional role conceptions of infertile subjects (with childbearing as a major element) and their inability to perform the childbearing function leads them to focus even more on their desire to have children and be traditional (which of course also intensifies the discrepancy).

It may also be that the traditional role conceptions actually contribute in some way to the infertility. For some infertile women, the ascribed, nonoptional nature of their traditional role conceptions (including childbearing) may somehow interfere with the conditions needed for conception to occur. As noted earlier, Rossi (1972) has argued that traditionally wifehood and motherhood are required, ascribed roles for women, and that therefore any ambivalence is unacceptance and tends to become covert, creating guilt and other negative consequences. Infertility might be one such possible consequence for women who hold nonoptional role expectations of childbearing, especially if they have cause for ambivalence about that role.

How, then, do the role conflict data fit into this emerging configuration? Infertility, in this sample, is associated with a greater traditionalism in the woman's role conceptions, which is consistent with the demands of woman's traditionally ascribed, nonoptional roles. If, as suggested above, infertility itself contributes to such traditionalism, and if such traditionalism suppresses ambivalence or conflict around their roles as women, then it follows that infertility functions indirectly to minimize the experience of role conflict.

The role discrepancy findings suggest that the infertile women's traditionalism functions to decrease the discrepancy between their own role conceptions and those that they perceive men to hold for them. It is the traditionalism that distinguishes the infertile group from the control group. Women's perception of "man's ideal woman" is almost the same between the two groups. It may be that the infertile women deny certain of their own individual, "self-achieving" needs, in an attempt to meet men's expectations as they perceive them. If this is true, then, infertility may also function as a somatic expression of the unmet personal, self-achieving needs that cannot be satisfied in their highly traditional women's role structure. The somatic reality of infertility is perhaps more tolerable for these women than the experience of role conflicts.

Although infertile women hold more traditional role conceptions, perhaps partially in response to their perception of what men want, the discrepancy data including husbands' own "ideal woman" role expectations indicate that the women actually have moved to a position more traditional than that which their husbands report they want. They are at least as discrepant from their husbands' self-reported expectations as the comparison group women are, but, unlike the comparison group, the infertile women do not reflect this wife–husband discrepancy in their *experience* of role conflict. This may be an example of a role-related pressure or conflict that is somatically expressed in their failure to conceive, rather than being experienced as a conflict of expectations. Of course, it could be that in some cases it is the husband himself who prevents conception.

Another source of potential role conflict for these women is a higher level of employment and occupational status, which is in distinct contrast with their significantly more traditional role conceptions.

Thus, it is suggested that the infertile woman is confronted with certain sources of potential role conflict, in an experiential context that makes the experience of role conflict intolerable. In part, this context consists of her already traditional role conceptions, which have an ascribed, nonoptional character. Infertility acts to remove the mother role from the arena of choice, which minimizes internal conflict in that area, since the woman can wholeheartedly *want* to fill the traditional role by having children. The more she is unable to do so, the more she is likely to want to do so, and this circular interaction becomes stabilized.

Limitations and Suggestions for Further Research

Since this exploratory study does not follow a true experimental design, the conclusions must be considered suggestive. Two methodological limitations are particularly noteworthy.

In this study, the infertile group consists only of infertile women who are seriously seeking pregnancy. The model for understanding infertility phenomenologically would certainly be at least somewhat different for women who do not want or are uninterested in having children.

Another consideration is that the infertile and comparison samples were not randomly selected groups, although they were not found to be statistically different on the demographic variables tested. One difference between the two samples was a far greater refusal rate among potential comparison subjects, probably attributable to the fact that the study was germane to the central concern for the infertile group while they were at the clinic.

The development of an instrument that quantifies and measures sources of role conflict is needed. This would preferably be a phenomenologically oriented instrument, so that researchers could base conclusions on the woman's own experiential context.

More research is needed on the role of the husband in infertility. A complete and sophisticated understanding of infertility would involve an understanding of each partner and of their interaction.

Finally, further research is needed concerning psychological interventions with infertile women or couples, in light of the relationship found here between role conceptions and conflict and infertility. If infertility is part of a coping system for these women, intervention should proceed with caution and should reflect an awareness of the interaction of the biological and social-psychological variables involved.

REFERENCES

Arnott, C. C. Husbands' and wives' commitment to employment. *Journal of Marriage and the Family*, 1972, 34, 673–684.

Bardwick, J. M. *The psychology of women: A study of bio-cultural conflicts*. New York: Harper & Row, 1971.

Bardwick, J. M., and Douvan, E. Ambivalence: The socialization of women. In V. Gornick and B. K. Moran (Eds.), *Woman in sexist society: Studies in power and powerlessness*. New York: Basic Books, 1971.

Bass, B. M., Krusell, J., and Alexander, R. A. Male managers' attitudes toward working women. *American Behavioral Scientist*, 1971, *15*, 221–236.

Beck, A. T. Cognition, anxiety, and psychophysiological disorders. In C. D. Spielberger (Ed.), *Anxiety—current trends in theory and research* (Vol. 2). New York: Academic Press, 1972.

Beckman, L. J. *Women's fertility, motivation for parenthood and work force participation*. Paper presented at the University of Oregon Psychology Department Colloquium, May 1974.

Bem, S. L. Sex-role adaptability: One consequence of psychological androgyny. *Journal of Personality and Social Psychology*, 1975, *31*, 634–643.

Bem, S. L., Martyna, W., and Watson, C. Sex typing and androgyny: Further explorations of the expressive domain. *Journal of Personality and Social Psychology*, 1976, *34* 1016–1023.

Benedek, T., and Rubenstein, B. B. The correlation between ovarian activity and psychodynamic processes: I. The ovulative phase. *Psychosomatic Medicine*, 1939, *1*, 245–270.

Benedek, T. The psychobiology of pregnancy. In E. J. Anthony and T. Benedek (Eds.), *Parenthood, its psychology and psychopathology*. Boston: Little Brown & Company, 1970.

Carr, G. D. *A psychosociological study of fertile and infertile marriages*. Unpublished doctoral dissertation, University of Southern California, 1963.

Clifford, E. Expressed attitudes in pregnancies of unwed women and married primigravida and multigravida. *Child Development*, 1962, *33*, 945–951.

Deaux, K. *The behavior of women and men*. Monterey, Calif.: Brooks/Cole, 1976.

Decker, A. Psychogenic infertility: Fact or fiction? *Medical Aspects of Human Sexuality*, 1972, *6*, 168–175.

Denber, H., and Roland, M. Psychologic factors and infertility. *Journal of Reproductive Medicine*, 1969, *2*, 29–34.

Deutsch, H. *The psychology of women* (2 vols.). New York: Grune & Stratton, 1944, 1945.

Eisner, B. G. Some psychological differences between fertile and infertile women. *Journal of Clinical Psychology*, 1963, *19*, 391–395.

Epstein, C. F. *Woman's place: Options and limits in professional careers*. Berkeley: University of California Press, 1970.

Ford, E. S. C., Forman, I., Wilson, J. R., Char, W., Mixson, W. T. and Scholz, C. A psychosomatic approach to the study of infertility. *Fertility and Sterility*, 1953, *6*, 456–465.

Freud, S. Female sexuality. In J. Strachey (Ed. and trans.), *Collected papers* (Vol. 5). New York: Basic Books, 1959 (Originally published in 1931). (a)

Freud, S. Some psychological consequences of the anatomical distinction between the sexes. In J. Strachey (Ed. and trans.), *Collected papers* (Vol. 5). New York: Basic Books, 1959 (Originally published in 1925.) (b)

Gordon, F. E., and Hall, D. T. Self-image and stereotypes of femininity: Their relationship to women's role conflicts and coping. *Journal of Applied Psychology*, 1974, *59*, 241–243.

Greenberg, N. H., Loesch, J. G., and Lakin, M. Life situations associated with the onset of pregnancy—1. The role of separation in a group of unmarried pregnant women. *Psychosomatic Medicine*, 1959, *21*, 296–310.

Hall, D. T., and Gordon, F. E. Career choices of married women: Effects on conflict, role behavior and satisfaction. *Journal of Applied Psychology*, 1973, *58*, 42–48.

Hampson, J. L. *Objective personality studies of infertile couples*. Unpublished manuscript, University of Washington School of Medicine, 1963.

Harmon, L. Anatomy of career commitment in women. *Journal of Counseling Psychology*, 1970, *16*, 77–80.

Hass, P. H. Maternal role incompatibility and fertility in urban Latin America. *Journal of*

Social Issues, 1972, 28, 111–127.

Hatcher, L. M. The adolescent experience of pregnancy and abortion: A developmental analysis (Doctoral dissertation, University of Michigan, 1972). *Dissertation Abstracts International*, 1973, 34, 4507B–4508B.

Hollingshead, A. B. *Two-factor index of social position*. Unpublished manuscript, 1957. (Available from 1965 Yale Station, New Haven, Connecticut.)

Jackson, E. F. Status consistency and symptoms of stress. *American Sociological Review*, 1962, 27, 469–480.

Jones, B. The dynamics of marriage and motherhood. In R. Morgan (Ed.), *Sisterhood is powerful*. New York: Vintage, 1970.

Kagan, J., and Moss, H. A. *Birth to maturity*. New York: Wiley, 1962.

Lacey, J. I. Somatic response patterning and stress: Some revisions of activation theory. In M. H. Appley and R. Trumbull (Eds.), *Psychological stress*. New York: Appleton-Century-Crofts, 1967.

Lott, B. E. Who wants the children? Some relationships among attitudes toward children, parents, and the liberation of women. *American Psychologist*, 1973, 28, 573–582.

Mai, F. M., Munday, R. N., and Rump, E. E. Psychiatric interview comparisons between infertile and fertile couples. *Psychosomatic Medicine*, 1972, 34, 431–440. (a)

Mai, F. M., Munday, R. N., and Rump, E. E. Psychosomatic and behavioral mechanisms in psychogenic infertility. *British Journal of Psychiatry*, 1972, 120, 199–204. (b)

Mandy, T. E., and Mandy, A. J. The psychosomatic aspects of infertility. *International Journal of Fertility*, 1958, 3, 287–295.

Markus, M. Women and work: Feminine emancipation at an impasse. *Impact of Science on Society*, 1970, 20, 61–72.

Mattson, M. R. *Objective personality studies of psychogenically infertile women*. Unpublished manuscript, University of Washington School of Medicine, 1963.

McDonald, R. L. The role of emotional factors in obstetric complications: A review. *Psychosomatic Medicine*, 1968, 30, 222–237.

Mead, M. Adolescence in primitive and modern society. In E. E. Maccoby, T. M. Newcomb and E. L. Hartley (Eds.), *Readings in social psychology*. New York: Holt, Rinehart & Winston, 1958.

Mitchell, J. *Woman's estate*. New York: Vintage, 1973.

Nevill, D., and Damico S. The development of a role conflict questionnaire for women: Some preliminary findings. *Journal of Consulting and Clinical Psychology*, 1974, 42, 743.

Nevill, D., and Damico, S. Role conflict in women as a function of marital status. *Human Relations*, 1975, 28, 478–498.

Noyes, R. W., and Chapnick, E. M. Literature on psychology and infertility—A critical analysis. *Fertility and Sterility*, 1964, 15, 543–558.

Richardson, I. M. A comparative study of personality characteristics of functionally infertile and fertile women (Doctoral dissertation, Texas Technical University, 1972). *Dissertation Abstracts International*, 1972, 33, 2772A–2773A.

Rossi, A. S. The roots of ambivalence in American women. In J. M. Bardwick (Ed.), *Readings on the psychology of women*. New York: Harper & Row, 1972.

Russo, N. F. The motherhood mandate. *Journal of Social Issues*, 1976, 32, 143–153.

Safilios-Rothschild, C. The relationship between work commitment and fertility. *International Journal of Sociology of the Family*, 1972, 2, 64–71.

Sandler, B. Emotional stress and infertility. *Journal of Psychosomatic Research*, 1968, 12, 51–59.

Sarbin, T. R., and Allen, V. L. Role theory. In G. Lindzey and E. Aronson (Eds.), *The handbook of social psychology* (2nd ed., Vol. 1). Reading, Mass.: Addison-Wesley Publishing Company, 1968.

Schacter, J., Williams, T. A., Rowe, R., Schacter, J. S., and Jameson, J. Personality correlates of physiological reactivity to stress: A study of 46 college males. *American Journal of Psychiatry*, 1965, *121*, 12–24.

Seward, G. H., Wagner, P. S., Heinrich, J. F., Bloch, S. K., and Myerhoff, H. L. The question of psychophysiologic infertility: Some negative answers. *Psychosomatic Medicine*, 1965, *27*, 533–547.

Steinmann, A., and Fox, D. J. *The male dilemma.* New York: Jason Aronson, Inc., 1974.

Stuckert, R. P. Role perception and marital satisfaction—A configurational approach. *Marriage and Family Living*, 1963, *25*, 415–419.

Vogel, S. R., Rosenkrantz, P. S., Broverman, D. M., and Clarkson, F. E. Sex-role self-concepts and life-style plans of young women. *Journal of Counseling and Clinical Psychology*, 1975, *43*, 427.

Weller, R. H. The employment of wives, dominance, and fertility. *Journal of Marriage and the Family*, 1968, *30*, 437–442.

Cinderella's Stepsisters

12

A Feminist Perspective on Anorexia Nervosa and Bulimia

MARLENE BOSKIND-LODAHL

> Reading the literature on female socialization reminds one of the familiar image of Cinderella's stepsisters industriously lopping off their toes and heels so as to fit into the glass slipper (key to the somewhat enigmatic heart of the prince)—when of course it was never intended for them anyway.[1]

During my early months of internship in 1974 in the mental health section of a university clinic, I encountered Anne, a lively, attractive, and slim young woman of 18. For three years she had been on a cycle of gorging and starving which had continued without relief. She felt desperate and out of control.

Anne was the first in a series of 138 binger-starvers that I was to treat. It became clear that the exaggerated gorging and purging reported by these patients was part of a self-perpetuating syndrome that was primarily a problem of women.[2] The women I interviewed were consumed by constant but self-defeating attempts to change their bodies so that they might each fit into the glass slipper. Anne was well informed about her symptoms. She even recommended books for me to read. I searched the traditional literature for insights into her problem. Bruch, who has written extensively on eating disorders, has most clearly diagnosed the starvation or anorexic aspect of this syndrome. According to her, characteristics of primary anorexia nervosa are: (1) severe weight loss; (2) a disturbance of body image and body concept which Bruch calls "delusional"; (3) a disturbance of cognitive interpretation of body stimuli, combined with the failure to recognize signs of nutritional need; (4) hyperactivity and denial of fatigue; (5) a paralyzing sense of ineffectiveness; (6) a family life in which (a) self-expression was neither encouraged nor reinforced, (b) the mother was frustrated in career aspirations, subservient to her husband, and generally conscientious and overprotective, (c) the father was preoccupied with outer appearances, admired fitness and beauty, and expected proper behavior and measurable achievements

Reprinted from *Signs: Journal of Women in Culture and Society* (2): 342–356, 1976. Copyright © 1976 by the University of Chicago. Reprinted by permission. This paper is dedicated to my original group of patients, for me the first of Cinderella's stepsisters.

from his children.[3] Little else, however, was helpful. Most writers treated the starvation and the binge-ing (bulimia) as separate and distinct diseases, although several researchers had noted in passing the compulsion of the self-starver to binge.

This paper is intended to provide the nucleus of a new approach. Relating anorexia to bulimia, it may also help to stimulate successful therapies for the young women whom I shall describe as "bulimarexics."

PSYCHOANALYTIC INTERPRETATION OF ANOREXIA AND BULIMIA

The view of anorexia as a rejection of femininity which often manifests itself as a fear of oral impregnation is widely held (see Figure 1). Szyrynski observes:

> They appear to be afraid of growing and maturation and they find it difficult to accept . . . their sexual identity. In the case of girls, fear of pregnancy often dominates the picture; pregnancy being symbolized by food, getting fat means becoming pregnant. Such fantasies are also quite often formulated as oral impregnation. The girl, after kissing a boy for the first time, gets panicky lest pregnancy should follow. She pays particular attention to her gaining weight and not infrequently a casual remark of a visitor, a relative, or a friend that she is looking well and probably has gained some weight will unleash the disastrous ritual of self-starvation.[4]

Behind such fears is said to be an unconscious hatred of the mother, who is ineffective and discontent but castrating. Wulff, writing in the early 1930s, describes such psychodynamics.

> This neurosis is characterized by the person's fight against her sexuality which, through previous repression, has become greedy and insatiable. . . . This sexuality is pregenitally oriented and sexual satisfaction is perceived as a "dirty meal." Periods of depression in which patients stuff themselves and feel themselves "fat," . . . "dirty," or "pregnant," . . . alternate with "good" periods in which they behave ascetically, feel slim and conduct themselves normally. . . . Psychoanalysis discloses that the unconscious content of the syndrome is a preoedipal mother conflict, which may be covered by an oral-sadistic Oedipus conflict. The patients have an intense unconscious hatred against their mothers and against femininity.[5]

Lindner, describing the case of Laura in *The Fifty-Minute Hour*, is a more modern proponent of traditional theory.[6] His patient, Laura, complained of the same gorging–fasting symptoms as my patient, Anne, but his interpretation of these symptoms diverges sharply from mine. He fits Laura neatly into a stereotyped feminine role, maintaining that her symptoms show a neurotic, unhealthy resistance to that role. His cure involves putting an end to that hatred of femininity by helping the woman learn to accept and to act out the traditional female role, often

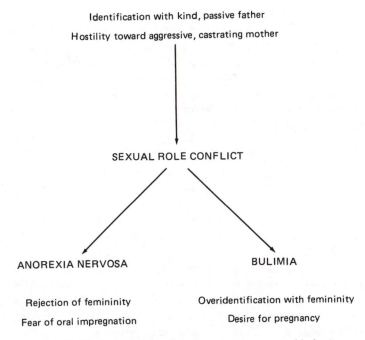

PREOEDIPAL RIVALRIES AND ORAL SADISTIC DRIVES

Identification with kind, passive father

Hostility toward aggressive, castrating mother

SEXUAL ROLE CONFLICT

ANOREXIA NERVOSA

Rejection of femininity

Fear of oral impregnation

BULIMIA

Overidentification with femininity

Desire for pregnancy

FIGURE 1. Psychoanalytic model of anorexia nervosa and bulimia.

described as accommodating, receptive, or passive. What Lindner's Laura "really wanted" was to become pregnant. He observes Laura's desperate desire for a man, but presupposes that it is healthy for a woman to feel desperate without a man and likewise to feel completely fulfilled once she is in a relationship.

Bruch writes more critically on the oral impregnation interpretation. She states that "modern psychoanalytic thinking has turned away from this merely symbolic, often analogistic etiological approach and focuses now on the nature of the parent–child relationship from the beginning." However, she confirms that "even today fear of oral impregnation is the one psychodynamic issue most consistently looked for."[7] The fact that most anorexic women suffer from amenorrhea, interruption of the menstrual cycle, is seen as further evidence that these women are rejecting their "femininity."[8] Medical evidence has shown, however, that amenorrhea is consistently observed in women with abnormally low body weight who do not have symptoms of primary anorexia. This suggests that it is low body weight that is the key factor in initiating hormonal changes associated with amenorrhea.[9]

WOMEN WHO BECOME BULIMAREXIC

My experience with bulimarexics contradicts standard psychoanalytic theory (see Figure 2). Far from rejecting the stereotype of femininity—that of the accommodating, passive, dependent woman—these young women have never questioned their assumptions that wifehood, motherhood, and intimacy with men are the fundamental components of femininity. I came to understand that their obsessive pursuit of thinness constitutes not only an acceptance of this ideal but an exaggerated striving to achieve it.[10] Their attempts to control their physical appearance demonstrate a disproportionate concern with pleasing others, particularly men—a reliance on others to validate their sense of worth.[11] They have devoted their lives to fulfilling the feminine *role* rather than the individual person. None has developed a basic sense of personal power or of self-worth.

Bruch says that these women have a basic *delusion* "of not having an identity of their own, of not even owning their body and its sensations, with the specific inability of recognizing hunger as a sign of nutritional needs." She attributes this to, among other things, "the mother's superimposing on the child her own concept of the child's needs."[12] Thus the child, believing that she is hungry because her mother says so, has little sense of what hunger is about internally. In my experience with these women, the feeling of not having any identity is not a delusion or a misperception but a reality which need not be caused solely by the stereotyped protective mother but by other cultural, social, and psychological pressures as well.

Anne, for example, was a good, generally submissive child. She had lived her life the way "she was supposed to"—precisely her problem. She had been socialized by her parents to believe that society would reward her good looks: "Some day the boys are going to go crazy over you." "What a face! With your good looks you'll never have to worry about getting a job." Clinging and dependent, she could not see herself as a separate person. Our early sessions had an unreal quality. I searched for a glimpse of unique character, but Anne had no identifiable sense of self from which to project a real person. Her dependency on others prevented any development of self. Most of the women in my study had been rewarded for their physical attractiveness and submissive "goodness," while characteristics such as independence, self-reliance, and assertiveness were generally punished by parents, grandparents, teachers, and peers. Peggy said, "I was always a tomboy. In fact at the age of ten to twelve I was stronger and faster than any of the boys. After I won a race against a boy, I was given the cold shoulder by the rest of the boys in my class. The girls teased me and my parents put pressure on me to 'start acting like a girl should.' I did, and stopped having as much fun."

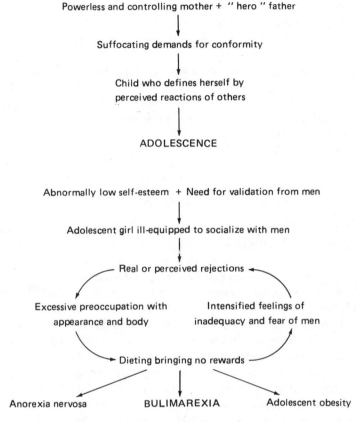

FIGURE 2. Development of bulimarexic behavior.

Wulff refers to an intense, unconscious mother hate in these women. In my experience they were, on the contrary, painfully conscious of despising their mothers, most of whom they described as weak and unhappy, women who had abandoned careers in order to raise children. "My mother wanted to be a lawyer but gave it all up when she married my father." Though the mothers are painted as generally ineffectual, they do exercise power in one limited realm: over their children. There, as if they are compensating for their misery elsewhere, they are often suffocating, dominating, and manipulative. Rather than rejecting the passive-aggressive behavior of their mothers and with it the more destructive results of such behavior, the women to whom I listened described their struggle for a social acceptance that would allow them to enact their mother's role. Most of them also strongly identified with their fathers, despite the fact that many fathers spent little time with their families. Instead, they concentrated on interests outside the home. Some of the women reported that the fathers were more persistent in their demands for prettiness and feminine behavior than the mothers. Fathers were objects of hero worship, even though they were preoccupied, distant, or emotionally rejecting.

A distorted concept of body size, a characteristic of the anorexics described by Bruch and of the bulimarexics I have studied, is related to the parental and societal expectations that emphasize physical appearance. At the first session with Anne, I was struck by the utter distortion of her body size. She complained frequently of how fat she was; I saw her as exceedingly thin.

> M. B.-L.: Why don't you stand up and point out to me where you experience
>   yourself as fat.
> ANNE: Here . . . here . . . everywhere. [She jabbed and pulled.]

I noted at this session that Anne's "distorted body image" was linked to a complete lack of confidence in her own ability to control her behavior. She reported that she felt inadequate as a woman and that she had never been able to sustain a loving relationship with a man.

As well as striving to perfect and control their physical appearance, the bulimarexics displayed a need for achievement. All the women were high achievers academically and above average in intellect. However, in most cases the drive to achieve had as its goal pleasing parents and marrying "well." Continued success in academe was essential to feelings of self-worth, but the pressure to achieve, with its rewards, was expected to be forgotten and tucked away in exchange for the fulfillments that marriage and childbearing could bring. These women saw achievement mainly in terms of what rewards it could provoke from others. For example, a doctor is more likely to meet and desire for a mate a woman who is educated; a woman is most likely to meet this man in a university. Achievement was not seen in terms of intrinsic rewards to the self.

Obviously, women who grew up struggling to perfect the female role expect that perfection to be rewarded by fulfillment. Their expectations are founded on what they perceive to be the expectations and standards of the rest of the world for them. It is expectation that has left the women I interviewed sadly vulnerable to rejection. In adolescence they begin to look eagerly for their reward, for the men who will see them as they have struggled to be seen. But rather than being offered rows of handsome princes waiting to court, many women suffer male rejection about this time. For others the rejection was *perceived* rather than actual (i.e., these adolescent girls felt rejected if they were not pursued by males and socially active). The experience of male rejection often precipitates dieting. The girl somehow believes that the appearance of her body must be related to the reason for her rejection. Bruch describes a young woman who could trace the beginning of her anorexic behavior to an incident she experienced as a rejection.

> Celia (No. 12) had begun her noneating regimen during her second year in college, when her boyfriend commented that she weighed nearly as much as he. He was of slight build weighing only 130 lbs. and was sensitive about this, feeling that his manliness was at stake. He expressed the desire that she lose a few pounds and she went on a diet in an effort to please him. However she resented that he had "fixed" their relationship at a certain weight. When she first talked about this she said, "I completely lost my appetite"; later she added that she had been continuously preoccupied with food but denied it to herself. . . . As she began to lose weight she experienced a great sense of strength and independence.[13]

Some women reported that they were, in fact, chubby at this time, but others described themselves as slim but not slim enough, according to their ideal image of what they believed a beautiful body should look like. Along with these slimming efforts, other attempts were sometimes made to beautify the body; three women reported having their noses straightened. However, these dieting attempts also do not produce anticipated rewards (i.e., male attentiveness).

When the expectations of these women of being desired and pursued by men did not materialize, they believed themselves to be undesirable, unattractive, and unworthy. These beliefs reinforced their already existing pervasive sense of inadequacy. Fear of rejection then became a crucial motivating force in their behavior. A rejection, real or perceived, shatters the self-image of the person who has constructed that image around the expectations of others. The person adopts a behavior that will protect her against future rejection. Lee supports this view: "There was an overwhelming preoccupation with weight and a tendency to view others according to their weight as a way of defending against feelings of inadequacy and fear of rejection by others. The struggle consists of a 'relentless pursuit of thinness.' "[14]

A fear of rejection as a source of Anne's symptoms appeared rather dramatically one day. After three months, she had not been able to recall her first food binge or the circumstances that had led to it. This day she was describing a binge she had had the night before. Using Gestalt techniques, I suggested she try a role-playing fantasy, something with which she was familiar.

> M. B.-L.: OK—in that chair is your *body*. The chair you are sitting in is *the food*. Now *be the "food"* and tell your body what you are doing and why.
> ANNE: I'm your food and I'm going into you now . . . stuffing you . . . making you disgusting . . . fat. I'm your shame and I'm making you untouchable.

No one will ever touch you now. That's what you want . . . that no one will touch you. [She looked up in surprise.]

M. B.-L.: Are you surprised about something you just said?

ANNE: Yes. About not being touched . . . [silence].

M. B.-L.: Is that something you feel you could get into talking about now?

ANNE: Yes, I guess it might be important . . . . When I was fifteen [three years ago] I was on a cruise down the Snake River. I impulsively decided I didn't want to be a virgin anymore and since I liked the boat man, I decided to let him make love to me. The only thing is I got drunk, passed out, and that's when he did it to me. I didn't remember anything the next day except feeling miserable and disgusted with myself. And the worst part was this guy didn't want anything to do with me after that. After this happened I lost some weight because I felt maybe I was too fat and that this is what had turned him off. Shortly after I lost weight I had my first binge, and it's gone on ever since.

The first rejection often becomes a pattern. Many women revert to dependent behavior, which assures the repetition of the rejection. Anne would meet a man, "fall in love," and eventually drive him away by growing increasingly possessive and clinging. She then tried to compensate for what she perceived as a failure, attempting to alter herself through fasting in order to accommodate to some mysterious standard of perfection men held. Other women become supercritical of most men they encounter, thereby eliminating the possibility of warm and loving relationships.

Another of my patients, Linda, petite, soft-spoken, and lovely, says of her first binge:

Well, my mother thinks it all started after I was rejected by a boy in my junior year of high school . . . [silence] . . . he was my first boyfriend, and I was really crazy about him. One day he just dropped me without any explanation. . . . I never did find out what I had done. It was so confusing. . . . I was really depressed. Shortly after I had my nose fixed and began to diet. I wasn't fat, but it was the Twiggy era, and I can't remember exactly, but I started to binge somewhere around that time, but I don't really know if there's any connection.

THE PSYCHODYNAMICS OF THE BINGE AND PURGE

The cycle the bulimarexic endures can be physically damaging (see Figure 3). The women report fasting, habitual forced vomiting, and amphetamine and laxative abuse as means to counteract a binge. However, for these young women who have been "good" girls, and who are afraid of parental disapproval and the rejection that might result from sexual activity, food is one of the few elements in their tightly regulated lives that they can choose to indulge excessively. For the person who is struggling to meet unrealistic goals by imposing severe and ascetic control over herself, the binge is a release.

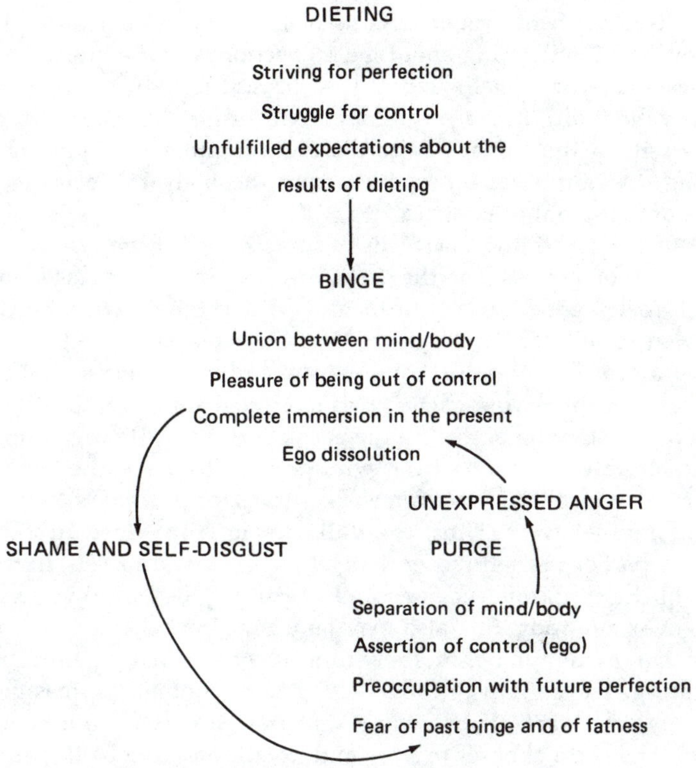

DIETING

Striving for perfection

Struggle for control

Unfulfilled expectations about the

results of dieting

BINGE

Union between mind/body

Pleasure of being out of control

Complete immersion in the present

Ego dissolution

UNEXPRESSED ANGER

SHAME AND SELF-DISGUST   PURGE

Separation of mind/body

Assertion of control (ego)

Preoccupation with future perfection

Fear of past binge and of fatness

FIGURE 3. The psychodynamics of bulimarexia.

ANNE: When I am into a binge it doesn't matter if I have just eaten . . . I just
go crazy . . . completely out of control. Whatever is around I eat . . .
candy . . . four or five bars . . . a whole quart of ice cream. If I am in the
cafeteria, I fill my plate with everything. I then go back for seconds,
thirds, and even more. I eat until I feel sick. After I binge I feel disgusted with myself and start my fast. I don't eat anything except liquids
for a few days. I usually stick to this for as long as a week.

Moreover, the binge brings about a union between the mind and body.
One gives one's self to the food, to the moment completely. There is a
complete loss of control (ego). It is an absolute here-and-now experience,
a kind of ecstasy.

However, the giving over of one's self to this kind of experience
leads to shame and guilt. Socialization and cultural pressures intrude to
initiate the purification rites, purging or fasting. The purging represents
a concentration on past and future. In reliving the past, the self is a helpless child, rewarded for beauty and feminine passivity, punished for
being assertive and rebellious. In anticipating the future, the self preoc-

cupies itself with the repercussions of having a fat body in American culture, which will bring about male rejection. For the bulimarexic, ego manifests itself in social symbols (i.e., beautiful body = male approval = self-validation). Because the binge will bring about an ugly body, it carries with it the threat of ego dissolution and social humiliation. In purging, the mind separates itself from the body by focusing on the shame of being out of control.

A feature of fasting that feeds the persistence of the syndrome is the false sense of power that the faster derives from her starvation. The woman feels "good," in control," and "disciplined" when her life has narrowed to self-denial. Bruch refers to anorexia as a "struggle for control for a sense of identity, competence, and effectiveness." She writes that many of these youngsters "had struggled for years to make themselves over and to be perfect in the eyes of others."[15] What her otherwise reasonable interpretation of the syndrome overlooks is the fact that the fasting behavior in this syndrome also strives for power and control over the bulimic behavior. Thus, the bulimarexic is involved in a struggle against a part of the self rather than a struggle toward a self. In the early stages of the syndrome, the adolescent girl may be asserting ownership rights over her body. She also may be using this behavior as a passive-aggressive reaction to her mother whom she perceives as controlling and suffocating. The refusal of food—along with compulsive masturbation, nailbiting, etc.—are all behaviors that the parents cannot completely control. The child chooses privacy and isolation for her acting out. However, when bulimia first occurs the nature of the syndrome undergoes a transformation. The underlying beliefs about one's self ("I am unlovable, unattractive, and inadequate") are pervasive and make the woman extraordinarily sensitive to the reactions of other people toward her. The most minor or insignificant slight is exaggerated and distorted, creating massive self-loathing, and is used as an *excuse* for binge-ing. The anger the women feels toward her imagined rejector is not acknowledged, and this unexpressed anger is turned inward, adding to the fury of the binge.

The fast–binge cycle of the bulimarexic is confining. It consumes enough energy to prevent the woman from looking beyond it or outgrowing it. It serves to keep her socially isolated. Binge-ing wards off people with a "wall of [perceived] fat." It is a way of "filling up " without needing others. A fairly typical example from Anne's case supports this hypothesis. Anne was invited to go out to dinner by a boy she really liked; she wanted to go but was on the fasting part of her cycle. She feared the temptation and thus worked herself into a high state of anxiety, fearing a binge and vacillating between going and staying home. On the date, she ate moderately and had an enjoyable time. When the man dropped her off, she proceeded to binge grotesquely.

The fact that the behavior is a secret one, carried out in private, further isolates the bulimarexic. For her food becomes a *fetish*, as Becker uses the term in "Fetishism as Low Self-Esteem."

> "General inactivity," "low self-esteem," and "sense of inadequacy" indicate that the fetishist is a person who has sentenced himself (herself) to live in a certain kind of object world. It will be shallow in terms of the complexity and richness of its objects; it will represent a narrow commitment instead of a broad and flexible one; yet it will be a segment of the world which has to bear a full load of life meaning. In other words, the fetishist will be a behaviorally poor person, who has the resourceful task of creating a rich world. As we said, the record of that resourceful contriving is the fetish behavior itself.[16]

A FEMINIST PERSPECTIVE

None of the women in this study had ever experienced a satisfying love relationship in spite of their attractiveness and high intelligence. All longed for one. Most were virgins. Others froze up when sexual overtures were made or developed severe anxiety or depression during or after sex. The sexual conflicts that are evident in these women do not reflect a rejection of femininity or a bizarre fear of oral impregnation.[17] Rather, these women have already learned a passive and accommodating approach to life from their parents and their culture. This accommodation is combined with two opposing tensions: the desperate desire for self-validation from a man, and an inordinate *fear of men* and their power to reject. Since most of the women have already experienced a real or perceived rejection by a male or males, this perpetuates the already larger than life belief in the power and importance of men. The sexual fears of these women are often associated with intercourse, which is viewed as an act of surrender exposing their vulnerability to rejection. Rather than finding an obsession with bizarre fantasies (oral impregnation), I found a preoccupation with the fear of rejection in sex, of not being good enough to please a man.

If the woman is able to find a male companion who loves her, in spite of the obstacles her behavior presents to the relationship, a remission of symptoms might occur. This relationship, while relieving the surface of the bulimarexic's problem, can be more ultimately destructive. If the woman has not strengthened her sense of self and self-worth, the future of the relationship can be at best uncertain; failure of the relationship can be devastating.

Why is it that the bulimarexic gives men the power to reject her? Why does she give up her own power and make men larger than life? A reasonable answer, one more direct than that found in a theory of the innate psychology of women, lies in our heritage of sexual inequality. As Miller says, "our male dominated society creates a system of values in which men and women tend to believe that the only meaningful relationships are with men. Men attempt to win esteem by achievement and their attention lies in the sphere outside the family. And since the women define themselves in terms of their success in holding the love of men, a system of mutual frustration develops and the children become the repository."[18] Between the ages of 13 and 17, these adolescent girls find that society in general and men in particular do not reward them as they have been socialized by both their parents and their culture to *expect*. Obviously, this image of men affects a woman not only as a daughter but as a mother. It is my conviction that the mothers of these women became what they are for the same reasons that their daughters became bulimarexics. Most women are socialized to dependency to some degree. Laws has summarized ways in which this affects women:

> Social dependence, as a habit of responding, has a number of consequences. . . . First, the reliance on rewards coming from others makes the individual very flexible and adaptable, ready to alter her behavior (or herself) in response to words and threats. Second, she is limited to others as a source of rewards, including self-esteem, for two reasons: (1) the necessity of being accommodating and responsive works against the development of a sense of self which might oppose the demands of others, and (2) any evidence of the development of the self as a source of approval or of alternative directions is punished by others. The "responsiveness" and the sole reliance on social support make the woman extraordinarily vulnerable to rejection (meaning failure).[19]

Many traditional approaches to therapy with women see men as solutions to problems of low self-esteem. Syzrynski exaggerates these assumptions when he suggests that "since a great majority of such patients are adolescent girls, a male therapist may be probably more effective than a woman. He can replace for the girl her inadequate father figure; on the other hand, he will not be identified by the patient with her hostile mother."[20] I believe, on the contrary, that female therapists can provide positive female role models for these women which are a marked contrast to the negative experiences they recount in relationships with their mothers. In addition, it is unrealistic to expect that the presence of a man, or any other person, can compensate for a nonexistent sense of self. It is equally unrealistic to expect a man to want to serve this function. I can only offer a pessimistic prognosis for the woman who looks at the accession of an approving man as the solution to her psychological conflicts.[21] Since anorexia nervosa and bulimarexia are appearing with greater frequency,[22] I can only hope that the increasing number of women suffering from these syndromes can avail themselves of a humane therapy to help alleviate the low self-esteem that is at the root of their problems.

NOTES

1. Judith Long Laws, "Woman as Object," *The Second XX* (New York: Elsevier Publishing Co., 1978).
2. Four men who reported the binge-ing–starving behavior were also treated. I saw three of these men in individual therapy. Since the writing of this paper I have been engaged in therapeutic interventions and research designed to test some of these theoretical arguments. Taking advantage of a new philosophical and innovative movement within our mental health clinic, I attempted an outreach program designed to break through the isolation and shame experienced by women who are food bingers. In September 1974, an ad was placed in our university newspaper describing the symptom and offering a group experience with a feminist orientation that would utilize Gestalt and behaviorist techniques. Sixty women responded; 15 were admitted to the group. Some of the before, after, and follow-up measurements administered were: questionnaires specifically dealing with the binge–fast behavior and early childhood training; a body cathexis test (P. Secord and S. Jourard, "The Appraisal of Body-Cathexis: Body-Cathexis and the Self," *Journal of Consulting Psychology* 17[1953]: 343–47); and the Sixteen Personality Factor questionnaire (R. B. Cattell. *The 16 P-F* [Champaign, Ill.: Institute for Personality and Ability Testing, 1972]). Based on the success of this initial group, two subsequent groups have been run and data collected. Our outreach program, designed as a preventive intervention, revealed a much larger population manifesting this behavior than had been suspected. After seeing 138 women and four men in two years at our clinic and systematically studying 80 of these with a variety of tests and other measurements, we are now working on developing an operational definition of the bulimarexic syndrome, analyzing our data for publication, and outlining a new therapeutic approach to this problem.
3. Hilda Bruch, *Eating Disorders* (New York: Basic Books, 1973), pp. 82, 251–54.
4. V. Szyrynski, "Anorexia Nervosa and Psychotherapy," *American Journal of Psychotherapy* 27, no. 2 (October 1973): 492–505.
5. M. Wulff, "Ueber einen interessanten oralen Symptomenkomplex und seine Beziehung zur sucht," in *The Psychoanalytic Theory of Neuroses*, ed. Otto Fenichel (New York: W. W. Norton & Co., 1945), p. 241
6. Robert Lindner, "The Case of Laura," *The Fifty-Minute Hour* (New York: Holt, Rinehart & Winston, 1955.)
7. Bruch, p. 217.
8. J. V. Waller, R. M. Kaufman, and F. Deutsch, "Anorexia Nervosa: A Psychosomatic Entity," *Psychosomatic Medicine* 2 (September 1940): 3–16.
9. R. M. Boyer et al., "Anorexia Nervosa: Immaturity of the 24-Hour Luteinizing Hormone Secretory Pattern," *New England Journal of Medicine* 291 (October 24, 1974): 861–65.
10. I am indebted to Dr. Ronald Leifer for his insights into the implications of bulimarexic behavior and to Janet Snoyer and Holly Bailey for their assistance.
11. The four male bingers I interviewed exhibited the following striking commonalities with the women in the study: (1) all complained of feelings of inadequacy and help-

lessness and exhibited abnormally low self-esteem: (2) all were extremely dependent and passive individuals who worked very hard at pleasing their parents through academic achievement; (3) all expressed feeling inadequate because they had never been able to sustain relationships with women, and, indeed, all had suffered female rejection in adolescence, which left them fearful of women and further encouraged their isolation; (4) all described their parents as excessively repressive. Unlike the women in the study, the men strongly identified with their mothers and expressed hostility toward their fathers whom they experienced as demanding and authoritarian. All had been pushed into athletics at an early age by their fathers. Although none were overweight as children and some were, in fact, slight of build, they became preoccupied with weight because of their desire to maintain slim and athletic bodies.

12. Hilda Bruch, "Children Who Starve Themselves," *The New York Times Magazine* (November 10, 1974), p. 70.

13. Bruch, *Eating Disorders*, p. 268.

14. A. O. Lee, "Disturbance of Body Image in Obesity and Anorexia Nervosa," *Smith College Studies in Social Work* 44(1973): 33–34.

15. Bruch, *Eating Disorders*, p. 251.

16. Ernest Becker, *Angel in Armor* (New York: Free Press, 1969), pp. 18–19.

17. Normal adolescent girls often express a fear of oral impregnation. These fears occur between the ages of 10 and 13 and usually are connected with inaccurate sexual information and imagined parental disapproval. Since such fears are so often experienced by normal women, I can see no basis for assuming that these fears foster anorexic behavior.

18. Jean B. Miller, "Sexual In-Equality: Men's Dilemma; a Note on the Oedipus Complex, Paranoia, and Other Psychological Concepts," *American Journal of Psychoanalysis* 32, no. 2 (April 1972): 140–55.

19. Laws (n.1.)

20. Szyrynski (n. 4), p. 502. In the cases of the three men I saw in individual therapy, the same Gestalt-behaviorist approach used with women was utilized. It emphasized awareness, responsibility, assertiveness training, and male consciousness raising. In all cases, at a particular stage in the therapy it was decided that a male therapist would be useful to deal with issues of sexuality, and these patients were then referred to a male counselor with a similar therapeutic orientation. All eventually gave up the bulimarexic behavior and reported many positive changes in their attitudes toward themselves, women, and their parents.

21. The extent to which such attitudes prevail in our culture is indicated by the account of a "cured" anorexic. "I fell in love. By no means do I want to suggest that love is the answer to everything. For me, loving someone shifted my attention away from the compulsive, convoluted world of self I had created inside me, toward another person. Finally, I felt some self-esteem because I had been found worthy by someone else" (Kathryn Lynch, "Danger! You Can Overdo Dieting," *Seventeen* 24 [March 1974]: 107).

22. With a few exceptions, most of the literature on these behaviors has not acknowledged this upward trend. One exception is the British study by May Duddle, "An Increase of Anorexia Nervosa in a University Population," *British Journal of Psychiatry* 123 (December 1973): 711–12. Most of the food bingers I have encountered know of other women who binge. I suspect that most cases are seen in a high school guidance office or college mental health service. Many more women probably suffer secretly from this compulsion and do not seek help because of inordinate shame about their behaviors.

Emotional Intimacy among Men   13

ROBERT A. LEWIS

This article is not about sexual behavior between men, nor about typical male friendships; it is concerned with something in between, i.e., emotional intimacy. Emotional intimacy is defined in behavioral terms as mutual self-disclosure and other kinds of verbal sharing, as declarations of liking or loving the other, and as demonstrations of affection such as hugging and nongenital caressing.

Cultural prohibitions in America, as well as in many other Western nations, frown strongly upon the demonstration of intimacy between men, such as adult males openly sharing affection in public. As a consequence, many American males in adult life have never had a close male friend nor known what it means to love and care for a male friend without the shadow of some guilt and fear of peer ridicule (Komarovsky, 1974; Pleck, 1975a; Goldberg, 1976). Because of these restrictive norms, even those who have male friends usually have experienced little trust, little personal sharing, and low emotional investments in these friendships (Jourard, 1971; Fasteau, 1972, 1974; Steinmann and Fox, 1974; Pleck, 1974, 1975a; Goldberg, 1976). There is more than a little irony in the keen observation that many American men report their closest male relationships as those discovered through war or sports, i.e., when they are bonded together to kill others (Fasteau, 1974).

Don Clark, a psychologist who has worked frequently with all-male groups, has reflected:

> Men need more from one another than they believe they are permitted to have. Expression of positive affect, or affection, between men is seriously inhibited in our culture. Negative affect is acceptable. Men can argue, fight, and injure one another in public view, but they cannot as easily hold hands, embrace, or kiss. When emotions in any area are blocked in expression, they seek other outlets, in distorted form if necessary. (1972, p. 368)

Reprinted from *Journal of Social Issues* 34(1):108–121, 1978. Copyright©1978 by The Society of the Psychological Study of Social Issues. Reprinted by permission.

DEFICITS IN EMOTIONAL INTIMACY

Research on male friendships suggests that most males are not very emotionally intimate with other males. Two studies (Olstad, 1975; Powers and Bultena, 1976) suggest that, although men may report more same-sex friendships than women do, these friendships are not close or intimate. For instance, Olstad's study of Oberlin college students reported that the majority of Oberlin males had more male best friends than female best friends. Yet these males tended to place greater confidence in, consulted more about important decisions, and spent more time together with their best female friends than with their best male friends. Powers and Bultena (1976) in a statewide study in Iowa interviewed 234 noninstitutionalized adults who were 70 years or older. Their findings suggested that the aged males had more frequent social contacts than did the aged females, but that the males basically limited their social interaction to their children and their children's families, and to spouses. The aged men also were less likely than the women to have intimate friends and were less likely to replace their lost friends.

Similar findings have been discussed by Knupfer, Clark, and Room (1966), who found unmarried males to have less close relationships with both sexes than females had. Finally, Nye (1976) reported that married men also went less to same-sex and other-sex friends for "therapeutic" purposes than their wives did.

Self-disclosure, a vital component of emotional intimacy, has been reported in many studies to be either very low or utterly lacking between males (Jourard, 1971). Similarly, in Komarovsky's survey of males at an Ivy League college (1974, 1976), college males disclosed themselves much more to their closest female friend than to their closest male friend. For most men, apparently, it is difficult and embarrassing to tell one's best male friend that he is liked. A recent nationwide survey (Peleck, Note 1) reported that a majority—58% of all males questioned—had not told their best male friend that they liked him. If the disclosure of liking one another is so difficult, it is little wonder that hugging, holding hands, caressing, and kissing, which are allowed between close male friends in some cultures, are not often observed in our own culture.

The lack of emotional intimacy between men is currently being decried from a number of quarters. Some writers have even taken the position that the absence of intimate behavior among men is a microcosm spreading to many social problems. Goldberg (1976) argues that the absence of a loving, close male relationship is strongly related to the significantly higher suicide rates among males, especially among divorced males. The Berkeley Men's Center Manifesto (1973), perhaps the first declaration of men's liberation, contains these words:

> We, as men want to take back our full humanity.... We want to relate to both women and men in more human ways—with warmth, sensitivity, emotion, and honesty. We want to share our feelings with one another to break down the walls and grow closer. We want to be equal with women and end destructive, competitive relationships between men.... We are oppressed by this dependence on women for support, nurturing, love, and warm feelings. We want to love, nurture, and support ourselves and other men, as well as women.... We want men to share their lives and experiences with each other in order to understand who we are, how we got this way, and what we must do to be free.

In a similar voice, Pleck and Sawyer have stated:

> Many of us are still working out in our own lives just what degree of emotional and sexual intimacy we want with others, both male and female. However each of us works this out, many of us already know that the traditional masculine role allows much less emotional expression with other males than we want, and that we must seek more. (1974, p. 75)

BARRIERS TO INTIMACY BETWEEN MEN

Competition

A number of recent essays have traced some of the barriers to male intimacy to norms prescribed by American society (Fasteau, 1974; Pleck, 1974, 1975b; Brannon, 1976; Goldberg, 1976). Pleck (1975b), for instance, attributes much affectional inhibition among men to our society's stress upon competition—what Brannon (1976) has called the "Big Wheel" dimension of the traditional male sex role. Pleck traces a number of ancient, as well as contemporary, fables about male–male relationships that have prescribed a heavy component of competition even among friends. In fact, he suggests that, since many "power trips" are directed toward other men, in order to win more approval, wealth, and status, it is very difficult for male friends to mutually disclose themselves, since disclosure amounts to increased vulnerability in a competitive mileu.

There is some empirical evidence that male children realize at an early age that part of being a man is to compete and win. Hartley (1959), for instance, suggested that her sample of 41 boys between the ages of 8 and 11 understood clearly that a man "is supposed to be rugged, independent, able to take care of himself, and to disdain 'sissies' ... [that] they have to be able to fight in case a bully comes along; they have to be athletic; they have to be able to run fast; they must be able to play rough games; they need to know how to play many games—curb-ball, baseball, basket-ball, football" (p. 460).

Vinacke (1959), with the backing of evidence from several experimental studies, concludes that "males are primarily concerned with winning, whereas females are more oriented towards working out an equitable outcome, as satisfactory as possible to all participants" (p. 359). In another study, Vinacke and Gullickson (1964) asked triads of same-sex subjects from ages 7 to 8, 14 to 16, and college students to play a game similar to Parcheesi through which they could operationalize competition/exploitation as well as cooperative/accommodative behavior. They concluded:

> Girls at all three age levels display the characteristics of accommodative strategy. Boys, however, appear to change drastically from behavior quite similar to that of girls to the contrasting strategy which we have called "exploitative." Competitiveness . . . such behavior so typical of adult males, appears to exist only in rudimentary form in small boys. (p. 1229)

Finally, Szal (1972) reported that, while pairs of females took turns in playing games of marbles so that each won an equal number of times, pairs of males competed so strongly that neither could win many games.

Clearly, it is hard to reach out affectionately to other males beyond a superficial level if one views all males as competitors in life. Komarovsky (1974) frequently noted college males suggesting that learning to let down their guard and trust other men came with great difficulty, since they had been taught to be alert for aggressive attacks even from their friends:

> The main disadvantage of a male friend, as confidant, was his threat as a competitor. "A guy means competition." One senior explained: "I have competed with guys in sports and for girls. Once you let your guard down, the guy can hurt you and take advantage of you. Your girl has your interest at heart." "Even your best (male) friend," remarked one senior wryly, "gets a certain amount of comfort out of your difficulty. A girl friend is readier to identify with your interests and to build you up." (p. 680)

In sum, competition, which is prescribed by the traditional male role, is a barrier to intimacy between men. As DeGolia (1973) has written: "Men are kept isolated from each other through competition and fear" (p. 16). And as Verser (Note 2) has commented: "Since a main form of winning is exploiting the opponent's weaknesses, men close themselves off from each other, so that they do not expose any vulnerabilities."

Homophobia

Another barrier to intimacy between men is homophobia. Homophobia, the fear of homosexuals or the fear of one's being or appearing to be homosexual, is still very strong within our culture; this is especially the case for males. This barrier to intimacy stems from both conscious and unconscious fears that any intimacy between men may color one's sexual identity with gay colors.

It was homophobia that restricted the growth of affection between two friends in James Kirkwood's *P. S. Your Cat is Dead*, a play in which the hero relates:

> One evening about three months into our friendship, after we'd taken our dates home, we stopped by a bar for a nightcap. We ended up having three or four and when we left and were walking down the street, Pete suddenly slipped his arm around my shoulder. He surprised me; there was extreme warmth and intimacy about the gesture. When I looked over at him, he grinned as casual as possible. "Why?" He shrugged in return, then gave my shoulder a squeeze. "Ever since I've known you, you got me pretending I don't have arms." (1973, p. 23)

The fear of touching another male, unless it is roughly done as in a game of football or other contact sport, undoubtedly derives not only from strong cultural prohibitions against male homosexuality, but also from many Americans' difficulty or inability to distinguish between the sensual and the sexual.

Nearly all of the data on homophobia or negative attitudes toward homosexuality are correlational, i.e., survey findings which relate personality, demographic, and other attitudes with homophobic attitudes. Morin and Garfinkle (1978), summarizing this research, report homophobia to be more characteristic of people who are likely also to be rural, white, male, first-born, reared in the Midwest and the South, more religious, and more conforming, with personality correlates which are more authoritarian, dogmatic, intolerant of ambiguity, status conscious, sexually rigid, guilty and negative about their own sexual impulses, and less accepting of others in general. Nevertheless, Morin and Wallace (Note 3) found through a multiple regression analysis that the single best predictor of homophobia was a belief in the traditional family ideology where the father is dominant and the mother is subservient.

There is some evidence that homophobia operates to maintain social distance between gays and straights. For instance, Wolfgang and Wolfgang (1971) used the placement of stick figures to measure social distance and found subjects placing themselves significantly further from marijuana users, drug addicts, obese persons, and present and former homosexuals than from "normal" peers. Similarly, Morin, Taylor, and Kielman (Note 4) found through the methodology of chair placement that males increased their social distance about three times more than did females where a male experimenter had been identified as a gay psychologist.

There is no experimental evidence to show that homophobia prevents emotional intimacy between heterosexual men, although such a connection has been long assumed (Pleck, 1975a). In fact most writers on this subject seem to agree with Morin and Garfinkle (1978) that "fear of being labeled homosexual . . . interferes with the development of intimacy between men."

Aversion to Vulnerability and Openness

Sexual stereotypes of males in the United States usually include some allusion to males being inexpressive or emotionally controlled. Bardwick and Douvan (1971) concluded that stereotypes of masculinity dictate that big boys are made of "aggression, competitiveness, task orientation, unsentimentality, and emotional control" (p. 225). Chafetz (1974) reports from group discussions of five to six undergraduate students that most Americans characterize males as "unemotional, stoic, and don't cry" (p. 35).

Brannon's (1976) characterization of American men as always having to be "the sturdy oak," i.e., having to maintain a "manly air of toughness, confidence, and self reliance," indicates another barrier to male-male intimacy. If a man must never show any weaknesses even with his friends, he is under the additional burden of keeping secrets about his weaknesses, his errors and his pains. The result of keeping these secrets is the "inexpressive male," as exemplified in the John Wayne "cowboy syndrome" and the James Bond "playboy syndrome," which have been well described by Balswick and Peek (1971). In fact, some men become so skilled in hiding their feelings and thoughts that even their wives and closest friends do not know when they are most depressed, anxious, or afraid.

Jourard's programmatic research on self-disclosure has documented the fact that males reveal much less personal information about themselves to others than do women (Jourard, 1971; Jourard and Lasakow, 1958; Jourard and Landsman, 1969; Jourard and Richman, 1963). Not only does the male aversion to vulnerability and openness handicap attempts to achieve emotional intimacy between men, but, as Jourard (1971) has suggested, always trying to be "manly" imposes a terrible burden upon many men, imposes extra stresses, consumes much personal energy, and consequently is a factor related to males' relatively shorter life-span.

Lack of Role Models

A fourth barrier to the expression of emotional intimacy between men is the fact that many men have been presented few models or examples of affection-giving between males. In the course of a series of intimacy workshops which this author led between 1975 and 1977, more than half of the male participants have reported that they do not remember their fathers hugging them, especially after they were somewhat older children.

Although current films and books have probably portrayed friendships between males more often than between females, our popular culture is seemingly devoid of interest in male–male affection. Outside of homoerotic literature, there is little to guide men who are trying to share intimacy without sex. In a number of recent novels, men come close but do not find permission to give each other affection. For example, in *Deliverance* (Dickey, 1970) men in the wilderness are allowed to rape and murder each other but not share more than a canoe. In the novel, *Radcliffe* (Storey, 1963), two boyhood friends eventually become involved in sexual intimacy, but apparently this must end "naturally" in the murder of one and the suicide of the other. A similar ending occurs for the young athlete in *The Front Runner* (Warren, 1974).

Although the barriers to male intimacy are undoubtedly more numerous than those described here, they illustrate well why most intimacy between males is confined in our culture to games that men can play together, e.g., sports. As many current observers have noted, without a game to play, men usually do not relate well together.

THE TRADITIONAL MALE ROLE AND INTIMACY

Three of the four barriers to emotional intimacy between males stem directly from the traditional male role into which most men in our society have been socialized. That is to say, a male's acceptance of traditional male role expectations strongly reinforces his efforts to be competitive, to fear homosexuality, and to avoid personal vulnerability and openness, all of which make emotional intimacy between men more difficult to attain. The fourth barrier, the scarcity of role models, is more of a cyclical effect of male role performances from previous generations; these have been documented for middle-aged men by Steinmann and Fox (1974).

Several writers have related males' difficulties in establishing relationships to the pressures and demands of the male sex role (Fasteau, 1974; Pleck, 1974). Brannon (1976) examines four themes of traditional American masculinity ("no sissy stuff," "be a big wheel," "be the sturdy oak," and "give 'em hell") and suggests similarly that they limit the development of meaningful relationships for men. Even earlier, Jourard (1971) had examined the "lethal aspects of the male role": the ways in which traditional expectations of manliness result for men in lower self-disclosure, a lack of self-insight and empathy, incompetence at loving others and self, and " dispiritation," i.e., the condition in which a man's morale and immunity to diseases decrease as a result of his not being able to live up to stringent masculine ideals.

A growing number of research findings appear to substantiate this linkage between the traditional male role and men's difficulties in relating to both women and other men. Mussen (1962) found that men who were more masculine in adolescence were rated 20 years later as less "sociable," less "self-assured," and less "self-accepting" than the men who had been less masculine in adolescence. Hartford, Willis, and Deabler (1967) found a negative relationship also between traditional masculinity and "sensitivity" among men. The methodology of these earlier studies was limited to paper and pencil techniques. However, a recent experimental study by Bem, Martyna, and Watson (1976) has demonstrated that more masculine males have higher thresholds than either androgynous or more feminine males for displaying emotionality. Bem et al. found that the more masculine men were significantly less responsive to a male stranger who needed to talk about his loneliness and to be supported. An observational study of interaction patterns in same-sex groups (Aries, 1976) likewise suggested that men in all-male college groups were much less intimate and open than were women in all-female groups. In fact, the men talked very little of themselves, their feelings, or their relationships with significant others, whereas the women frequently did. It seems, therefore, that the sex-role demands of conventional American society powerfully limit the degree of intimacy that males may attain, especially in their relationships with other men.

INTIMACY WORKSHOP EXPERIENCES

Since 1975 I have conducted a number of workshops at men's conferences around the United States and Canada. The focus of these workshops has been the development of openness and intimacy between males. The increasing number of men who have been attracted to these workshops is some evidence that many men are desirous of closer relationships with other men.

Self-Disclosure

The first major objective in these workshops has been the opening of communication between men, most of whom are strangers. Working within small groups of two or three, the participants have been asked first to introduce themselves to one other person in the room and to tell as much about themselves as is possible within a 10 minute period. At the end of this time, each participant is then asked to introduce the other person to the larger group. The typical introduction involves a man's name, his occupation, his marital status, his residence, the number of his children if any, and sometimes even a list of his hobbies or leisure-time pursuits. All of these are predictable masculine disclosures, predictable because they involve the roles a man plays in society. In addition, these first disclosures are usually relatively "safe"—a fact which is quickly brought to the group's awareness, along with an appeal to risk more during the next group experience, such as telling things about themselves that they usually would tell only a very close friend.

Some risk-taking usually proceeds with haste and is evident in the number of self-disclosures which are indicated, although not always shared with the entire group, during the second reporting period. About this time the intensity of the small group interaction usually breaks forth in very spontaneous and unpredictable fashion. In spite of the fact that the workshop is a relatively artificial social group of strangers, the breakthroughs in terms of self-disclosure are amazing. Participants have described later to us how for the first time in their life they were able to share thoughts and feelings about which they had never before spoken. One man described it this way:

> I have never even told my wife about that feeling I have often had. Now, I cannot wait to get home and tell her. What a relief this is for me.

Self-disclosure is probably one of the most difficult forms of intimacy to initiate and facilitate between men. This is probably due to the fact that even as young boys, men have been taught to play it "cool and tough" (Hartley, 1959). No wonder that by the time most men are adults, they disclose much less about themselves than women do, especially to other males. And yet, we have found that many of the barriers to self-disclosure melt away in these workshops where permission is given to disclose oneself and one is surrounded by the acceptance and warm support of other men.

Extending Affection

A second series of exercises usually focuses upon the achievement of some physical intimacy, such as touching hands. In spite of many initial inhibitions, we have found most groups eager to be involved in a physical way. Although there are still signs of embarrassment and timidity for some men, most are able to complete the remaining intimacy exercises which involve further self-disclosure while touching or holding hands and looking directly into another man's eyes. The averting of eyes is another barrier to male intimacy (Argyle , 1967) which takes concerted efforts to break.

The greatest breakthroughs to demonstrating affection, however, usually are achieved through a larger group experience of affection. One of the most popular is the group hug, a configuration formed by men holding hands and winding themselves into a tight human coil. As some participants have related: "You lose contact of where you begin and end in the group hug," and "If this is what a football huddle feels like, I wish I had gone out for the varsity." An activity such as the group hug or any of the many trust exercises used in growth groups usually gives visual evidence of a sudden release from inhibitions which were still evident in the smaller dyadic and triadic groups. Whether this dynamic release from earlier inhibitions is due to the greater anonymity within the larger group or due to the total accumulation of experiences is not known. The final products, however, have been a proliferation of many spontaneous acts of intimacy witnessed throughout the room, amid laughing and hugging. Fairly common have been open-ended invitations by one or more of the participants, such as overt requests for the demonstration of affection. One typical comment has been: "I never get enough hugs, so, anyone who wants to hug me can." And, interestingly, not one of these invitations has ever been ignored.

COPING WITH INVITATIONS TO INTIMACY

One concern which has not yet risen in these workshops but which seems to be a problematic area voiced by individuals who are learning to be emotionally intimate is the question: how do males cope with unwanted invitations to intimacy? Also, how do I know the amount and type of intimacy that I wish from a male friend? Finally, how can I keep the intimacy to a level and kind that I also desire, that will not threaten other intimate relationships, such as a marriage or other meaningful relationships with women? In particular, the opening of emotionally warm relationships between males may also involve the exposing of one's life to many new relationship problems, such as jealousy, rejection, and the fear of rejection.

Some men have experienced one or more of these problems firsthand in their early attempts at learning to relate to another male at a more intimate level. For instance, some have taken risks later in their ongoing friendships by honestly sharing their feelings of liking or loving. Fortunately, none of these revelations have been met with physical violence or reactions that have threatened these ongoing friendships.

Out of all possible reactions to overt male protestations of liking or loving one could envision the following points along an entire continuum of reactions: (a) Physical violence or other hostile rejection, e.g., the revealee beating up the revealor; (b) obvious repulsion experienced by the revealee toward revealor with subsequent attempts to avoid revealor; (c) no reaction, such as attempts to ignore the message and the sender or creating a momentary diversion so that revealee does not have to deal with an uncomfortable situation; (d) acceptance of the message with no reciprocity of similar feelings of love or liking; and (e) acceptance with reciprocity of similar protestations.

The finding of most responses from my friends falling into category (d) perhaps tells more about my friends than about the process of coping with typical invitations to intimacy, since many are counselors and therapists who have learned to handle feelings of transference and countertransference. However, that which my ethnomethodological experiments have thus far not taught is how to handle rejection from males. Upon entering the dating game in adolescence, men learn to cope with rejections by females. But how do men learn to cope with personal rejections by males? It may be that the male ego may prove too fragile or friendships too few to allow many of us to continue these attempts at establishing greater emotional intimacy with other men.

For some men, learning to extend the boundaries of friendship in new directions has not only become a fresh way to know themselves but also the opening of a new universe of experiences in emotional intimacy. However, this virgin territory already appears to be mixed bag of positive and negative elements.

In respect to negative outcomes, some men have vocalized their having been hurt in terms of: (a) being openly rejected by one who was formerly their friend; (b) being open to negative labeling by friends and others who either misunderstand one's motivations or are threatened by them; (c) being susceptible to easy manipulation by those one has attempted to trust and with whom one has risked some deeper interaction; and (d) having to define themselves as persons who are dependent to some degree upon other men for emotional support.

The positive outcomes of initiating intimacy with other men have been described to us in terms of: (a) discovering new parts of the personality through learning to share and care for other males, (b) opening oneself to a novel range of previously unknown feelings and experiences, and (c) the growth of very satisfying and meaningful relationships with other men.

As one male participant evaluated his workshop experiences: "It's a shame that all my life I've been taught that I could love only one half of the human race, the female half. I'm really grateful that I'm now free of that limitation on my life."

REFERENCE NOTES

1. Pleck, J. *Male sex role behaviors in a representative national sample.* Paper presented at the Conference on New Research on Women, University of Michigan, 1975
2. Verser, J. *Men and competition.* Unpublished manuscript, 1976.
3. Morin, S., and Wallace, S. *Traditional values, sex-role stereotyping and attitudes toward homosexuality.* Paper presented at the meeting of the Western Psychological Association, Los Angeles, April 1976.
4. Morin, S., Taylor. K., and Kielman, S. *Gay is beautiful at a distance.* Paper presented at the meeting of the American Psychological Association, Chicago, August 1975.

REFERENCES

Argyle, M. *The psychology of interpersonal behavior.* Baltimore: Penguin, 1967.

Aries, E. Male–female interpersonal styles in all male, all female and mixed groups. In A. G. Sargent (Ed.) *Beyond sex roles.* St. Paul: West & Co., 1976.

Balswick, J., and Peek, C. The inexpressive male: A tragedy of American society. *The Family Coordinator,* 1971, *20,* 363–368.

Bardwick, J., and Douvan, E. Ambivalence: The socialization of women. In V. Gornick and B. Moran (Eds.)., *Women in sexist society. New York: American Library, 1971.*

Bem, S., Martyna, W., and Watson, C. Sex typing and androgyny: Further explorations of the expressive domain. *Journal of Personality and Social Psychology,* 1976, *34* 1016–1023.

Berkeley Men's Center. Berkeley Men's Center Manifesto. In J. H. Pleck and J. Sawyer (Eds.), *Men and masculinity.* Englewood Cliffs, N.J.: Prentice-Hall, 1974.

Brannon, R. The male sex role: Our culture's blueprint of manhood, and what it's done for us lately. In D. David and R. Brannon (Eds.), *The forty-nine percent majority: The male sex role.* Reading, MA: Addison-Wesley, 1976.

Chafetz, J. *Masculine/Feminine or human.* Itasca, Il: F. E. Peacock, 1974.

Clark, D. Homosexual encounter in all-male groups. In L. Solomon and B. Berzon (Eds.), *New perspectives on encounter groups.* San Francisco: Jossey-Bass, 1972.

DeGolia, R. Thoughts on men's oppression. *Issues in Radical Therapy,* 1973, 14–17.

Dickey, J. *Deliverance.* New York: Dell, 1970.

Fasteau, M. F. Why aren't we talking? *MS.,* July 1972.

Fasteau, M. F. *The male Machine.* New York: McGraw-Hill, 1974.

Goldberg, H. *The hazards of being male: Surviving the myth of masculine privilege.* New York: Nash, 1976.

Hartley, R. Sex role pressures in the socialization of the male child. *Psychological Reports,* 1959, *5,* 457–468.

Harford, T., Willis, C., and Deabler, H. Personality correlates of masculinity-femininity. *Psychological Reports, 67,5,* 457–468.

Jourard, S. *The transparent self.* New York: D. Van Nostrand, 1971.

Jourard, S., and Landsman, M. Cognition, cathexis, and the "dyadic effect" in men's self-disclosing behavior. *Merrill-Palmer Quarterly,* 1969, *6,* 178–186.

Jourard, S., and Lasakow, P. Some factors in self-disclosure. *Journal of Abnormal and Social Psychology,* 1958, 56, 91–98.

Jourard, S., and Richman. P. Disclosure output and input in college students. *Merrill-Palmer Quarterly,* 1963, 9, 141–148.

Kirkwood, J. *P.S. your cat is dead.* New York: Warner Communications, 1973.

Komarovsky, M. Patterns of self-disclosure of male undergraduates. *Journal of Marriage and the Family,* 1974, *36,* 677–686.

Komarovsky, M. *Dilemmas of masculinity: A study of college youth.* Norton, 1976.

Knupfer, G., Clark, W., and Room, R. The mental health of the unmarried. *American Journal of Psychiatry,* 1966, *122,* 841–851.

Morin S., and Garfinkle, E. M. Male homophobia. *Journal of Social Issues,* 1978, *34* (1).

Mussen, P. Long-term consequents of masculinity of interests in adolescence. *Journal of Consulting Psychology,* 1962, *26,* 435–440.

Nye, F. I. *Role structure and analysis of the family.* Beverly Hills, CA: Sage, 1976.

Olstad, K. Brave new men: A basis for discussion. In J. Petras (Ed.), *Sex: Male/Gender: Masculine.* Port Washington, NY: Alfred, 1975.

Pleck, J. My male sex role—And ours. *Win,* 1974 *10,* 8–12.

Pleck, J. Male–male friendship: Is brotherhood possible? In M. Glazer (Ed.), *Old family/ New family: Interpersonal relationships.* Van Nostrand Reinhold, 1975. (a)

Pleck, J. Issues for the men's movement: Summer, 1975. *Changing Men: A Newsletter for Men Against Sexism,* 1975, 21–23. (b)

Pleck, J., and Sawyer, J. (Eds.). *Men and masculinity.* Englewood Cliffs, NJ: Prentice-Hall, 1974.

Powers, E., and Bultena, G. Sex differences in intimate friendships of old age. *Journal of Marriage and the Family,* 1976, *38,* 739–747.

Steinmann, A., and Fox, D. *The male dilemma.* New York: Jason Aronson, 1974.

Storey, D. *Radcliffe.* New York: Avon Books, 1963.

Szal, J. *Sex differences in the cooperative and competitive behaviors of nursery school children.* Unpublished master's thesis, Stanford University, 1972.

Vinacke, W. E. Sex roles in a three-person game. *Sociometry,* 1959, *22,* 343–360.

Vinacke, W. E., and Gullickson, G. R. Age and sex differences in the formation of coalitions. *Child Development,* 1964, *35,* 1217–1231.

Warren, P. N. *The front runner.* Bantam Books, 1974.

Wolfgang, A., and Wolfgang, J. Exploration of attitudes via physical interpersonal distance toward the obese, drug users, homosexuals, police and other marginal figures. *Journal of Clinical Psychology,* 1971, *27,* 510–512.

C. Violence and Psychiatric Disorders

It is in the body of work on victimization of females (rape, incest, wife abuse) that the most extensive reformulation of traditional psychological theories of women's pain and suffering has occurred. In the previous section, we discussed the limitations of theories of masochism for explaining these phenomena. Using an alternative model, this group of articles conceptualizes violence against women as one of the most destructive consequences of the inequality in existing social institutions. Unfortunately, it is within the institutions of marriage and family that females are most vulnerable to physical and sexual assault.

The first article, "Victims of Violence and Psychiatric Illness," by Elaine (Hilberman) Carmen, Patricia Perri Rieker, and Trudy Mills, explores the relationship between physical and sexual abuse and the subsequent development of psychiatric disorders serious enough to require hospitalization. This is one of the few studies that compare the experiences of males and females in terms of both patterns of abuse and responses to the abuse. We found that almost half of the inpatient sample had histories of physical and/or sexual abuse, and 90% of the abuse occurred in the context of family. Female patients were much more likely than males to have histories of abuse and to be vulnerable to abuse throughout their lives.

We observed some differences in the behavioral responses to victimization in males and females that parallel differences in sex-role socialization. Abused females generally became more passive and internalized their anger, while abused males more often directed their anger toward others. We want to emphasize, however, that the psychic trauma that arises from abuse is similar for males and females and has important implications for treatment. These include victims' inability to trust, which delays or prevents the development of a therapeutic liaison; impaired self-esteem, in which abused patients judge themselves as undeserving of treatment; and, finally, difficulty in coping with aggression, in which anger is destructively directed toward the damaged self or others.

It is when we look at specific forms of abuse, as the next three chapters do, that we see more clearly how violence against women and children is generated by patriarchal family structures. Elaine Hilberman, in "Overview: The 'Wife-Beater's Wife' Reconsidered," presents alternative social and psychological perspectives for understanding and treating abused wives. She makes a compelling case for why traditional psychiatric theories that view the violence as representing "some intrapsychic liability on the part of the victim" not only are inadequate causal explanations but also have serious treatment implications: "if the victim can be seen as provoking or needing the abuse, mental health professionals can more comfortably focus on the 'meaning' of the violence than on the fact of the violence per se."

In reconsidering why women remain in violent relationships, Hilberman suggests that "clinicians must identify the woman's internal and external barriers to self-protection in order to help her become capable of action to terminate the violence or the marriage." She defines a specific traumatic stress disorder in abused wives that is one of the important internal deterrents to self-protection, and links this syndrome to fears of losing control of aggression. Finally, she describes the expanded options available for therapeutic interventions when the problem of marital violence is located in the structures of inequality rather than solely within the victim.

It is important to recognize that women who are unable to protect themselves from violent relationships are also unable to protect their daughters from incest and both daughters and sons from abuse. The two articles by Judith Herman and Lisa Hirschman, "Father–Daughter Incest" and "Families at Risk for Father–Daughter Incest," analyze the parental roles and power relationships that are associated with incestuous families. The most distinguishing characteristic of overtly incestuous fathers is that "they tend to use physical force and intimidation to dominate their families." A large proportion of the mothers in these families are estranged from their daughters and are incapable of fulfilling their maternal roles. They "are rendered unusually powerless, whether through battering, physical disability, mental illness, or the burden of repeated childbearing. . . . " This alternative view of incest has significant treatment implications that are eloquently described in Herman's book *Father–Daughter Incest* (Harvard University Press, 1982).

Physical and sexual abuse occur in poor, middle-class, and wealthy families, some of which are highly disorganized and some of which appear to be in no way out of the ordinary or deviant. As a result, clinicians cannot rely on stereotypes to identify victims, and they will have to learn how to ask routinely about rape, incest, wife abuse, and child abuse. Although males are socialized to be aggressive and are more likely to be the abusers, it is clear that they are also vulnerable to victimization. In contrast, although women are socialized to inhibit anger and aggression and are more often abused, they can also be violent toward others. Successful treatment requires knowledge of the abuse and the extraordinary damage to the self that follows. Clinicians must have a social and psychological perspective for understanding the abuse so that neither victim-blaming nor identification with victims or aggressors interferes with treatment. As Carmen, Rieker, and Mills conclude: "From our perspective, a major focus of treatment must be to help victims become survivors. This transformation is contingent on recognizing how chronic abuse constructs the individual's social identity as a victim and how the survival strategies employed by victims interfere not only with emotional development but with the therapeutic alliance and process."

Victims of Violence and Psychiatric Illness

14

ELAINE (HILBERMAN) CARMEN,
PATRICIA PERRI RIEKER, AND TRUDY MILLS

The growing body of knowledge about victims of violence strongly suggests that physical and sexual abuse may be frequent, if not inevitable, life experiences for many people. However, psychological and social conditions that link such victimization to subsequent psychiatric illness have only recently been identified as subjects for clinical investigation. As a result, the importance of the victim-to-patient process is neither appreciated by clinicians nor adequately conceptualized by researchers. This lack of recognition persists in spite of an extensive, but unsynthesized, literature on the psychosocial consequences of child abuse, spouse abuse, rape, and incest. As a way of addressing this gap in our knowledge, in this paper we report the results of an investigation into the relationship between physical and sexual abuse and psychiatric illness in a psychiatric inpatient population.

ABUSE AND PSYCHIATRIC ILLNESS

Only in the last decade have mental health professionals begun to examine the extent to which victims are represented in a variety of clinical settings. For example, Rounsaville and Weissman[1] reported that 3.8% of the women presenting to an emergency trauma service and 3.4% of the women presenting to an emergency psychiatric service had been battered by men with whom they were intimate. However, when Stark and associates[2] analyzed new data from the same emergency trauma service, they concluded that "where physicians saw 1 out of 35 of their patients as battered, a more accurate approximation is 1 in 4; where they acknowledged that 1 injury out of 20 resulted from domestic abuse, the actual

Reprinted from *American Journal of Psychiatry* 141:378–383, 1984. Copyright © 1984 by the American Psychiatric Association. Reprinted by permission. The authors thank Jean Gross, A.C.S.W., and Leonora Stephens, M.D., for their contributions to the research.

figure approached 1 in 4. What they described as a rare occurrence was in reality an event of epidemic proportions."

Rosenfeld,[3] in a review of all of his female psychotherapy patients seen in a group practice setting over one year, found that 6 of the 18 women were incest victims, only one of whom offered this information spontaneously. The underreporting of victims in psychiatric samples is consistent with the finding of Hilberman and Munson[4] that half of all women referred for psychiatric consultation in a rural medical clinical were in battering relationships. Post and associates,[5] in a preliminary report on the prevalence of domestic violence among psychiatric inpatients, further substantiated the relationship of abuse and psychological disorder. Of the 60 patients (38 women and 22 men), 48% gave histories of a battering relationship; 50% of the women had been battered and 21% reported abusing their partners; 14% of the men had been battered and 27% reported abusing their partners. Post and associates did not discuss other forms of abuse in their paper.

Several studies[2,6-8] provide evidence of the profoundly self-destructive behaviors that emerge after victimization. These are the behaviors that demonstrate a clear link between abuse experiences and psychiatric illness. Green[6] compared 59 abused and neglected children with 29 neglected children and 30 children who were neither abused nor neglected. Self-destructive behaviors (biting, cutting, burning, head banging, suicide attempts) were exhibited by 40.6% of the abused children, 17.2% of the neglected children, and 6.7% of the controls. Green concluded that "the abused child's sense of worthlessness, badness, and self-hatred as a consequence of parental assault, rejection, and scapegoating formed the nucleus for subsequent self-destructive behavior" (6, p. 581). The new research on violence against women not only corroborates this pattern but also provides a vivid psychological portrait of female victims of incest, spouse abuse, and rape.[7-11]

METHOD

To explore the relationship between violence and psychiatric disorder, we reconstructed the life experiences of patients through an in-depth examination of psychiatric inpatient records. To clarify this relationship, it was necessary to compare male and female patients as well as to compare abused and nonabused patients.

The nonrandom sample for this retrospective study included all patients discharged over 18-months from one of three adult psychiatric inpatient units in a university teaching hospital. The final sample consisted of 188 adult and adolescent male and female patients. Multiple discharges were treated as one case. A comparison of the demographic characteristics of this sample with those inpatients from all wards during the previous two years confirms that the study sample was representative in terms of race and sex.

A standardized coding instrument developed by the research team (two psychiatrists, two sociologists, and one social worker) was used to analyze the following content of the discharge summary and other patient records: demographic information; social, medical, and psychiatric histories; behavior before and during hospitalization; and details on the type and extent of violence. Clinicians were interviewed to verify ambiguous details or to supply missing data.

Violence was defined as any form of serious physical or sexual abuse described in the discharge summary or in the record. These abuse events included child abuse, incest, marital violence, and assault or rape occurring outside of the family. Instances in which abuse was suspected but not confirmed in the records were not coded as violence. Decisions about what behaviors constituted abuse were conservative, and ambiguous cases were discussed until the research team reached a consensus. In this way, a high degree of intercoder consistency was achieved. We collected data about the type of abuse, the severity and duration of the abuse, and the relationship of the patient to the abuser. Similar data were collected for those patients who were abusers. In addition, a scale was constructed for measuring the patient's ability to cope with anger and aggression during the hospitalization.

Cross-tabulation and multivariate techniques were used to analyze the data. Chi-square analyses were used to compare the abused and non-abused patients. We used the 0.05 level of significance to point out important differences between groups. Because this was an exploratory study with a nonrandom sample, the chi-square values are presented as descriptive statistics and not as statistical tests conducted to retain or reject null hypotheses. We will report the results of additional analyses of these data elsewhere.

RESULTS

Description of the Sample

The patients in the study were a diverse group. Eighty percent were white and 20% were black; 65% were female and 35% were male. Their ages ranged from 12 to 88 years. Adolescents made up 15% of the sample and the elderly made up 4%. Only 25% of the patients were married; 47% had never been married. Educational and occupational data showed that 26% had not graduated from high school (some were students) and that 18% were college graduates; 21% were professionals and 33% worked in clerical, sales, craft, or unskilled jobs. Fifty-two percent had annual incomes of less than $10,000. The low income of the patients may reflect the substantial percentage (35%) who were disabled or unemployed before hospitalization. However, the income data were less accurate than the educational and occupational data, and should be interpreted cautiously. Half of the patients had affective disorders, and the other half was divided among psychoses (18%), personality disorders (13%), adjustment reactions (11%), substance abuse (5%), and psychosomatic disorders (2%).

Extent of Abuse

Given our conservative coding of abuse, the prevalence appears quite high. Eighty of the 188 patients (43%) had histories of physical or sexual abuse or both. Abuse was suspected but not confirmed in enough detail in the records of an additional 7%. Of the 80 abused patients, 53% (N = 42) had been physically abused, 19% (N = 15) had been sexually abused, and 29% (N = 23) had been physically and sexually abused. The majority of sexual abuse (71%) had occurred more than a year before admission compared with 40% of physical abuse. Forty-one percent of the abused patients had been abused by more than one person.

Ninety percent (N = 72) of the abused patients had been abused by family members. Fifty-one percent had been abused by husbands or former husbands, 40% by fathers or stepfathers, and 23% by mothers or stepmothers. Sixty-six percent (N = 25) of those who had been sexually abused had been abused by family members. The largest group of sexually abused patients had been abused by fathers (34%); siblings accounted for 16% of sexual abuse cases and strangers for 29%.

Female patients were much more likely than males to have histories of abuse. Fifty-three percent (N = 65) of the females and 23% (N = 15) of the males had been abused. There were also differences between sexes in the patterns of abuse. Males (mainly teenagers) were most frequently abused by parents during childhood and adolescence, whereas females were abused by parents, spouses, and strangers. For the females, abuse had started in childhood and continued through adulthood. Only 4 of the 38 patients who had been sexually abused were males, as were their assailants. Teenagers were much more likely than adults to have been abused. Seventy-five percent of the 28 teenagers had been abused, compared with 39% of the adults. The blacks were slightly more likely than the whites to have been victims of abuse (50% compared to 41%), but this reflects the fact that the blacks in this sample were predominantly female (85%) and the females were more likely than the males to have histories of abuse.

Comparison of Abused and Nonabused Patients

Can abused patients be differentiated from nonabused patients in a clinical setting? To answer this question, we made comparisons on the basis of social history data, behaviors at the time of admission, behaviors during the hospitalization, and diagnoses. In the analysis, diagnoses did not differentiate between abused and nonabused patients.

One significant family characteristic of the abused patients was the excessive use of alcohol by parents. Thirty percent of the abused patients had alcoholic fathers, compared with 13% of the nonabused patients. The figures for alcoholic mothers were 13% and 5%, respectively. Table 1 provides a further comparison of social history characteristics of abused and nonabused patients. We found that abused patients were more likely than nonabused patients to have past histories of suicidal and assaultive behaviors and criminal justice involvement.

The patients displayed a wide range of behaviors and symptoms at the time of admission to the hospital. As Table 1 indicates, these behaviors did not differentiate abused from nonabused patients. At the time of admission, precipitants for hospitalization were equally likely to include

TABLE 1. Social History and Admission Behaviors of Abused and Nonabused Psychiatric Patients

Behavior	Abused patients ($N = 80$)		Nonabused patients ($N = 108$)		χ^2
	N	$\%^a$	N	$\%^a$	
Social history					
Abuse of alcohol	17	21	38	35	3.665
Abuse of illicit drugs	14	18	26	24	0.826
Suicide attempt(s)	36	45	32	30	4.061[b]
Criminal justice involvement	12	15	5	5	4.814[b]
Abuse of others	20	25	14	13	3.719[b]
Admission					
Suicidal	35	44	45	42	0.019
Aggressive/destructive	20	25	20	19	0.798
Depressive symptoms	49	61	66	61	0.000
Substance abuse	19	24	25	23	0.000
Organic symptoms/confusion	2	3	15	14	5.929[b]
Conduct disorder	12	15	9	8	1.441
Anxiety/agitation	25	31	33	31	0.000
Psychosomatic	13	16	13	12	0.377
Psychotic	19	24	41	38	3.64

[a]Percentages do not total 100% because some patients exhibited more than one behavior.
[b]$p < 0.05$.

suicidal behavior, aggressiveness, depression, drug abuse, disordered conduct, anxiety, and psychosomatic symptoms. The patients differed only with respect to organic symptoms. However, this may be a spurious finding that derives from limitations in the data.

Two important differences emerged when we examined various behaviors *during* the hospitalization. First, abused patients tended to remain in the hospital longer than the nonabused group. Twenty-six percent of the abused group were hospitalized longer than 90 days, whereas only 9% of the nonabused group were hospitalized for that length of time. The average stay for nonabused patients was 43 days, and for the abused patients it was 58 days.

Second, abused and nonabused patients differed in how they dealt with anger and aggression during the hospitalization. This is especially pertinent to our study, since anger is an expected response to abusive events. We developed a measure of the coping behavior of the inpatients that focused on whether the anger was mainly directed inward or outward and whether behavioral control of aggressive impulses was maintained. Four categories were used to measure this aspect of hospital behavior.

Category 1 describes a behavior pattern in which the anger was directed inward in a passive, overcontrolled manner. These generally depressed, frightened, and withdrawn patients felt worthless, hopeless, and undeserving but were not actively suicidal. Although these passive patients were not behavioral problems on the ward, the passivity frustrated clinicians' attempts to establish therapeutic relationships.

Category 2 patients directed their anger inward, but in a more overt, active fashion. This coping style was characterized by active suicidal intent and/or savage self-hatred, with loss of control reflected in a variety of self-destructive and self-mutilating behaviors. At times, some of these patients alarmed even experienced clinicians with their uncontrollable self-mutilation and their resolutely maintained unempathic attitude toward themselves.

Category 3 patients directed their anger outward in a controlled manner. Some of these patients expressed anger appropriately, while others displaced and projected their anger and hostility elsewhere (most prominently toward hospital staff). In all cases, however, control of aggressive impulses remained intact.

Category 4 patients directed their anger outward, with aggressive and sometimes violent behaviors toward others. Such loss of control was reflected in outbursts of barely contained murderous rage, threats to harm others, and actual assaults. The four behavior patterns were not mutually exclusive and some patients displayed aspects of more than one type of coping behavior. For some patients, the information available was insufficient for classification.

A higher percentage of abused patients (20%) than of nonabused patients (10%) displayed the behavior pattern of category 2, that is, directed their anger inward in an actively self-destructive fashion. This finding will be discussed further as we examine the issue of sex differences.

Comparison of Abused Males and Females

As noted earlier, abused patients were more likely to be female. In this section we will compare the 65 abused females and the 15 abused males.

The majority of abused males were teenagers (60%), and the majority of abused females were adults (81%). There were other differences betwen male and female abused patients. First, they presented themselves differently at the time of hospitalization (see Table 2). The behavior of the abused females resembled that of the other females at the time of hospitalization, that is, they were equally likely to be suicidal, depressed, and so forth.

Abused males, however, differed from the other males, as shown in Table 2. The small number of abused males in the study decreased the likelihood that the findings would be statistically significant. Nevertheless, three of the relationships were statistically significant and three of the remaining comparisons showed substantial differences between percentages of abused and nonabused males. The abused males were less likely to appear depressed, suicidal, or psychotic at the time of hospitalization (see Table 2). They were more likely than nonabused males to be aggressive or to have disordered conduct or psychosomatic symptoms. Since the majority of abused males were teenagers, the increase in disordered conduct reflected age as well as abuse.

Other differences between the abused males and females emerged when behaviors before hospitalization were examined. Table 2 shows that the abused males were much more likely than the abused females (and other males) to have abused others. Sixty percent of the abused males had been violent toward others, while only 17% of the abused females had been violent. Abused males were also more likely than abused females (and other males) to have had criminal justice involvement.

Perhaps the most important characteristic that distinguished the behavior of the abused males and females was that the males had become more aggressive while the females had become more passive. In some ways the sex-role stereotypes seemed to be exaggerated in this sample. This was evident in the way that the abused males and females coped

Table 2. Social History and Admission Behaviors of Abused and Nonabused Male and Female Psychiatric Patients

Behavior	Males					Females				
	Abused (N = 15)[a]		Nonabused (N = 50)			Abused (N = 65)		Nonabused (N = 58)		
	N	%	N	%	χ^2	N	%	N	%	χ^2
Social history										
Alcohol abuse	4	27	27	54	2.447	13	20	11	19	0.000
Abuse of illicit drugs	4	27	17	34	0.047	10	15	9	16	0.000
Suicide attempts	8	53	14	28	2.272	28	43	18	31	1.419
Criminal justice involvement	6	40	3	6	8.513[b]	6	9	2	3	0.869
Abusive to others	9	60	11	22	6.139[b]	11	17	3	5	3.111
Admission										
Suicidal	4	27	21	42	0.589	31	48	24	41	0.272
Aggressive/destructive	6	40	10	20	1.526	14	22	10	17	0.139
Depressive symptoms	4	27	30	60	3.889[b]	45	69	36	62	0.417
Substance abuse	4	27	15	30	0.000	15	23	10	17	0.334
Organic symptoms/confused	0		4	8	0.269	2	3	11	19	6.591[b]
Conduct disorder	6	40	3	6	8.513[b]	6	9	6	10	0.000
Anxiety/agitation	3	20	16	32	0.328	22	34	17	29	0.119
Psychosomatic	4	27	7	14	0.569	9	14	6	10	0.100
Psychotic	0		18	36	5.778[b]	19	29	23	40	1.054

[a] These columns should be interpreted with caution since the number of abused males was small.
[b] $p < 0.05$ level.

TABLE 3. Anger/Aggression Coping Behavior of Abused and Nonabused Male and Female Psychiatric Patients

Anger/aggression coping behavior	Males				Females			
	Abused (N = 15)		Nonabused (N = 50)		Abused (N = 65)		Nonabused (N = 58)	
	N	%	N	%	N	%	N	%
Directed inward								
Controlled (category 1)	2	13	17	34	27	42	21	36
Uncontrolled (category 2)	1	7	6	12	15	24	5	9
Directed outward								
Controlled (category 3)	0		2	4	7	11	5	9
Uncontrolled (category 4)	5	33	9	18	9	14	7	12
Directed both inward and outward	4	27	10	20	5	8	9	16
None of the categories	3	20	6	12	2	4	11	19

with anger (see Table 3). Thirty-three percent of abused males coped with anger by directing it aggressively toward others (category 4), but only 14% of the abused females did so. The majority of abused females (66%) directed their anger inward (categories 1 and 2), compared with only 20% of the abused males. As shown in Table 3, abused males, more than nonabused males, coped with anger by aggressively directing it toward others, while abused females were more likely than other females to turn their anger inward. For example, 24% of the abused females, compared with 9% of the nonabused females, were actively self-destructive during hospitalization.

DISCUSSION

Our finding that almost half of the psychiatric inpatients in this sample had histories of physical or sexual abuse should not come as a surprise, given the prevalence of violence in the general population. As this study demonstrates, most of the abuse occurred in the context of family. Although families are usually viewed as providing the primary support networks for individuals, our data confirm the findings of other researchers[7,9,12,13] that female adults and children of both sexes are at highest risk for violence within the family. In a retrospective study of 40 patients with multiple personality disorder, Putnam[14] found that 80% had been severely abused by family members during childhood. It is important to bear in mind that victims of family violence might be overrepresented in any psychiatric sample because violent family systems may produce a population at risk for chronic abuse as well as for psychiatric illness.

Victims of physical and sexual abuse are faced with an extraordinary task of conflict resolution as they look for a context in which bodily harm and threats to life can be understood. When the assailant is an intimate or a family member, this process is immeasurably complicated by the profound betrayal of trust. Such victims must also cope with ongoing vulnerability to physical and psychological danger when the abuser has continuing access to the victim. It was not uncommon, in our sample, for a patient to have experienced multiple kinds of abuse. There were numerous cases of women who were physically or sexually abused as children and subsequently raped or abused by spouses and others in adulthood. This pattern of increased vulnerability of female victims to other kinds of abuse was also described in Herman's study of incest victims[7] and Hilberman's review of research on battered women.[8] It is unclear if such vulnerability to multiple abuse is the same among men with prior histories of victimization, since the number of males was small and the majority were adolescents.

What is clear, from the inpatient summaries and our clinical experiences, is that the psychological and behavioral manifestations of chronic abuse reflect extraordinary damage to the self, which then becomes the object of the victim's hatred and aggression. While there are psychodynamic issues specific to each kind of abuse, our observations indicate a common pattern of responses to chronic victimization. Although these psychosocial responses may have different behavioral manifestations in abused males and females, the psychic trauma is similar. These victims have extreme difficulties with anger and aggression, self-image, and trust.

In contrast to the outrage and disgust experienced by others hearing of the abuse, victims do not usually acknowledge their anger toward their abusers, in part because their rage is perceived as dangerous and potentially uncontrollable and in part because of the complex relationship between victim and abuser. After years of abuse, victims blame themselves as they come to believe that the abuse can be explained only by their essential "badness."

In our sample, the abused females directed their hatred and aggression against themselves in both overt and covert ways. These behaviors formed a continuum from quiet resignation and depression to repeated episodes of self-mutilation and suicide attempts. Self-destructive behaviors were related to feelings of worthlessness, hopelessness, shame, and guilt. These affects escalated when anger threatened to surface and, at such times, often culminated in impulsive self-destructive episodes. Markedly impaired self-esteem was prominent among these patients as they conveyed a sense that they were undeserving of any empathic understanding or help by clinicians.

In comparison, the mainly adolescent male victims, although experiencing many of the same feelings of self-hatred, more often directed their aggression toward others. It is likely that these outward displays of aggression were defenses against intolerable feelings of helplessness and vulnerability. In the hospital this internal dynamic was reflected in alternating expressions of anguish and despair followed by threatening "macho" behavior and displays of physical prowess. Patterns of sex-role socialization obviously shape the differential responses to abuse of males and females.

The social histories and inpatient process notes provide impressive evidence of the abused patients' lack of trust and the way in which inability to trust complicates the evaluative and treatment processes. Herman[7] reported the same finding in her study of father–daughter incest, in which she described a dual pattern of inability to feel trust when this would be appropriate and to protect oneself when trust is inappropriate. In our sample, expectations of abandonment and exploitation by the clinician were prominent, hence victims did not spontaneously reveal the abuse or easily form therapeutic alliances.

In the absence of direct information about past or current abuse, our data suggest that abused patients are not easily distinguished from nonabused patients at the time of admission to the hospital. Rather, the significant differences between abused and nonabused patients emerged during the course of hospitalization and were reflected both in the treatment difficulties and the greater length of time that abused patients remained in the hospital. These outcomes may be the end result of victims' (1) inability to trust, which delays or prevents the development of a therapeutic liaison, (2) impaired self-esteem, whereby abused patients judge themselves as undeserving of treatment, and (3) difficulty in coping with aggression, whereby anger is destructively directed toward the damaged self or others.

CONCLUSIONS

Clinicians generally ask patients about abuse experiences *if* they have some reason to suspect abuse. However, these suspicions are often based on unfounded stereotypes about victims and violent families. Increasing awareness of the extent of violence in this society leads us to suspect that psychiatric patients are more likely to have experienced physical and/or sexual violence than to hear voices, yet clinicians are systematic in their inquiries about hallucinations while overlooking the reality and importance of violent assaults. Our research underscores the discrepancy between the alarming numbers of people who are physically and sexually abused and the relative lack of attention that is given to these topics in taking routine psychiatric histories.

Clinicians are largely unaware of the psychosocial consequences of abuse because the victim-to-patient process is an area of clinical research that has been underconceptualized. Thus, even when abuse is identified, clinicians' confusion about the role of abuse in psychiatric illness leaves them unprepared to implement special treatment approaches for what appears to be a large proportion of psychiatric patients. In a separate paper, we will analyze a series of inpatient case examples that illustrate and capture the complexity of the victim-to-patient process and its implications for treatment. From our perspective, a major focus of treatment must be to help victims become survivors. This transformation is contingent on recognizing how chronic abuse constructs the individual's social identity as a victim and how the survival strategies employed by victims interfere not only with emotional development but with the therapeutic alliance and process.

Because the theoretical understanding of the victim-to-patient process lags behind clinical experiences with victims, our research raises more questions than it answers about the effects of abuse and the conditions that leave some, but not all, victims vulnerable to psychiatric illness. We believe we have provided a realistic description of the lives of chronically abused females whose self-destructive behaviors and silence make them hard to identify and treat. However, because most of the abused males in our population were adolescents, we can only conjecture about their fates as adult men. It may be that, if the behavioral response pattern of the abused adolescent males seen in our population continues into adulthood, they become inmates in other structured environments, such as state mental hospitals and prisons. It is possible that these men are coerced into treatment only after they have become dangerous and assaultive, hence the treatment focus is on their abusive behaviors while their histories of victimization go unrecognized. The large population of Viet Nam veterans in prisons and psychiatric hospitals would provide a relevant sample of adult male victims for further study.

References

1. Rounsaville B., Weissman M. M.: Battered women: a medical problem requiring detection. *Int J Psychiatry Med* 8:191–202, 1977–78.
2. Stark E., Flitcraft A., Frazier W.: Medicine and patriarchal violence: the social construction of a "private" event. *Int J Health Serv* 9:461–493, 1979.

3. Rosenfeld A. A.: Incidence of a history of incest among 18 female psychiatric patients. *Am J Psychiatry* 136:791–795, 1979.

4. Hilberman E., Munson K.: Sixty battered women. *Victimology: An International Journal* 2:460–471, 1977–78.

5. Post R. D., Willett A. B., Franks R. D., et al: A preliminary report on the prevalence of domestic violence among psychiatric inpatients. *Am J Psychiatry* 137:974–975, 1980.

6. Green A. H.: Self-destructive behavior in battered children. *Am J Psychiatry* 135:579–582, 1978.

7. Herman J. L.: *Father–Daughter Incest*. Cambridge, Mass., Harvard University Press, 1981.

8. Hilberman E.: Overview: the "wife-beater's wife" reconsidered. *Am J Psychiatry* 137:1336–1347, 1980.

9. Dobash R. E., Dobash R.: *Violence Against Wives: A Case Against the Patriarchy*. New York, Free Press, 1979.

10. Burgess A. W., Holmstrom L. L.: *Rape: Victims of Crisis*. Bowie, Maryland, Robert J. Brady Co. 1974.

11. Symonds M.: The rape victim: psychological patterns of response. *Am J Psychoanalysis* 36:27–34, 1976.

12. Carmen E. (H.), Russo N. F., Miller J. B.: Inequality and women's mental health: an overview. *Am J Psychiatry* 138:1319–1330, 1981.

13. Gelles R. J., Straus M. A.: Family experience and public support of the death penalty. *Am J Orthopsychiatry* 45:596–613, 1975.

14. Abused child, multiple personality tied. *Clinical Psychiatry News* September, 1982, p. 2..

Overview: The "Wife-Beater's Wife" Reconsidered

15

ELAINE HILBERMAN

Wife-beating, although not a new phenomenon, has been largely ignored by mental health professionals. Until recently the literature and research on family violence were limited to child abuse and murder, since these categories alone were generally accepted as serious problems deserving of public attention and intervention. Although extensive research and service efforts have focused on family dynamics that foster child abuse and alcoholism, there has been inadequate recognition of the aggression that is often directed toward the wives and mothers in such families. This "selective inattention" has been noted by most contemporary researchers and writers[1-3] and was documented by O'Brien's finding[4] that the index of the *Journal of Marriage and the Family* from its inception in 1939 through 1969 contained no references to "violence."

Wife abuse, when it was identified, was generally assumed to represent some intrapsychic liability on the part of the victim. This psychiatric labeling or attribution of blame reflected and reinforced the societal belief that spouse abuse was an isolated problem in unusually disturbed couples in which the violence was viewed as "fulfilling masochistic needs of the wife and necessary for the wife's (and the couple's) equilibrium."[5] Several important clinical implications follow from these explanations of causality. First, when spouse abuse is perceived as occurring only infrequently and in deviant relationships, it is defined as a private rather than a public problem. Second, if the victim can be seen as provoking or needing the abuse, mental health professionals can more comfortably focus on the "meaning" of the violence than on the fact of the violence per se. Third, since women themselves are aware of and even share these attitudes, they are reluctant to reveal the abuse and are most usually "silent victims." Thus there has been a covert alliance between victims and clinicians, in which treatment of symptoms is offered as an alternative to the more direct identification of the problem and the appropriate intervention and protection of abused women.[3,6,7]

Reprinted from *American Journal of Psychiatry* 137(11):1336–1347, 1980. Copyright © 1980 by the American Psychiatric Association. Reprinted by permission. The author wishes to thank Elissa Benedek, M.D., Margaret J. Gates, J.D., Carol Nadelson, M.D., and Leonore Walker, Ph.D., for their critical review and discussion of an earlier draft of this article.

Because spouse abuse is usually wife abuse, I will focus on the female victims of marital violence. The intent of this overview is to present a context in which the physical abuse of women as wives can be understood. A review of the pertinent literature is summarized in terms of information that is essential for the assessment and treatment of victims in danger. Although the sociological and feminist literature on this topic has expanded rapidly in the last decade,[1-3,7-13] the clinical and psychiatric literature is relatively new and is often found outside traditional sources.[6,14-22]

I will discuss societal attitudes that normalize the use of family violence as well as attitudes about women, men, and sex roles that leave women vulnerable to assaults by significant other men. I will summarize clinical research reports about abused wives; these suggest alternative theoretical constructs to explain why women remain in violent marital relationships. A more detailed account of my own clinical experiences is offered and includes the identification of a specific stress response syndrome that is the direct result of violent abuse.[19] I will discuss treatment implications and recommendations, clarify the role of the mental health professional, and elaborate the problems posed for clinicians working with abused wives. I hope that this article will mobilize the interests and capabilities of the psychiatric community for urgently needed clinical services and research in this area.

THE SOCIETAL CONTEXT

Violence as a Norm

There is considerable irony in our lack of attention to family violence at a time of great public concern and fear about violence in general. As Straus noted in the foreword to Gelles' *The Violent Home*,[1] the social definition of the family as nonviolent "causes a perceptual blackout of the family violence going on daily all around us in 'normal' families." Although the concept of family is cherished as a source of nurturance and mental health, the family is the most frequent single locus for violence of all types, including homicide.[23] Violence is said to occur in 50% of American families, so that the marriage license might be viewed as a "hitting license."[1,21,23,24]

Family violence, in contrast to violence outside the family, is more often perceived as normal, legitimate, and instrumental.[1,2,23] This attitude is most evident in the corporal punishment of children. That violence between spouses is also socially condoned is reflected in results of the 1968 interview survey conducted for the National Commission on

Causes and Prevention of Violence. This survey of a representative national sample of adult women and men found that 20% approved of husband- and wife-hitting.[25] Spouse abuse is not limited to a particular social class or ethnic group, although the highest reported incidence is among the poor. Poor people are more likely to come to the attention of a public agency, while the privacy of middle- and upper-class women is protected by their personal physicians or attorneys. In a study of 600 couples who were in the process of divorce,[26] 40% of lower-class women and 23% of middle-class women reported physical abuse by spouses. A 1979 survey of wife abuse in Kentucky[27] found that income levels were not good predictors of family violence. School dropouts with less than an eighth-grade education appeared to be less violence-prone than those who had some college education.

Family violence has several important societal ramifications beyond the suffering of individuals[28]:

1. *Injury and death.* Of all murders in this country, 20%–50% occur within the family. Police are called to intervene in domestic disputes more often than in all other criminal incidents combined,[2,29–32] and 20% of all police fatalities occur during such interventions.[3,28] A Kansas City, Mo., police study[33] reported that 40% of the city's homicides were between spouses. In more than 85% of these homicides police had been called in at least once before the fatal episode, and in half of these cases they had been called in five times during the 2 years before the murder.[33]

Although reports consistently reveal that the home is a violent setting, Dobash and Dobash[30,34] have observed that researchers often fail to note that this violence is not evenly distributed among family members but is disproportionately directed toward women. Female victims of homicide are more often killed by a spouse, while the majority of male victims are killed by someone outside the family. According to Dobash and Dobash,[30,34] about 40% of all female homicide victims were killed by husbands, but only 10% of male victims were killed by wives. It has also been reported[35] that among those who murder spouses, wives were seven times more likely than husbands to have murdered in self-defense. Thus, men are much more likely to commit homicide than women and women victims are usually married to their assailants.

2. *Violence as learned behavior.* Gelles and Straus[23] noted that the family is the primary training ground for violent behavior: "A person is more likely to observe, commit, and to be the victim of violence within the family than in any other setting." Beating of women in the home is often accompanied by physical and/or sexual abuse of the children.[15,19,20] Children who are abused often grow up to abuse their offspring, and children who see violent parental interactions often have physically abusive relationships in adulthood. Thus violence breeds violence.[1,7,23]

Violence against Women

The recent attention to wife abuse is the direct result of the women's movement and follows on the heels of the anti-rape movement. It is best understood as an expansion of the concern about female sexual abuse to encompass the broader category of violence against women. The large majority of victims of spouse abuse, incest, and rape are female, and their assailants are most often men who (with the possible exception of rapists) are trusted relatives and intimates. In all of these acts of violence, women and girls are perceived by their assailants as legitimate targets for male aggression.[3,36-40] The basic fact of the victim's femaleness is used by the offender to justify the assault, and the complaining woman is suspected of fabrication, provocation, or seduction, while the assailant is protected.

Wife-beating has had social and legal sanction throughout history.[3,30,36,41,42] Martin[3,43] noted that the word "family," derived from the Latin *familia*, in Roman culture connoted the totality of slaves belonging to an individual. As early as 753 B.C., married women were defined as "necessary and inseparable possessions" of their husbands.[30] There is ample documentation of the wife's obligation to obey her husband and of the husband's legal and moral responsibility to control his wife. The husband's authority to chastise his wife was explicitly written into the laws of church and state and later incorporated into English common law. Blackstone, in 1763, explained the husband's right of chastisement: "For, as he is to answer for her misbehaviours, the law thought it reasonable to entrust him with his power of restraining her by domestic chastisement."[30]

The husband's right to hit his wife was written into law in the United States in 1824 with the restriction that "he ... [use] a switch no bigger than his thumb."[3] This law was overturned in 1874 when the North Carolina Supreme Court ruled that "the husband has no right to chastise his wife under any circumstances." The importance of this judgment was unfortunately undone by the court's qualifying statement: "If no permanent injury has been inflicted, nor malice, cruelty nor dangerous violence shown by the husband, it is better to draw the curtain, shut out the public gaze, and leave the parties to forget and forgive."[3]

Although wife-beating is no longer legitimized by statute, current criminal justice procedures are consistent with "drawing the curtain." Field and Field[44] commented that

> the evolution of a system in which criminal enforcement is left entirely to the whim of the victim ... implies official acceptance of our acquiescence to the policy that violence between "consenting" adults is a private affair. ... The poles of enforcement are the rigorous prosecution of the person accused of assaulting a stranger and the non-prosecution of the one who assaults a marital partner.

Violent marriages are currently maintained by pervasive patterns of sex discrimination.[3,38,39,43] Men use violence as a way of maintaining a superior power position in the family. Their wives understand that neither separation nor legal intervention will necessarily end the violence.[28,44,45] The man is protected, and the abused woman comes to believe that marital violence is the norm and that she deserves the abuse. This self-blame is reinforced by "helping" agencies that ignore and demean the victim or accuse her of provoking the assault.[37] The woman who leaves a violent home is denied child-care facilities; equal educational, vocational, and economic opportunities; and a legitimate self-supporting and autonomous role outside the home.[38,39]

DEFINING WIFE ABUSE

Most clinicians who study spouse abuse have arrived at similar working definitions of marital violence.[6,15,18,20] (The term "marital" does not imply a legal relationship but includes any relationship involving cohabitation and sexual intimacy.) In general, an abused or battered wife is one who is subjected to serious and/or repeated physical injury as a result of deliberate assaults by her spouse. Scott[20] graded the severity of such abuse along the following continuum: (1) not requiring medical attention, (2) requiring outpatient attention, and (3) requiring hospitalization. He also categorized the frequency of abuse as (1) regular, (2) episodic (situational), (3) increasing, and (4) terminal.

There is considerable semantic and attitudinal confusion about these definitions of violence. Pushing and shoving may not constitute a threat to life and may be considered permissible by a couple, but the same behaviors would be considered violent acts if the assailant were a stranger. As another example, Gelles[1] commented that individuals do not label the use of physical force on children as "violence" because of the "powerful pro-use-of-physical-force-on-children norms." He asserted that if violence is defined as an act with the intent of physically injuring the victim, then the physical punishment of children is violent.

THE FAMILY CONTEXT AND THE CONSEQUENCES

In this section I will describe the family setting and the psychological and behavioral consequences of wife-beating, as derived from clinical research reports.[1,7,14−21,46−48] One of the largest clinical samples has been reported by Gayford,[15−17] who studied 100 battered women admitted to a shelter in England. British psychiatrists have been somewhat more aware of this problem because of Pizzey's efforts to initiate a network of shelters for abused women and their children.[7,46] Gelles's 1974 sociological study of 80 families[1] was the first important clinical research effort in the United States.

A 1977–1978 study by Munson and myself of 60 battered women in a general medical clinic setting[19] is similar to work reported by Dewsbury[6] in that the abused women were not selected by virtue of admission to a shelter or by awareness that the abuse they suffered warranted attention. The history of violence was known to the referring clinician in only 4 of our 60 cases, although most of these women and their children had received ongoing medical care at the clinic. Information about the women was acquired by dialogue with them, while material about spouses was almost always indirect because these men adamantly rejected attempts to engage them in medical or psychiatric treatment. Involvement with husbands was further limited by the women's need to maintain silence about clinic visits and by our concern that conjoint treatment in the absence of provisions for safety might result in an escalation of violence. Other researchers have also found that husbands are unwilling to participate in interviews about family violence. Gelles[1] abandoned initial plans for conjoint interviews because early interviews with couples suggested the potential for precipitation of further violence.

Families of Origin

Munson and I[19] found that lifelong violence was a frequent pattern for many abused wives. Half of the women we studied reported violence between parents (usually the father assaulting the mother), paternal alcoholism, and their own physical and/or sexual abuse as children. The women's husbands were said to have had even more early exposure to emotional deprivation, alcoholism, lack of protection, and violence, both as witnesses and as objects of abuse. Suicides and homicides among family members and neighborhood acquaintances were common occurrences and were usually committed with guns, which were normal household possessions. These findings about violence in families of origin are consistent with other reports. Of the sample studied by Gayford,[15] 23% gave histories of parental violence; violent backgrounds were even more prevalent for their husbands, half of whom were said to come from violent families. Scott[20] also described a pattern of violent fathers and passive mothers in families of origin.

Most of the women we studied[19] left home at an early age to escape from violent, jealous and seductive fathers who kept their wives and daughters imprisoned. Marriage during teenage years was the norm for these women, and many were pregnant at the time of marriage or had had children before marriage. They viewed pregnancy as the only way they would be allowed to leave the family—the alternative to paternal control was paternal rejection and a way out of the home. In Gayford's sample,[15] 60% of the women reported premarital pregnancies. Rounsaville[48] described these marriages as occurring precipitously and during stressful periods. Most usually, the future husbands did not exhibit violent behavior toward the women until they were married, and the women ignored other evidence of the men's potential for violence because of the urgent need to marry in order to "escape" from home. Once married, these women found themselves with jealous and assaultive husbands, often replicating their lives before marriage.

Alcohol and Violence

An association between alcohol use by the batterer and marital violence has been noted in all of the relevant studies. Drinking accompanied the violence in 44% of Gelles' sample[1] and 93% of our sample.[19] Gayford[15] described drunkenness as occurring regularly in 52% of the men and occasionally in an additional 22%. In a survey of 100 wives of alcoholics, none of whom had been identified as victims of marital violence, Scott[20] found that 72% of the women had been threatened, 45% were beaten, and 27% described potentially lethal assaults. Drunkenness is not always accompanied by violent behavior, however, and wife abusers who drink heavily also beat their wives when they are sober. Because of this variability, Gelles[1] hypothesized that wife abusers become intoxicated in order to carry out a violent act. Drinking is thus used to disavow the deviant behavior and to provide a "time out" during which the assailant is not responsible for his actions.

The Marriage

The violent relationship is one of extraordinary intensity.[19,21] When they are not behaving aggressively, wife abusers have been described as childlike, remorseful, and yearning for nurturance. This picture of fragility was confirmed in our study[19] by occasional reports of a husband's suicidal or psychotic behavior when his wife threatened to dissolve the relationship. The women felt quite sorry for their spouses because of their histories of deprivation and abuse. These men could never understand or acknowledge a termination without murderous rage, so marriage became a life sentence for their wives.[7,19] When husbands threatened homicide, they were taken literally because threats and wishes became a reality with explosive suddenness in these relationships. Many women left their marriages for brief periods but invariably returned because of economic and emotional dependence on husbands and threats of further violence from which they had no protection. For example, one woman made active plans to leave her marriage despite her husband's threats of violence but retreated abruptly when her closest friend, also an abused woman, was murdered by a violent spouse.

In many violent marital relationships, there seems to be a cycle of violence, with three phases that vary in time and intensity. There is a phase in which tension builds, a phase in which violence erupts, and a phase of relief from tension. In this last phase, the husband is often kind, loving, and remorseful. This postviolence reconciliation leaves the woman hopeful that her husband will change and serves as a powerful reinforcer for her to continue the marital relationship.[21,49] Battered women are most often seen by clinicians toward the end of the first phase or during the last phase. When the anticipatory anxiety becomes intolerable, women sometimes act to precipitate the inevitable assault. In contrast, during the reconciliation period victims often appear unconcerned about the violence. It is possible that both of these behaviors may be misinterpreted as masochistic by clinicians.

Jealousy

Extreme jealousy was reported in 57 of the 60 marriages that Munson and I studied,[19] with husbands making active and successful efforts to keep their wives ignorant and isolated. If the women left the house for any reason, they were met with accusations of infidelity that culminated in assault. Clinic visits were often made in secrecy, and some women were beaten regularly when they returned from the clinic. Other channels of communication were also closed off. Friendships with women were discouraged either by the husband's embarrassing his wife in front of her friends or by his accusations that the wife's friends were lesbians or "trash." Many husbands refused to allow their wives to work, and others tried to ensure that both partners worked at the same place so they could monitor the woman's activities and friends. Thus for these women isolation was complete and potential support unavailable. The women were painfully aware of this; one commented, "He'd do anything he could to get me down to where I would not go out in the world."

This extraordinary possessiveness was apparent in Gayford's sample[15]—66% of the women said their husbands accused them of infidelity or checked on their activities. Gelles[1] and Scott[20] have identified the "third degree," a phenomenon in which a husband interrogates his wife for hours until she admits to some infidelity simply to end the argument. In reality, many of the husbands studied engaged in extramarital liaisons, while few of the women did so. Gayford[15] and Scott[20] have both suggested that extreme cases of delusional jealousy warrant immediate separation because of the potential for homicidal violence.

Marital Violence

The women we studied[19] reported that violence erupted any time a husband did not immediately get his way. A common pattern was for the husband to come home late after being with another woman and to goad his wife into an argument that ended in violence. The assaults usually occurred at night and on weekends, so children were witnesses and participants.[1,19] In many cases, the oldest child had not been fathered by the husband, and violence toward the wife was extended to the "bastard kid." Older children also became involved when they attempted to defend or protect the mother.

Some women were assaulted daily, while others were beaten intermittently; they therefore lived in constant anticipatory terror. There was also a subgroup of victims who had sustained one life-threatening injury, e.g., a subdural hematoma or a gunshot wound to the chest. Although there was no further violence in these cases, this was a powerful learning experience for the victim, who behaved thereafter as if she were always in danger.

Assault weapons included hands, feet, fists, rocks, bottles, telephones, iron bars, knives, and guns. Scratching, slapping, punching with fists, throwing down, and kicking were prevalent, with faces and breasts the most frequently mentioned sites of assault.[1,3,6,14,15,19-21] These assaults led to multiple bruises, black eyes, fractured ribs, subdural hematomas, and detached retinas. Some victims also reported having been strangled and choked until consciousness was impaired. Sexual assaults were common, and women described being beaten and raped in front of the children. Guns were available in most of these homes and were constant threats—some men kept guns in bed to intimidate their wives.[19] We know of one woman who slept with her shoes on to permit a "fast getaway."[19]

Most women reported changes in the pattern of violence during pregnancy.[19] There was increasing abuse for some, with the abdomen replacing the face and breasts as the target for battering. This often led to abortions and premature births.[1,15,19,21] It has been hypothesized that this behavior represents a prenatal form of infanticide or child abuse.[1,50] A smaller number of women reported less abuse with pregnancy, and one women deliberately stayed pregnant to avoid violence.[19]

The coping strategy used most often during the assault was to get away temporarily, although the women found there were few places to go. Some women sought recourse through the criminal justice system, but these attempts were frustrated by the unresponsiveness of magistrates and law enforcement officials, as well as the husband's retaliative violence[8,19,21,28,42,44] The few women who resorted to counterviolence did so in desperation when other options had failed. In contrast to the husband's violent behavior, these women used violence in response to a direct threat to life. Their behavior usually came as a surprise to them because they had been unaware of the extent of their rage and their own capacity for violence.[19]

The Children

Almost all clinicians are impressed with the correlation between child abuse and spouse abuse. Gayford[15] reported, in his study of battered women, that 37% of the women and 54% of the men beat the children. Munson and I[19] identified the physical and/or sexual abuse of children in a third of the families we studied. Whether the children were themselves battered or were onlookers to parental violence, they were deeply affected by the climate of violence in which they lived.[51] Emotional neglect, abuse, and frequent separations were the norms—the children were never certain who would leave and when. Thus, children in violent homes, as witnesses and targets of abuse, are quite vulnerable.[1,15,19–21]

A high incidence of somatic, psychological, and behavioral dysfunctions has been described in such children.[15,19] Psychosomatic illnesses were especially prominent in the children we studied and included headaches, abdominal complaints, asthma, peptic ulcer, rheumatoid arthritis, stuttering, and enuresis.[19] Depression, suicidal behavior, and overt psychosis were seen in a few of these children and adolescents.

The following portrait of the children emerged from our study.[19] Preschool and young school children in violent homes had somatic complaints, school phobias, enuresis, and insomnia. The insomnia was often accompanied by intense fear, screaming, and resistance to going to bed at night. This behavior was temporally related to the violence in the home—much of the wife-beating occurred when the children were in bed. Most children had impaired concentration and difficulty with school work. Older children began to show differential behavior patterns that divided along gender lines. The most frequently reported cluster for boys—aggressive disruptive behavior, stealing, temper tantrums, truancy, and fighting with siblings and schoolmates—was notably absent in girls.

As Gayford[15] observed, "Some children were so disruptive that they could not be contained at normal schools, primarily because of their violence toward other children and, in some cases, their teachers." In a 1977 personal communication Pizzey confirmed the effectiveness of this training for violence, noting that her network of crisis shelters could not contain the adolescent boys from violent homes because of their uncontrollable aggression. Separate housing and personnel were necessary for these boys, who invariably destroyed furniture and possessions and broke windows until they had gone through a period of resocialization.

In contrast, teenage girls continued to have an increasing array of somatic symptoms and became withdrawn, passive, clinging, and anxious (this pattern also occurred in a smaller number of boys). Teenage girls further suffered from the perpetual surveillance and accusations of sexual activity by their fathers, who were seductive and, in some cases, overtly incestuous. Finally, there were reports of married daughters who were battered and of grown sons who were alcoholic and violent, thus completing the cycle.

Battered Women: Psychological Consequences

In our sample,[19] the reasons for psychiatric referral usually clustered around physical symptoms or mixed anxiety/depressive symptoms that the women related to marital problems. Marital problems were generally defined in terms of the husband's alcoholism, financial irresponsibility, and promiscuity; the battering was never mentioned. Women with physical symptoms had been referred because of chronic use or abuse of tranquilizers or analgesics, unremitting symptomatology, treatment noncompliance, and frequent clinic visits.

Somatic complaints, conversion symptoms, and psychophysiologic reactions were abundant, as evidenced by frequent clinic visits for headaches, choking sensations, hyperventilation, asthma, gastrointestinal symptoms, allergic phenomena, and chest, pelvic, and back pain. Symptoms were often connected to previous sites of battering. One husband regularly scratched and gouged his wife's back to the point of bleeding and scarring; when there was increased tension at home her back "broke out" in giant urticaria.[19]

Treatment of preexisting chronic disease was complicated by the affective states of these women. For example, an epileptic woman required multiple hospitalizations for seizures. Noncompliance in the use of anticonvulsants was her only escape from a savagely brutal husband who refused to allow her to leave the house unless she needed medical attention. Some women were unable to leave battering marriages because of physical disabilities that left them helpless, such as blindness and Huntington's chorea.[19]

Psychiatric histories suggested prior psychological dysfunction for more than half of the women in our study.[19] Depressive illness was the single most frequent diagnostic category, with manic-depressive psychosis, schizophrenia, alcoholism, and personality disorders all represented to a lesser degree. There were relatively few alcoholic women in this sample, but the women patients in a nearby alcoholic rehabilitation program were almost all victims of parental and marital violence. Some women in our study had been hospitalized repeatedly, often because of the acute onset of a reactive psychosis in which they lost control of aggressive impulses. Others had sought help from crisis lines, outpatient mental health facilities, and emergency rooms. Almost all of these women had made frequent visits to local physicians for somatic complaints, anxiety, insomnia, or suicide attempts, usually by drug overdoses. Most had been treated intermittently or chronically with sedative-hypnotics, tranquilizers, and/or antidepressants. Although these women had had multiple contacts with various clinicians over the years, they did not tell the physicians of the violence, nor did the physicians ask them.[6,19]

These findings of a high incidence of depressive symptoms, treatment with psychoactive drugs, and suicidal behavior are consistent with other reports.[6,15–17,19,20,48] Of Gayford's sample of 100 women,[15] 71 had symptoms that were treated with antidepressants and tranquilizers, 42 had attempted suicide, usually by overdose, 46 at some time had been referred to a psychiatrist, and 21 had a diagnosis of depression. Half of Dewsbury's sample of 15 women[6] had a history of psychiatric hospitalization.

The Impact of Violence: A Stress-Response Syndrome

Munson and I[19] have described a uniform psychological response to violence that was identical for the entire sample of battered women. These women were a study in paralyzing terror that was reminiscent of the rape trauma syndrome,[52] except the stress was unending and the threat of assault ever present. Agitation and anxiety bordering on panic were almost always present. Events even remotely connected with violence—sirens, thunder, a door slamming—elicited intense fear. There was chronic apprehension of imminent doom, of something terrible always about to happen. Any symbolic or actual sign of potential danger resulted in increased activity, agitation, pacing, screaming, and crying. The women remained vigilant, unable to relax or to sleep. Sleep, when it came, brought no relief. Nightmares were universal, with undisguised themes of violence and danger.

In contrast to their dreams, in which they actively attempted to protect themselves, the waking lives of these women were characterized by overwhelming passivity and inability to act. They were drained, fatigued, and numb, without the energy to do more than minimal household chores and child care. They had a pervasive sense of hopelessness and despair about themselves and their lives. They saw themselves as incompetent, unworthy, and unlovable and were ridden with guilt and shame. They thought they deserved the abuse, saw no options, and felt powerless to make changes.

Like rape victims, battered women rarely experienced their anger directly,[53] although their stories elicited anguish and outrage in the listener. It is probable that the constellation of passivity, guilt, intense fear of the unexpected, and violent nightmares reflected not only fear of another assault but a constant struggle with the self to contain and control aggressive impulses. The violent encounter with another person's loss of control of aggression precipitates great anxiety about one's own controls. We know from rape victims that one such encounter is sufficient to bury aggression.[54] In the life experiences of battered women, there is little perceived or real difference between affect, fantasy, and action. Thus it is not surprising that fear of loss of control was a universal concern. These fears were often expressed in vague, abstract terms but were unmistakably linked to aggression.

A minority of women did lose control of aggressive impulses. Some women became frankly homicidal and others fantasized detailed plans for murdering their husbands as a way of coping with their anger. They locked up guns and knives to prevent easy access to weapons, without knowing why they did so. Some displayed aggression by becoming adept at verbal retaliation, while others fought back physically. However, these cases were the exceptions; passivity and paralysis of action more accurately described the majority of these women. Aggression was most consistently directed against themselves, in the form of suicidal behavior, depression, grotesque self-imagery, alcoholism, or self-mutilation. One woman's face and body were covered with self-inflicted scratches and scars. Passivity and denial of anger do not imply that the battered woman is adjusted to or likes her situation. These are the last desperate defenses against homicidal rage.[19]

TREATMENT ISSUES

The Clinician's Response

The response of health professionals to wife-battering has generally been characterized by inattention, blame, and disbelief. Explanations for the extraordinary difficulty experienced by clinicians in confronting these issues are complex and multidetermined. First, both male and female clinicians share the pervasive cultural biases and myths that stereotype and denigrate women (e.g., the ambivalent image of woman as virgin or seductress). Second, female victims of male aggression may not feel safe in revealing the abuse to male clinicians. Third, even when clinicians are sensitive to the possibility of such victimization, they may find it difficult to initiate direct questions because the details of such savage abuse can be overwhelming, and the clinician may feel as anguished or helpless as the patient. Finally, the frequency with which family violence occurs makes it likely that an individual clinician may have personally experienced a violent family or may have a friend or family member who was abused. It is not surprising, then, that the pressure on the clinician is to achieve some distance from the victim. This distancing is achieved by disbelief, labeling, accusations that the victim "needs" the abuse or could have controlled or prevented it by being less provocative, and the unfounded assumption that most victims come from poor or black families and are thus different from the clinician.

Identification

Clinicians must be aware of the prevalence of family violence and the variety of ways in which victims may present themselves. The portal of entry to health care is determined by the nature of the presenting symptom. Victims with physical injuries are seen on emergency and trauma services and are then referred to surgical subspecialists and dentists.[14,22] Those with chronic psychosomatic symptoms, anxiety, and insomnia make multiple visits to general practitioners and family doctors. Battered women who are severely depressed, anxious, or suicidal are referred to crisis intervention units or psychiatrists for evaluation, while those with functional psychoses enter psychiatric hospitals. Victims who are substance abusers may come to the attention of drug or alcohol programs. Some victims can be identified by virtue of their relationship to other identified patients, such as alcoholic husbands and abused or disturbed children. A high index of suspicion facilitates victim identification, but there is no substitute for a direct inquiry about violence. Clinicians must be aware that victims for whom violence has become a way of life do not define the abuse as "violence" and will deny its occurrence. Thus it is more helpful and productive to base questions on behavioral descriptions, e.g., "Is anyone at home hitting you?"

Once established, marital violence tends to escalate, and the possibility of a lethal outcome must be considered throughout the diagnostic and treatment process. This is especially important in the usual clinical situation, in which only the abused wife is in treatment and the violence at home is continuing. In theory, the aim of treatment might be to terminate the violence or the marital relationship. In practice, however, the husband usually does not perceive his behavior as a problem requiring intervention, and his wife maintains secrecy about any intervention to avoid further violence or interference with her treatment. Removal of women and children from the home to a safe environment is therefore essential to adequate long-term treatment and rehabilitation.[3,7,12,15,19,21,39,46,55–58] In the absence of such shelter, battering men will continue to follow, harrass, and assault their families wherever they go.

Why Do They Stay?

Women are trapped in violent homes by a complex interplay of intrapsychic and external constraints. Gelles[59] cited three major factors that influence the abused woman's likelihood of staying in the marriage:

1. The less severe and less frequent the violence, the more likely the woman is to stay.
2. The more a woman was struck by her parents as a child, the more likely she is to stay.
3. The fewer her resources and the less her power, the more probable it is she will stay.

Clinicians must identify the woman's internal and external barriers to self-protection in order to help her become capable of action to terminate the violence or the marriage.

Among contemporary researchers, there has been little enthusiasm or supporting data for the theories of masochism that have been traditionally invoked to explain why women remain in violent relationships.[15,20,39,48,49,59,60] Clinicians and social scientists highlight the absence of economic resources as a factor that severely limits the options of women attempting to leave their marriages. Most women are economically dependent on their husbands and have neither the job skills nor opportunities that are necessary for financial independence. The economic realities for female-headed single-parent families are well documented.[58]

In an elegant critical review of theories of female masochism, Waites[60] argued:

> Female motivation, like motivation generally, must be studied in the context of external constraints such as social choices available and the consequences of particular choices. In this light, the masochistic woman often appears as an individual who has almost no choice, given the lack of social support for extricating herself from her situation or who is confronted with alternatives which are, for the most part, negatively valued.

She concluded that theories of female masochism are inadequate as explanations of actual behavior because "in situations in which choice is externally restricted, the question of internal motivation approaches irrelevance."[60]

The combination of continuing threats and violence by the husband and the absence of provisions for safety is universally identified as a deterrent to action. As Martin[3] asserted, "Battered women give many reasons or rationalizations for staying, but fear is the common denominator. Fear immobilizes them, ruling their actions, their decisions, their very lives." She cited Maccoby and Jacklin,[61] who suggested that while fear is an arousal state, "the possibility exists that females show immobilization and other 'passive' behavior primarily when they are afraid." In a paper presented to the Association for the Advancement of Psychoanalysis in October 1977 Symonds also concluded, "The response of women to the violence of the immature, impulsive and exploitive husband is to be profoundly terrorized and traumatized by this violence"; they are "brainwashed by terror." He conceptualized this fear as a form of traumatic psychological infantilism or frozen fright, which in other reports[62,63] he described as the acute psychological response to rape and other violent crimes.

There has also been increasing interest on the part of several authors[21,49,60,64] in Seligman's concept of learned helplessness[65] as an explanation of the abused wife's continued passivity when external options seem possible or are made available:

> When an organism has experienced trauma it cannot control, its motivation to respond in the face of later trauma wanes. Moreover, even if it does respond and the response succeeds in producing relief, it has trouble learning, perceiving, and believing that the response worked. (pp. 22–23)

Battered women do not believe that they can escape from the batterer's domination.[49] This expectation of powerlessness and inability to control one's destiny, whether real or perceived, prevents effective action. Traditional sex-role socialization norms further reinforce the idea that women's needs are fulfilled and their identities derived only indirectly through their men. As a consequence women have inadequate preparation for independence and inadequate skills for assertive problem-solving behavior.

These descriptions of the victim's immobilization and inability to leave the violent home are reminiscent of the pathological transference that develops between hostages and hostage-takers. According to Ochberg,[66] the "Stockholm syndrome" includes positive feelings on the part of the hostage toward the captor, negative feelings on the part of the hostage toward the authorities responsible for rescue, and reciprocation of positive feelings by the hostage-taker toward the captive. He suggested that this pathological transference is based on the captive's terror, infantile dependence, and gratitude and that this relationship may, in fact, promote the survival of the hostage.

The constructs offered as explanations of why women remain in destructive relationships are not mutually exclusive and have important implications for the choice of treatment models and the availability and nature of programs for battered women.[49,57,60,64,67] The most significant treatment implication derives from the way in which the locus of the problem is defined. Theories of masochism, which locate the problem within the victim, lead to certain assumptions about victim–offender relationships and programmatic responses that have been described by Lynch and Norris.[67] For example, if the victim is held responsible for the abuse, there will be no support for spouse-abuse programming, and existing helping agencies will set the victim up for further abuse.[67]

Clinicians working with battered women comment on the frequency with which helpers become frustrated and angry with their clients.[7,19,49] Even victims who initiate the request for assistance and shelter and who are provided with resources often show a pattern of secrecy, continued protection of the assailant, and failure to follow through. It often takes four or five separations from an abusive spouse before the fantasy of change within the marriage ends and a decisive separation occurs.[19,21]

As Walker[49] pointed out, "It is probable that battered women do not accept the helper's assistance because they do not believe it will be effective. This can be attributed to the learned helplessness hypothesis in which their cognitive set tells them that no one can help them." One treatment implication of this learning theory is that clinicians may need to view changes in behavior and cognitive sets as primary, with the expectation that motivational and affective correlates will follow. In order to reverse this conditioning for helplessness, clinicians must find new ways to motivate clients to try new behaviors.[45]

Clinicians who work with battered women are aware of the temptation to take excessive responsibility for the victim's treatment in response to her presentation of herself as incompetent and unable to help herself. These attempts to "rescue" the victim may lead her to shift her dependence from the abusive husband to the therapist or agency,[57,64] thus reinforcing her passivity and helplessness. Personnel in refuges and shelters are especially sensitive to the importance of achieving "a reconceptualization of self from 'victim' and 'failure' to competent, autonomous person" and have developed a variety of environmental models in which women "come to define their own acts, to accept responsibility for them, and see themselves as capable of acting independently."[57]

Thus the evaluation of battered women must include a careful assessment of those intrapsychic and environmental factors which limit or can be mobilized to facilitate constructive solutions. Limiting factors may be intrapsychic, such as severe depression, passivity, or self-blame, or external, such as economic dependence on the spouse, physical disability, or homicidal threats by the husband. Potential resources include personal strengths, talents, and capacities, as well as concerned family and friends and institutional means for economic, legal, educational, and vocational support. In describing the direct treatment situation, Waites[60] concluded that

> an awareness of external constraints can be helpful in raising the self-esteem of the client as well as in helping her sort out the extent to which her own actions do interact with circumstances to keep her in a destructive situation.... Once reality is acknowledged ... irrational behavior patterns can be examined both from the standpoint of how such patterns were originally acquired and how they may be changed.

Victims' Needs for Intervention and the Clinician's Role

Victims have both short- and long-term needs that include immediate protection and crisis intervention; food, clothing, and shelter; medical, psychiatric, and legal interventions; psychotherapy and counseling; and the mobilization of resources that support an alternative choice to living with an abusive spouse. The extent of these needs will vary according to an individual's life circumstances, adaptive capacities, and psychological status—one client may need all of these resources, while another may need few.

Emergency Protection/Crisis Intervention. An understanding of the immediate determinants of a call for help is crucial to any assessment. Some women come to law enforcement or health facilities when the violence has escalated to a point where their lives are endangered. Others come when they are losing control of their aggressive impulses toward self, spouse, or children. These are emergencies in which immediate protection is imperative. It may be necessary for the clinician to intervene directly with hospitals, law enforcement, child protection, and social service agencies, and/or emergency shelters. The lack of emergency housing for women in crisis has complicated disposition planning enormously,[68] and the experiences of the current shelter movement underscore the necessity for a safe milieu in which a woman can begin the process of regaining control of her life without fear. When emergency protection is not needed early in treatment, it may become necessary later, as will be discussed in the section on psychotherapy and counseling issues. Personnel who work with battered women are keenly aware that intervention involves "anticipating the worst and preparing for it."[64]

Treatment of Mental Illness and Stress Syndromes. Diagnosis of any clinical psychopathologic syndrome for which a specific treatment modality exists will obviously enhance the battered woman's ability to take control of her life. Hospitalization is indicated when there is acute decompensation or loss of control. I have not found hospitalization useful beyond these urgent needs, perhaps because the hospital environment often tends to reinforce helpless and dependent behavior. As noted earlier, depressive reactions are especially prevalent among abused women and respond to tricyclic antidepressant treatment. However, clinicians should be aware when prescribing such medications of the frequency with which abused women attempt suicide by drug overdose.

The stress syndrome that occurs in response to the violence itself seems to abate only with removal of the threat of violence. The agitation and sleep disturbances have been treated with low doses of antianxiety agents and antidepressants. However, when there may be dangerous consequences if the woman goes to sleep or decreases her vigilance, medication is usually ineffective and is contraindicated.

Psychotherapy and Counseling Issues. The battered woman has often experienced a lifetime of abuse and neglect by significant others and in her contacts with medical, social, and criminal justice agencies. She thus comes to believe that she deserves such treatment and to expect no empathy from clinicians. Her feelings of helpless rage, which she may have acted out against her children or herself, further intensify her belief that she is unworthy or bad. To tell the clinician about the spouse's violence or her own frightening impulses is to risk yet another confirmation of her harsh self-judgment. The core issues for psychotherapeutic work, then, are the woman's markedly impaired self-esteem, emotional isolation, and mistrust.

There is a complex mythology about wife-beating that must be identified and challenged early in the treatment of battered women. The victim uses this group of beliefs to "explain" the brutality:

1. The violence is "normal," a perception seen most often in victims who come from violent families of origin.
2. The violence is rationalized: the husband is not responsible because he is sick, mentally ill, alcoholic, unemployed, or under stress.
3. The violence is justified: the woman deserves it because she is bad, provocative, or challenging.
4. The violence is controllable: if the woman is good, quiet, and compliant, her husband will not abuse her.

These beliefs reinforce the battered woman's tenuous denial and protect her husband and her marriage, at the expense of her self-esteem and autonomy and, possibly, her life. They allow her to remain totally enslaved while she believes that she is in control.

In a therapeutic relationship, the battered woman becomes aware of the extent of her rage and its relationship to her guilt, passivity, and fears of losing control. Understandably, this is a crisis point for some women, who may require hospitalization or intensive outpatient work to support their controls. This is also a time when the woman begins to take a more assertive position, with tentative plans for employment, vocational training, education, and termination of the marriage. Because the woman's behavioral changes may lead to escalation of her husband's violent behavior, she should not be pushed to move beyond her perceived "safe boundaries" in acknowledging her anger or confronting her husband. The clinician must assume that the woman is accurate in her assessment of her controls, the extent of the danger to herself and her children, and her husband's potential for violence.

This discussion of treatment issues has been based on the assumptions that the abused woman's living situation continues to leave her vulnerable to violent abuse and that her husband does not think he needs treatment, which are the most common conditions in cases of spouse abuse. Treatment options may expand if the victim is protected from further violence and/or her husband is motivated to seek help. The latter situation is more likely to occur when the assailant no longer has access to the victim. Treatment modalities may then include couples work, individual or group therapy with the abusing spouse, or a shelter for violent husbands. Our knowledge of these treatment options is preliminary and beyond the scope of this paper. However, some observations on this subject are relevant.

Commenting on her research with couples therapy, Walker[49] noted that battered women are more successful at reversing helplessness when they leave the relationship than when they remain with their partners and try to change the relationship to a nonbattering one. She suggested that before couples therapy can begin, the symbiotic dependency bonds that have developed must be severed by treating the couple as two individuals, with a focus on enhancing independent behavior and teaching new communication skills. In a study designed to test the hypothesis that treatment approaches which encourage ventilation of anger may be dangerous, Straus[69] found that increases in verbal aggression resulted in dramatic increases in physical aggression. Thus clinicians must exert caution in devising treatment strategies for aggressive clients.

Identification of Life Alternatives. Adequate rehabilitative efforts often require information and assistance from a variety of community resources with which both the battered woman and the clinician may have contact, including (1) medical facilities for reproductive control and medical and mental health care, (2) social service agencies for financial aid, housing, emergency shelter, food stamps, clothing, day care, and child protective services, (3) criminal justice agencies for protection against further violence, (4) legal aid for assistance with warrants, court procedures, and separation and divorce agreements, (5) vocational rehabilitation programs for financial aid and information about educational pursuits, job training, and employment counseling, and (6) women's groups for information, support, and shelter.[19,67]

Consultation and Collaboration. Thus far, the role of mental health professionals has been discussed in terms of direct services to victims. There is also a broad spectrum of consultative roles with other clinicians and agencies and in collaborative efforts to develop innovative programs. Within the hospital setting, mental health professionals can use their consultative and liaison skills to educate the staff of emergency, trauma, and general medical services in the identification and assessment of "silent victims" and in the variety of treatment options and community programs.

Outside of the medical setting, there is a growing need for mental health consultation to criminal justice agencies. Appropriate areas for consultation include crisis intervention training for law enforcement personnel, with emphasis on strategies to de-escalate violence and to mediate disputes, and prosecutor and court diversion programs that provide victims and offenders with referrals to helping agencies and special treatment facilities.[28,70–72] A newer area for psychiatric consultation and education is the courtroom. Attorneys are increasingly requesting pretrial psychiatric evaluations and consultations in preparing the defense of the battered wife who kills her husband after years of abuse.[73] These women usually do not have extensive criminal records, and the homicide often reflects the failure of law enforcement personnel and the courts to protect such women, especially those who are poor and/or minority group members. Psychiatrists can help to educate prosecutors, defense attorneys, judges, and juries about the social and psychological aspects of wife-beating and the context in which a fatality can occur in the absence of insanity or premeditation. Through testimony, they can assist in the determination of a therapeutic rather than a punitive disposition.

The widespread development of shelters for abused women and their children has given rise to another area for mental health consultation. Evaluation services for victims and their children are needed, as are programs that focus on unlearning aggressive behavior patterns and teaching nonviolent models for relationships. Shelters are a singularly important therapeutic and rehabilitative experience for battered women and their children. As Vaughan[56] noted,

> A shelter is not a treatment center, residents are not described as clients, battering is not described as a syndrome. . . . In the operation of the house every attempt is made to avoid labels that stereotype. A woman at the shelter said once, "It belittles you to admit you're a battered woman. I don't like the name. I'd rather be referred to as temporarily abused."

REFERENCES

1. Gelles R. J.: *The Violent Home: A Study of Physical Aggression Between Husbands and Wives.* Beverly Hills, Sage Publications, 1974
2. Steinmetz S. K., Straus M. A. (eds): *Violence in the Family.* New York, Harper & Row, 1974
3. Martin D.: *Battered Wives,* San Francisco, Glide, 1976
4. O'Brien J. E.: Violence in divorce prone families. *Journal of Marriage and the Family* 33(4):692–698, 1971
5. Snell J. E., Rosenwald R. J., Robey A.: The wife-beater's wife, *Arch Gen Psychiatry* 11:107–112, 1964
6. Dewsbury A.: Family violence seen in general practice. *R Soc Health J* 95:290–294, 1975
7. Pizzey E.: *Scream Quietly or the Neighbors will Hear.* Essex, England, Anchorage, 1974
8. Chapman J. R., Gates M. (eds): *The Victimization of Women.* Beverly Hills, Sage Publications, 1978
9. Lystad M.: Violence at home: a review of the literature. *Am J Orthopsychiatry* 45:328–345, 1975
10. Russell D. E. H., Van de Ven N. (eds): *Crimes Against Women: Proceedings of the International Tribunal.* Millbrae, Calif. Les Femmes, 1976
11. Stahly G. B.: A review of select literature of spousal abuse. *Victimology: An International Journal* 2(3/4):591–607, 1977–1978
12. *Battered Women: Issues of Public Policy.* Washington, D.C., U.S. Commission on Civil Rights, 1978
13. Roy M. (ed): *Battered Women: A Psychosociological Study of Domestic Violence.* New York, Van Nostrand Reinhold, 1977
14. Fonseka S.: A study of wife beating in the Camberwell area. *Br J Clin Pract* 28:400–402, 1974
15. Gayford J. J.: Battered wives, *Med Sci Law* 15:237–245, 1975
16. Gayford J. J.: Research on battered wives. *R Soc Health J* 95:288–289, 1975
17. Gayford J. J.: Wife battering: a preliminary survey of 100 cases. *Br Med J* 1:194–197, 1975
18. Hanks S. E., Rosenbaum P.: Battered women: a study of women who live with violent alcohol-abusing men. *Am J Orthopsychiatry* 47:291–306, 1977
19. Hilberman E., Munson K.: Sixty battered women. *Victimology: An International Journal* 2(3/4):460–471, 1977–1978
20. Scott P. D.: Battered wives. *Br J Psychiatry* 125:433–441, 1974
21. Walker L. E.: *The Battered Woman.* New York, Harper & Row, 1979
22. Stark E., Flitcraft A., Frazier W.: Medicine and patriarchal violence: the social construction of a "private" event. *Int J Health Serv* 9:461–493, 1979
23. Gelles R. J., Straus M. A.: Family experience and public support of the death penalty. *Am J Orthopsychiatry* 45:596–613, 1975
24. Straus M. A.: Wifebeating: how common and why? *Victimology: An International Journal* 2(3/4):443–458, 1977–1978
25. Stark R., McEvoy J.: Middle class violence. *Psychology Today,* November 1970, pp. 52–65
26. Levinger G.: Sources of marital dissatisfaction among applicants for divorce. *Am J Orthopsychiatry* 36:803–807, 1966
27. Schulman M. A.: *A Survey of Spousal Violence Against Women in Kentucky Conducted for the Kentucky Commission on Women.* New York, Louis Harris and Associates, July 1979
28. Gates M. J.: *The battered woman: criminal and civil remedies.* Presented at the 130th annual

meeting of the American Psychiatric Association, Toronto, Ont, Canada, May 2-6, 1977

29. Boudouris J.: Homicide and the family. *Journal of Marriage and the Family* 33(4):667–682, 1971

30. Dobash R. E., Dobash R. P.: Wives: the "appropriate" victims of marital violence. *Victimology: An International Journal* 2(3/4):426–442, 1977–1978

31. Goode W.: Force and violence in the family. *Journal of Marriage and the Family* 33(4):637–648, 1971

32. Truninger E.: Marital violence: the legal solutions. *Hastings Law Review* 23:259–276, 1971

33. *Conflict Management: Analysis/Resolution.* Kansas City, Mo, Kansas City Police Department, 1973

34. Dobash R. E., Dobash R. P.: *Violence Against Wives.* New York, Free Press, 1979

35. National Commission on the Causes and Prevention of Violence: *Staff Report.* Washington, D.C., U.S. Government Printing Office, 1969

36. Brownmiller S.: *Against Our Will: Men, Women, and Rape.* New York, Simon and Schuster, 1975

37. Weis K., Borges S. S.: Victimology and rape: the case of the legitimate victim. *Issues in Criminology* 8(2):71–115, 1973

38. Straus M. A.: Sexual inequality, cultural norms, and wifebeating. *Victimology: An International Journal* 1(1):54–76, 1976

39. Straus M. A.: A sociological perspective on the prevention and treatment of wifebeating, in *Battered Women.* Edited by Roy M. New York, Van Nostrand Reinhold, 1977

40. London J.: Images of violence against women. *Victimology: An International Journal* 2(3/4):510–524, 1977–1978

41. Davidson T.: Wifebeating: a recurring phenomenon throughout history, in *Battered Women.* Edited by Roy M. New York, Van Nostrand Reinhold, 1977

42. Eisenberg S., Micklow P.: The assaulted wife: "Catch 22" revisited. *Women's Rights Law Reporter* 5(3/4):138, 1976

43. Martin D.: Overview: scope of the problem, in *Battered Women: Issues of Public Policy.* Washington, D.C., U.S. Commission on Civil Rights, 1978

44. Field M., Field H.: Marital violence and the criminal process: neither justice nor peace. *Social Service Review* 47:221–240, 1973

45. Field M. D.: Wife beating: government intervention policies and practices, in *Battered Women: Issues of Public Policy.* Washington, D.C., U.S. Commission on Civil Rights, 1978

46. Pizzey E.: Chiswick Women's Aid: a refuge from violence. *R Soc Health J* 95:297–298, 308, 1975

47. Parker B., Schumacher D. N.: The battered wife syndrome and violence in the nuclear family of origin: a controlled pilot study. *Am J Public Health* 67:760–761, 1977

48. Rounsaville B. J.: Theories in marital violence: evidence from a study of battered women. *Victimology: An International Journal* 3(1/2):11–29, 1978

49. Walker L. E.: Battered women and learned helplessness. *Victimology: An International Journal* 2(3/4):525–534, 1978

50. Gelles R. J.: Violence and pregnancy: a note on the extent of the problem and needed services. *Family Coordinator* 24:81–86, 1975

51. Pfouts J. H.: Violent families: coping responses of abused wives. *Child Welfare* 57:101–111, 1978

52. Burgess A. W., Holmstrom L. L.: Rape trauma syndrome. *Am J Psychiatry* 131:981–986, 1974

53. Notman M. T., Nadelson C. C.: The rape victim: psychodynamic considerations. *Am J Psychiatry* 133:408–413, 1976

54. Hilberman E.: The impact of rape, in *The Woman Patient*, vol 1. Edited by Notman M. T., Nadelson C. C. New York, Plenum Press, 1978

55. Walker L. E.: Treatment alternatives for battered women, in *The Victimization of Women*. Edited by Chapman J. R., Gates M. Beverly Hills, Sage Publications, 1978

56. Vaughan S. R.: *The last refuge: shelter for battered women*. Presented at the 130th annual meeting of the American Psychiatric Association, Toronto, Ont, Canada, May 2–6, 1977

57. Ridington J.: The transition process: a feminist environment as reconstitutive milieu. *Victimology: An International Journal* 2(3/4):563–575, 1977–1978

58. *Report of the Subpanel on Women's Mental Health of the President's Commission on Mental Health*, vol III (Appendix). Washington, D.C., U.S. Government Printing Office, 1978

59. Gelles R. J.: Abused wives: why do they stay? *Journal of Marriage and the Family* 38:659–668, 1976

60. Waites E. A.: Female masochism and the enforced restriction of choice. *Victimology: An International Journal* 2(3/4):535–544, 1977–1978

61. Maccoby E. E., Jacklin C. N.: *The Psychology of Sex Differences*. Stanford, Calif, Stanford University Press, 1974

62. Symonds M.: Victims of violence: psychological effects and after-effects. *Am J Psychoanal* 35:19–26, 1975

63. Symonds M.: The rape victim: psychological patterns of response. *Am J Psychoanal* 36:27–34, 1976

64. Ball P. G., Wyman E.: Battered wives and powerlessness: what can counselors do? *Victimology: An International Journal* 2(3/4):545–552, 1977–1978

65. Seligman M. E.: *Helplessness: On Depression, Development, and Death*. San Francisco, W. H. Freeman & Co, 1975

66. Ochberg F. M.: Victims of terrorism (editorial). *Journal of Clinical Psychiatry* 41:73–74, 1980

67. Lynch C. G., Norris T. L.: Services for battered women: looking for a perspective. *Victimology: An International Journal* 2(3/4):553–562, 1977–1978

68. Sutton J.: The growth of the British movement for battered women. Ibid, pp 576–584

69. Straus M. A.: Leveling, civility, and violence in the family. *Journal of Marriage and the Family* 36:13–29, 1974

70. Bard M., Zacker J.: The prevention of family violence: dilemmas of community intervention. *Journal of Marriage and the Family* 33:677–682, 1971

71. Bard M., Connolly H.: The police and family violence: policy and practice, in *Battered Women: Issues of Public Policy*. Washington, D.C., U.S. Commission on Civil Rights, 1978

72. Laszlo A. T., McKean T.: Court diversion: an alternative for spousal abuse cases. Ibid

73. Schneider E. M., Jordan S. B.: *Representation of Women Who Defend Themselves in Response to Physical or Sexual Assault*. New York, N.Y., Center for Constitutional Rights, 1978

Father–Daughter Incest

16

JUDITH HERMAN AND LISA HIRSCHMAN

A FEMINIST THEORETICAL PERSPECTIVE

The incest taboo is universal in human culture. Though it varies from one culture to another, it is generally considered by anthropologists to be the foundation of all kinship structures. Lévi-Strauss describes it as the basic social contract; Mead says its purpose is the preservation of the human social order.[1] All cultures, including our own, regard violations of the taboo with horror and dread. Death has not been considered too extreme a punishment in many societies. In our laws, some states punish incest by up to 20 years' imprisonment.[2]

In spite of the strength of the prohibition on incest, sexual relations between family members do occur. Because of the extreme secrecy which surrounds the violation of our most basic sexual taboo, we have little clinical literature and no accurate statistics on the prevalence of incest. This paper attempts to review what is known about the occurrence of incest between parents and children, to discuss common social attitudes which pervade the existing clinical literature, and to offer a theoretical perspective which locates the incest taboo and its violations within the structure of patriarchy.

The Occurrence of Incest

The Children's Division of the American Humane Association estimates that a minimum of 80,000–100,000 children are sexually molested each year.[3] In the majority of these cases the offender is well known to the child, and in about 25% of them, a relative. These estimates are based on New York City police records and the experience of social workers in a child protection agency. They are, therefore, projections based on observing poor and disorganized families who lack the resources to preserve secrecy. There is reason to believe, however, that most incest in fact

Reprinted from *Signs: Journal of Women in Culture and Society* 2(4):735–756, 1977. Copyright © 1977 by the University of Chicago. All rights reserved. Reprinted by permission. The authors gratefully acknowledge the contributions of the incest victims themselves and of the therapists who shared their experience with us. For reasons of confidentiality, we cannot thank them by name.

occurs in intact families and entirely escapes the attention of social agencies. One in 16 of the 8000 white, middle-class women surveyed by Kinsey et al. reported sexual contact with an adult relative during childhood.[4] In the vast majority of these cases, the incident remained a secret.

A constant finding in all existing surveys is the overwhelming predominance of father–daughter incest. Weinberg, in a study of 200 court cases in the Chicago area, found 164 cases of father–daughter incest, compared with two cases of mother–son incest.[5] Maisch, in a study of court cases in the Federal Republic of Germany, reported that 90% of the cases involved fathers and daughters, stepfathers and stepdaughters, or (infrequently) grandfathers and granddaughters.[6] Fathers and sons accounted for another 5%. Incest between mothers and sons occurred in only 4% of the cases. Incest appears to follow the general pattern of sexual abuse of children, in which 92% of the victims are female, and 97% of the offenders are male.[7]

It may be objected that these data are all based on court records and perhaps reflect only a difference in complaints rather than a difference in incidence. The Kinsey reports, however, confirm the impression of a major discrepency between the childhood sexual contacts of boys and girls. If, as noted above, more than 6% of the female sample reported sexual approaches by adult relatives, only a small number of the 12,000 men surveyed reported sexual contact with any adult, relative or stranger. (Exact figures were not reported.) Among these few, contact with adult males seemed to be more common than with adult females. As for mother–son incest, the authors concluded that "heterosexual incest occurs more frequently in the thinking of clinicians and social workers than it does in actual performance."[8] None of the existing literature, to our knowledge, makes any attempt to account for this striking discrepancy between the occurrence of father–daughter and mother–son incest.

Common Attitudes toward Incest in the Professional Literature

Because the subject of incest inspires such strong emotional responses, few authors have even attempted a dispassionate examination of its actual occurrence and effects. Those who have approached the subject have often been unable to avoid defensive reactions such as denial, distancing, or blaming. We undertake this discussion with the full recognition that we ourselves are not immune to these reactions, which may be far more apparent to our readers than to ourselves.

Undoubtedly the most famous and consequential instance of denial of the reality of incest occurs in Freud's 1897 letter to Fliess. In it, Freud reveals the process by which he came to disbelieve the reports of his female patients and develop his concepts of infantile sexuality and the infantile neurosis: "Then there was the astonishing thing that in every case blame was laid on perverse acts by the father, and realization of the unexpected frequency of hysteria, in every case of which the same thing applied, though it was hardly credible that perverted acts against children were so general."[9]

Freud's conclusion that the sexual approaches did not occur in fact was based simply on his unwillingness to believe that incest was such a common event in respectable families. To experience a sexual approach by a parent probably *was* unlikely for a boy: Freud concluded incorrectly that the same was true for girls. Rather than investigate further into the question of fact, Freud's followers chose to continue the presumption of fantasy and made the child's desire and fantasy the focus of psychological inquiry. The adult's desire (and capacity for action) were forgotten. Psychoanalytic investigation, then, while it placed the incest taboo at the center of the child's psychological development, did little to dispel the secrecy surrounding the actual occurrence of incest. As one child psychiatrist commented: "Helene Deutsch and other followers of Freud have, in my opinion, gone too far in the direction of conceptualizing patients' reports of childhood sexual abuse in terms of fantasy. My own experience, both in private practice and with several hundred child victims brought to us . . . [at the Center for Rape Concern] . . . in Philadelphia, has convinced me that analysts too often dismissed as fantasy what was the real sexual molestation of a child. . . . As a result, the victim was isolated and her trauma compounded."[10]

Even those investigators who have paid attention to cases of actual incest have often shown a tendency to comment or make judgments concerning the guilt or innocence of the participants. An example:

> These children undoubtedly do not deserve completely the cloak of innocence with which they have been endowed by moralists, social reformers, and legislators. The history of the relationship in our cases usually suggests at least some cooperation of the child in the activity, and in some cases the child assumed an active role in initiating the relationship. . . . It is true that the child often rationalized with excuses of fear of physical harm or the enticement of gifts, but there were obviously secondary reasons. Even in the cases where physical force may have been applied by the adult, this did not wholly account for the frequent repetition of the practice.
>
> Finally, a most striking feature was that these children were distinguished as unusually charming and attractive in their outward personalities. Thus, it was not remarkable that frequently we considered the possibility that the child might have been the actual seducer, rather than the one innocently seduced.[11]

In addition to denial and blame, much of the existing literature on incest shows evidence of social and emotional distancing between the investigators and their subjects. This sometimes takes the form of an assertion that incestuous behavior is accepted or condoned in some culture other than the investigator's own. Thus, a British study of Irish working-class people reports that father–daughter incest, which occurred in 4% of an unselected outpatient clinic population, was a "cultural phenomenon" precipitated by social isolation or crowding, and had "no pathological effects."[12] The several investigators who have also reported instances where children, in their judgment, were not harmed by the incest experience do not usually state the criteria on which this judgment is based.[13] Still other investigators seem fearful to commit themselves to an opinion on the question of harm. Thus, for example, although 70% of the victims in Maisch's survey showed evidence of disturbed personality development, the author is uncertain about ascribing this to the effects of incest per se.

A few investigators, however, have testified to the destructive effects of the incest experience on the development of the child. Sloane and Karpinski, who studied five incestuous families in rural Pennsylvania, conclude: "Indulgence in incest in the post-adolescent period leads to serious repercussions in the girl, even in an environment where the moral standards are relaxed."[14] Kaufman, Peck, and Tagiuri, in a thorough study of 11 victims and their families who were seen at a Boston clinic, report: "Depression and guilt were universal as clinical findings. . . . The underlying craving for an adequate parent . . . dominated the lives of these girls."[15]

Several retrospective studies, including a recent report by Benward and Densen-Gerber, document a strong association between reported incest history and the later development of promiscuity or prostitution.[16] In fact, failure to marry or promiscuity seems to be the only criterion generally accepted in the literature as conclusive evidence that the victim has been harmed.[17] We believe that this finding in itself testifies to the traditional bias which pervades the incest literature.

Our survey of what has been written about incest, then, raises several questions. Why does incest between fathers and daughters occur so much more frequently than incest between mothers and sons? Why, though this finding has been consistently documented in all available sources, has no previous attempt been made to explain it? Why does the incest victim find so little attention or compassion in the literature, while she finds so many authorities who are willing to assert either that the incest did not happen, that it did not harm her, or that she was to blame for it? We believe that a feminist perspective must be invoked in order to address these questions.

Incest and Patriarchy

In a patriarchal culture, such as our own, the incest taboo must have a different meaning for the two sexes and may be observed by men and women for different reasons.

Major theorists in the disciplines of both psychology and anthropology explain the importance of the incest taboo by placing it at the center of an agreement to control warfare among men. It represents the first and most basic peace treaty. An essential element of the agreement is the concept that women are the possessions of men; the incest taboo represents an agreement as to how women shall be shared. Since virtually all known societies are dominated by men, all versions of the incest taboo are agreements among men regarding sexual access to women. As Mitchell points out, men create rules governing the exchange of women; women do not create rules governing the exchange of men.[18] Because the taboo is created and enforced by men, we argue that it may also be more easily and frequently violated by men.

The point at which the child learns the meaning of the incest taboo is the point of initiation into the social order. Boys and girls, however, learn different versions of the taboo. To paraphrase Freud once again, the boy learns that he may not consummate his sexual desires for his mother because his mother belongs to his father, and his father has the power to inflict the most terrible of punishments on him: to deprive him of his maleness.[19] In compensation, however, the boy learns that when he is a man he will one day possess women of his own.

When this little boy grows up, he will probably marry and may have a daughter. Although custom will eventually oblige him to give away his daughter in marriage to another man (note that mothers do not give away either daughters or sons), the taboo against sexual contact with his daughter will never carry the same force, either psychologically or socially, as the taboo which prohibited incest with his mother. *There is no punishing father to avenge father–daughter incest.*

What the little girl learns is not at all parallel. Her initiation into the patriarchal order begins with the realization that she is not only comparatively powerless as a child, but that she will remain so as a woman. She may acquire power only indirectly, as the favorite of a powerful man. As a child she may not possess her mother *or* her father; when she is an adult, her best hope is to *be* possessed by someone like her father. Thus, according to Freud she has less incentive than the boy to come to a full resolution of the Oedipus complex.[20] Since she has no hope of acquiring the privileges of an adult male, she can neither be rewarded for giving up her incestuous attachments nor punished for refusing to do so. Chesler states the same conclusion more bluntly: "Women are encouraged to commit incest as a way of life. . . . As opposed to marrying our fathers, we marry men like our fathers . . . men who are older than us, have more money than us, more power than us, are taller than us, are stronger than us . . . our fathers."[21]

A patriarchal society, then, most abhors the idea of incest between mother and son, because this is an affront to the father's prerogatives. Though incest between father and daughter is also forbidden, the prohibition carries considerably less weight and is, therefore, more frequently violated. We believe this understanding of the asymmetrical nature of the incest taboo under patriarchy offers an explanation for the observed difference in the occurrence of mother–son and father–daughter incest.

If, as we propose, the taboo on father–daughter incest is relatively weak in a patriarchal family system, we might expect violations of the taboo to occur most frequently in families characterized by extreme paternal dominance. This is in fact the case. Incest offenders are frequently described as "family tyrants": "These fathers, who are often quite incapable of relating their despotic claim to leadership to their social efforts for the family, tend toward abuses of authority of every conceivable kind, and they not infrequently endeavor to secure their dominant position by socially isolating the members of the family from the world outside. Swedish, American, and French surveys have pointed time and again to the patriarchal position of such fathers, who set up a 'primitive family order.' "[22] Thus the seduction of daughters is an abuse which is inherent in a father–dominated family system; we believe that the greater the degree of male supremacy in any culture, the greater the likelihood of father–daughter incest.

A final speculative point: since, according to this formulation, women neither make nor enforce the incest taboo, why is it that women apparently observe the taboo so scrupulously? We do not know. We suspect that the answer may lie in the historic experience of women both as sexual property and as the primary caretakers of children. Having been frequently obliged to exchange sexual services for protection and care, women are in a position to understand the harmful effects of introducing sex into a relationship where there is a vast inequality of power. And, having throughout history been assigned the primary responsibility for the care of children, women may be in a position to understand more fully the needs of children, the difference between affectionate and erotic contact, and the appropriate limits of parental love.

A CLINICAL REPORT

The following is a clinical case study of 15 victims of father–daughter incest. All the women were clients in psychotherapy who reported their incest experiences to their therapists after the fact. Seven were women whom the authors had personally evaluated or seen in psychotherapy. The remaining eight were clients in treatment with other therapists. No systematic case-finding effort was made; the authors simply questioned those practitioners who were best known to us through an informal network of female professionals. Four out of the first 10 therapists we questioned reported that at least one of her clients had an incest history. We concluded from this admittedly small sample that a history of incest is frequently encountered in clinical practice.

Our combined group of six therapists (the authors and our four informants) had interviewed close to 1000 clients in the past five years. In this population, the incidence of reported father–daughter incest was 2–3%. We believe this to be a minimum estimate, since in most cases no particular effort was made to elicit the history. Our estimate accords with the data of the Kinsey report,[23] in which 1.5% of the women surveyed stated that they had been molested by their fathers.

For the purposes of this study, we defined incest as overt sexual contact such as fondling, petting, masturbation, or intercourse between parent and child. We included only those cases in which there was no doubt in the daughter's mind that explicit and intentionally sexual contact occurred and that secrecy was required. Thus we did not include in our study the many women who reported seductive behaviors such as verbal sharing of sexual secrets, flirting, extreme possessiveness or jealousy, or intense interest in their bodies or their sexual activities on the part of their fathers. We recognize that these cases represent the extreme of a continuum of father–daughter relationships which range from the affectionate through the seductive to the overtly sexual. Information about the incest history was initially gathered from the therapists. Those clients who were willing to discuss their experiences with us in person were then interviewed directly.

The 15 women who reported that they had been molested during childhood were in other respects quite ordinary women. Nothing obvious distinguished them from the general population of women entering psychotherapy (see Table 1). They ranged in age from 15 to 55. Most were in their early 20's at the time they first requested psychotherapy. They were all white. Four were single, seven married, and four separated or divorced. Half had children. The majority had at least some college education. They worked at common women's jobs: housewife, waitress, factory worker, office worker, prostitute, teacher, nurse. They complained mostly of depression and social isolation. Those who were married or recently separated complained of marital problems. The severity of their complaints seemed to be related to the degree of family disorganization and deprivation in their histories rather than to the incest history per se. Five of the women had been hospitalized at some point in their lives; three were or had been actively suicidal, and two were addicted to drugs or alcohol. Seven women brought up the incest history among their initial complaints; the rest revealed it only after hav-

Table 1. Characteristics of Incest Victims
Entering Therapy

Characteristic	Victims (N)
Age (years)	
15–20	3
21–25	7
26–30	2
30+	3
Marital Status	
Single	4
Married	7
Separated or divorced	4
Occupation	
Blue collar	4
White collar	4
Professional	3
Houseworker	1
Student	3
Education	
High school not completed	4
High school completed	2
1–2 years college	3
College completed	5
Advanced degree	1
Presenting complaints	
Marital problems	5
Depression	3
Anxiety	3
Social isolation	4
Drug or alcohol abuse	4
Suicide attempt	2

ing established a relationship with the therapist. In some cases, the history was not disclosed for one, two, or even three years after therapy had begun.

The incest histories were remarkably similar (see Table 2). The majority of the victims were oldest or only daughters and were between the ages of 6 and 9 when they were first approached sexually by their fathers or male guardians (nine fathers, three stepfathers, a grandfather, a brother-in-law, and an uncle). The youngest girl was 4 years old; the oldest 14. The sexual contact usually took place repeatedly. In most cases the incestuous relationship lasted three years or more. Physical force was not used, and intercourse was rarely attempted with girls who had not reached puberty; the sexual contact was limited to masturbation and fondling. In three cases, the relationship was terminated when the father attempted intercourse.

> LENORE: I had already started to develop breasts at age nine and had my period when I was eleven. All this time he's still calling me into bed for "little chats" with him. I basically trusted him although I felt funny about it. Then one time I was twelve or thirteen, he called me into bed and started undressing me. He gave this rationale about preparing me to be with boys. He kept saying I was safe as long as I didn't let them take my pants down. Meantime he was doing the same thing. I split. I knew what he was trying to do, and that it was wrong. That was the end of the overt sexual stuff. Not long after that he found an excuse to beat me.

In all but two of these 15 cases the sexual relationship between father and daughter remained a secret, and there was no intervention in the family by the courts or child-protection authorities. Previous studies are based on court referrals and therefore give the erroneous impression that incest occurs predominantly in families at the lower end of the

TABLE 2. Characteristics of the Incest History

Characteristic	Incidence
Daughter's place in sibship	
Oldest daughter	9
Only daughter	3
Middle or youngest daughter	1
Unknown	2
Daughter's age at onset of incestuous relationship (years)	
4	1
5	0
6	2
7	3
8	4
9	2
10	0
11	1
12	0
13	0
14	1
Unknown	1
Duration of incestuous relationship (years)	
Single incident	1
1–2	1
3–4	3
5–6	5
7–10	2
Unknown	3

socioeconomic scale. This was not the case in the families of our victims. Of these, four fathers were blue-collar workers, two were white-collar workers, six were professionals, and the occupations of three were not known. The fathers' occupations cut across class lines. Several held jobs that required considerable personal competence and commanded social respect: college administrator, policeman, army officer, engineer. Others were skilled workers, foremen, or managers in factories or offices. All the mothers were houseworkers. Five of the 15 families could certainly be considered disorganized, with histories of poverty, unemployment, frequent moves, alcoholism, violence, abandonment, and foster care. Not surprisingly, the women who came from these families were those who complained of the most severe distress. The majority of the families, however, were apparently intact and maintained a facade of respectability.

The Incestuous Family Constellation

Both the apparently intact and the disorganized families shared certain common features in the pattern of family relationships. The most striking was the almost uniform estrangement of the mother and daughter, an estrangement that preceded the occurrence of overt incest. Over half the mothers were partially incapacitated by physical or mental illness or alcoholism and either assumed an invalid role within the home or were periodically absent because of hospitalization. Their oldest daughters were often obliged to take over the household duties. Anne-Marie remembered being hidden from the truant officer by her mother so that she could stay home and take care of the younger children. Her mother had tuberculosis. Claire's mother, who was not ill, went to work to support the family because her father, a severe alcoholic, brought home no money. In her absence, Claire did the housework and cooking and cared for her older brother.

At best, these mothers were seen by their daughters as helpless, frail, downtrodden victims, who were unable to take care of themselves, much less to protect their children.

> ANNE-MARIE: She used to say, "give with one hand and you'll get with the other" but she gave with two hands and always went down. . . . She was nothing but a floor mat. She sold out herself and her self-respect. She was a love slave to my father.
> CLAIRE: I always felt sorry for her. She spent her life suffering, suffering, suffering.

Some of the mothers habitually confided in their oldest daughters and unburdened their troubles to them. Theresa felt her mother was "more like a sister." Joan's mother frequently clung to her and told her, "You're the only one who understands me." By contrast, the daughters felt unable to go to their mothers for support or protection once their fathers had begun to make sexual advances to them. Some feared that their mothers would take action to expel the father from the house, but more commonly these daughters expected that their mothers would do nothing; in many cases the mothers tolerated a great deal of abuse themselves, and the daughters had learned not to expect any protection. Five of the women said they suspected that their mothers knew about the incest and tacitly condoned it. Two made attempts to bring up the subject but were put off by their mother's denial or indifference.

Only two of the 15 women actually told their mothers. Both had reason to regret it. Paula's mother reacted by committing her to an institution: "She was afraid I would become a lesbian or a whore." Sandra's mother initially took her husband to court. When she realized that a conviction would lead to his imprisonment, she reversed her testimony and publicly called her 12-year-old daughter a "notorious liar and slut."

The message that these mothers transmitted over and over to their daughters was: your father first, you second. It is dangerous to fight back, for if I lose him I lose everything. For my own survival I must leave you to your own devices. I cannot defend you, and if necessary I will sacrifice you to your father.

At worst, the mother–daughter relations were marked by frank and open hostility. Some of the daughters stated they could remember no tenderness or caring in the relationship.

> MARTHA: She's always picking on me. She's so fuckin' cold.
> PAULA: She's an asshole. I really don't like my mom. I guess I am bitter. She's very selfish. She did a lousy job of bringing me up.

The most severe disruption in the mother–daughter relationship occurred in Rita's case. She remembers receiving severe beatings from her mother, and her father intervening to rescue her. Though the physical attacks were infrequent, Rita recalls her mother as implacably hostile and critical, and her father as by far the more nurturant parent.

Previous studies of incestuous families document the disturbance in the mother–daughter relationship as a constant finding.[24] In a study of 11 girls who were referred by courts to a child guidance center, Kaufman et al. reported that the girls uniformly saw their mothers as cruel, unjust, and depriving, while the fathers were seen much more ambivalently: "These girls had long felt abandoned by the mother as a protective adult. This was their basic anxiety. . . . Though the original sexual experience with the father was at a genital level, the meaning of the sexual act was pregenital, and seemed to have the purpose of receiving some sort of parental interest."[25]

In contrast, almost all the victims expressed some warm feelings toward their fathers. Many described them in much more favorable terms than their mothers. Some examples:

Anne-Marie: A handsome devil.
Theresa: Good with kids. An honest, decent guy.
Lenore: He was my confidant. .
Rita: My savior.

Although it may seem odd to have expressed such attitudes toward blatantly authoritarian fathers, there are explanations. These were men whose presentation to the outside world made them liked and often respected members of the community. The daughters responded to their fathers' social status and power and derived satisfaction from being their fathers' favorites. They were "daddy's special girls," and often they were special to no one else. Feelings of pity for the fathers were also common, especially where the fathers had lost social status. The daughters seemed much more willing to forgive their fathers' failings and weaknesses than to forgive their mothers, or themselves.

Sandra: He was a sweet, decent man. My mother ruined him. I saw him lying in his bed in the hospital, and I kept thinking why don't they let him die. When he finally did, everyone cried at the funeral but me. I was glad he was dead. He had a miserable life. He had nothing. No one cared, not even me. I didn't help him much.

The daughters not only felt themselves abandoned by their mothers, but seemed to perceive their fathers as likewise deserted, and they felt the same pity for their fathers as they felt for themselves.

The victims rarely expressed anger toward their fathers, even about the incestuous act itself. Two of the three women who did express anger were women who had been repeatedly beaten as well as sexually abused by their fathers. Not surprisingly, they were angrier about the beatings than about the sexual act, which they viewed ambivalently. Most women expressed feelings of fear, disgust, and intense shame about the sexual contact and stated that they endured it because they felt they had no other choice. Several of the women stated that they learned to deal with the sexual approach by "tuning out" or pretending that it was not happening. Later, this response generalized to other relationships. Half of the women acknowledged, however, that they had felt some degree of pleasure in the sexual contact, a feeling which only increased their sense of guilt and confusion.

Kitty: I was in love with my father. He called me his special girlfriend.

LENORE: The whole issue is very complicated. I was very attracted to my
   father, and that just compounded the guilt.
PAULA: I was scared of him, but basically I liked him.

Though these women sometimes expressed a sense of disappoint-
ment and even contempt for their fathers, they did not feel as keenly the
sense of betrayal as they felt toward their mothers. Having abandoned
the hope of pleasing their mothers, they seemed relieved to have found
some way of pleasing their fathers and gaining their attention.

Susan Brownmiller, in her study of rape as a paradigm of relations
between men and women, refers briefly to father–daughter incest.
Stressing the coercive aspect of the situation, she calls it "father-rape."[26]
To label it thus is to understate the complexity of the relationship. The
father's sexual approach is clearly an abuse of power and authority, and
the daughter almost always understands it as such. But, unlike rape, it
occurs in the context of a caring relationship. The victim feels overwhelmed by her father's superior power and unable to resist him; she
may feel disgust, loathing, and shame. But at the same time she often
feels that this is the only kind of love she can get, and prefers it to no
love at all. The daughter is not raped, but seduced.

In fact, to describe what occurs as a rape is to minimize the harm to
the child, for what is involved here is not simply an assault, it is a
betrayal. A woman who has been raped can cope with the experience in
the same way that she would react to any other intentionally cruel and
harmful attack. She is not socially or psychologically dependent upon
the rapist. She is free to hate him. But the daughter who has been
molested is dependent on her father for protection and care. Her mother
is not an ally. She has no recourse. She does not dare express, or even
feel, the depths of her anger at being used. She must comply with her
father's demands or risk losing the parental love that she needs. She is
not an adult. She cannot walk out of a situation (though she may try to
run away). She must endure it, and find in it what compensations she
can.

Although the victims reported that they felt helpless and powerless
against their fathers, the incestuous relationship did give them some
semblance of power within the family. Many of the daughters effectively
replaced their mothers and became their fathers' surrogate wives. They
were also deputy mothers to the younger children and were generally
given some authority over them. While they resented being exploited
and robbed of the freedom ordinarily granted to dependent children,
they did gain some feeling of value and importance from the role they
were given. Many girls felt an enormous sense of responsibility for holding the family together. They also knew that, as keepers of the incest
secret, they had an extraordinary power which could be used to destroy
the family. Their sexual contact with their fathers conferred on them a

sense of possessing a dangerous, secret power over the lives of others, power which they derived from no other source. In this situation, keeping up appearances and doing whatever was necessary to maintain the integrity of the family became a neccessary, expiating act at the same that it increased the daughters' sense of isolation and shame.

> THERESA: I was mortified. My father and mother had fights so loud that you could hear them yelling all over the neighborhood. I used to think that my father was really yelling at my mother because she wouldn't give him sex. I felt I had to make it up to him.

What is most striking to us about this family constellation, in which the daughter replaces the mother in her traditional role, is the underlying assumption about that role shared apparently by all the family members. Customarily, a mother and wife in our society is one who nurtures and takes care of children and husband. If, for whatever reasons, the mother is unable to fulfill her ordinary functions, it is apparently assumed that some other female must be found to do it. The eldest daughter is a frequent choice. The father does not assume the wife's maternal role when she is incapacitated. He feels that his first right is to continue to receive the services which his wife formerly provided, sometimes including sexual services. He feels only secondarily responsible for giving care to his children. This view of the father's prerogative to be served not only is shared by the fathers and daughters in these families, but is often encouraged by societal attitudes. Fathers who feel abandoned by their wives are not generally expected or taught to assume primary parenting responsibilities. We should not find it surprising, then, that fathers occasionally turn to their daughters for services (domestic and sexual) that they had formerly expected of their wives.

The Victims

The 15 women who reported their incest experiences were all clients in psychotherapy. That is to say, all had admitted to themselves and at least one other person that they were suffering and needed help. Although we do not know whether they speak for the vast majority of victims, some of their complaints are so similar that we believe that they represent a pattern common to most women who have endured prolonged sexual abuse in childhood at the hands of parents.

One of the most frequent complaints of the victims entering therapy was a sense of being different, and distant, from ordinary people. The sense of isolation and inability to make contact was expressed in many different ways:

> KITTY: I'm dead inside.

LENORE: I have a problem getting close to people. I back off.
LOIS: I can't communicate with anyone.

Their therapists described difficulty in forming relationships with them, confirming their assessment of themselves. Therapists frequently made comments like "I don't really know whether I'm in touch with her," or "she's one of the people that's been the hardest for me to figure out." These women complained that most of their relationships were superficial and empty, or else extremely conflictual. They expressed fear that they were unable to love. The sense of an absence of feeling was most marked in sexual relationships, although most women were sexually responsive in the narrow sense of the word; that is, capable of having orgasms.

In some cases, the suppression of feeling was clearly a defense which had been employed in the incestuous relationship in childhood. The distance or isolation of affect seemed originally to be a device set up as protection against the feelings aroused by the molesting father. One woman reported that when she "shut down," did not move or speak, her father would leave her alone. Another remembered that she would tell herself over and over "this isn't really happening" during the sexual episode. Passive resistance and dissociation of feeling seemed to be among the few defenses available in an overwhelming situation. Later, this carried over into relations with others.

The sense of distance and isolation which these women experienced was uniformly painful, and they made repeated, often desperate efforts to overcome it. Frequently, the result was a pattern of many brief unsatisfactory sexual contacts. Those relationships which did become more intense and lasting were fraught with difficulty.

Five of the seven married women complained of marital conflict, either feeling abused by their husbands or indifferent toward them. Those who were single or divorced uniformly complained of problems in their relationships with men. Some expressed negative feelings toward men in general:

STEPHANIE: When I ride the bus I look at all the men and think, "all they want to do is stick their pricks into little girls."

Most, however, overvalued men and kept searching for a relationship with an idealized protector and sexual teacher who would take care of them and tell them what to do. Half the women had affairs during adolescence with older or married men. In these relationships, the sense of specialness, power, and secrecy of the incestuous relationship was regained. The men were seen as heroes and saviors.

In many cases, these women became intensely involved with men who were cruel, abusive, or neglectful, and tolerated extremes of mistreatment. Anne-Marie remained married for 20 years to a psychotic husband who beat her, terrorized their children, and never supported the family. She felt she could not leave him because he would fall apart without her. "We were his kingdom," she said, "to bully and beat." She eventually sought police protection and separation only after it was clear that her life was in danger. Her masochistic behavior in this relationship was all the more striking, since other areas of her life were relatively intact. She was a warm and generous mother, a valued worker, and an active, respected member of her community. Lois was raped at age 19 by a stranger whom she married a week later. After this marriage ended in divorce, she began to frequent bars where she would pick up men who beat her repeatedly. She expressed no anger toward these men. Three other women in this group of 15 were also rape victims. Only one expressed anger toward her attackers; the others felt they "deserved it." Some of the women recognized and commented on their predilection for abusive men. As Sandra put it: "I'm better off with a bum. I can handle that situation."

Why did these women feel they deserved to be beaten, raped, neglected, and used? The answer lies in their image of themselves. It is only through understanding how they perceived themselves that we can make sense of their often highly destructive relations with others. Almost every one of these 15 women described herself as a "witch," "bitch," or "whore." They saw themselves as socially "branded" or "marked," even when no social exposure of their sexual relations had occurred or was likely to occur. They experienced themselves as powerful and dangerous to men; their self-image had almost a magical quality. Kitty, for instance, called herself a "devil's child," while Sandra compared herself to the 12-year-old villainess of a popular melodrama, *The Exorcist*, a girl who was possessed by the devil. Some felt they were invested with special seductive prowess and could captivate men simply by looking at them. These daughters seemed almost uniformly to believe that they had seduced their fathers and therefore could seduce any man.

At one level, this sense of malignant power can be understood to have arisen as a defense against the child's feelings of utter helplessness. In addition, however, this self-image had been reinforced by the long-standing conspiratorial relationship with the father, in which the child had been elevated to the mother's position and did indeed have the power to destroy the family by exposing the incestuous secret.

Moreover, most of the victims were aware that they had experienced some pleasure in the incestuous relationship and had joined with their fathers in a shared hatred of their mothers. This led to intense feelings of shame, degradation, and worthlessness. Because they had enjoyed their fathers' attention and their mothers' defeat, these women felt responsible for the incestuous situation. Almost uniformly, they distrusted their own desires and needs and did not feel entitled to care and respect. Any relationship that afforded some kind of pleasure seemed to increase the sense of guilt and shame. These women constantly sought to expiate their guilt and relieve their shame by serving and giving to others and by observing the strictest and most rigorous codes of religion and morality. Any lapse from a rigid code of behavior was felt as confirming evidence of their innate evilness. Some of the women embraced their negative identity with a kind of defiance and pride. As Sandra boasted: "There's *nothing* I haven't done!"

Those women who were mothers themselves seemed to be preoccupied with the fear that they would be bad mothers to their children, as they felt their mothers had been to them. Several sought treatment when they began to be aware of feelings of rage and resentment toward their children, especially their daughters. Any indulgence in pleasure seeking or attention to personal needs reinforced their sense that they were "whores" and unfit mothers. In some, the fear of exposure took the form of a constant worry that the authorities would intervene to take the children away. Other mothers worried that they would not be able to protect their daughters from a repetition of the incest situation. As one victim testified:

> I could a been the biggest bum. My father called me a "big whore" and my mother believed him. I could a got so disgusted that I could a run around with anyone I saw. I met my husband and told him about my father and my child. He stuck by me and we was married. I got to the church and I'm not so shy like I was. It always come back to me that this thing might get on the front pages and people might know about it. I'm getting over it since the time I joined the church.

Her husband testified:

> The wife is nervous and she can't sleep. She gets up yesterday night about two o'clock in the morning and starts fixing the curtains. She works that way till five, then she sleeps like a rock. She's cold to me but she tells me she likes me. She gets cold once in a while and she don't know why herself. She watches me like a hawk with those kids. She don't want me to be loving with them and to be too open about sex. It makes her think of her old man. I got to take it easy with her or she blows up.[27]

In our opinion, the testimony of these victims, and the observations of their therapists, is convincing evidence that the incest experience was harmful to them and left long-lasting scars. Many victims had severely impaired object relations with both men and women. The overvaluation of men led them into conflictual and often intensely masochistic relationships with men. The victims' devaluation of themselves and their mothers impaired development of supportive friendships with women.

Many of the victims also had a well-formed negative identity as witch, bitch, or whore. In adult life they continued to make repeated ineffectual attempts to expiate their intense feelings of guilt and shame.

Therapy for the Incest Victim and Her Family

Very little is known about how to help the incest victim. If the incestuous secret is discovered while the victim is still living with her parents, the most common social intervention is the destructon of the family. This outcome is usually terrifying even to an exploited child, and most victims cooperate with their fathers in maintaining secrecy rather that see their fathers jailed or risk being sent away from home.

We know of only one treatment program specifically designed for the rehabilitation of the incestuous family.[28] This program, which operates out of the probation department of the Santa Clara County Court in California, involves all members of the incestuous family in both individual and family therapy and benefits from a close working alliance with Daughters United, a self-help support group for victims. The program directors acknowledge that the coercive power of the court is essential for obtaining the cooperation of the fathers. An early therapeutic goal in this program is a confrontation between the daughter and her mother and father, in which they admit to her that she has been the victim of "poor parenting." This is necessary in order to relieve the daughter from her feeling of responsibility for the incest. Mothers appear to be more willing than fathers to admit this to their daughters.

Though this program offers a promising model for the treatment of the discovered incestuous family, it does not touch the problem of undetected incest. The vast majority of incest victims reach adulthood still bearing their secrets. Some will eventually enter psychotherapy. How can the therapist respond appropriately to their needs?

We believe that the male therapist may have great difficulty in validating the victim's experience and responding empathically to her suffering. Consciously or not, the male therapist will tend to identify with the father's position and therefore will tend to deny or excuse his behavior and project blame onto the victim. Here is an example of a male therapist's judgmental perception of an incest victim:

> This woman had had a great love and respect for her father until puberty when he had made several sexual advances toward her. In analysis she talked at first only of her good feelings toward him because she had blocked out the sexual episodes. When they were finally brought back into consciousness, all the fury returned which she had experienced at the age of thirteen. She felt that her father was an impotent, dirty old man who had taken advantage of her trusting youthful innocence. From some of the details which she related of her relationship to her father, *it was obvious that she was not all that innocent.* [Our italics][29]

Not surprisingly, the client in this case became furious with her therapist, and therapy was unsuccessful.

If the male therapist identifies with the aggressor in the incest situation, it is also clear that the female therapist tends to identify with the victim and that this may limit her effectiveness. In a round-table discussion of experiences with incest victims, most of the contributing therapists acknowledged having shied away from a full and detailed exploration of the incestuous relationship. In some cases the therapist blatantly avoided the issue. In these cases, no trust was established in the relationship, and the client quickly discontinued therapy. In effect, the therapists had conveyed to these women that their secrets were indeed too terrible to share, thus reinforcing their already intense sense of isolation and shame.

Two possible explanations arise for the female therapist's flight. Traditional psychoanalytic theory might suggest that the therapist's own incestuous wishes and fantasies are too threatening for her to acknowledge. This might seem to be the most obvious reason for such a powerful countertransference phenomenon. The second reason, though less apparent, may be equally powerful: the female therapist confronting the incest victim reexperiences her own fear of her father and recognizes how easily she could have shared the victim's fate. We suspect that many women have been aware of, and frightened by, seductive behavior on the part of their own fathers. For every family in which incest is consummated there are undoubtedly hundreds with essentially similar, if less extreme, psychological dynamics. Thus the incest victim forces the female therapist to confront her own condition and to reexperience not only her infantile desires but also her (often realistic) childhood fears.

If the therapist overcomes this obstacle, and does not avoid addressing the issue with her client, another trap follows. As one therapist put it during the round-table discussion: "I get angry *for* her. How can she *not* be angry with her father?" Getting angry for a client is a notoriously unsuccessful intervention. Since the victim is more likely to feel rage toward the mother who abandoned her to her fate than toward her father, the therapeutic relationship must provide a place where the victim feels she can safely express her hostile feelings. Rage against the mother must be allowed to surface, for it is only when the client feels she can freely express her full range of feelings without driving the therapist away that she loses her sense of being malignantly "marked."

The feminist therapist may have particular difficulty facing the degree of estrangement between mother and daughter that occurs in these families. Committed as she is to building solidarity among women, she is bound to be distressed by the frequent histories of indifference, hostility, and cruelty in the mother–daughter relationship. She may find herself rushing to the defense of the mother, pointing out that the

mother, herself, was a victim, and so on. This may be true, but not helpful. Rather than denying the situation or making excuses for anyone, the
therapist must face the challenge that the incestuous family presents to
all of us: How can we overcome the deep estrangement between mothers
and daughters that frequently exists in our society, and how can we better provide for the security of both?

Beyond Therapy

For both social and psychological reasons, therapy alone seems to be
an insufficient response to the situation of the incest victim. Because of
its confidential nature, the therapy relationship does not lend itself to a
full resolution of the issue of secrecy. The woman who feels herself to
be the guardian of a terrible, almost magical secret may find considerable
relief from her shame after sharing the secret with another person. However, the shared secrecy then recreates a situation similar to the original
incestuous relationship. Instead of the victim alone against the world,
there is the special dyad of the victim and her confidant. This, in fact,
was a difficult issue for all the participants in our study, since the victims
once again were the subject of special interest because of their sexual
history.

The women's liberation movement has demonstrated repeatedly to
the mental health profession that consciousness raising has often been
more beneficial and empowering to women than psychotherapy. In particular, the public revelation of the many and ancient sexual secrets of
women (orgasm, rape, abortion) may have contributed far more toward
the liberation of women than the attempt to heal individual wounds
through a restorative therapeutic relationship.

The same should be true for incest. The victims who feel like bitches,
whores, and witches might feel greatly relieved if they felt less lonely,
if their identities as the special guardians of a dreadful secret could be
shed. Incest will begin to lose its devastating magic power when women
begin to speak out about it publicly and realize how common it is.

We know that most cases do not come to the attention of therapists,
and those that do, come years after the fact. Thus, as a social problem
incest is clearly not amenable to a purely psychotherapeutic approach.
Prevention, rather than treatment, seems to be indicated. On the basis of
our study and the testimony of these victims, we favor all measures
which strengthen and support the mother's role within the family, for it
is clear that these daughters fell prey to their fathers' abuse when their
mothers were too ill, weak, or downtrodden to protect them. We favor
the strengthening of protective services for women and children, including adequate and dignified financial support for mothers, irrespective of

their marital status; free, public, round-the-clock child care; and refuge facilities for women in crisis. We favor the vigorous enforcement (by female officials) of laws prohibiting the sexual abuse of children. Offenders should be isolated and reeducated. We see efforts to reintegrate fathers into the world of children as a positive development, but only on the condition that they learn more appropriate parental behavior. A seductive father is not much of an improvement over an abandoning or distant one.

As both Shulamith Firestone and Florence Rush have pointed out, the liberation of children is inseparable from our own.[30] In particular, as long as daughters are subject to seduction in childhood, no adult woman is free. Like prostitution and rape, we believe father–daughter incest will disappear only when male supremacy is ended.

NOTES

1. Claude Lévi-Strauss, *The Elementary Structures of Kinship* (Boston: Beacon Press, 1969),p.481; Margaret Mead, "Incest," in *International Encyclopedia of the Social Sciences*, ed. David L. Sills (New York: Crowell, Collier & Macmillan, 1968).
2. Herbert Maisch, *Incest* (London: Andre Deutsch, 1973), p. 69
3. Vincent De Francis, ed., *Sexual Abuse of Children* (Denver: Children's Division of the American Humane Association, 1967).
4. Alfred Kinsey, W. B. Pomeroy, C. E. Martin, and P. Gebhard, *Sexual Behavior in the Human Female* (Philadelphia: Saunders & Co., 1953), pp. 116–122.
5. S. Kirson Weinberg, *Incest Behavior* (New York: Citadel Press, 1955).
6. See n. 2 above.
7. De Francis.
8. Alfred C. Kinsey, W. B. Pomeroy, and Clyde Martin, *Sexual Behavior in the Human Male* (Philadelphia: Saunders & Co., 1948), pp. 167, 558.
9. Freud, *The Origins of Psychoanalysis: Letters to Wilhelm Fliess, Drafts and Notes; 1887–1902* (New York: Basic Books, 1954). p. 215.
10. Joseph Peters, "Letter to the Editor," *New York Times Book Review* (November 16, 1975).
11. L. Bender and A. Blau, "The Reaction of Children to Sexual Relations with Adults," *American Journal of Orthopsychiatry* 7 (1937): 500–518.
12. N. Lukianowitz, "Incest," *British Journal of Psychiatry* 120 (1972): 301–313.
13. Yokoguchi, "Children Not Severely Damaged by Incest with a Parent," *Journal of the American Academy of Child Psychiatry* 5(1966): 111–124; J. B. Weiner, "Father–Daughter Incest," *Psychiatric Quarterly* 36 (1962): 1132–1138.
14. P. Sloane and E. Karpinski, "Effects of Incest on the Participants," *American Journal of Orthopsychiatry* 12 (1942): 666–673.
15. I. Kaufman, A. Peck, and L. Tagiuri, "The Family Constellation and Overt Incestuous Relations between Father and Daughter," *American Journal of Orthopsychiatry* 24 (1954): 266–279.
16. J. Benward and J. Densen-Gerber, *Incest as a Causative Factor in Anti-social Behavior: An Exploratory Study* (New York: Odyssey Institute, 1975).
17. Weinberg.
18. Juliet Mitchell, *Psychoanalysis and Feminism* (New York: Pantheon Books, 1974).

19. Freud, *Three Essays on the Theory of Sexuality* (New York: Avon Books, 1962).
20. Freud, "Some Psychical Consequences of the Anatomical Distinction between the Sexes" (1925), "Female Sexuality" (1931), and "Femininity" (1933), all reprinted in *Women and Analysis*, ed. Jean Strouse (New York: Viking Press, 1974).
21. Phyllis Chesler, "Rape and Psychotherapy," in *Rape: The First Sourcebook for Women*, ed. Noreen Connell and Cassandra Wilson (New York: New American Library, 1974), p. 76.
22. Maisch, p. 140.
23. Kinsey et al. (n. 4 above), p. 121.
24. Maisch.
25. Kaufman et al., p. 270.
26. S. Brownmiller, *Against Our Will: Men, Women and Rape* (New York: Simon & Schuster, 1975),p. 281.
27. Weinberg, pp. 151–152.
28. H. Giarretto, "Humanistic Treatment of Father–Daughter Incest," in *Child Abuse and Neglect—the Family and the Community*, ed. R. E. Helfer and C. H. Kemp (Cambridge, Mass.: Ballinger Publishing Co., 1976).
29. R. Stein, *Incest and Human Love: The Betrayal of the Soul in Psychotherapy* (New York: Third Press, 1973), pp. 45–46.
30. Shulamith Firestone, *The Dialectic of Sex: The Case for Feminist Revolution* (New York: Bantam Books, 1970); Florence Rush, "The Sexual Abuse of Children: A Feminist Point of View," in Connell and Wilson.

Families at Risk for Father–Daughter Incest

17

JUDITH HERMAN AND LISA HIRSCHMAN

Sexual abuse of children within their families is a common problem that is only beginning to gain the attention of the mental health professions. As recently as 1975, the *Comprehensive Textbook of Psychiatry*[1] contained an estimated prevalence of all forms of incest of one case per million population. This estimate is most likely in error by four or five orders of magnitude. Several large surveys[2-6] of predominantly white, middle-class women have indicated that between 20% and 35% of all women have had a childhood sexual encounter with an adult male, that 4%–12% of all women have had such an experience with a relative, and that about 1% of all women have been involved in father–daughter incest. The great majority of these sexual encounters are not disclosed at the time of occurrence and have never come to the attention of any social agency.

Almost all previous clinical studies of incestuous families are based on cases reported to courts,[7] child protection agencies,[8] or public mental health facilities.[9-12] They therefore describe a group that is quite atypical of the common run of incestuous families. Poor and disorganized families that lack the resources to preserve secrecy are heavily overrepresented. In addition, with two exceptions,[13,14] previous clinical studies lack any sort of control or comparison group. Thus it has been difficult to define specific attributes of families in which incest is most likely to occur. The goal of the present study was to identify factors in the family constellation that might be associated with a high risk for the development of overt incest.

METHOD

Forty women who reported having had a sexual relationship with their fathers during childhood were compared with 20 women who

Reprinted from *American Journal of Psychiatry* 138(7):967–970, 1981. Copyright © 1981 by the American Psychiatric Association. Reprinted by permission. Presented at the 133rd annual meeting of the American Psychiatric Association, San Francisco, May 3–9, 1980. The research reported in this article was supported in part by grant MH-29407 from NIMH.

reported that their fathers had been seductive but had stopped short of overt incest. By choosing this comparison group, we hoped to be able to define those factors most commonly associated with the development of incest, as well as those factors which seemed to protect against this outcome in vulnerable families.

We defined incest as any physical contact between father and daughter that had to be kept a secret. The activities most commonly reported were fondling, masturbation, and oral–genital contacts. Behaviors that did not include physical contact and a requirement for secrecy but were clearly sexually motivated were included in the seductive category. Common examples were peeping, exhibitionism, leaving pornographic materials for the daughter to find, sharing confidences of sexual exploits, or demanding detailed descriptions of the daughter's real or imagined sexual activities.

All the subjects were outpatients in psychotherapy. They were recruited through an informal network of therapists in private practice. In each case, an initial case review was conducted with the therapist. Some subjects were then interviewed personally. The semi-structured interview protocol elicited information on the subject's current functioning, a developmental history, a description of each member of the family of origin, and an extensive description of family roles and interactions. Information was generally gathered in a single interview lasting 2 to 3 hours.

The two groups were roughly matched by age, social class, and religious background. All the women were white. The mean age was 27.7 years in the incest group and 26.8 in the comparison group. About 45% of the women were from Catholic, 40% from Protestant, and 15% from Jewish families. Roughly half the women in each group came from working-class and half from middle-class backgrounds, as defined by Braverman.[15] Working-class fathers were generally skilled tradesmen, salesmen, or public service employees. Middle-class fathers ran small businesses or were middle-level executives or professionals. About three-quarters of the mothers in both groups were full-time houseworkers. The great majority of families in both groups were intact and presented a conventional appearance, and over 90% of the cases were unknown to mental health facilities or social service agencies

RESULTS

Most of the women in both groups described their fathers as the dominant parent. However, incestuous fathers, far more than their seductive counterparts, tended to use physical force and intimidation to dominate their families. Fifty percent of the women in the incest group but only 20% of the comparison group reported that their fathers had been violent ($\chi^2 = 3.83$, $df = 1$, $p < 0.05$). The assaultive behavior, although frightening to all family members, was not completely uncontrolled. None of the fathers was so violent as to provoke outside intervention in the family, and most were quite discriminating in their attacks, singling out one family member to bear the brunt of their rage. Many daughters reported having seen their mothers being beaten; in some cases siblings were beaten as well. The daughter chosen as the object of the father's sexual attention was usually exempted from physical attack. Some daughters reported that they tolerated the father's sexual advances in order to preserve this privileged position.

Some previous studies[16–18] have noted a high incidence of alcoholism in incestuous fathers. In our study, however, the father's drinking pattern did not differ significantly between the two groups. About 35% of women in both groups described their fathers as problem drinkers. In most cases, the father's alcoholism was not severe enough to result in loss of a job or major medical complications. Thus the fathers' drinking, like the violence and the inappropriate sexual behavior, escaped detection outside the family.

Except for violence, we were not able to identify any characteristic of the fathers that distinguished the two groups. Significant differences, however, were noted between the mothers. Mothers in the incestuous families were more often described as ill or disabled and were more often absent for some period of time. Fifty-five percent of the women in the incest group but only 15% of the comparison group reported that their mothers had been seriously ill ($\chi^2 = 7.21$, $df = 1$, $p < 0.01$). Undiagnosed alcoholism, psychosis, and depression were among the problems most commonly reported. Thirty-eight percent of the women in the incest group and none of the comparison group had been separated from their mothers for some period of time during childhood ($\chi^2 = 8.10$, $df = 1$, $p < 0.01$). The separation occurred either because the mother was hospitalized or because she felt unable to cope with her child care duties and temporarily placed the daughter in the care of relatives. Three mothers in the incest group died before their daughters were grown, 1 by suicide. Another mother committed suicide after her daughter left home. There were no maternal deaths in the comparison group.

Mothers in the incestuous families also had more pregnancies and more children to care for. The mean number of children in the incestuous families was 3.6, significantly different from the national mean of 2.2 ($t_n = 3.442$, $df = 39$, $p \leq 0.01$). The mean for the comparison group was 2.85. The incest group included 5 families with 8 or more children. In the comparison group, there were no families of this size. In some cases, the daughters saw their mothers' repeated pregnancies as evidence of their helplessness and inability to protect themselves. As one daughter testified,

After the seventh child, they found out she had cancer, and they told her not to get pregnant again. But she couldn't control it, my father being the man he is. His attitude is, if you're going to have sex, you have to have the child. And he was the type of man who would say if I can't get it from my wife, I'll go elsewhere. He's also the type of man where, if she didn't want to open her legs, he'd pinch her thighs. He told me so himself.

In families where the mothers were ill, disabled, or overwhelmed by child care responsibilities, the fathers characteristically did not assume a nurturing parental role. Rather, the burden of the mother's traditional duties was most often imposed on the oldest daughter. Forty-five percent of the women in the incest group, as opposed to only 5% in the comparison group, reported that they took on a maternal role within their families ($\chi^2 = 8.10$, $df = 1$, p < 0.01); often by the time they were 8 or 9, they had assumed major responsibility for housework and/or child care. Providing sexual services to their fathers seemed to develop as an extension of their maternal family role.

The mean age of the daughters at the onset of the incestuous relationship was 9.4 years, and the relationship lasted on the average 3.3 years. Fifty-eight percent of the daughters never told anyone about the sexual relationship until they had already left home. The minority of children who told did so only after the abuse had been going for a long time: 3.8 years on the average. Only 3 cases (8%) were reported outside the family. Twenty-eight percent of the incest victims reported that their sisters had been molested as well as themselves; another 25% suspected that this was the case but were not certain. In 33% of the families there was no repetition of the incestuous relationship because there were no sisters.

Fathers commonly began by singling out the oldest daughter both to fill a maternal family role and to participate in the secret sexual relationship. As that daughter advanced into adolescence and became more rebellious, the father often moved on to the younger sisters.

Brothers were not molested, according to our informants. However, a number of brothers were physically abused, and several women described their brothers as developing assaultive and abusive behavior in identification with their fathers. One woman in the incest group was molested by an older brother as well as her father; 6 others were also molested by close relatives or family friends. None of the women in the comparison group reported similar incidents.

Given the stress of the maternal family role and the incestuous relationship, it was not surprising to find that the women in the incest group had had a much more turbulent adolescence than those in the comparison group. There were significant differences in the percent who attempted to run away (33% versus 5%; $\chi^2 = 4.20$, $df = 1$, $p < 0.05$), attempted suicide (38% versus 5%; χ^2 5.64, df = 1, $p < 0.02$), and became pregnant before reaching adulthood (45% versus 15%; $\chi^2 = 4.04$, $df = 1$, $p < 0.05$). There were nonsignificant differences in the percent who abused drugs or alcohol (20% versus 5%) or had periods of careless and indiscriminate sexual behavior (in their own judgment) (35% versus 15%).

Women in the incest group also tended to marry and begin their own families earlier than the comparison group. Marriage was often perceived as the only realistic means of escape from the incestuous family. Thus, although the two groups came from similar class and ethnic backgrounds, more of the women in the comparison group than in the incest group had remained single (55% versus 38%), had not yet had children (75% versus 50%), and had continued their education past college level (30% versus 8%).

Although these last differences do not individually reach the level of statistical significance, taken together they suggest a tendency toward early foreclosure of major developmental stages in the incest group.

DISCUSSION

Our results suggest certain circumstances in which the clinician should be particularly alert to the possibility of father–daughter incest. Families in which mothers are rendered unusually powerless, whether through battering, physical disability, mental illness, or the burden of repeated childbearing, seem to be particularly at risk. Thus, for example, whenever a mother is treated for severe chronic illness of any sort, the family's adaptation to the mother's disability should be assessed. If the father has not assumed a maternal role or sought help from appropriate adults, and especially if one daughter has taken on major household responsibilities, the suspicion that the daughter is also fulfilling a sexual role should be entertained.

Although incest most commonly involves the oldest daughter, once the first sexual relationship has been established, all the daughters in the family should be considered at risk, since the behavior is often repeated. Our data also suggest that the father's incestuous behavior may place the daughters at greater risk of sexual abuse by other male relatives and family intimates.

Incest should be suspected as a precipitant of impulsive, self-destructive behavior such as suicide attempts, drug abuse, attempts at running away, and what is commonly called "sexual acting out" in adolescent girls. Questions regarding sexual abuse within the family should be incorporated into routine history-taking whenever such high-risk populations are encountered.

Our findings have implications both for treatment of incestuous families and for efforts at prevention of sexual abuse. Our results suggest that mothers who function competently within their families, who do not themselves submit to abuse, and who are able to preserve a more nearly equal balance of parental power effectively protect their daughters from overt incest, even in situations where the father's sexual interest in the daughter is quite apparent. Thus any measures that strengthen the position of mothers within their families might be expected indirectly to benefit their daughters.

Services designed to meet previously undetected mental health needs of women, such as women's alcoholism programs and shelters for battered women, may be especially significant for prevention or early detection of incest. Programs for the rehabilitation of incestuous families should place major emphasis on strengthening the role of the mother. Both treatment of the mother's previously neglected medical or psychiatric problems and development of an adequate social support system for the mother may be required.

Our data do not lend themselves to firm conclusions about treatment of incestuous fathers. They suggest, however, that incestuous child abuse and wife abuse may be related problems. Many experimental programs for men who batter are now in the developmental stages.[19] Such programs may offer a promising model for the treatment of men who commit incest as well.

REFERENCES

1. Henderson DJ.: Incest, in *Comprehensive Textbook of Psychiatry*, 2nd ed. Edited by Freedman AM., Kaplan HI., Sadock BJ. Baltimore, Williams & Wilkins Co, 1975
2. Landis C: *Sex in Development*. New York, Harper & Brothers, 1940
3. Kinsey A, Pomeroy W, Martin C, et al: *Sexual Behavior in the Human Female*. Philadelphia, WB Saunders Co, 1953
4. Landis J: Experiences of 500 children with adult sexual deviation. *Psychiatric Q Suppl* 30:91–109, 1956
5. Gagnon J: Female child victims of sex offenses. *Social Problems* 13:176–192, 1965
6. Finkelhor D: *Sexually Victimized Children*. New York, Free Press, 1979
7. Maisch H: *Incest*. New York, Stein & Day, 1972
8. DeFrancis V: *Protecting the Child Victim of Sex Crimes Committed by Adults*. Denver, American Humane Association, 1969
9. Kaufman I, Peck A, Tagiuri C: The family constellation and overt incestuous relations between father and daughter. *Am J Orthopsychiatry* 24:266–279, 1954
10. Cormier B, Kennedy M, Sangowicz J: Psychodynamics of father–daughter incest. *Can Psychiatr Assoc J* 7:203–217, 1962
11. Lustig N, Dresser J, Spellman S, et al: Incest: a family group surival pattern. *Arch Gen Psychiatry* 14:31–40, 1966
12. Lukjanowicz N: Incest. *Br J Psychiatry* 120:301–313, 1972
13. Tormes Y: *Child Victims of Incest*. Denver, American Humane Associaion, 1968
14. Meiselman K: *Incest*. San Francisco, Jossey-Bass, 1978
15. Braverman H: *Labor and Monopoly Capitalism*. New York, Monthly Review Press, 1974
16. Virkkunen M: Incest offenses and alcoholism. *Med Sci Law* 14:124–128, 1974
17. Browning DH., Boatman B: Incest: children at risk. *Am J Psychiatry* 34:69–72, 1977
18. Rada R, Kellner D, Winslow W: Drinking, alcoholism and the mentally disordered sex offender. *Bull Am Acad Psychiatry Law* 6:296–300, 1978
19. Center for Women Policy Studies: Programs for men who batter. *Response to Violence in the Family* 3 (3,4):6–7, 1980

Implications for Treatment and Training

IV

A. Doing Psychotherapy

Throughout this book, we have been asking therapists to examine their own unconscious biases as well as the gender values concealed in psychological theories. We have attempted to present alternative explanations for understanding psychological distress that emphasize the importance of sociocultural realities along with intrapsychic processes. Many of these reconceptualizations are not fully developed theories, nor has there been enough time for clinicians to adopt and apply them extensively in treatment. As a result, there are no research studies that compare the effectiveness of the new perspectives with more traditional perspectives. However, we remain convinced that the elimination of sexism from psychotherapy can only improve the outcome. We include this group of articles because they represent creative attempts by therapists to clarify values and to apply the new perspectives in clinical practice.

In "Special Issues for Women in Psychotherapy," Harriet E. Lerner points out that whether feminist or traditional, "every therapist has an implicit concept of 'normality' for men and women that . . . continuously affects the nature of the interventions that are made (or not made) in the course of the therapeutic process." She shows how these often unconscious norms and values have a subtle but powerful influence on how therapists interpret and misinterpret conformity to and rebellion against traditional feminine roles. To illustrate the subtle forms this takes in the therapeutic encounter, Lerner demonstrates how therapists with different perspectives might evaluate the same data. Finally, she discusses the characteristics of a competent therapist and the potential advantages of female therapists for female patients. Although there are real differences between male and female therapists in the treatment of women that need to be explored, it is important to keep in mind that neither sex nor ideology guarantees one's skill as a clinician.

Nanette Gartrell, in "Issues in the Psychotherapy of Lesbians, " further extends definitions of normality to include sexual preference. She points out that even most feminist scholars have failed to identify the pervasive concealed assumption that "relationship maturity is possible only through heterosexual union." She argues, as does Adrienne Rich, that heterosexuality is a patriarchal ideology that functions to keep women dependent on men. Lesbian relationships, by creating alternative cultural patterns, threaten societal values about sexuality, sex roles, and family structures. At the same time they challenge the implicit homophobic attitudes that help to maintain existing social arrangements. Homophobia, then, becomes a crucial aspect of the psychotherapeutic process for both patient and therapist. Although Gartrell limits her discussion to lesbians, many of the issues she raises apply to gay men as well. Indeed, in a male-dominated world, the homophobic responses to gay men are even more intense.

Gartrell discusses the advantages of "out" lesbian therapists treating lesbian clients and cautions that closeted therapists may also have homophobic attitudes that interfere with treatment. She believes that being out is necessary for a healthy adaptation to lesbian and gay life. Hence, it is mandatory to explore with clients the risks and benefits of coming out with an understanding of both intrapsychic prohibitions and external realities. Although Gartrell suggests that lesbians are more likely than heterosexuals to have egalitarian relationships, we would argue that gay and lesbian relationships, like all relationships, are subject to the same power struggles that derive from differences in status characteristics (e.g., age, wealth, occupation) and personality traits.

The last two chapters in this section discuss roles and relationships within families and the tension and conflict that develop when one or both partners try to change their sex-typed roles. It should be noted that the authors of both articles have assumed that a family refers to a man and a woman in a heterosexual relationship. In spite of this unquestioned assumption, these articles reconceptualize the roles of men and women within families and discuss the implications for therapy.

Rachel T. Hare-Mustin, in "A Feminist Approach to Family Therapy," argues that the unequal distribution of power that derives from patriarchal family structures and stereotyped sex roles must be a central part of family therapy. She notes that power aspects of sex roles are generally overlooked by family therapists. However, a significant exception occurs when women in families are seen as having a disproportionate amount of power, for which the "dominant-mother" formulation is invoked to explain all family psychopathology. In contrast, Hare-Mustin defines certain areas of intervention in families in which she believes a feminist orientation is important—for example, negotiating a contract that equalizes power between the father who pays for the sessions and family members with no income. Other areas in which she rethinks the therapists's role are shifting tasks in the family, communication patterns, generational boundaries, relabeling deviance, modeling, ownership and privacy, and the therapeutic alliance with different family members.

Just as Lerner and Gartrell have been concerned with the characteristics of a good therapist, Hare-Mustin also comments about this, emphasizing the importance of the sex of the therapist and his or her gender values. She cautions that male/female cotherapy teams do not necessarily guarantee therapeutic effectiveness: "If there are differences in experience, training, and status of the cotherapy pair, there is a basis for inequality that is not lost on family members, no matter what roles the cotherapists imagine they are playing in the therapy sessions."

In "Men's New Family Roles—Some Implications for Therapists," Michael Berger discusses the issues facing men who want to extend their family roles to include responsibility for child care and household tasks. These men in transition, who elect to change their own roles and the inequitable structures at home and work, are clearly in the minority. The author describes how "individuals in transition experience both institutional constraints on their ability to change, and internal doubts as to the 'rightness' of their changing. . . ." Men who are highly invested in their families meet considerable resistance and hostility from colleagues and employers who view them as less committed to work and achievement.

In addition to these external prohibitions against men changing their priorities about work and family, they also must cope with the internal and interpersonal conflicts that result from this process. Since male identity is defined in part by being "not-female" (e.g., not emotional, vulnerable, nurturant) and by doing work that is reserved for men, it is not surprising that the adoption of new family roles is accompanied by profound pain and confusion about identity. Although wives and partners want men to change, they may have ambivalent responses to these new behaviors based on their own cultural definitions of masculinity and femininity. As men turn to parents and friends, they receive little validation and support for their nontraditional gender behaviors. This is in contrast to women's changing roles, where there is considerable support provided by other women. In the absence of support for men, the therapist has a critical role in understanding the internal and external dimensions of the problems that men in transition face. Berger calls on therapists to clarify their own gender values so that they do not unwittingly restrict their clients' choices. This involves recognizing the limitations of therapy in resolving these issues, and encouraging men to find personal support groups and to become politically active in changing the institutional structures that restrict their roles.

All of the chapters in this section are examples of some of the ways that the new perspectives can be translated into clinical practices. We know from our own experiences that there are no formulas for integrating the new knowledge into psychotherapeutic work. In addition, the continuous self-monitoring of personal and professional values as they influence clinical perspectives is hard work. As a result, even well-intentioned clinicians find this a difficult and confusing process, both emotionally and intellectually.

Special Issues for Women in Psychotherapy

18

In recent years the practice of psychotherapy came under heavy fire from feminist critics, who turned in large numbers to women's rap groups or feminist therapy as alternatives to more established modes of treatment.[1] Concern about widespread sexist practices in the treatment of women was also voiced by mental health professionals from traditional training programs and work settings as well[2-4] This chapter explores the nature and legitimacy of such complaints and identifies special issues of relevance to all women seeking psychotherapy.

Of the many criticisms leveled against traditional psychotherapies, a few may be summarized briefly. First, traditional psychotherapy—and in particular, psychoanalysis—tends to focus primarily, if not exclusively, on internal or intrapsychic conflicts rather than on the cultural context that has produced them. Such a therapeutic bias not only diverts energy away from potential social and political change but may also foster in the woman a sense of "uniqueness" regarding her "pathology" rather than helping her to recognize that her symptoms, which may be ubiquitous among women, stem naturally from patriarchal society's neglect and distortion of women's true intellectual, sexual, and social needs. Perhaps the most serious accusation against traditional psychotherapy is that in subtle but powerful ways, it may lead women to conform to male-defined notions of femininity and may discourage rebellion from the "feminine role" by interpreting such rebellion as pathological.

For many therapists, however, such accusations do not ring true. As a staff psychologist in a traditional psychoanalytic institution, I can personally vouch for the good intentions of my colleagues. Well-trained psychoanalytic therapists do not strive to send their female patients back to the kitchen. Rather, the task of a good psychotherapy, psychoanalytic or otherwise, is to provide women with the opportunity to overcome the barriers that interfere with the full utilization of their capacities. This, in theory, is to be done in an atmosphere of therapeutic neutrality in which

Reprinted from *The Woman Patient, Volume 3: Aggression, Adaptations, and Psychotherapy.* Edited by Malkah T. Notman and Carol C. Nadelson. New York, Plenum Press, 273–286, 1982. Copyright © 1982 by Plenum Press. Reprinted with permission.

a woman is free to find a comfortable and honest definition of her femininity, based neither on predominant stereotypes about women nor on
rancor and rebellion against them.

With such purity of intention, most therapists do not view sexism in
treatment as a serious problem. Feminist concerns may be written off as
naive, outdated, or simply misguided. It is indeed difficult for therapists
to examine openly and critically how their own unconscious biases and
perceptions adversely affect and limit their treatment of female patients.
Yet, no longer can we close our eyes to the fact that every therapist has
an implicit concept of "normality" for men and women that arises out of
the cultural context in which she or he is embedded. As we will see in
the pages following, a therapist's implicit (and often unconscious)
absorption of cultural norms and values continuously affects the nature
of the interventions that are made (or not made) in the course of the
therapeutic process.

PSYCHOTHERAPY WITH WOMEN: DIFFERING IDEOLOGICAL PERSPECTIVES

Traditional therapists* tend to view women's symptoms and dissat-
isfactions as an expression of individual psychopathology, to be analyzed
and understood in light of the patient's unique individual history. Even
those therapists who are sympathetic toward feminist goals may not view
"cultural factors" as the "real" or primary determinants that interfere
with women's fulfillment. While cultural limitations on women may be
superficially acknowledged, a patient's anger in response to these factors
may be said to reflect an unhealthy sense of passive victimization that
militates against constructive personal change. Thus, a patient's sensitivity to the social and cultural roots of her difficulties may not be legitimized by the therapist as an important focus for treatment. Rather, feminist concerns may be interpreted as the patient's defensive attempt to
avoid painful inner conflict by placing the blame for her unhappiness
outside herself.

In contrast, those who identify themselves as feminist therapists
view the social and cultural context of the patient's problems as a legitimate and important focus of treatment. Indeed, to deny or minimize
these sources of conflict is seen "as inappropriate as attempts to treat
black persons while denying that racism is an ugly reality that affects us
all."[5] The patient's capacity to identify and respond to ways in which

---

*By *traditional therapists*, I mean psychotherapists whose conceptualization of their
patients' difficulties and their own therapeutic goals or clinical techniques has not been
significantly altered or influenced by the past two decades of feminism. My experience
with traditional therapists is largely with colleagues whose individual or group work is
psychoanalytically based.

women are depreciated, trivialized, scapegoated, or falsely defined in work and family is not viewed as peripheral to therapeutic work. Rather, the patient's expanded awareness of false and constricting values, myths, and pressures, which pervade the systems in which she operates, is seen as crucial to the process of self-definition and growth. It is when a therapist fails to legitimize the patient's realistic anger and protest that the patient becomes further inhibited in her capacity for creative and free-ranging thought and action.[5]

Most sophisticated therapists, whether feminist or traditional, do not maintain a narrow, single-minded focus on either intrapsychic or socio-cultural realities, which would, in either case, be akin to listening for "the sound of one hand clapping." But therapists all differ, if not in conscious beliefs, then in the nature of their interventions and their approach to women's struggles during this period of social change. There still exists much controversy about whether women who angrily protest societal definitions of femininity and the feminine role are themselves expressing neurotic conflicts, or whether, on the other hand, it is our very definitions of femininity and the feminine role that are a pathogenic cause of female symptomatology. This is not simply a matter of theoretical interest, for a therapist's position regarding this controversy (whether conscious and explicit or unexamined and unconsciously held) determines the very course and process of treatment despite that therapist's very best intentions to "help patients make their own choices" in an atmosphere that is "value-free."[6] To illustrate this point, let us consider the hypothetical case of Janet:

> Janet, a 34-year-old homemaker, has two healthy children and an ambitious, successful, and concerned husband. Janet tells herself that she "has everything"; yet she seeks psychotherapy because of feelings of depression and malaise as well as a growing anger and resentment toward her children and husband. From her own perspective, her dissatisfaction is entirely irrational, and she begins her first therapy hour by telling her psychotherapist, "I have nothing to be angry and depressed about." Her goal for treatment, as she initially states it, is to be a better and more satisfied wife and mother. Let us examine how two different therapists, Therapist A (traditional) and Therapist B (feminist), might conceptualize and work with Janet's problems.

> *Therapist A*
> Therapist A views Janet's anger and depression as a symptom reflecting unconscious conflicts that interfere with her capacity to nurture and care for others. Therapist A may explore with Janet deep-rooted feelings of neglect and deprivation from her own childhood, which now make it difficult for her to provide for her children without resentment and hostility. If Janet's anger at her husband is associated with the envious wish that she, too, would like to achieve and compete in the world outside the home, these "masculine strivings" may be interpreted in light of Janet's neurotic discomfort with her own feminine role.

Therapist A may also reassure Janet that a mother's job is a difficult one, particularly in her children's early years and may reassure Janet that to some degree her anger and ambivalence are a natural part of the difficult and challenging career of motherhood. In addition, Janet may be encouraged to find some time away from the children that is just hers alone, or perhaps to take up some independent hobby or activity. In a supportive and nonjudgmental context, therapist and patient may together explore a range of early conflicts and relationship paradigms with the goal (as Janet herself has stated it) of helping the patient to become a better and more satisfied wife and mother.

Therapist B

Therapist B may agree that Janet (like every human being) has neurotic conflicts that prevent her from parenting her children more competently and comfortably. However, these conflicts may not be viewed as a primary or even an important focus of treatment. Indeed, Therapist B may consider Janet's anger and depression healthy, legitimate, and realistic, despite Janet's own protests that it is "irrational." This therapist may first choose to explore with Janet the internal pressures and the external realities that caused her to lose sight of her own hopes, aspirations, and dreams for herself and to choose instead to live vicariously through her husband and her children. Expressions of anger, competitiveness, or envy in regard to her husband, or men in general, may be interpreted as healthy strivings for mastery, success, and self-sufficiency, which are frightening for Janet to acknowledge. Historical and intrapsychic determinants may be explored at length—however, not with the goal of making Janet "a better wife and mother," in the conventional sense. Rather, this therapist may use her or his skills to analyze the unconscious anxiety and guilt that prevent Janet from acknowledging and expressing more autonomous, self-seeking strivings for mastery and success.

In addition, Therapist B will help Janet to identify the familial and institutional realities that interfere with her potential fulfillment in both parenting and work pursuits. Therapist B may question Janet's assumption that the "good mother" (in singular contrast to the "good father") always puts the needs of her young children before her own growth and creative development. While Therapist B will recognize that Janet has her own private neurosis, it is not this neurosis that the therapist believes to be at the core of the problem. Rather, Janet's difficulties are seen as a symptom of the institution of motherhood and family (as it has been defined by male "experts"), which has excused the male sex from the real day-to-day task of child rearing, while demanding that a mother's growth and development be exchanged for the growth and development of the child she has borne.

The striking difference in focus between these two therapists illustrates the fact that we are living in a time of considerable controversy regarding our basic understanding of women's pleasures and problems. In the pages following I continue to demonstrate how psychotherapy invariably reflects the cultural context in which it is embedded. Every therapist, whether feminist or "Freudian," will express, in the course of treatment, her or his own values and visions for women. There is no "value-free" psychotherapy.

The Masculine–Feminine Dichotomy: Implications for Therapeutic Practice

Many therapists have absorbed culturally defined notions of masculinity and femininity and consciously or unconsciously view these concepts as reflecting what is healthy or "natural" for men and women. Therapists who explicitly label, or even privately conceptualize, certain of women's wishes, strivings, and behaviors as being "unfeminine" may unwittingly exacerbate their patients' inhibitions rather than increasing their options.[7] In certain cases, women may become further constricted in treatment as their aggressive strivings for dominance and power (which may indeed have certain pathological aspects) are labeled as *masculine* or *phallic* by the therapist, often without acknowledgment of the healthy and adaptive components of such behaviors. While purportedly providing insight, therapeutic interpretation may subtly be aimed at encouraging the patient to "stop" her aggressive, controlling, or competitive behaviors.[8] With men, however, the therapeutic goal would more typically be to help the patient achieve a healthier and more comfortable, conflict-free integration and expression of these same qualities or behaviors.

Failure to Analyze Conformity to Traditional Feminine Scripts

It is important to recognize that most good therapists do not consciously hold to narrow, stereotypical ideas about women; rather, they respect the patient's right to pursue treatment goals that may be out of keeping with the traditional feminine role. However, a subtle, serious, and more pervasive problem arises for the psychotherapy patient who does indeed fit the cultural stereotype, but for the wrong reasons (e.g., the traditional "feminine" woman who opts for full-time motherhood out of neurotic anxieties about competition, success, and intellectual achievement). In these cases, many therapists fail to analyze the conflicts and anxieties that keep the woman in her role and restrict her choices.[6,9] I have noted that unhealthy degrees of self-sacrifice, dependency, and underachievement in women (except in their extreme and most conspicuous "masochistic" forms) are often not recognized or questioned by the therapist since these may strike one as quite "natural" characteristics of the female sex. The failure of therapists to analyze sufficiently the defensive and maladaptive determinants underlying a patient's choice to conform to culturally prescribed notions of femininity is a common phenomenon in psychotherapy. The following clinical vignette offers an example of skillful therapeutic work, which unfortunately may be more the exception than the rule:

Ms. B., a 28-year-old woman in intensive psychotherapy, announced to her therapist that she would be moving to a new city at the end of the year because of her husband's professional advancement. Although she was sad about leaving psychotherapy as well as her friends and her teaching job in a Montessori school, she expressed excitement about the challenges that the move would bring and pride in her husband's success. Initial inquiry by the therapist as to any less enthusiastic feelings she might have met with a restatement of her positive reaction to the anticipated change. Certainly, it entailed losses for her, but these were well overshadowed by the gains. Further, Ms. B was thinking about starting a family soon and thought she might stop work entirely for several years. She communicated clearly that she would like the issue dropped, and it was dropped for some time.

Months later, when Ms. B was discussing some pains and pleasures of her work, the therapist once again commented that he was struck by how easily she had made her own job unimportant in regard to the planned move, and how adept she was at convincing him that this was the case. He also speculated as to why she might need to avoid taking her own professional life seriously and commented that it was difficult for her to be in competition with her husband or to ask him to make professional sacrifices for her, although she had done so earlier for him. The therapist's questioning, which occurred in the face of her initial insistence that there were no further issues to discuss, led to her increased understanding of the neurotic anxieties that caused her to devalue her work, to treat it as less important than her husband's, and even to be ready to drop it entirely. The therapist's persistence in this line of questioning also had significant transference implications, since it communicated to the patient that he took her work seriously. The fact that he had dropped the issue, even though she had more than invited him to do so, had for her the unconscious meaning that he, like her mother, did not really want her to be a fulfilled individual. Ms B. and her husband did not move, and she has continued to advance professionally and now has a challenging position with considerable authority.*

In contrast to the therapeutic work presented above, many therapists fail to recognize, and thus to analyze, the patient's defensive or neurotic conformity to the feminine role and to false and confining definitions of femininity. These errors of omission affect great numbers of female patients, for most women entering treatment are themselves unable to consciously acknowledge wishes or longings that are out of keeping with traditional feminine scripts. Indeed, many women who seemingly "choose" to relinquish self-seeking professional or autonomous strivings do so because they cannot freely, and without guilt and anxiety, fulfill themselves through personal achievement.[10] In my experience, it is not

*This vignette was previously published in the *American Journal of Psychiatry* 135(1):51, January 1978 (H. Lerner, "Adaptive and Pathogenic Aspects of Sex-Role Stereotypes: Implications for Parenting and Psychotherapy.")

uncommon for a bored, exhausted, intellectually impoverished, and isolated mother of small children to begin treatment with the following goal, "Make me a better wife and mother to my husband and children." She may, quite literally, have no other vision for herself that feels acceptable, and the only form of protest she can voice is her symptoms, which frequently take the form of an unconscious wildcat strike against her "sacred calling"[11] (i.e., "I am too depressed/fatigued/confused to run the household and care for my children").

Traditional therapists, especially those who believe that small children need their mothers continually at home, often fail to skillfully explore with the patient other alternatives and options.[9] Further, they may not help her to clarify the nature of her legitimate anger and complaints against her "prescribed role," which the patient dare not herself express, except through her symptoms.

THE FEMALE-PATIENT–MALE-THERAPIST DYAD: REPLICATING PATRIARCHAL ARRANGEMENTS

Some feminist critics have warned that psychotherapy for women may entail a potential reenactment of male–female relationship paradigms as they exist in the culture at large.[1] It is indeed true that many women in psychotherapy become intensely dependent on an idealized male therapist, who may become the center of their fantasy life. If the relationship is eroticized, it may, much like an affair, dilute and eclipse other important relationships and pursuits in the patient's life and serve as a resistance to change. It may be so gratifying for a woman to receive support and empathic understanding from a warm, nurturant, male authority (and so gratifying for a male therapist to be able to comfortably express and be appreciated for these "maternal" qualities) that the therapeutic relationship itself may foster dependency without facilitating autonomous solutions.

Women have a long history of experiencing unegalitarian relationships with males as "natural" and of following leaders and "experts" compliantly. Cultural pressures on women to "please men" are so profound that the woman's desire to be attractive and admired by her therapist may override a more honest process of self-definition and self-determination. Women's attempt to fit themselves to definitions of femininity that are implicitly communicated by their therapist is often unconscious and subtle and may thus go unrecognized by both therapist and patient. I have spoken to a number of women who have participated in both individual treatment and feminist consciousness-raising groups, and who have stated in retrospect that the latter allowed them a greater opportunity to explore personal issues with real honesty and depth. Some of these women saw the limitations of their psychotherapy as stemming from their own deep-seated and often unconscious need to please the male therapist and to remain unthreatening. Others reported that their dependent, nonthreatening behaviors were induced, or at least unconsciously rewarded, by the therapist himself. Experienced supervisors do indeed report that male therapists may covertly and unwittingly encourage compliant behaviors and discourage a challenging, independent stance in female patients.[8]

While female therapists are hardly immune from adopting such attitudes, it is my observation that the problem occurs most intensely and with least conscious recognition in the male-therapist–female-patient dyad. Of significance is the fact that the feminine socialization process teaches females to protect the male ego at all costs by inhibiting any traits, qualities, and behaviors that may be threatening to men. Cultural pressures to "play dumb," "let the man win," or "pretend he's boss" are all crude, if not comic, expressions of a more subtle but powerful cultural injunction that states that in intimate male–female dyads, the man should be (or at least should feel like) the more capable, successful, and dominant partner. For the many couples who deviate from this arrangement, psychiatry has designed such terms as *role reversal, role confusion,* or *matriarchal family,* all of which are mildly pejorative terms suggesting that things are not in their natural place. Indeed, women who dare to compete openly with men on issues of competence and power may be labeled *castrating* or *unfeminine* and have their very attractiveness and love of humankind brought into question. As many authors have noted,[5,12–14] this patriarchal arrangement reflects, in part, men's persistent irrational anxieties about the dreadful effects of female aggression and dominance, as well as women's related irrational fears of their own destructive, "castrating" potential. These shared fears of female destructiveness date back to our long years of helpless dependency on women (i.e., our mothers and other female caretakers) and are rarely recognized consciously by either sex. Rather, these anxieties are contained and held in check by social arrangements that allow men to maintain power and control over women, who are discouraged from expressing aggression and dominance except in indirect, covert, or manipulative ways.

Given such intrapsychic and cultural pressures, it is hardly surprising that male therapists, in particular, may encourage a patient to be self-assertive and autonomous in her family and work life but may subtly encourage her to have a "nice relationship" (e.g., to follow his advice and to accept and value his interpretations) within the therapeutic hour. The paradox of therapeutic interpretations that are purportedly in the service of fostering the patient's independence, while subtly patronizing her or undermining her autonomy within the therapeutic relationship, may go unnoticed by both therapist and supervisor ("No matter how much I interpret, or try to push her, she still won't be assertive with her husband!") Further, the woman's healthy expressions of anger, criticalness, or competitiveness directed toward the therapist may be felt by him as an unhealthy display of aggression or an attempt to control. If the woman is, in fact, hostile and controlling, he may interpret accurately the pathogenic components of such behavior, but without recognizing the positive and adaptive aspects of what the patient is attempting to communicate or accomplish.[8] Bernardez-Bonesatti[8] has commented on the especially strong feelings of revulsion and disapproval that male therapists may feel when confronted with openly hostile and domineering behavior in their women patients. Because women themselves have enormous unconscious fears regarding their own destructiveness and the related fragility of the male ego, both patient and therapist may fail to recognize the subtle ways in which the woman is being a "good patient" at the expense of her own autonomy and growth.

Bernardez-Bonesatti[8] has noted that women therapists may also be prone to excessive disapproval of their female patient's anger or competitiveness, especially if the target of the patient's hostility is a male. Not only is a protectiveness for males aroused, but the female therapist who unconsciously fears that her own unrestrained anger may be hurtful to men is threatened by her identification with a female patient whom she perceives as "destructive" or "castrating." I have also been impressed by the need of female therapists to avoid identifying with women who are angry at men, even if they perceive them as having a legitimate cause.

SEX OF THERAPIST

Advantages of Female Therapist

A significant number of factors go into the making of a good psychotherapist that far outweigh the matter of one's sex. It is my opinion opinion, however, that other things being equal (level of skill, experience, quality of training, etc.) female patients may have much to gain in working with a woman therapist. At the risk of offering somewhat oversimplified generalizations, I would briefly outline certain advantages as follows:

1. Many women find it difficult to be open with a male therapist. For example, their frankness and specificity regarding sexual experiences may be limited. In general, a more honest exploration of self may be

facilitated by work with a same-sex therapist. With a female therapist, the patient is less pulled to unconsciously fulfill stereotypical feminine behavior (e.g., "protectiveness" of the male therapist's ego and sense of importance, avoidance of direct confrontation and competition) that will block more creative, free-ranging work.

In intimate dyadic relationships, men have very little experience relating to women in a truly egalitarian manner, although many men may consider themselves exceptions to this rule. As noted earlier, men are more likely than women to overlook subtle aspects of female compliance, dependency, deskilling, etc., since these are the expectable and familiar ways that women relate to men in close dyadic relationships.

2. With a female therapist, sexualization of the relationship, which may serve as a major resistance against learning, is characteristically avoided. While homosexual feelings and fantasies may emerge with a same-sex therapist, these are usually not used defensively and seductively in the service of warding off anxiety and the threat of confrontation.

3. The opportunity to identify with a female therapist's professional skills and competence is extremely helpful for many women, particularly in instances where there is deep guilt and anxiety over issues of achievement and autonomous functioning. Some patients are better able to consciously acknowledge and express jealous and competitive feelings toward a therapist of their own sex, without having to feel "castrating" or unfeminine.

4. The firsthand experience of women therapists with specifically female emotional, physical, sexual, and spiritual experiences may facilitate a greater depth and intensity of clinical work. Women have incorporated a great number of male-defined myths regarding the "feminine experience," which can best be explored with a female therapist who has herself taken seriously the task of her own consciousness-raising.

5. Women's conflicts and inhibitions often have their roots in unresolved issues of autonomy and separation from the mother, although these conflicts may be masked by the girl-woman's transfer of dependency onto male authority figures and a premature flight into heterosexual relationships.[15,16] A female therapist may allow for a richer and deeper exploration of the mother–daughter relationship and may facilitate an affective reexperiencing of the profoundly complex and ambivalent nature of this bond.

6. Affirmation by a same-sex therapist has especially significant meanings for certain women. To be accepted by another woman in the context of a close relationship characterized by trust and mutual respect may be more "validating" of one's worth and self-esteem than working with a cross-sex therapist. This, I have noted, is especially the case for

narcissistic women with poor self-esteem who unconsciously experience male therapists (or men in general) as relatively more seducible, easily flattered, or fooled by appearances than are women.

7. A same-sex therapist offers greater opportunities for identification. While this is an advantage for all patients, it may be especially critical for the more disturbed individuals, who have not consolidated a stable and coherent sense of gender identity.

Paradoxically, the potential advantages of same-sex therapy, outlined above, are also associated with unconscious threats that may lead certain women to seek out male therapists. For example, a woman who is involved in an intense, unresolved struggle to separate from her own mother may experience considerable anxiety in anticipating dependency on the female therapist. Women who lack a stable and coherent sense of identity and fear themselves to be without substance and depth usually have consolidated a repertoire of cross-sex behaviors that make it easier to begin treatment with a male therapist, with whom these behaviors may help to control the anxieties inherent in beginning a therapy relationship. Women with unconscious conflicted wishes to achieve and succeed in the world outside the home may wish to avoid a relationship with a professional woman in which these conflicts will inevitably be stirred. In sum, many women consider a male therapist "safer" than a female therapist, although this feeling may not be their conscious experience. Rather, unconscious fears of women may be defensively masked by an experience of female professionals as less capable or authoritative than their male counterparts.

Prospective psychotherapy patients who voice a strong preference for male therapists may do so for adaptive, constructive reasons (e.g., a woman whose family life has included a psychologically or physically absent father may need to experience male nurturance.) It is my clinical opinion that when a woman feels strongly that she wishes to see a therapist of a particular sex, male or female, her choice should be respected. While such preferences invariably include both adaptive and defensive components, the patient's anxieties should not be overriden or prematurely interpreted, and the wisdom of the patient's unconscious should not be ignored.

Additional Remarks

As is true of all generalizations, those stated here tell us nothing about the advantages or disadvantages of a particular therapist or the unique needs of an individual patient. Surely, being male does not condemn one to tunnel vision or to a rigid and unexamined adherence to patriarchal attitudes. Nor does being female guarantee one's freedom from unconscious biases and prejudices against women. As Alonso and Rutan[17] pointed out, there are female therapists who are male-identified, who look on their female patients with some measure of scorn, or who may lack empathy for women who have struggled less successfully than they have. Certainly, not all women therapists, by virtue of their female-ness, have their empathic understanding of women enhanced. Some, for example, may be vulnerable to greater distortion through overidentifi-cation and a reliance on projection, which may lead to a false assumption of "sameness" or understanding where it does not exist.

Similarly, a therapist's being a feminist tells us little about her professional expertise. While some feminist therapists have had excellent training, others have not, perhaps because they have avoided traditional, male-dominated institutions at a time when there are few alternative programs available that offer the opportunity for intensive, high-level clinical training. Certain feminist therapists, following an egalitarian treatment model that stresses demystification of the therapist's expertise, may engage in nontherapeutic openness and self-disclosure that blur the appropriate boundaries and fail to provide for the patient the optimal conditions for free-ranging fantasy and exploration. Feminist therapists, like traditional therapists, may be competent or not.

In light of the individual differences between psychotherapists and the many important factors that go into the making of a skilled profes-sional other than his or her sex, it may be tempting to deny real differ-ences between female and male therapists in the treatment of women. As Alonso and Rutan[17] noted, it is difficult for all of us to come to terms with the limitations of our own capacity to empathize and identify with patients whose experience we cannot enter. In discussing such limita-tions of empathy, these authors have reminded us of the painful expe-rience that white liberals had during the racial tensions of the 1960s, and I recall vividly my own defensive reaction to being informed that blacks could not deal effectively with issues of power and self-definition in groups that included white members, and especially white "experts." Women, like blacks, have learned in the past decades of feminism that there is a certain development of consciousness and self-definition that can be achieved only in all-female groups. Along these lines, Bernardez-Bonesatti[16] has described the special advantages and benefits that an all-women's therapy group can provide for its members. Yet, perhaps because of unconscious fears about hurting or excluding men and incur-ring their anger and disapproval, even female mental-health profession-als may deny or minimize the potentially powerful therapeutic benefits of same-sex therapy.

Conclusion

Psychotherapy can be a creative, expanding process of unfolding from the center, or it may reinforce conformity to constricted and externally defined notions of femininity. Similarly, the therapeutic process may free a woman to identify more clearly the sociocultural context of her difficulties, or it may "cool the mark" by encouraging her to cultivate her personal neurosis like a little flower garden, while minimizing the pathogenic effects of the system in which she is operating. To write off the more unhappy of these outcomes as isolated instances of "bad therapy" is tempting, for it allows therapists to avoid taking seriously the difficult task of critically evaluating their work with female patients. As I have tried to show here, good intentions and dedication to helping women become all they can be hardly ensure nonsexist work. It is only through a deeply felt commitment to one's own consciousness-raising that therapists can even begin to gain freedom from the unconscious biases and assumptions that adversely affect the treatment of women.

References

1. Chesler P.: *Women and madness.* Garden City, N.Y., Doubleday, 1972.
2. Symonds A.: Psychoanalysis and women's liberation, *Journal of the American Academy of Psychoanalysis 6* (4):429–431, 1978.
3. American Psychological Association: Report of the Task Force on Sex Bias and Sex-Role Stereotyping in Psychotherapeutic Practice, *Am Psychol* 30:1169–1175, 1975.
4. American Psychological Association: Report of the Task Force on Sex Bias and Sex-Role Stereotyping in Psychotherapeutic Practice, Guidelines for Therapy with Women, *Am Psychol* 33:1122–1123, 1978.
5. Bernardez-Bonesatti T.: Women and anger: Conflicts with aggression in contemporary women, *Journal of the American Medical Women's Association* 33 (5):215–219, 1978.
6. Lerner H.: Adaptive and pathogenic aspects of sex-role stereotypes: Implications for parenting and psychotherapy, *American Journal of Psychiatry* 135 (1):48–52, 1978.
7. Kronsky B.: Feminism and psychotherapy, *Journal of Contemporary Psychotherapy 3* (2):89–98, 1971.
8. Bernardez-Bonesatti T.: Unconscious beliefs about women affecting psychotherapy, *North Carolina Journal of Mental Health* 7 (5):63–66, 1976.
9. Group for the Advancement of Psychiatry, Committee on the College Student: *The educated woman: Prospects and problems,* GAP Report 92, New York, GAP, 1975.
10. Chasseguet-Smirgel J.: Feminine guilt and the Oedipus complex. In *Female sexuality: New psychoanalytic views.* Edited by Chasseguet-Smirgel J. Ann Arbor, University of Michigan Press, 1970.
11. Rich A.: *Of woman born,* New York, W. W. Norton, 1976.
12. Lerner H. E.: Early origins of envy and devaluation of women: Implications for sex-role stereotypes, *Bulletin of the Menninger Clinic* 38:538–553, 1974.
13. Lerner H. E.: Taboos against female anger, *Menninger Perspective* 8 (4):4–11, 1977.

14. Dinnerstein D.:*The mermaid and the minotaur: Sexual arrangements and human malaise.* New York, Harper & Row, 1976.
15. Lerner H. E. On the comfort of patriarchal solutions: Some reflections on Brown's paper, *Journal of Personality and Social Systems* 1 (3):47–50, 1978.
16. Bernardez-Bonesatti T.: Women's groups: A feminist perspective on the treatment of women. In *Changing approaches to the psychotherapies.* Edited by Grayson H., Loew C. New York, Spectrum Publications, 1978.
17. Alonso A., Rutan J. S.: Cross-sex supervision for cross-sex therapy, *American Journal of Psychiatry* 135 (8):929–931, 1978.

Issues in the Psychotherapy of Lesbians

19

Nanette Gartrell

Introduction

One needs only to take a cursory look through the literature on the psychology of women from the last decade to realize that women's struggle to establish intimacy and mutuality in their relationships with men has been the subject of extensive investigation. One is likewise struck by the paucity of literature on relationships between women which have been mutual, egalitarian and fulfilling. Why, one might ask, have we consistently focused our writing, thinking, and teaching on power struggles in heterosexual relationships, and ignored the egalitarian models which have been created in lesbian relationships? The answer, I suspect, is that most feminist theorists fail to recognize the extent to which they have accepted the myth that relationship maturity is possible only through heterosexual union. Heterosexuality must be recognized as a powerful patriarchal institution which has been "imposed, managed, organized, propagandized, and maintained by force," says Adrienne Rich, in order to ensure that women are physically, economically, and emotionally dependent on men.[1] Whereas bonding between women is often experienced as mutual, supportive, and nurturing, the institution of compulsory heterosexuality has forced most women to seek sexual complementarity from men who are incapable of providing emotional fulfillment. As a result, heterosexual women routinely find themselves struggling to understand the discrepancy between the myth of heterosexual romance and the reality of heterosexual relationships.

Not surprisingly, lesbians are seen as a direct threat to the institution of compulsory heterosexuality. Lesbians are women who, in their selection of other women as lovers, partners, and companions, make a clear statement of resistance to economic, emotional and sexual dependence upon men. The price of this resistance to compulsory heterosexuality has been enormous. Lesbians have been burned as witches, sentenced to prison and concentration camps, and more recently kidnapped and "deprogrammed" by gang rape. Lesbianism has been called sinful, evil, perverted, deviant, and antisocial. It has been defined as a psychiatric illness requiring treatment by institutionalization, drugs, electroshock, and sometimes lobotomy. Documents such as letters, poetry, books, and journals written by lesbians have been destroyed[1] or reinterpreted heterosexually. Clearly, the existence of egalitarian, fulfilling lesbian relationships represents a significant threat to the patriarchal exploitation and subjugation of women.

In psychotherapy with lesbian clients, it is essential that the therapist understand the etiology of compulsory heterosexuality and the homophobia* which perpetuates this patriarchal ideology. The therapist must also be skilled at facilitating an exploration of the impact of homophobia on the lives of lesbian clients. I have been working as an "out" lesbian psychotherapist for the past five years, and I would like to discuss some of the treatment goals and strategies which I have developed to assist lesbians in understanding homophobia and maintaining a positive self-image in an oppressively heterosexist world.

WORKING AS AN "OUT" LESBIAN THERAPIST

Regardless of the problem which brings a lesbian into treatment, her experiences of homophobia inevitably become a focus of attention during the treatment process. Since an understanding of the personal, economic, social, and political ramifications of homophobia is essential in working with clients who are struggling with these issues, I believe that lesbian clients should be treated by "out" lesbian psychotherapists.

There have been a number of studies evaluating the effect of therapist–client similarity on the treatment process.[2] There is evidence that when the therapist and client have the same racial or ethnic background, the commonality of experience—and not simply a theoretical understanding of it—produced a more favorable therapeutic outcome.[3-4] Liljestrand et al. examined the relationship between sexual orientation of therapist and client and found that therapist–client similarity in sexual orientation was correlated with a more successful treatment outcome than therapist–client difference in sexual orientation.[5] My clinical work with lesbian clients, as well as their reports of previous treatment experiences with heterosexual therapists, supports this finding.

Women frequently seek treatment at the time that they first become aware of their sexual and emotional attraction to other women. Gener-

*In this article "homophobia" refers to the fear of, hatred of, or aversion to lesbianism.

ally, they are frightened about these feelings, and concerned that they will end up as social outcasts if they pursue relationships with women. Since many of these clients have no prior information about my sexual orientation, they express considerable anxiety when describing their feelings about women to me. They are afraid that I will be offended by their attraction to women and that I will view them as emotionally disturbed.

I make every attempt during the initial interview to convey my comfort with these clients' feelings about women. After obtaining information about the current relationship or potential relationship, I take a history of past relationships, making it clear that I am interested in *any* person—female or male—for whom the client has had strong feelings. In inquiring about past relationships, I intentionally do not ask a separate question about heterosexual relationships, since such questions are interpreted by lesbian clients as a value judgment about the primacy of heterosexuality. At some point during the initial interview, I comment on the fact that there are a variety of cultural myths about lesbianism which are sometimes hard to ignore since they are so ingrained in our thinking. I then ask the client to describe her own perceptions and fears about lesbianism. At the end of the interview, I provide a brief summary of factual information about lesbianism which is pertinent to any negative attitudes, stereotypes, and fears the client has expressed. Additionally, I inform the client about my clinical training, the type of therapy I provide, and my areas of expertise. Most clients who are concerned that they might be lesbians, and all clients who have already identified themselves as lesbians, are informed that I am a lesbian. I explain that I specialize in psychotherapy for lesbians and that my clinical experience, as well as my personal and political understanding of lesbianism, will be important assets to the treatment. For the client who is conflicted about sexual orientation, I add the statement that I feel comfortable working with her regardless of her eventual sexual orientation—lesbian, bisexual, or heterosexual. I explain that the most important aspect of trying to explore various sexual orientations is to be able to do so in a nonjudgmental atmosphere.

My heterosexual colleagues have expressed considerable concern about the disclosure of my lesbianism to my lesbian clients. Many of them aspire to conducting treatment in a setting in which the client has very little information about the therapist. By means of analogy, they claim they would never discuss their marital status with their clients. What these individuals fail to recognize is the fact that most people in our society are *assumed* to be heterosexual, unless otherwise identified. Furthermore, wedding rings and office pictures of spouses and children are not invisible to clients. I interpret discomfort with the disclosure of my lesbianism to clients as an indication of homophobia on the part of therapists who subtly or blatantly advertise their heterosexuality in the treatment setting.

I should mention that I occasionally see clients who are conflicted about their sexual orientation whom I do not inform of my lesbianism. These are clients who are extremely horrified at the prospect of being identified as lesbian and who are terrified of having any contact with other lesbians. In these cases, it has been clear that these women would have been too frightened of me to continue treatment. Generally, these clients have been able to explore their own homophobia in the course of therapy and become more comfortable with their attraction to women without knowing about my lesbianism.

For the most part, I have experienced very positive responses from clients to whom I have disclosed my lesbianism. The following comment is typical of those I have received from lesbian clients who have just been informed that I am a lesbian: "I feel very relieved to hear this. I feel like you won't consciously or unconsciously be judgmental of me about my feelings for women." A number of my clients who had been unable to establish an alliance with previous heterosexual therapists expressed the feeling that they knew that things would be different working with me, because they felt that I, as a lesbian, could understand them. As one client put it: "I have seen four different 'straight' therapists for one or two sessions each. Every one of them seemed to focus on my lesbianism and the family dynamics which made me that way. When you told me in the first session that you were a lesbian, I knew that I had finally found the right therapist. I was sure that you wouldn't interpret every problem in my life as connected to my lesbianism, whether it was or not." Generally, I have found that the disclosure of my lesbianism has been a critical first step in building a therapeutic alliance with lesbians—particularly with those who enter treatment feeling socially isolated or alienated because of their attraction to women.

Positive identification with a therapist can have a major impact on a client who is suffering from low self-esteem. Unlike racial or ethnic minorities, lesbians generally do not grow up in family or social groups where other members are lesbian or gay. Identifying oneself as a lesbian in a social atmosphere of homophobia, without family or peer support, can be a very devastating experience. For the lesbian who seeks treatment at this time, the availability of a therapist who can be a positive lesbian role model is important. The fact that I am a lesbian who is "out," who has completed medical school to become a psychiatrist, a teacher, and a researcher, is tremendously helpful in dispelling the myth that lesbians are incapable of functioning as successful, competent, and contributing members of society.

There are many times in the course of treatment that the experience of being a lesbian is essential to the treatment process. As a lesbian, I am able to empathize with the pain of secrecy as well as the liberation of coming out. I can understand the complexities of lesbian life-styles and the importance of community activites. I also speak the same language as my clients. I know what it means when lesbians use words such as "dyke," "butch," and "femme." My clients have expressed appreciation that they do not have to change their vocabulary when speaking to me. For example, one client informed me that she felt that her previous heterosexual therapist would interpret her use of the word "dykish" pejoratively, so she instead used the phrase "somewhat masculine," even though she felt that it never quite captured the concept she had been trying to present.

Riddle and Sang have observed that the therapist's having a personal understanding of lesbian life experiences seems to accelerate the treatment process.[6] I have also found this to be the case, particularly when I have been able to assist clients in taking advantage of community resources. I had one case which clearly illustrates this point. A woman came to see me because she was considering dropping out of school to move to another city with her woman lover. When she first came to see me, she gave me only a false first name. She explained that she had never discussed her seven-year relationship with anyone other than her lover. She was terrified that the school administration might find out about her relationship if she had a mental health record with her name on it. She did not see herself as a lesbian, because she had never felt attracted to any women other than her current lover.

From my personal and clinical experiences with homophobia, I was aware of the fact that denying one's lesbianism, even in the context of a lesbian relationship, is a common phenomenon. This denial enables a woman to see herself as "different" from all of the negative stereotypes about lesbians which exist in our culture. Beneath this denial is generally a very poor self-image, which is fed by a constant struggle to keep one's relationship hidden. This client had even resorted to changing pronouns, so that her friends at school would believe that she was involved with a man rather than a woman.

The therapeutic intervention in this case consisted primarily of educating her about lesbianism. I began by providing information to assuage her fears about lesbian psychopathology. I then recommended books for her to read and suggested community activities she might wish to attend. Before leaving the first session, she informed me of her real name. When she returned for the second session, she had read *Our Right to Love*, a lesbian resource book produced in cooperation with the women of the National Gay Task Force. She had also decided to attend a "Coming Out" group at a local women's center. Most of the second session was focused on her anxiety about attending this group and her concern that perhaps she was a lesbian after all. The following week she attended the "Coming Out" group, where she met three other women she described as "just like me." They took her to a women's concert where she saw thousands of lesbians celebrating their love of women. She decided at the concert to acknowledge her own lesbianism and join in the celebration. She informed me during our third meeting that she appreciated the opportunity to talk with me, but that she now had friends with whom she could discuss her lesbianism, and that she no longer needed to see me. She said she felt so good about her new contacts with the lesbian community that she had decided to stay in Boston until she finished school. She was no longer fearful that her school administration would discover that she was a lesbian, because she had been informed that her school had an official policy of nondiscrimination against gays and lesbians. I never saw her again, but she did call me a year later to thank me for my helpfulness and to tell me that her life was going very well. The treatment process would obviously never have proceeded this rapidly if I had not been able to validate this client's lesbianism and refer her to the appropriate community resources.

It is of course important to understand that psychotherapeutic training does not automatically qualify a lesbian as an expert in lesbian psychotherapy. Every therapist working with lesbian clients must have an understanding of her own internalized homophobia in order to make certain that it does not affect the treatment process. Therapists—lesbian and heterosexual alike—often become defensive at the suggestion that they have internalized negative feelings about lesbianism. It is difficult for most of us to acknowledge that just because one does not *want* to be homophobic, one can automatically eliminate all homophobic feelings. Understanding cultural homophobia from the perspective of living in that same culture requires rigorous training and study.[7]

Obviously, if a therapist and a client share the same homophobic attitudes, these will not be challenged in the treatment process.[7] For example, one of my lesbian clients had been actively discouraged from childbearing by her previous therapist. Whenever the client brought up her fears about the difficulty of raising a child in a homophobic society, her therapist would validate her fears. The therapist told her that she should not subject a child to the psychic trauma of growing up as a social outcast. In fact, studies have shown that the children of lesbian mothers are no different from the children of heterosexual parents on a variety of developmental measures.[8,9] Clearly, the former therapist's communication that children raised in lesbian households would be incapable of coping with cultural homophobia was a reflection of her personal bias rather than scientific evidence. A more helpful and effective treatment intervention would have involved examining the client's concerns about childrearing in relation to the existing data.

Treatment aimed at uncovering the "etiology" of a client's lesbianism is an obvious indication of therapist homophobia. Before entering treatment with me, a number of my clients had seen other therapists who viewed lesbianism as a developmental disorder. These therapists had insisted on exploring family and relationship dynamics which predisposed to the clients' lesbianism. Needless to say, clients who entered this type of treatment with homophobia-induced low self-esteem were *not* helped to overcome these feelings. Many reported that they felt unhappier about their lesbianism when they terminated than they had when they began this treatment. Since studies[10] have repeatedly refuted psychodynamic theories about the "etiology" of lesbianism (etiology by definition implying that lesbianism is pathological), there is currently no indication for treatment based on the assumption of lesbian psychopathology.

It is not uncommon for lesbians who are having a particularly difficult time with internalized homophobia to develop symptoms which inhibit their ability to function in relationships. Ferreting out the homophobia in these cases requires an understanding of the impact of discrimination on intrapsychic functioning. One of my clients had been in treatment previously because of her inability to have orgasms with her lover. Although she had been orgasmic at the onset of their relationship and she continued to be orgasmic while masturbating, she had become progressively unable to be aroused by her lover. This client's previous therapist utilized the techniques developed by Masters and Johnson to assist her and her lover in improving their sexual relationship. Unfortunately, this client was unable to move beyond the sensate focus exercises despite weeks of patient effort on the part of her lover. When this client entered treatment with me a year later, her sexual dysfunction had not resolved. However, it became clear to me that she was deeply troubled about her family's rejection of her because of her lesbianism. Her treatment with me was focused initially on developing strategies for managing the conflict with her family. I also encouraged this client to expand her network of support within the lesbian community so that the absence of family approval would feel less devastating to her. As her own negative feelings about lesbianism began to diminish, she realized that her inorgasmia had enabled her to avoid sexual contact with her lover and therefore to feel less vulnerable to her family's disapproval of their relationship. That realization led to a gradual return of her sexual functioning. Although the previous therapist had had good intentions in her efforts to assist this client and her lover in resolving their sexual conflict, the therapist was inexperienced in working with lesbian clients and did not understand the fact that homophobia could present as a sexual dysfunction.

In any discussion of therapist homophobia, the subject of the closeted lesbian therapist inevitably arises. There are many more closeted lesbian therapists in existence than "out" lesbian therapists. One might ask whether it would be better for a lesbian client to be seen by a closeted therapist than a nonlesbian therapist, since the closeted lesbian therapist at least has the benefit of understanding lesbianism from her own personal experience. The problem with this line of reasoning, as I mentioned earlier, is that simply being a lesbian is not the only prequisite for understanding homophobia. One must also make a concerted effort to be educated about the personal, political, social, and cultural ramifications of homophobia. The lesbian therapist who remains in the closet believes that she will lose respect from her colleagues and her clients, among others, if her sexual orientation becomes known. Because she allows her own fears of homophobia to dictate a life of secrecy, the closeted lesbian therapist may be unable to offer unbiased assistance to lesbian clients who are struggling with the risks of coming out. Some closeted lesbian therapists have been known to counsel lesbian clients against ever coming out. Since coming out is a positive step toward self-affirmation for most lesbians, closeted lesbian therapists must make every effort to guard against perpetuating their own fears when working with lesbian clients.

Another difficulty which arises when a lesbian therapist is closeted is that most lesbian communities are small, and therefore a client may learn of her therapist's lesbianism via a mutual acquaintance. This presents a particular strain on the therapeutic relationship, especially when the therapist does not acknowledge her lesbianism. If the therapist denies her lesbianism or refuses to reply when asked if she is a lesbian, she makes a clear statement of discomfort about her life-style to the client. Denial of her lesbianism will seriously threaten the therapeutic alliance because the client will then know that she cannot trust her therapist to be honest. If she acknowledges her lesbianism but requests that the client keep this information confidential, she disrupts the therapeutic relationship by placing the client in the special role of "secret-keeper." Giving a client the "gift" of secret information about the therapist's private life will inhibit the client's ability to express negative affects toward the therapist. Clearly, unless a closeted therapist leads such an isolated life that her clients would never find out that she is a lesbian, the likelihood of a client's discovery of the therapist's lesbianism impacting negatively on the treatment process is high.

As an "out" lesbian therapist, I have found advantages and disadvantages to living and working within the lesbian community. My experiences have been similar to those described by Anthony, another "out" lesbian therapist.[11] Since I participate in a variety of lesbian social and political activities, I occasionally encounter clients at these functions. Although running into me at activites reinforces my clients' image of me as a therapist who affirms her own lesbianism and relates comfortably to the community, it sometimes creates problems in the transference. Topics which arise after such encounters include comfort or discomfort with how I am dressed, the company I keep, and my level of commitment to political activities. At these times I make every effort to explore clients' feelings about these issues without becoming defensive or attempting to justify my own behavior. Even when I am successfully able to do this, it is not without some regret that the lesbian community is not large enough to allow me to participate in activities more anonymously.

The size of the community and the possibility that my friends may meet or know my clients or my clients' friends make confidentiality a very important issue. I make it a policy never to identify my clients or discuss them in social situations. I ask my clients early in treatment if they would like me to acknowledge them if I encounter them outside of treatment. If they do wish to be acknowledged, I inform them that I will simply say "hello," and that I will not engage in any further conversation with them or their companions. I also make every effort to launder the identities of my clients out of case presentations, papers, or lectures so that any client who may be present at a lecture or who may stumble across this paper at a later point will be unable to identify herself in the text.

Every therapist encounters erotic transference which sometimes blocks treatment. Anthony reported that erotic transference produced a therapeutic impasse only in cases where her client was relatively alienated from the lesbian community.[11] I have encountered only two cases in which an erotic transference temporarily blocked the treatment. In both of these cases, the clients were lesbians who had been experiencing major difficulty in their attempts to establish relationships. They had also isolated themselves from the community because of their internalized homophobia. Although the treatment was eventually able to proceed after exploring their need to see me as an idealized, eroticized object, I did find it necessary to be quite explicit about the ethical prohibitions against therapist–client physical contact in both cases.

Erotic transference is obviously not unique to psychotherapy with lesbian clients. However, because the institution of compulsory heterosexuality has allowed lesbianism to be defined only as a sexual behavior—and not as a life-style with social, political, and economic as well as sexual components—lesbian clients who do not have a sophisticated understanding of this particular form of homophobia are likely to interpret the therapist's acknowledgment of her own lesbianism as a sexual come-on. Increasing their exposure to the lesbian community via books, articles, and activities enables these clients to view the sexual component of lesbianism from a more appropriate perspective.

COMING OUT AS A TREATMENT GOAL

I emphasize the importance of lesbian clients being treated by "out" lesbian therapists because I believe that being out is necessary for a healthy adaptation to lesbian life. I have found from my clinical and personal experience that self-esteem and self-image increase in direct proportion to increasing visibility and openness about one's lesbianism. The improvement in psychological well-being as one sheds the constraints of secrecy makes exploration of the risks and benefits of coming out mandatory in the treatment of lesbian clients.

Most closeted lesbians have developed a system of defenses that allows them to function as if being closeted were ego-syntonic. These defenses must be identified so that the client can explore the possibility of coming out with an understanding of both intrapsychic and extrapsychic prohibitions. One of the most common defenses is to deny that living in the closet requires any special effort. When I first explore the possibility of coming out with clients, many of them inform me that the issue is irrelevant because they never engage in intimate conversations with family members or work associates. They express pride in their ability to sidestep questions about their personal lives, and deny that their inability to be honest has any negative impact on their associations with friends and family members. On further questioning, the enormous effort required to conceal their lesbianism becomes apparent. Clients begin to acknowledge how terrified they feel whenever they are asked about their personal lives. They report feeling extremely anxious whenever anyone even mentions boyfriends, marriage, and children in their presence. They describe how painful it is to make their relationships invisible and to act as if their lovers were merely friends. Eventually, most clients admit that living in the closet not only feels bad but also requires a tremendous expenditure of energy.

The next step in the process of exploring coming out options involves a careful assessment of risks. The obvious risks in terms of personal and economic loss can be relatively easily identified. For some women, the potential losses are so great that coming out cannot be considered at that time. These are women who are at serious risk of losing their lives, their jobs, their homes, or their children if their lesbianism becomes known. However, it is still important to help these clients plan toward future changes which will allow them fewer restrictions because of their lesbianism. For example, a third-year medical student I saw in treatment had decided that her last two years of medical school would be too painful if she were out. At her medical school, evaluations were completely subjective for the third and fourth years. She knew that confronting every resident and attending who made homophobic comments on rounds would put her at risk of receiving poor evaluations. She expressed a wish to be out after medical school, but she was concerned about the impact of being out on her medical career. Since I had treated a number of lesbian clients for depression secondary to career choices which had taken them deeper and deeper into the closet, I pointed out to this medical student that it was important to follow a career path which allowed for greater rather than lesser openness. Her ensuing treatment focused on the ways that she could merge her career and coming out goals into a life-style which felt comfortable to her. She is currently practicing as an out lesbian internist in a large metropolitan area.

In my practice, I more frequently encounter clients who have a generalized fear of coming out than clients who have clearly identifiable risks associated with coming out. There are clients who may realistically fear personal rejection, but who do not risk major physical or economic hardship if they were to come out. For these clients, it is not sufficient to assess only the risks and benefits of coming out in each interpersonal situation. It is equally important to evaluate the long-term social and psychological consequences of remaining closeted. The cost of this secrecy *cannot* be underestimated. The constant need to lie, to be on guard, and to pretend heterosexuality must be understood by clients in terms of the toll on psychic energy and injury to self-esteem. Weinberg[12] contends that the amount of psychological damage caused by lying is directly proportional to the amount of self-contempt which motivates the lie. I would add that the amount of damage is also proportional to the amount of the time maintaining the lie. Obviously, the longer a lesbian has lived in the closet, the greater her guilt will be when coming out and informing those around her of past deceptions. Lesbian clients who have some choice about coming out (and again, this does not mean coming out risk-free; it only means that they are not likely to suffer major physical or economic hardships) must be educated about the long-term potential for stress, anxiety, and depression if they remain closeted.

One of my clients was a successful attorney in a corporate law firm. She concealed her lesbianism from both her work colleagues and her family. During the initial history, I noted that she had been abusing alcohol during the three years she had worked for the firm. When I confronted her about her alcohol abuse, she related it to the stress of work. Eventually, she was able to see that being closeted was also contributing to the anxiety which she treated with alcohol. However, she was unwilling to explore the possibility of coming out as a means of alleviating stress. She agreed to cut down on her alcohol consumption, but she refused to consider AA.

During the second session, the client informed me that she had just discovered a breast lump. She was scheduled for a lumpectomy the next day. Despite her young age, she was found to have breast cancer, which required radiation and chemotherapy. During her hospitalization, both her colleagues who visited her and her family learned that she was a lesbian through a physician's indiscretion (i.e., via a note in the chart.) All continued to be extremely supportive of her even after they were aware of her lesbianism. In the psychotherapy which followed, this client reported feeling extremely relieved that she no longer had to hide. She was finally able to acknowledge the degree to which the stress of being closeted had contributed to her alcoholism. She began to attend AA, and she has been dry for the past two years. If she had not been forced out by a physician's indiscretion, the struggle around her alcohol abuse would undoubtedly have been greatly prolonged in the treatment.

I find that it is particularly helpful for clients to have worked through some of their internalized homophobia and to feel good about being lesbian prior to coming out publicly. It is obviously very stressful to confront blatant homophobia when coming out, and therefore I encourage clients to begin this undertaking from a position of as much strength and pride as possible. Coming out to one's parents after a recent relationship loss, for instance, is likely to be far more stressful than coming out to them when one is involved in a good relationship. Even if the client generally feels happy about being a lesbian, confronting typical parental concerns that she will have a more difficult life as a lesbian at a time that she is experiencing the acute pain and loneliness of a relationship loss inevitably generates unnecessary self-doubt. Selecting the appropriate time and setting for coming out will enable the client to withstand anticipated confrontations and criticisms with the least amount of psychic trauma and damage to self-esteem.

Once a client has decided that she would like to venture out of the closet, the therapist should be able to provide some useful coming out strategies. Together the client and the therapist can develop a sequence from high- to low-priority persons to whom the client will come out. The therapist should point out that it often takes weeks or months to resolve feelings around a particular coming out experience. Therefore, the coming out strategy should not involve coming out to every significant person in the client's life simultaneously. The therapist should explain that the client is likely to have much more positive experiences in coming out if she can take the time to educate the important people in her life whom she will need for support if she encounters any major homophobia or discrimination down the line.

The particular sequence for coming out will vary from client to client. Most clients feel the need to inform close friends and family members about their lesbianism prior to coming out at work. In preparation for coming out to friends and family members, we discuss the client's expectations about how each person will respond. We evaluate these expectations in terms of any previous homophobic or supportive statements the person may have made in the client's presence. I may then role-play the coming out conversation between the client and this person. I attempt to role-play the various ways one can acknowledge one's lesbianism in a manner which is *not* confessional. I explain that acknowledging one's lesbianism proudly, affirmatively, and directly (i.e., in person) not only bolsters one's own self-esteem but also makes it clear that the client feels good about her life. This is an important communication, since she should not put herself in a position of having to defend her lesbianism. Instead, the person to whom she has come out must be assisted in acknowledging her or his own homophobia. The client must facilitate this person's understanding that her/his future relationship with the client is largely dependent upon her/his willingness to eliminate homophobia through self-examination and education. I encourage clients to provide books and articles containing up-to-date information about lesbianism to interested friends and family members. Having good resource materials on hand not only relieves the client of the responsibility of being the sole educator but also provides information about topics which may be difficult to discuss in person.

Parents usually feel guilty about or responsible for their daughter's lesbianism. Most parents believe the myth that childrearing practices determine sexual orientation. As a result, when they learn that their daughter is a lesbian, parents often blame each other and themselves for not being passive enough, assertive enough, masculine enough, or feminine enough when their daughter was growing up. I warn clients that providing information and reading materials may not be enough to counteract the feelings of guilt and failure which their parents may experience when they learn of their daughter's lesbianism. I explain that parents may need support groups (such as Parents of Gays groups which meet regularly in most major cities in the United States) or psychotherapy to work out their own conflicts about having a lesbian daughter. Clients may be able to help their parents locate support groups and nonjudgmental psychotherapists to help them with this process.

When clients are considering coming out at school or at work, I emphasize the importance of doing so only when they feel academically or occupationally secure. I saw two clients who had come out when they were in academic difficulty. Where as other students in similar difficulty had been placed on academic probation, both lesbian students were informed that they would be asked to withdraw from school if their grades did not improve significantly within one semester. Obviously, the risk of homophobia compounding academic or occupational insecurity is great.

Beyond the major obstacles of friends, family, and work, lesbians will make choices about being out every day of their lives. One must decide when, where, and how to express affection toward a lover in public. One must also develop a casual way of informing acquaintances of one's lesbianism when asked the inevitable questions about marriage and family. I encourage clients to correct heterosexist assumptions in as casual a manner as they would correct any other erroneous assumption. For example, I suggest that when asked if they are married, they respond, "Oh, no, I'm a lesbian. But I am involved in a relationship," if they are, just as calmly and directly as they would respond to a mistaken assumption about where they grew up. In interactions with people who are relatively inconsequential in one's life, I stress that it is important to protect oneself from unnecessary vulnerability. One can do this by presenting one's lesbianism in a directly factual manner with no invitation for detailed or intimate discussion.

Although it is often tempting to avoid disclosing one's lesbianism to people whom one does not know well, I remind clients that they will be likely to come away feeling bad from every situation in which they have deferred to heterosexist assumptions. Generally, the decision to conceal one's lebianism—even in a casual encounter—is accompanied by an internalization of the negative attitudes which one assumes other people would express if one's lesbianism were acknowledged. By making a promise to oneself that one will be honest about one's lesbianism as often as possible, one avoids returning to the closet with an impaired self-image. Being out allows one to externalize rather than internalize the anger one feels in response to homophobia; it also enables one to develop more open and honest friendships with those who are supportive.

Before terminating with lesbian clients who have recently come out, I point out the importance of protecting themselves from future insults or difficulties in their lives. Although they may be fairly adept at living in a homophobic world by then, I stress the need to maintain a viable lesbian support network. I remind them that as long as we live in an oppressively heterosexist world, lesbians will be victimized in order to keep women in a subservient role. I encourage them to continue resisting this tyranny by being out, by participating in the lesbian community, and by lending a hand to other lesbians who are struggling with the same obstacles they have now overcome. I express the hope that being out will enable them to enjoy a greater sense of personal freedom than they have previously experienced.

CONCLUSION

In closing, I would like to say that one cannot possibly cover in a single article all of the issues which come up in psychotherapy with lesbian clients. Certainly, the criticism may be raised that I have not cited examples of poor or working-class women in my discussion. Since I work largely in an academic environment, most of my referrals are students or professionals. Although the issues I have raised are relevant to all lesbians, class privilege cannot be overlooked as a major factor affecting coming out choices.

I have limited my focus further to a discussion of the treatment of lesbian clients by "out" lesbian therapists who can assist clients in the process of coming out themselves. I have pointed out some of the ways in which coming out has a positive impact on self-esteem and self-image in lesbians. I have also discussed being out in the sociopolitical context of compulsory heterosexuality. It is my hope not only that increasing lesbian visibility will dispel destructive stereotyping and homophobia, but also that it will demonstrate to nonlesbian women that there *are* models for intimate, egalitarian, and emotionally fulfilling relationships.

REFERENCES

1. Rich A.: Compulsory heterosexuality and lesbian existence. *Signs* 5(4):631–660, 1980.
2. Rochlin M.: Sexual orientation of the therapist and therapeutic effectiveness with gay clients. *J Homosex* 7(2/3):21–30, 1982.
3. Jones A., Seagull A. A.: Dimensions of the relationship between the black client and the white therapist. *Amer Psychol* 32:850–855, 1977.
4. Roll S., Millen L., Martinez R.: Common errors in psychotherapy with Chicanos: Extrapolations from research and clinical experience. *Psychother: Theory, Research, Practice* 17:158–168, 1980.
5. Liljestrand P., Gerling E., Saliba P. A.: The effects of social sex-role stereotypes and sexual orientation in psychotherapeutic outcomes. *J Homosex* 3(4):361–372, 1978.
6. Riddle D. I., Sang B.: Psychotherapy with lesbians. *J Soc Iss* 34(3):84–100, 1979.
7. Martin A.: Some issues in the treatment of gay and lesbian patients. *Psychother: Theory, Research, Practice* 19(3):341–348, 1982.
8. Green R.: Children raised by homosexual or transsexual parents. *A J P* 135(6):692–697, 1978.
9. Kirkpatrick M., Smith C., Roy R.: Lesbian mothers and their children: A comparative study. *Am J Orthopsych* 51(3):545–551, 1981.
10. Gartrell N.: The lesbian as a "single" woman. *Am J Psychother* 35(4):502–516, 1981.
11. Anthony B. D.: Lesbian client–lesbian therapist: Opportunities and challenges working together. *J Homosex* 7(2/3):45–57, 1982.
12. Weinberg G.: *Society and the Healthy Homosexual.* New York: St. Martin's, 1972.

A Feminist Approach to Family Therapy

20

Rachel T. Hare-Mustin

One might well ask what family therapy has to do with feminist therapy. Have not the family and the institutions that support it been the primary cause of maintaining women in their stereotyped sex roles? As feminists can readily point out, "The family has been the principal arena for the exploitation of women, and however deeply rooted in social structure that exploitation may be, it is through family structure that it makes its daily presence felt."[10] Chase's question, "What does feminism demand of therapy?"[10] is the question I would like to examine in the form, "What does feminism demand of family therapy?"

In discussing family therapy from a feminist point of view, I will first briefly consider the principles of feminist therapy and review the structure of the family as we know it today. I will then discuss how family therapy has evolved. Some of the ways in which family therapy differs from the feminist approach will be examined. Finally, I will present in greater detail the ways feminist values can be translated into techniques for working with families.

Feminist Therapy

Feminist therapy grew out of the theory and philosophy of consciousness-raising. Central to feminist therapy is the recognition that (a) the traditional intrapsychic model of human behavior fails to recognize the importance of the social context as a determiner of behavior, and (b) the sex roles and statuses prescribed by society for females and males disadvantage women.[29,30,42,45]

Feminism sees as the ideal for the individual the ability to respond to changing situations with whatever behavior seems appropriate, regardless of the stereotyped expectations for either sex. This idea of the androgynous personality reflects a recent shift away from dualistic notions of masculine-feminine personality types.[21] In helping women develop in line with an androgynous model, feminist therapy has

Reprinted from *Family Process* 17(2):181–194, 1978. Copyright © 1978 by Family Process, Inc. Reprinted by permission.

encouraged women not only to become aware of the oppressiveness of traditional roles but also to gain experiences that enhance their self-esteem as they try new behaviors as part of gaining self-definition. The feminist therapeutic relationship itself embodies these principles in its emphasis on greater equality between the therapist and the client. By differentiating what is personal from what is external, feminist therapy may be distinguished from nonsexist therapy or humanistic therapy. These approaches may encourage individual development free of gender-prescribed behaviors, but they do not (a) examine and (b) seek to change the conditions in society that contribute to the maintenance of such behaviors.

THE FAMILY

The American family as we know it from research and clinical practice is one in which the husband bears the main responsibility for the economic maintenance of the family and the wife bears primary responsibility for domestic work and child care. The nature of the family today is a consequence of the dramatic changes that took place during the 19th century, chief among which was the separation of work from the home.[41] Where productivity was rewarded by money, those who did not earn money, such as women, children and old people who were left at home, had an ambiguous position in the occupational world.[22] The instrumental role for males and the expressive role for females that evolved were held up as normative by Parsons and Bales[40] and even necessary for the well-being of individuals, the family, and society.

The employment of women outside the home has not released women from the assigned expressive role that accompanies homemaking responsibility. Employed wives labor longer then either employed men or full-time housewives, and the fact that child care is not available for working women in the United States reinforces the idea that women are not about to be released from their primary responsibility in the home merely because they work outside.[6] Recent work patterns for women are actually not innovative but regressive in terms of the decreasing proportion of women in any but low-paying jobs.[44] Being female is regarded as uniquely qualifying a woman for domestic work, no matter what her interests, aptitudes, or intelligence.[5] Equalitarian arrangements by which both parents share equally in domestic areas or by which contributions to the family are based on personal preferences and individual capabilities are rare when these preferences diverge from traditional role expectations.

In marriage, the power of the male in the family is guaranteed by society's expectation that he will be older, bigger, have more education, and come from a higher social class than his wife. This tends to assure that he has the strength, credentials, experience, special knowledge, and training on which power in part is based. Marriages in which this is not the case are regarded as deviant. The power in the female role that derives from the woman's responsibility in organizing the household, the children, and the husband has depended on being married and having children.[22] With the decline in the importance of the family, such power has been reduced. Women's lack of power is obscured and attributed to women's being more emotional and less able to "handle power" than men. As in other unequal relationships, the dominant group defines the "acceptable" roles for the less powerful, which are those activities like domestic work that the dominant group does not choose to do. There is research demonstrating that loss of power and chronic powerlessness are frequent precursors of psychological disorder.[31]

Marriage typically demands that women give up their activities or place of residence to adjust to the needs of men. It has been observed that the partner who sacrifices or gives up the most for the marriage must of necessity be the one most committed to it.[37] The woman, who may have given up her occupation, family closeness, or residence for marriage, must rely more on the marriage to fulfill her needs. The expectation that women will adjust to men's patterns leads to an often unrecognized difference in the number of stressful life events impacting on men and women. Dohrenwend[11] has found that women are exposed to a relatively higher rate of change or instability in their lives compared with men, which can be seen as contributing to frequent psychosomatic symptoms and mood disorders.

The inequality in the traditional family is rarely recognized by individual or family therapists. It has been observed that power aspects of sex roles are largely disregarded or denied, except when women have power.[35] The formulation of dominant-mother/ineffectual-father as the cause of practically every serious psychological difficulty is made without regard for the underlying inequality that leads to such a situation. Few therapists recognize that the stress on family members and particularly on women from required sex roles that assign them an inferior position has led to the family becoming the arena of conflicts that arise from the inequity sanctioned by the larger society.[34]

FAMILY THERAPY

In the late 1940s and 1950s, researchers such as Wynne, Lidz, and others, focusing on the schizophrenic patient, identified the overinvolved mother as the source of pathology. In terms of the social events of the time, women who had been more fully involved in activities outside the home during World War II were now being encouraged to return to their natural feminine occupations as wives and mothers and to apply themselves to these responsibilities. The profound impact on the field of Parsons and Bales[40] idea of fixed sex roles, with males having the instrumental role and females the expressive, has been pointed out.[24] Observations of these stereotyped sex roles in the American family were then used by researchers and therapists as the basis for the argument that these were the necessary conditions for normal family life and successful child rearing. Advances in the 1960s saw the application of principles of general systems theory to the understanding of the family. The most notable change in family therapy in the 1970s, and one that has implications for women, is the growing acceptance of the family developmental point of view that follows from the work of Hill and other sociologists.[19]

The family developmental orientation is analogous to the individual life cycle perspective in its focus on the stages in family development over the family life span—from the initial courtship phase to the death of the last member of the couple. Stages are defined in terms of the dominant developmental tasks faced by individual members of the family and the family as a system at that point. "Normal" crises in family development are usually identified as those that occur around the addition or loss of a member, whether actually by birth or death, or symbolically by change in activity or residence. The importance of this model is that it can provide an orientation toward prevention rather than pathology by identifying predictable crisis points in advance. Therapeutic interventions are directed at preparing the family for such stress points as well as helping the system move on from crises to resume its characteristic functioning.

If the systems approach to family therapy has adopted a prevention model of mental health and has shifted from a focus on the individual to recognizing social systems as determinants of behavior, one might ask why has it not been discovered and acclaimed by feminists as sex-fair therapy? In point of fact, while espousing a theory that might seem to assure equality for family members, family therapists in practice share the same biases and prejudices as others in the society and often have not freed themselves from their past training in a traditional orientation that views the mental health of males as akin to adulthood and that of females as not.[9] For example, Bowen's Differentiation of Self Scale[8] can readily be identified as a sex-stereotyped masculinity-femininity scale with femininity at the devalued end. Bowen's approach is akin to the Ego Strength Scale based on the Minnesota Multiphasic Personality Inventory

(MMPI), which is biased in favor of males by including more masculine than feminine scored items.[32] Bowen ignores the fact that women's socialization encourages them to be emotional and intuitive rather than rational.

To restore the family to healthy functioning, family therapists often intentionally or unwittingly reinforce stereotypic role assignments for man, the doer, and woman, the nurturer, assuming that the traditional roles are the basis for healthy functioning. That some people are more comfortable in these roles for which they were trained cannot be denied, but, as suggested earlier, they may pay a price in psychological functioning. The fact that married women have a higher incidence of mental illness than men but single women do not[15] should lead family therapists to question the structure of the traditional family as it affects women. Representative of family therapists who support sex-stereotyped roles as important for healthy development are Boszormenyi-Nagy and Spark.[7] They point out that "a heterosexual [therapy] team permits each individual to function more comfortably in his or her life-long assigned biological-emotional role. . . . Mutual respect is needed to confirm the differences between masculinity and femininity" (p. 204). They criticize women who live vicariously through their husbands and children, thus avoiding facing their own lack of identity; however, they also criticize women who seek identity elsewhere, as in the following example.

> A young married woman who received superior ratings as a school teacher refused to cook or shop for food since she considered this beneath her. . . . She seemed to expect the therapist as well as her family to be completely accepting of her passive, dependent attitude that it was beneath her dignity to fulfill this aspect of a woman's role. (p. 203)

Minuchin[37] sees himself as modeling the male executive functions, forming alliances, most typically with the father, and through competition, rule-setting, and direction, demanding that the father resume control of the family and exert leadership as Minuchin leads and controls the session. In a comparable manner, Forrest[12] describes the female therapist as using her feminine warmth, wisdom, and interest in men to appeal to their masculine instincts.

These illustrations reveal how the unquestioned acceptance and reinforcement of stereotypic sex roles takes place in much of family therapy, despite the possibilities inherent for change in the systems point of view. As Klapper and Kaplan[24] point out in their survey of sex-role stereotyping in family therapy literature, current writing has been minimally affected by the emerging consciousness. "Someone being trained as a family therapist would have to maintain stern vigilance in order not to be caught up in the oftentimes subtle reinforcement of behavior patterns which are so debasing and humiliating to women" (p. 28).

TECHNIQUES FOR FAMILY THERAPY

Despite the fact that a feminist approach to family therapy has not developed, I would contend that such an approach is possible. The obstacles can be summed up as (a) the socially reinforced sex roles that exist in the family; (b) the therapist's own family and clinical experience that renders her or him unaware of and insensitive to alternatives to stereotyped sex roles; and (c) the family's concerns, which are rarely identified as related to traditional sex-role assignments. My purpose in what follows is not to analyze family therapy techniques, per se, but rather to consider certain areas of intervention in which a feminist orientation is important. These areas are: the contract, shifting tasks in the family, communication, generational boundaries, relabeling deviance, modeling, ownership and privacy, and the therapeutic alliance with different family members.

The Contract

Feminists stress the equality in the relationship between the therapist and the client as a departure from the paternalistic medical model in which the doctor is presumed to always know best. Recognizing that the capacity to influence people comes in part from their expectations (the placebo effect), feminists are contending that an equal relationship with mutual respect can still raise expectations that are beneficial in achieving goals.[13] One method of attaining equality is by use of a contract.

Many family therapists use an informal or unwritten contract with families that come for help that facilitates agreement on arrangements for treatment and goals.[18] As has been pointed out by the Nader group, a contract that is written assures the protection of client rights to an even greater extent.[1] The contract is probably not intended to be legally binding, but it does establish a mutual accountability between the therapist and the family. Furthermore, the negotiation of the contract can be an important part of the therapeutic process itself. The contract can include arrangements for treatment, the amounts and kinds of responsibility to be assumed by the therapist and by the family, issues of confidentiality, the goals of therapy and measurement of their accomplishment, and provisions for renegotiation of the contract.

One of the problems in contracting with families is the need to involve all family members, some of whom are more reluctant to participate than others. Hines and Hare-Mustin[20] have pointed out the ethical problems in requiring reluctant children and adolescents to participate in family therapy. Most families come because the mother is distressed about something in the family. The father, from his less involved position, feels that there is nothing to worry about, while the children have little choice. Too strong initial support by the therapist of any one member's point of view is likely to alienate the other members and lead to sabotaging or early termination of treatment. The therapist must reach some shared agreement with all family members.

To the extent that the father is paying for the sessions, he controls the sessions. It is hard to complain about the person paying the bills, as women and children are well aware. Part of the therapeutic process that relates to the contract and the setting of fees is the shifting of the conventional idea that the one who contributes money to the family is the only meaningful contributor. Unpaid services of other family members, primarily the mother, must be viewed as contributing to and subsidizing the person who is bringing in the money. Another aspect of the money economy is the inflexibility of most job schedules that can be pointed out to the family in connection with scheduling appointment times that the father can attend. In like manner, when babysitting arrangements are necessary, the value of the mother's unpaid work should be focused on, rather than merely her traditional responsibility for locating babysitters.

Beginning with the contract helps the family learn about negotiation and makes explicit the "rules" for the therapy. From the negotiations about the contract, the family can begin to understand how rules regulate the behavior of family members. Many family conflicts center about what the rules are and who makes them, which is basically the issue of power. In family conflicts, Zuk[49] has pointed out that the weak person traditionally espouses values such as justice, compassion, and relatedness, while the powerful person advocates control, rationality, law, and discipline. In husband–wife conflicts, wives usually espouse values concerned with caring, while husbands espouse rationality. In parent–child conflicts, children espouse the relatedness values, while their parents stress control and discipline. The family therapist can help the family recognize the value differences that accompany the shifts in power among participants in family conflicts.

Shifting of Tasks in the Family

Family therapists recognize that it is impossible to change the role of one family member without changing the role of another. However, the division of labor and functions in the family is often looked at in a very limited perspective. Therapists who ask about the sharing of chores in the family may not recognize that the division of labor in the home is in part a result of the separation of paid work from the home and the consequent devaluing of domestic work. Traditional therapists who see some women having a greater share of responsibility and power within the home than men overlook the fact that men typically have power and status elsewhere. Family therapists should not rush to "restore" the power in the family to the father, thus further reducing the mother's self-esteem and limited authority. As noted earlier, the observation that fathers typically have the instrumental role and mothers the expressive role in families has led family and child care experts to assume that these role assignments are necessary for normal functioning, an assumption for which the evidence is at best equivocal.

Many couples share responsibilities without regard for traditional stereotypes until the birth of the first child.[43] The arrival of a child precipitates a change in power and relationship status between the partners. Resentment can build up at this point in the person who has to shift to the major child care responsibilities—resentment that can lead to the breakdown of the bonds of affection established in the previous period. At the same time, the woman with authority is too often seen as a monster by her family and by therapists because for a woman to have authority deviates from the stereotype. In point of fact, the limited power that women have to make decisions and guide the lives of family members has declined as the family has declined in importance.

Often, women would like others to share more of the decision-making in the family.[36] Mothers are burdened with many small decisions, but the fact that fathers do not participate signals to the mother as well as to the children that the decisions are about matters that are not really important. The family therapist needs to help family members examine how decisions are made and who shares in the process.

The practice of the mother's thanking other family members for household chores also needs to be examined. As long as the mother thanks others and they expect to be thanked, the implication is that they are doing her work, rather than family work, and they are doing it as a favor to her. In addition, children are not going to participate willingly in chores that the father signifies by his nonparticipation are demeaning.

What should take precedence, the job or the family? The feminist therapist needs to be aware of the complexities of this question. The intense pressure on the person working with technology in the money economy often results in a choice having been made in favor of the job. Because men bring in the money, it is expected that women and children will adjust to their needs. Yet, when a woman works, the family still demands primary allegiance.[6] Women who work are expected to be interrupted by and respond to the demands of the family. I had a case in which an unemployed father and the teenage daughter waited for the working mother to come home and cook supper. Not all therapists would have questioned this practice.

Family therapists need to be aware of the options for women as well as men and not oversell work for women outside the home when the jobs available are frequently repetitious, demeaning, and underpaid. In addition, there are women whose socialization is such that they are genuinely happy with the "professionalization" of housework in their current lives. The encouragement of women to go out to work without a reduction of their work load at home may be but a thinly disguised punitive act. The economic realities are also such that if both individuals work part time or if the woman works full time instead of her husband, there will be a loss in family income owing to the differentials in earning power of men and women and the loss of fringe benefits for part time work. Despite these limitations, outside work can be an enhancing experience. Therapists need to help the family recognize not only the positive aspects but also the enormous societal barriers operating against meaningful change in the family and not advocate facile solutions that may have slight chance of success. On the other hand, counseling women to remain in traditional roles can have repercussions for their families in terms of anger, frustration, and a smothering overinvolvement with their children.[47]

The mother, as well as other family members, needs to give up the view that she should be totally available to respond to every demand family members make upon her. If she is to give up some of the power associated with being central in the family, she must be connected with areas outside the home where she can have autonomy, respect, earning power, and opportunities to develop her capabilities. Women's ambivalence and resistance to giving up responsibility in the family is often a defense against the guilt they feel about not fulfilling their traditional sex roles and the anxiety they experience when departing from the familiar patterns of wife and mother. Some of the specific directions the therapist can take with the family are drawing up and trying out new schedules of household chores, involving the father in home tasks, child care, and decision-making, assigning age-appropriate responsibilities to the children, and helping the family develop network supports that will be encouraging of the anticipated changes. More appropriate assertive behaviors can be developed by the mother at the same time she is learning to set more realistic goals for herself. One of the first things that signals change may be a reduction in the mother's behavior as a critic, which is an often unacknowledged consequence of her inferior position. All family members can benefit from consciousness-raising as a part of family therapy. Understanding of different roles develops as parents and children are asked to examine what they like and do not like about being male or female.

Communication

Many family therapists focus on communication, but few have analyzed the relation of communication styles to male and female roles. Women are typically not listened to as having something important to say because the woman in a family or marital relationship is viewed as an adjunct. ("Hello, Mrs. Smith. What does your husband do?") Like children, women are not taken seriously, or when they talk about serious things, are accused of imitating a man.[4] Research on nonverbal communication consistently shows that women are treated and behave as inferiors.[33] There are several consequences of this lack of confirmation experienced by women that therapists should be aware of: women are regarded as nags because they talk constantly in seeking to be attended to or as devious or vague because they express themselves indirectly and tentatively in order to avoid disapproval.

The transactional nature of family therapy reveals habitual family communication patterns as no other approach has been able to do. For example, the nagging person can be viewed not only in terms of the withdrawn or disinterested partner that provokes the nagging behavior, but also in terms of the third person in the triangle who is being given a lesson, drawn in, distanced, supported, alienated, or the like. Changing communication patterns in the family is regarded by some family theorists as the single most important technique for changing behaviors and attitudes.[16,48] The family can practice new ways of communicating, shifting roles through role play, critique, and practice in order to learn new ways of interacting and to understand the confining aspects of one's own or another's traditional role.

Rules for communication have been developed by women's consciousness-raising groups to help women express themselves and be heard. Some of these are similar to those used by family therapists, such as not interrupting, relating the particular experience to the universal (generalizing), becoming specific ("What does that mean to you?"), and attaching significance to feelings, not just to facts. The latter leads to less disqualifying of women's experiences or style of expression than the rational mode to which men have been socialized. The therapist can also reinforce a greater range of genuine emotional expression and sensitivity to emotions in men who have avoided or disparaged emotional expression.

Generational Boundaries

Clear generational boundaries are often seen as congruent with healthy family functioning.[37] The breakdown in boundaries can occur when one of the parents is more closely allied with a child than with the spouse. The therapist who is not sensitive to the power differences in family roles may not understand the alliance of the powerless mother and child against the powerful father or the father and child against the demanding mother. Sometimes there seem to be no generational boundaries but an amorphous unit consisting of parents and children in which the parents avoid the burden of decisions and responsibility by a spurious equality. Children may find themselves parenting the parent with exaggerated dependency needs. The low status accorded to older people in our society and particularly to older women needs to be kept in mind by the therapist who sees a mother trying to be an age mate to her daughter. The therapist should work to restore the alliance between the parents without the exaggerated status differences that have evolved between adults and children in modern times.

It has been pointed out that children have a deteriorating effect on the marital relationship in terms of a decline in understanding, love, and general satisfaction.[19] This could well be a consequence of the mother's dissatisfaction with the burden of her assigned role and the lack of genuine sharing and interest in child care by the father. The availability of the mother to the children leads to close alliances as well as the perpetuation of stereotyped sex roles. Mothers tend to use their daughters (or sons) as confidants because their isolation in the home from other adults confines them to housewife and mothering functions. In this way, women pass on their sense of worthlessness and denigration to both daughters and sons. The unavailability of fathers affects sons and daughters as well as mothers, sons because the unavailable father does not provide a model for learning, daughters because the father's unavailability leads them to develop an image of the male as a romantic stranger, an unrealistic ideal that cannot be satisfied when they reach adult life.

During adolescence, daughters are particularly torn between identification with the mother and with the father. This is the time when it becomes increasingly apparent to young women that career paths may be closed to them. The daughter who has a close relationship with her mother but is interested in a life different from her mother's may see herself as betraying and competing with her mother. If she aspires to a career path and identifies with her father, this can interfere with her relationship with her mother as well as with the development of feminine aspects of her identity.[38] The therapist who is sensitive to the confusion of young women during this period can provide support to the girl as a facilitative model who values both career and family.

Siblings can sometimes develop a strong subsystem independent of the parents. Freedom from assigned sex roles among siblings can be supported by the therapist and the parents. It is frequently not recognized how much siblings contribute to one another's development through socialization, control, and rescuing operations.

Younger children are often coopted by one or both of the parents in terms of their own needs. Therapists need to be aware of the extent to which children bring zest and life to a family and misbehave to keep the family system functioning. A range of behaviors should be equally allowed both girls and boys. Children's disturbing behavior may be subtly encouraged by the parents who can be united only when dealing with a child's misbehavior. School refusal and other disruptive behaviors may actually be supportive of a depressed parent, usually the mother. To the extent the family therapist can help the mother develop independence and self-esteem, as well as gain the positive regard of the father, the therapist frees the children from the need to rescue the mother by "bad" behavior.

Relabeling Deviance

Diagnostic labels are not useful in a family systems approach because they carry intrapsychic and causal connotations that do not fit into a systems model. Like the feminist therapist, the family therapist can avoid labels implying that the attribute belongs to the individual rather than the situation. Diagnostic labels, by focusing on the individual, serve to mask the prevalence of particular conditions in society that stress individuals. That behavior has become habitual as a result of socialization patterns of reinforcement does not mean that the therapist should shift to the intrapsychic model. For example, it should be recognized that the unhappiness of women in families is too widespread to be viewed as an individual weakness or defect. As Halleck[17] has emphasized, treatment that does not encourage the patient to examine and confront her environment merely strengthens the status quo.

The use of language is important because in this way sex differences can be exaggerated, often with disparaging connotations.[14] Some of the pejorative labels used are imposed by the male-dominated culture such as pretty, sexy, ugly, blonde, dumpy, and the like.[23] Others clearly reflect the double standard of terminology for men and women. The use of the generic masculine pronoun denies women's experiences. Consider also, for example, "father absence" and "maternal deprivation." or the fact that a family is called traditional when the man is breadwinner but matriarchal when the woman is the breadwinner.[35] "Weak" is a label applied to women and pejoratively to men, but like "strong," its meaning can only be understood in transactional terms. All too often, the weak person in the family, by appearing incompetent, is shoring up the strong one in order to prevent the latter's true frailty from becoming apparent.

In this way, the inadequate housekeeper or the fearful woman is making her partner as well as other family members appear strong, and so in reality, she is protecting them.

An example of a pejorative and overused label in contemporary society is "passive-aggressive." What the therapist needs to do is examine the conditions that make individuals use covert and indirect means rather than direct means for gaining their ends. Some behaviors, such as phobic behaviors, can be understood as exaggerations of the dependency and timidity that women are taught or as a consequence of women's inexperience and the taboos against women successfully coping with and overcoming obstacles in a "man's world." Too often therapists, like others, blame women for the dependency in which they have been trained.

There are a number of ways by which therapists who are sensitive to the misuse of labels can bring about change. They can help both women and men free themselves from stereotypic expectations that lead them to try to hide attributes in themselves they have been taught are unacceptable. In addition, therapists can often perceive attributes of family members that are not usually noticed and by drawing attention to them can shift family members' ways of perceiving and interacting. Labels of "good" and "bad" illustrate how labels deny the complexity of persons. In the case of an older "bad" sister who was always in trouble, I was able to shift some of the "good" from the younger "good" child to the "bad" one by drawing the family's attention to the contribution that older children make to younger ones by testing the limits and the rules in the family. This emphasized the similarities between the children rather than their differences.

Modeling

Feminists recognize that one of the important aspects of consciousness-raising groups is the opportunity for women to model for each other. There are a variety of successful male models available in public life, business, the professions, and the media, but women have lacked female models because of the relatively few women in positions of prominence. Women have also been isolated from others in their daily lives in their homes. The female therapist can model a successful woman for clients. I have found that it is hard for even the most liberal male to acknowledge that a female therapist could provide something that he could not. Some male therapists claim that they are better therapists for female clients because they can provide a different kind of male model than the client is accustomed to.[26] What goes unrecognized is that the male therapist, in providing a different male model, is reinforcing traditional stereotypes by assuming that the female client needs a special male who will treat her differently than other males have done. What a woman needs to learn is not that some men are different but how she can become a different woman.

By modeling different behaviors, the female therapist can help women free themselves from minority group traits that they have developed because of lack of power and secondary status, traits such as dislike of one's own sex, a negative self-image, "shuffling," insecurity, low aspirations, and appeasing behaviors.[23] Another quality that female therapists can model for all the family is competency in a woman. However, in family therapy, the therapist needs to be careful not to render family members incompetent by being a better parent, a better mother, or a better partner—more wise, just, and all-seeing. Traditional therapy has too often fostered the woman's view of herself as incompetent. The therapist who can acknowledge a lack of knowledge in some areas is a better model for parents and family members than one who is either a superwoman or a superman.

Ownership and Privacy

Just as Gestalt therapists have sought to develop ownership of an individual's feelings and attitudes by "I" statements, so family therapists can encourage ownership. Women typically have not been sure of their share in family resources that relate to the money world. Therapists may need to help women negotiate with other family members to gain ownership of many aspects of their lives. Women often lack ownership of the means of privacy, such as personal space, their space being that associated with their household job, like kitchen or sewing room.[28] They also do not own personal time without feelings of guilt or the use of money without accountability. A sensitive therapist can also encourage a woman to own and develop her talents and hobbies, as well as her thoughts and feelings. By encouraging ownership in other areas, the therapist may be able to help women assert ownership of their own bodies. Experiences like menstruation, menopause, hot flashes, tension around menstrual periods, impregnation, lactation, and childbirth can be crisis situations that women never discuss with male therapists.

Is family solidarity incompatible with individual ownership in the family? The therapist needs to point out that personhood for the mother as well as other family members is important, that the family need not be either a fortress or a prison. Since women have been raised to believe that their self-worth and identity is inextricably bound to finding the right husband and caring for a family, they may use therapy to talk about relationships with men rather than about their own identity.[3] The family therapist de-emphasizes "talking about" in the favor of interaction and can be influential in reinforcing assertive steps toward a sense of self that does not result solely from identification with family goals, family service, and family responsibility.

Therapeutic Alliances

An issue raised in modeling and in the interventions and alliances of the family therapist is the therapist's own gender. Does the therapist interact differently with men and women? Can a male be a feminist therapist? Certainly a nonsexist male therapist is better than a sexist female one. The power differential between males and females is still an enormous obstacle. Furthermore, because the stereotyped male role requires men always to appear competent, it may be that men find it harder than women to recognize and acknowledge sex biases in themselves. These therapist blind spots lead to reinforcing traditional patterns, whether the male therapist is allying with a woman to "protect" her, which is really a competitive move against her husband, or allying in a male bond with the husband, against the wife.

An essential aspect of family therapy is that the therapist must be committed to each person in the family.[20] This means the therapist must frequently shift alliances congruent with therapeutic goals. An alliance does not necessarily mean an "agreement" with. The experienced family therapist can ally with one family member in terms of feelings, attention, or emphasis on syntonic aspects of therapist and client personalities, while supporting the views and attitudes of another family member. For example, an initial alliance of one kind may need to be made with the typically reluctant father in order to assure his attendance and participation in the beginning stages of therapy.

The female therapist will frequently be viewed as allied with the mother because of their common gender just as the male therapist will be perceived as allied with the male when sometimes this is not the case. The husband and the therapist as the two reasonable (powerful) persons are often assumed to have a natural alliance. Rawlings and Carter[42] report a family therapy session with two therapists, a psychiatrist and a social worker, both males, where the mother felt like a rabbit being attacked by a wolf pack. Women may need the support of a female therapist to oppose traditional alliances and to be able to release pent-up rage, helplessness, and envy of men.[25]

Many married couples who do cotherapy assume that they provide a model of a normal or a liberated couple, as the case may be. I would agree with Sager[46] that "the therapy couple's use of themselves as role models is a dubious procedure based on the treating couple's idealization of their own self-image" (p. 188). Marriage per se of a cotherapy team is no guarantee of therapeutic effectiveness.[27] If there are differences in experience, training, and status of the cotherapy pair, there is a basis for inequality that is not lost on family members, no matter what roles the cotherapists imagine they are playing in the therapy sessions. Male-female cotherapy teams have been found to reinforce patterns of behavior that are oppressive to women.[2] The cotherapy team in which the female rather than the male therapist is the senior member is virtually unheard of. Some therapists prefer a cotherapist because they recognize that family therapy can take on aspects of an adversary proceeding in which each spouse is seeking an ally for a scolding match.[42]

The family therapist needs to be aware of the alliance-seeking behaviors of some family members who draw the therapist into a triangle at the expense of other family members. Therapists who expect and assume that female behaviors toward males are basically envious or seductive are themselves locked into stereotyped thinking that will interfere with their capacity to be helpful. Nor can one disregard the enormous emotional significance of men qua men in our society. Orlinsky and Howard[39] have pointed out that the client's emotional reactivity solely to the sex of the therapist may override the experience, talent, and warmth that the therapist brings to bear. A problem for the male therapist may be to deal with the woman's anger as she recognizes the irrelevance and goallessness of the activities that are her daily lot. A problem for the female therapist is the lack of respect and questions of therapeutic competence that are leveled at the female professional. As the husband and children learn to deal with the competent female therapist, they will learn to deal with the wife and mother in the family in a new way.

CONCLUSION

Family therapy provides opportunities for social change unavailable in other therapeutic approaches. The therapist is addressing problems in the family that reflect the traditional norms and expectations the parents bring from their own families of origin and attempt to maintain in their current family. The systems approach to family therapy is congruent with feminist therapy in examining behavior in terms of its economic and social determinants rather than using an individual-centered approach. A feminist-oriented family therapist can intervene in many ways to change the oppressive consequences of stereotyped roles and expectations in the family. As consciousness-raising takes place in families, family members come to recognize the sociocultural pressures that perpetuate traditional sex roles and seek ways to free themselves from these pressures. A review of family techniques from a feminist perspective indicates that family therapy is indeed possible without encouraging stereotyped sex roles.

REFERENCES

1. Adams, S. and Orgel, M., *Through the Mental Health Maze*, Washington, Public Citizen's Health Research Group, 1975.
2. American Psychological Association, *Report of the Task Force on Sex Bias and Sex Role Stereotyping in Therapeutic Practice*, Washington, Author, 1975.
3. Barrett, C. J.; Berg, P. I.; Eaton, E. M.; and Pomeroy, E. L., "Implications of Women's Liberation and the Future of Psychotherapy," *Psychother.: Theo. Res. Pract.* 11:11–15, 1974.
4. Beauvoir, S. de, *The Second Sex*, New York, Bantum Books, 1970.
5. Bem, S. L. and Bem, D. J., "We're All Nonconscious Sexists," *Psychol. Today*, November 1970, p. 22.
6. Bernard, J., *The Future of Motherhood*, New York, Dial Press, 1974.
7. Boszormenyi-Nagy, I. and Spark, G. M., *Invisible Loyalties: Reciprocity in Intergenerational Family Therapy*, New York, Harper & Row, 1973.
8. Bowen, M., "The Use of Family Theory in Clinical Practice," *Compr. Psychiat.* 7:345–374, 1966.
9. Broverman, I. K.; Broverman, D. M.; Clarkson, F. E.; Rosenkrantz, P. S.; and Vogel, S. R., "Sex Role Stereotypes and Clinical Judgments of Mental Health," *J. Consult. Clin. Psychol*, 34:1–7, 1970.
10. Chase, K., "Seeing Sexism: A Look at Feminist Therapy," *State and Mind*, March–April 1977, pp. 19–22.
11. Dohrenwend, B. S., "Social Status and Stressful Life Events," *J. Pers. Soc. Psychol.* 28:225–235, 1973.
12. Forrest, T., "Treatment of the Father in Family Therapy," *Fam. Proc.* 8:106–117, 1969.
13. Frank, J. D., *Persuasion and Healing*, Baltimore, Johns Hopkins University Press, 1973.
14. Gingras-Baker, S., "Sex Role Stereotyping and Marriage Counseling," *J. Marr. Fam. Couns.*, 2:355–366, 1976.
15. Gove, W. R., "The Relationship between Sex Roles, Marital Status, and Mental Illness," In A. G. Kaplan and J. P. Bean (Eds), *Beyond Sex-Role Stereotypes: Reading toward a Psychology of Androgyny*, Boston, Little, Brown, 1976.
16. Haley, J. (Ed.), *Changing Families*, New York, Grune & Stratton, 1971.
17. Halleck, S. L., *Politics of Therapy*, New York, Science House, 1971.
18. Hare-Mustin, R. T.; Marecek, J.; Kaplan, A.; and Liss-Levinson, N., "Rights of Clients, Responsibilities of Therapists," *Am. Psychol.* 34: 3–16, 1979.
19. Hill, R. and Rodgers, R. H., "The Developmental Approach," in H. T. Christensen (Ed.), *Handbook of Marriage and the Family*, Chicago, Rand McNally, 1964.
20. Hines, P. and Hare-Mustin, R. T., "Ethical Concerns in Family Therapy," *Profess. Psychol.*, 1978, 9:165–171, 1978.
21. Kaplan, A. G., "Clarifying the Concept of Androgyny: Implications for Therapy," Paper presented in Symposium on Applications of Androgyny to the Theory and Practice of Psychotherapy at the meeting of the American Psychological Association, Washington, September 1976.
22. Keller, S., "The Female Role: Constants and Change," in V. Franks and V. Burtle (Eds.), *Women in Therapy*, New York, Brunner/ Mazel, 1974.
23. Kirsh, B., "Consciousness-Raising Groups as Therapy for Women," in V. Franks and V. Burtle (Eds.), *Women in Therapy*, New York, Brunner/Mazel, 1974.

24. Klapper, L. and Kaplan, A. G., "The Emerging Consciousness of Sex-role Stereotyping in the Family Literature," Unpublished manuscript, 1977.

25. Kronsky, B. J., "Feminism and Psychotherapy," *J. Contemp. Psychother.* 3:89–98, 1971.

26. Lazarus, A. A., "Women in Behavior Therapy," in V. Franks and V. Burtle (Eds.), *Women in Therapy*, New York, Brunner/Mazel, 1974.

27. Lazarus, L. W., "Family Therapy by a Husband–Wife Team," *J. Marr. Fam. Couns.*, 2:225–235, 1976.

28. Lennard, S. H. C., and Lennard, H. L., "Architecture: Effect of Territory, Boundary, and Orientation on Family Functioning," *Fam. Proc.*, 16:49–66, 1977.

29. Lerman, H., "What Happens in Feminist Therapy," Paper presented in Symposium on Feminist Therapy in Search of a Theory at the meeting of the American Psychological Association, New Orleans, 1974.

30. Marecek, J., "Dimensions of Feminist Therapy," Paper presented in Symposium on Liberating Psychotherapy: Changing Perspectives and Roles among Women, at the meeting of the American Psychological Association, Montreal, September 1973.

31. Marecek, J., "Powerlessness and Women's Psychological Disorders," *Voices: J. Am. Acad. Psychotherapists* 12:50–54, 1976.

32. McAllister, A. and Fernhoff, D., "Test on the Bias: An Experiential Assessment of Sex Bias in the Psychological Battery," *Division 35 Newsletter*, American Psychological Association, 3(4):10–12, 1976.

33. Mehrabian, A., *Nonverbal Communication*, Chicago, Aldine-Atherton, 1972.

34. Miller, J. B. and Mothner, I., "Psychological Consequences of Sexual Inequality," *Am. J. Orthopsychiat.*, 41: 767–775, 1971.

35. Millman, M., "Observations on Sex Role Research," *J. Marr. Fam.*, 33: 772–775, 1971.

36. Minturn, L. and Lambert, W. W., *Mothers of Six Cultures, Antecedents of Child Rearing*, New York, Wiley, 1964.

37. Minuchin, S., *Families and Family Therapy*, Cambridge, Mass., Harvard University Press, 1974.

38. Nadelson, C. M., "Adjustment: New Approaches to Women's Mental Health," in M. L. McBee and K. A. Blake (Eds.), *The American Woman: Who Will She Be?*, Beverly Hills, Glencoe Press, 1974.

39. Orlinsky, D. E. and Howard, K. I., "The Effects of Sex of Therapist on the Therapeutic Experiences of Women," *Psychother.: Theo Res. Pract.* 13: 82–88, 1976.

40. Parsons, T. and Bales, R. F., *Family, Socialization, and Interaction Process*, Glencoe, Ill., Free Press, 1955.

41. Peal, E., "'Normal' Sex Roles: An Historical Analysis," *Fam. Proc.*, 14:389–409, 1975.

42. Rawlings, E. I. and Carter, D. K., *Psychotherapy for Women*, Springfield, Ill., Thomas, 1977.

43. Rice, D. G. and Rice, J. K., "Non-Sexist 'Marital' Therapy," *J. Marr. Fam. Couns.*, 3: 3–10, 1977.

44. Rosenthal, E. R., *Structural Patterns of Women's Occupational Choice*, Ph.D. dissertation, Cornell University, 1974.

45. Sachnoff, E., "Toward a Definition of Feminist Therapy," *AWP Newsletter*, Fall 1975, pp. 4–5.

46. Sager, C. J., *Marriage Contracts and Couple Therapy*, New York, Brunner/Mazel, 1976.

47. Smith, J. A., "For God's Sake, What Do Those Women Want?" *Personnel and Guidance J.*, 51:133–136, 1972.

48. Watzlawick, P.; Weakland, J. H.; and Fisch, R., *Change*, New York, Norton, 1974.

49. Zuk, G. R., "Family Therapy: Clinical Hodgepodge or Clinical Science?" *J. Marr. Fam. Couns.*, 2:229–304, 1972.

Men's New Family Roles

21

Some Implications for Therapists

MICHAEL BERGER

> By the waters of Babylon, we sat down, yea, we wept when we remembered Zion.
> We hanged our harps upon the willows in the midst thereof.
> For they that carried us away captive required of us a song; and they that wasted
> us required of us mirth, saying, Sing us one of the songs of Zion.
> How shall we sing the Lord's song in a new land?
>
> PSALMS 137, VERSES 1–4

The lament of the Psalmist was caused by the consequences of the Baby-
lonian Captivity—the removal of the Jews from the land (and perhaps

Reprinted from *The Family Coordinator* 28(4):638–646, 1979. Copyright © 1979 by the
National Council on Family Relations, 1219 University Avenue, SE, Minneapolis, Minnesota 55414. Reprinted by permission.

Two points need to be made with regard to the title and subject matter of this paper.
First, by "new family roles," I refer primarily to men assuming responsibility for child
care and household tasks, though I also include men taking on more nurturant or expressive functions in their family generally, e.g., counseling a parent who is divorcing or
comforting a sibling who has lost a spouse or a job. Secondly, in order to keep this paper
within manageable limits, I have limited it to a discussion of issues facing men who wish,
of their own free choice, to take on new family roles. I am aware (e.g., Berger and Wright,
1978) that such men are *not* in the majority, and I think they will not be in the majority
for a long time. I am aware that many men see no need to take on roles thought of as
traditionally feminine, or are extremely ambivalent about the price of assuming these
new roles, or feel pressured to act as if they wish to assume these roles in order to pacify
their wives (see the interviews in Rubin, 1976). Therapists working with such men will
face different issues and will, undoubtedly, need to use different strategies than therapists
seeking to be helpful to men who choose to take on new family roles.

I am most grateful to friends and colleagues for their help. Martha Foster, Luciano
L'Abate, Maggie Turkheimer, Larry Wright, Jeannette Sarbo, Lyn Sommer, Greg Jurkovic,
Ingrid Kraus, Debbie Dingman, and Michael O'Shea commented on earlier drafts of the
paper. Discussions with them and with Stephen Berger and Margaret Napier have helped
clarify my thinking. Reviewers' comments on an earlier draft alerted me to some of its
weaknesses, though I am, of course, responsible for weaknesses which remain. Vicki Lan-
ier, Jann Manderson, and Robin Young both typed drafts of this paper and put up with
me while I was writing it, as did my wife. Lastly, the support of Joseph Pleck for my work
has been important to me.

319

the heart) of their Lord. The task posed for the Jews by their captivity was how to create anew a state of grace between themselves and their Lord, a state in which the Lord's song could again be properly sung.

So it is with men now. For the pattern of institutional behavior and sex-role socialization which maintained a situation in which most men and women believed that men were, by nature, dominant and women subordinate, which held that it was natural for men to invest in work and to define themselves through achievement in the public world while women defined and created themselves through supporting the wishes and activities of others (Berger and Wright, 1978; Miller, 1976; Young and Willmott, 1973), which taught us that while women felt, men thought and acted—that world is dying. Men have been thrust out of this world (in large measure because of the actions of women who refuse to tolerate the assumptions and inequities of the old dispensation) and must struggle to help create a new one.* This paper examines some of the therapeutic implications of one major aspect of this struggle—men's new family roles. Since, in our view, individuals in transition experience both institutional constraints on their ability to change, and internal doubts as to the "rightness" of their changing, delineating the therapeutic implications of these new roles necessitates an examination of institutional arrangements affecting men's family roles and of likely interpersonal and intrapsychic consequences of these new roles.

INSTITUTIONAL LINKAGES

Work and family are the central spheres of life for most adults in this society. They are the arenas in which adults act and create themselves, the spheres through which they are defined (Berger and Wright, 1978; Pleck, 1977; Rapoport and Rapoport, 1965, 1971, 1976, 1978). A number of recent writers have examined the nature of the connections between work and family and their effect on the lives of men and women (Bailyn, 1978; Berger, Foster, and Wallston, 1978; Coser and Rokoff, 1971; Pleck, 1977, Note 1; Pleck and Lang, Note 2; Rapoport and Rapoport, 1971; Young and Willmott, 1973). As Pleck (1977) has stressed, the character of these linkages has been different for men and women. For women, family involvements have been seen as primary; family con-

---

*We will not finish this struggle in our lifetime. Probably our thinking will change first; our feelings and the institutional arrangements of the culture will only change much later. One hopes our children will have it better.

cerns have had the right to spill over into the other settings in which women were involved. Hence, women's work involvements should not jeopardize their family ties: women may work so long as nothing or no one in the family suffers. For men, the relationship is reversed: work investments are primary and are expected to spill over into the family world, while family investments should not intrude upon the work space.

The asymmetrical nature of these connections means that as men and women work to invest more of themselves in the sphere that has hitherto been less central for them, they will experience increasing tension as the demands of the new role are added to or conflict with those of the old one. Many women, for example, have felt it necessary to become "superwomen," women who successfully meet the "greedy" demands of work and family domains as the price of remaining in the work setting (Coser and Coser, 1974; Miller, 1976; Rapoport and Rapoport, 1976). Men who invest more in their families, who create new family roles, will increasingly find themselves meeting resistance or opposition from their colleagues and from institutional procedures at work. Several recent studies (Rosen, Jerdee, and Prestwich, 1975; Wright and Berger, Note 3) have demonstrated employer resistance to promoting males who are seen as unduly (i.e., heavily) invested in their families; other recent work (Bear, Berger, and Wright, 1979; Berger and Wright, 1978; Pleck, 1977) has noted the hostility displayed by colleagues to men who are seen as subordinating work demands to family responsibilities.

The particular price that many men and women are paying and will pay for caring both about their work and their families is not inherent in the nature of the world, but is caused by the way in which this society has structured the relationship between work and family concerns.* This societal arrangement, this pattern of payoffs and punishments, can be altered. Miller has put it beautifully:

> It is easy to devise work schedules and arrangements that will allow both men and women to share in child-rearing and fully participate in the life of our time, if both desire to do so. But to bring these changes about for any large numbers of people will require more changes in social and economic arrangements than other oppressed groups have had to accomplish. It requires us to ask, not how can women fit into, and advance in, the institutions as organized for men, but how should these institutions be reorganized

---

*As one reviewer of an earlier draft of this paper correctly noted, any societal arrangement, even the one dreamt of in this paper, will be punishing to some members of the society. I am grateful to the reviewer for that comment.

so as to include women. For example, the question is still asked of women: "How do you propose to answer the need for child care?" That is an obvious attempt to structure the question in the old terms. The questions are rather: "If we as a *human community want* children, how does the total society propose to provide for them? How can it provide for them in such a way that women do not have to suffer or forfeit other forms of participation and power, and opportunities for genuine leadership? How does society propose to organize so that men can benefit from equal participation in child care?" (1976, pp. 127–128)

INTERPERSONAL CONSEQUENCES

Nuclear Family

The effects of men's new family roles on their immediate families can best be understood by looking first at the traditional definition of family roles. One major aspect of this definition has been noted above: men have been expected to be primarily involved in work while women were supposed to be primarily involved with the family. Within the boundaries of the family itself, a similar segregation of primary roles has been demanded: men are responsible for linking the family into the world outside the family (instrumental functions) while women are primarily responsible for understanding and administering to the emotional needs of family members (expressive functions).* An analogous segregation extends to the domain of intimate experience itself. As Miller (1976) notes, emotionality in general, and the most problematic emotions (vulnerability, weakness, helplessness, the need for affiliation) in particular, have been assigned as the province of women alone. Men, therefore, have not had to deal with major portions of themselves. They lack skill in doing so, and have been socialized to believe that doing so will make them unmanly, will make them like women, the subordinate and inferior sex (L'Abate, 1977).

It should not be suprising, therefore, that changes in men's family roles are likely to create difficulties. As men seek to become more nurturant with their wives, their children, and themselves, as they take on more responsibility for the day-to-day work of running a household and providing the organizational and emotional resources which support the growth and activities of household members, they face dangerous con-

---

*The language used here is that of the sociologist, Talcott Parsons, with whom the above description of family roles is most closely associated.

sequences if they fail and also if they succeed. For men have been trained not to fail, not to admit to vulnerability or weakness in themselves (L'Abate, 1975). A failure in a new family role, therefore, is likely to be seen as revealing one's lack of manliness. So, paradoxically, failure to succeed at family tasks "traditionally" associated with women will likely result in men feeling less manly. As one colleague, describing his discomfort with his (self-perceived) lack of rapport with his young child put it: "I know men haven't been trained to play and be expressive with their kids, but, damn it, *I* should be able to do it." Success in this area is not an unmixed blessing, either, for given traditional gender socialization, success in family roles which require access to and expression of emotionality is likely to make men feel that they have become more like women, and thus, because the society has defined the natures of men and women as mutually exclusive, less manly.

Sex, at times, will be a problematic area since it is the domain, we have learned, in which intimacy is most likely to occur. But, for individuals in our culture, intimacy is linked to the terrifying possibility of engulfment or fusion (Bowen, 1976; Napier, 1978), of becoming so close to another person that one loses one's unique self. As men take on new family roles and engage in behavior previously considered as feminine, they will seem to become more like women and the possibility of fusion will become more likely, and because fusion seems more likely, fear of fusion will become more intense. Further, since most individuals have been socialized to associate appropriate sexual feelings and behavior with only some of the feelings and behavior of which they are capable (e.g., it's okay for men to be assertive and women dependent in bed), feeling and acting like the opposite sex will be frightening to them. Such behavior may be frightening to their partners as well. For example, a number of men have found, as they struggle to be vulnerable with women, that their vulnerability is hard for the woman to respond to.

Changing men's roles will affect women in other ways as well. Wives who have wanted their husbands to share in family tasks to a greater extent may yet criticize husbands, when they begin to do so, for not immediately assuming the new roles with grace and excellence. Out of legitimate anger at past inequities, out of anger at oneself for having tolerated these inequities, and out of a fear that clumsiness in the new roles is a sign that men "really" do not want to take on the new roles, wives may punish their husbands for these failures. In addition, as some recent observers (e.g., Rapoport and Rapoport, 1978) have noted, wives may react with mixed feelings to the success of husbands in some new family roles, particularly success in childrearing.* For women have been so strongly socialized to believe that childrearing is both their responsibility and their unique way of demonstrating worth that their husbands' ability in this role may be threatening to them, taking away the conventional means of demonstrating their worth and competence at a time when alternate means are not yet fully available.

These particular marital difficulties are vicious but predictable consequences of the traditional organization of sex-role relationships. For the changes required by men's new family roles or by other efforts to create more symmetrical family roles necessitate couples' becoming more interdependent, and interdependence requires that both men and women become more able to use previously forbidden aspects of themselves. Weingarten (1978) has noted that interdependence includes not only mutual dependence but also the capacity to be independent in the context of an intimate relationship. Interdependence, she argues, is the capacity to tolerate all of the following relationship patterns: (a) both husband and wife dependent; (b) both husband and wife independent; (c) husband dependent, wife independent; and (d) husband independent, wife dependent. Each of these patterns will be hard for some men. Mutual independence may require long separations so that each spouse may pursue his/her separate interests, may require that men act independently in areas thought to be feminine such as child care or housework, and may place men in situations where their behavior will be negatively evaluated by other men (Bear, Berger, and Wright, 1979; Weingarten, 1978). Any pattern in which men are dependent is likely to be problematic since men are not supposed to acknowledge that they need others or that they can be weak or vulnerable. Many men thus fight any sign of dependence in themselves and permit their wives to care for them only for short periods of time or under special circumstances, such as after an operation (Weingarten, 1978).

Lastly, child care will be an area of difficulty for some families. In the first place, men who invest in children as well as their work will find what women have found—they have only a finite amount of energy available and energy that goes into child care is diverted from work, or oneself, or one's marriage (Bailyn, 1978; Levine, 1976; Rapoport and Rapoport, 1976, 1978). Moreover, child care is an easy place for spouses to fight out the aspects of difference between them which are problematic, the differences which make one think that "something is wrong with him/her" rather than "(s)he is different than me on this dimension." This will be especially likely since couples in which men are heav-

---

*Some men wishing to espouse new family roles will be involved with women who prefer traditional roles. I suspect this is an uncommon situation, but it will be problematic when it occurs.

ily involved in child care are probably couples who do not wish their children to learn the conventional ideas about appropriate gender behavior. But a clearly established new set of ideas does not exist yet, so such couples will have to be inventive and there will be many muddy areas about which they can argue. Since parents often play out their own concerns and confusions through their children, arguments about childrearing may be especially intense since not only the correctness of one's own views but the part of oneself projected onto the child is at stake.

My emphasis on problematic consequences for marriage of men's new family roles does not mean that I believe men should not espouse these new roles. Men and women striving for new roles are uprooted now, cast adrift from the old dispensation but not yet within an established world of new values, supports, and institutions. Because of this, they are often ambivalent. Expressions of this ambivalence can include a longing for past securities or an overemphasis on the difficulties which arise whenever values and roles change. Even when men and women attempting to live out new roles are not ambivalent, they may lack the skills to live out the new roles perfectly. Further, the content of the new roles is unclear and the resources necessary to anchor new roles in a supportive context are lacking. What Miller (1976) has said with regard to women is true for any person espousing a new role: "Many women have now moved on to determine the nature of their affiliations, and to decide for themselves with whom they will affiliate. As soon as they attempt this step, they find the societal forms standing in opposition. In fact, they are already outside the old social forms looking for new ones. . . . No one can take this formidable task alone. [Therapy, even if we knew how to do it in some near perfect way—which we do not—is not enough]" (p. 95).

So it is predictable that men espousing new family roles will often encounter problems in their family life. There will also be satisfactions which arise from these new roles, satisfactions for both men and women. Men will have a greater chance of learning that they can feel, that their feelings are not overwhelming, that they can care, that caring will not unman them, that they can think *and* act *and* feel without coming apart. And this learning will be supportive to women who are already working to cease to play stupid, to cease to define themselves through their men, to become more comfortable learning what *they* want and seeking out ways to fulfill these wants. And it is even possible, as Miller (1976) suggests, that men and women who can support one another in stepping outside the boundaries of the world defined by the men-dominant and women-subordinate roles, can create a world in which it is more likely that people can affiliate with one another and still act powerfully, can use the feelings of vulnerability which accompany change and yet not be paralyzed with fear of change, can finally learn, in Blake's marvelous words, that "We are put on earth a little space/That we may learn to bear the beams of love" (1946, p. 86).[5]*

Family of Origin

Men espousing new family roles, like all human beings standing outside the old social forms and striving to create new ones, need support. We have already considered some difficulties that prevent their unequivocally supporting themselves or receiving unequivocal support from their wives. There are two other likely sources of support—one's family of origin and one's friends.

The importance of connection with one's family of origin has been stressed in recent years by a number of prominent family therapists (e.g., Bowen, 1978; Fogarty, 1976; Napier and Whitaker, 1978). Two assumptions, I think, underlie this focus: (a) a belief that many of the qualities sought for and many of the issues played out with one's spouse derive their intensity from unfinished business with one's family of origin. It is assumed that individuals strive to complete these matters with their spouse but cannot do so; rather only by striving for and achieving new kinds of contact with their families of origin can these issues be resolved; (b) a belief that human beings need close affiliations and that one's family of origin is the most likely place to get such affiliation (Bowen, 1976), or that few people have long-lasting intense friendships which means, consequently, that one's family of origin is one of the few places where one *could* have an intense relationship.

The validity of these assumptions is supported by recurring accounts from friends and clients of deceptions they have employed in order to conceal untraditional sex-role behavior from their or their spouse's family of origin. For example, one man who had given up an excellent job to follow his wife and was home writing a novel routinely took both sets of visiting parents to her office, simulating it as his. I am impressed also by the frequency with which friends and clients tell me that their parents do not understand (and, one gathers, do not support) their untraditional gender behavior. Few men I know receive validation from their parents for the excellence of their cooking or their child care. Instead, these efforts are ignored or disparaged.

The difficulties experienced by men in receiving support for new roles from their parents are not surprising. Conventional gender behavior is a core aspect of traditionally appropriate adult behavior (Miller, 1976). The parents of most men want them to do well, and doing well means acting in an appropriate manly fashion. Thus, new family roles or other untraditional sex-role behavior on the part of the man is likely to

*But see the point made in the footnote on p. 324.

be interpreted by their family of origin as an indication that they are not sufficiently manly. Moreover, the adoption of new family roles by men is likely to threaten their parents, to call into question the parents' own marriages, and the parents' sense of appropriate gender and family roles. When first threatened, people don't usually behave in a kindly manner.

However understandable the causes of these difficulties, they increase the price men pay for assuming new family roles. Support from one's own family of origin is crucial for men in helping them feel rooted and helping them feel all right about the changes they are endeavoring to make. It is hard to live outside the old social forms without support and not feel crazy. So deceiving one's family of origin about the way one is living will not work, for the lack of support undermines one's sense of rightness about the way one is trying to live.

Friends

The impact of lack of support from family of origin is intensified by the fact that few men espousing new family roles have contact with other men who will support them in their new roles and who will discuss with them the issues that arise as a consequence of these new roles. Both in my studies of men in dual-career couples (Berger, Foster, and Wallston, 1978; Berger, Foster, Wallston, and Wright, 1977) and in my own experience, I have been saddened by how seldom men seek or find opportunities to share experiences of trying on new roles with other men. There is a kind of support and comradeship that is available only from those who share one's own experience.

INTRAPSYCHIC CONSEQUENCES

Assuming new roles in the family will expose men to new parts of themselves and will alter men. Some of the changes will be painful, some frightening. There is also the prospect of glory.

Taking on new roles will be painful because, insofar as they step outside the old social forms, men will relinquish structures that, limited and costly as they are, provide sense and shape to their lives. It is no accident that in recent novels which have spoken to the changes in gender roles such as *The Golden Notebook* (Lessing, 1962), *Small Changes* (Piercy, 1972), and *The Women's Room* (French, 1977), only female characters go mad. The men in these novels are far from admirable, are often despicable and shallow, but because they continue to adhere to the rules of the traditional sex-role game, they are not unmoored and are not crazy. Stepping outside the forms opens the door to growth and to something akin to madness. One of the charcters in *The Four-Gated City* (Lessing, 1969) puts it perfectly: "There is a point where you choose to know the things which you know and risk going mad or you give up on yourself and the truth." Taking on new roles will be particularly difficult and painful for men, for men have been trained to shun vulnerability and weakness, to deny the existence or even the possibility of these feelings within themselves. But these feelings, as Miller (1976) notes, are implacably linked to change: "The ability to grow psychologically... is necessarily an ongoing process, involving repeated feelings of vulnerability all through life.... It is necessary to 'learn' in an emotional sense that these feelings are not shameful or abhorrent but ones from which the individual can move on—if the feelings are experienced for what they are. Only then can a person hope to find appropriate paths to new strengths. Along with new strength will come new areas of vulnerability, for there is no absolute invulnerability" (p. 31).

Challenging the limits of conventional sex-role ideology will increase the chance that men and women can find out what they really are like, that people can learn what they truly love and can, however haltingly, embody in action. This is an opportunity which, like all opportunities, has its price. Throughout this paper we have talked of the likelihood that assuming new roles will result in men discovering within themselves feelings, commitments, and behavior that are unmanly in the conventional terms. This knowledge will often be terrifying. More subtly, but not less painfully, trying on new roles exposes one to the possibility of experiencing one's limits, the ways in which one cannot meet the demands of one's values and ideology. Just as people are more than they are defined to be by the conventional sex-role standards, each of us is different than we are defined as being by any set of general standards. For example, men espousing new roles may also be men who are quite traditionally masculine in some areas of their lives, men who are quite competitive about their work or who have (comparatively) great difficulty in voicing their feelings. Similarly, women who are very invested in their careers and in the women's movement may also be very invested in how their homes look. Our task is not to stamp out every vestige of conventional sex-role behavior but to create conditions which do not arbitrarily limit the development of individuals on the basis of presumed gender distinctions.

I do not know what people will be like under a more equitable dispensation, and I do not believe that such a dispensation would be the new Jerusalem. Other societal organizations will create other problems. Still, I would hope that we will become more clear that it is possible to be powerful without using that power to limit or hurt others, that it is possible to be separate and yet to affiliate, and that pursuing one's own dream is compatible with supporting the dreams of others (Miller, 1976).

Suggestions for Therapists*

How can therapists be helpful to men espousing new family roles? The first task for therapists is to become more clear about their own values and commitments. Therapists, like everyone else in this society, have been socialized into the conventional notions of sex-role behavior. While individual therapists may pride themselves on ways in which they have overcome the limits of conventional sex-role stereotypes (male therapists, for example, citing their own openness and sensitivity and female therapists noting their own assertiveness) it is still the case that most therapists are part of the culture, benefit from the current organization of the culture, and share the traditional values of the culture. Therapists, therefore, may find it difficult to support clients espousing untraditional gender aspirations, for the values of such clients may threaten the therapist's own life choices (Bear, Berger, and Wright, 1979; Berger and Wright, 1978). Therapists wishing to behave responsibly toward such men need to be clear concerning their own values so that they do not limit the choices open to clients, so that they can support behavior which is reasonable to the client although the therapist would not choose it for him/herself.†

Value clarity on the therapist's part is necessary for another reason as well. Men in transition (and those involved with such men) will experience a great deal of pain and confusion. The therapist's values will determine how (s)he responds to this pain and confusion, whether (s)he sees it as futile or misguided and thus interprets it as a cue that the client should alter his behavior, or whether (s)he sees it as an unfortunate but implacable consequence of role transition and thus works to help the client correctly label the sources of his difficulty and supports the client in working toward creating new situations and tolerating the turmoil and confusion of the transitional times (Rapoport and Rapoport, 1978).‡

Attention to the sources of difficulties confronting men espousing new roles will be a major task for therapists. In my experience, when men attempting new roles experience difficulty in meeting the demands of these new roles, their characteristic response is to blame themselves or those close to them (e.g., their wives). Rarely is the response to blame the set of institutional arrangements and socialization patterns which make it difficult for men and women espousing new roles both to achieve

---

*More detailed suggestions can be found in Bear, Berger, and Wright (1979).

†Therapists concerned with changing their own gender definitions should likewise act responsibly and not impose those values on their clients. I am indebted to Martha Foster for this point.

‡Therapists need to help clients assimilate the painful knowledge that the period of transition will likely last their lifetime.

their aims and to find support. For example, dual-career couples who fail to find two acceptable jobs in the same location often, instead of attributing their failure to a tight job market or to the discriminatory practices of specific employers, blame themselves for their failure to be so competent in their field that they can find acceptable jobs under all circumstances (Berger, Foster, Wallston, and Wright, 1977; Berger, Foster, and Wallston, 1978). Similar responses have been reported with regard to women working to change their situations at work or at home; when they meet resistance in these attempts to change, one of their initial responses is to doubt or blame themselves (Miller, 1976).

It should be clear by now that this self-doubting response is a predictable consequence of the conventional sex-role ideology. It should be clear also that this response is another and particularly vicious example of blaming the victim (Ryan, 1971) because it is a response through which the victim condemns himself and stops him/herself from changing.

Moreover, since men espousing new roles will not move directly from the old social forms into a new world which organizes around and supports these new roles but rather must live with the confusion and pain of trying to create a new world while still living with the old, they will need support from therapists in bearing with pain and confusion and in understanding it. So long as institutional behavior and the linkages between institutions constitute one of the major barriers to new gender behavior (Berger, Foster, and Wallston, 1978; Miller, 1976; Pleck, 1977; Rapoport and Rapoport, 1976, 1978), therapists who wish to provide this help must learn to focus on more than intrapsychic or interpersonal behavior. Therapists must learn that it is therapeutic both to help clients examine the connections between their individual worlds, their families, and the structures of work, and to support clients in efforts aimed at altering the character of these linkages. Changing institutions and linkages between institutions are not the only tasks facing men espousing new roles, but they are essential ones. Therapists can support men facing these tasks by considering them as one of the legitimate foci in therapy, for considering these issues in therapy validates them as areas in which change can be sought.

It will be difficult for therapists to do this. In general, therapists have not been trained to deal with issues arising in areas other than intrapsychic or interpersonal domains. In addition, men will need therapists who not only consider the above issues in therapy but will recognize the limitations of therapy in solving these issues. Therapists will be most helpful to men attempting new roles, I believe, if they recognize, for example, that finding and maintaining support groups of friends or organizing with others to change work structure may be more useful at times than anything which occurs during the treatment hour (Miller, 1976). I realize that I am recommending that therapists place very hard demands upon themselves. Still, I think that meeting these demands is the best way for therapists to help men who are seeking to change and grow. And in a sense it is appropriate that therapists will have to transform themselves, for that is the task which our clients face and it is fitting that we participate with them in their efforts.

REFERENCE NOTES

1. Pleck, J. *Men's new roles in the family: Housework and children.* Wellesley, Massachusetts: Wellesley College Center for Research on Women, 1976.
2. Pleck, J., and Lang, L. *Men's family role: Its nature and consequences.* Wellesley, Massachusetts: Wellesley College Center for Research on Women, 1978.
3. Wright, L., and Berger, M. *The effects of employer attitudes and behaviors on the employment of dual-career couples.* Unpublished manuscript, 1978. (Available from Department of Psychology, Georgia State University, Atlanta, Georgia 30303.)

REFERENCES

Bailyn, L. Accommodation of work to family. In R. Rapoport and R. Rapoport, (Eds.), *Working couples.* New York: Harper, 1978.

Bear, S., Berger, M., and Wright, L. Even cowboys sing the blues: Difficulties facing men espousing untraditional gender aspirations and what therapists can do about it. *Sex Roles: A Journal of Research,* 1979, **2,** 191–197.

Berger, M., Foster, M., and Wallston, B. Finding two jobs. In R. Rapoport and R. Rapoport (Eds.), *Working couples.* New York: Harper, 1978.

Berger, M., Foster, M., Wallston, B., and Wright, L. You and me against the world: Dual-career couples and joint job-seeking. *Journal of Research and Development in Education,* 1977, **10,** 30–37.

Berger, M., and Wright, L. Divided allegiance: Men, work, and family life. *The Counseling Psychologist,* 1978, **4** (2), 50–53.

Blake, W. The little black boy. In A. Kazin (Ed.), *The Viking portable William Blake.* New York: Viking, 1946.

Bowen, M. Theory in the practice of psychotherapy. In P. Guerin (Ed.), *Family therapy.* Long Island, New York: Gardner, 1976.

Bowen, M. *Family therapy in clinical practice.* New York: Aronson, 1978.

Coser, L., and Coser, R. The housewife and her "greedy" family. In L. Coser (Ed.), *Greedy institutions.* New York: Free Press, 1974.

Coser, R., and Rokoff, G. Women in the occupational world: Social disruption and conflict. *Social Problems,* 1971, **18,** 535–554.

Fogarty, T. Marital crisis. In P. Guerin (Ed.), *Family therapy.* Long Island, New York: Gardner, 1976.

French, M. *The women's room.* New York: Summit, 1977.

L'Abate, L. Pathogenic role rigidity in fathers: Some observations. *Journal of Marriage and Family Counseling,* 1975, **1,** 69–79.

L'Abate, L. Intimacy is sharing hurt feelings: A reply to David Mace. *Journal of Marriage and Family Counseling,* 1977, **3,** 13–16.

Lessing, D. *The golden notebook.* New York: Simon & Schuster, 1962.

Lessing, D. *The four-gated city.* New York: Knopf, 1969.

Levine, J. *Who will raise the children?* Philadelphia: Lippincott, 1976.

Miller, J. B. *Toward a new psychology of women.* Boston: Beacon, 1976.

Napier, A. The rejection-intrusion pattern: A central family dynamic. *Journal of Marriage and Family Counseling,* 1978, **4,** 5–12.

Napier, A., and Whitaker, C. *The family crucible.* New York: Harper, 1978.

Piercy, M. *Small changes.* New York: Doubleday, 1972.

Pleck, J. The work-family role system. *Social Problems,* 1977, **24,** 417–427.

Rapoport, R. and Rapoport, R. Work and family in contemporary society. *American Sociological Review,* 30, **3,** 1965.

Rapoport, R., and Rapoport, R. *Dual-career families.* Baltimore: Penguin, 1971.

Rapoport, R., and Rapoport, R. *Dual-career families reexamined.* New York: Harper, 1976.

Rapoport, R., and Rapoport, R. (Eds.). *Working couples.* New York: Harper, 1978.

Rosen, B., Jerdee, T., and Prestwich, T. Dual-career marital adjustment: Potential effects of discriminatory managerial attitudes. *Journal of Marriage and the Family,* 1975, **37,** 565–572.

Rubin, L. *Worlds of pain: Life in the working class community.* New York: Basic, 1976.

Ryan, W. *Blaming the victim.* New York: Random, 1971.

Weingarten, K. Interdependence. In R. Rapoport and R. Rapoport (Eds.), *Working couples.* New York: Harper, 1978.

Young, M., and Willmott, P. *The symmetrical family.* New York: Pantheon, 1973.

B. Gender and Psychiatric Education

In the chapters in this section, we consider selected aspects of psychiatric education that are necessary for the development of clinical competence. We are convinced that the training of mental health professionals must include methods through which trainees learn to clarify their own values in addition to acquiring new knowledge and skills. We also examine some of the ethical consequences for the mental health professions if value clarification does not become an integral part of clinical training.

In "Teaching Value Clarification: The Example of Gender and Psychotherapy," we present a unique model for teaching a course on gender and psychotherapy in which a central feature is team teaching by a psychiatrist and a sociologist. Clarification of values and attitudes about gender is a learning process that has intellectual, affective, and ethical components. We have conceptualized the cognitive–affective interplay that is so essential to learning as a series of stages or turning points in the process of value change and professional resocialization. Although the article adequately describes the course objectives and format, we want to emphasize the efficacy of limiting the course enrollment, having a balance of men and women, and maintaining confidentiality regarding all patient and personal material discussed in class.

We have found that traditional sex-role behaviors and conflicts are reenacted in class, in psychotherapy, and in supervision, much as they occur in the daily lives of the trainees and in the wider social context. Although it is not critical that such a gender course be taught exclusively by women, we found: "The powerful affective responses of both male and female residents to two women in positions of authority provided the experiential data through which each participant came to confront deeply embedded sex-role stereotypes and behavioral norms." The chapters by Mayes (7) and Lerner (8), presented earlier in this book, are particularly helpful in explaining the intensity and form of the confrontations that participants had with the self and with us.

As a psychiatrist/sociologist team, we were able to clarify the distinction between psychological and social explanations of behavior and to demonstrate the value of combining the two perspectives in clinical practice. One of the important course outcomes is that participants understand that there is a social context for viewing both patient experiences and the therapist–patient interaction. As we conclude in our article, "a requirement for effective therapeutic role performance is the ability to stand outside the self, to observe the cognitive–value interaction, and to question one's values and intellectual framework without paralyzing fear of personal or professional annihilation."

Although formal courses are one mode of teaching clinicians, psychotherapy supervision remains at the heart of professional training. We include Alexandra G. Kaplan's article, "Toward an Analysis of Sex-Role-Related Issues in the Therapeutic Relationship," as an example of the influence of gender on the dynamics of the therapeutic alliance. Supervisors will find Kaplan's sex-role analysis valuable in understanding transference and countertransference phenomena in the psychotherapy cases that trainees present. Further, her analysis can be used to illuminate certain gender aspects of supervisory relationships—for example, the expectation that good female supervisors must be not only competent but also nurturant.

Kaplan defines the therapist's role as having a structural (authority) dimension and a functional (empathic) dimension. Although effective clinicians need to employ both qualities in the performance of their roles, Kaplan shows how sex-role socialization, by reinforcing different characteristics in men and women, complicates the integration of empathy and authority in clinical work. Similarly, patients also bring expectations about appropriate sex-role behaviors to therapeutic encounters.

As one illustration of gender effects, patients may be reluctant to accept the authority of their female therapists but would be likely to expect and reinforce empathic qualities. These expectations of patients, in combination with women's inexperience and discomfort with exercising authority, may encourage female therapists to rely mainly on empathy as a therapeutic tool. Conversely, the cultural conditioning of males, which, as Kaplan says, discourages "the open expression of feelings, intimate sharing between peers, or a sensitivity to the emotional states of others" and defines such behaviors as unmanly, may inhibit the male therapist's capacity for empathy. These gender aspects of transference and countertransference demonstrate the futility of denying the existence of concealed values in psychotherapy and the importance, in supervision, of exploring these values.

The last two articles, Virginia Davidson's "Psychiatry's Problem with No Name: Therapist–Patient Sex" and Alan A. Stone's "Sexual Misconduct by Psychiatrists: The Ethical and Clinical Dilemma of Confidentiality," discuss the sexual abuse of patients by psychiatrists and the ramifications of this unethical behavior for the patient, the psychiatrist, and the profession. We believe that the social and psychological perspectives presented in this book provide a context for analyzing sexual misconduct and, we hope, preventing it in the future.

Davidson sees the sexual exploitation of female patients by male therapists as a direct outcome of structures of inequality. She maintains that even when the existence of therapist–patient sex was documented in case histories, the issue was perceived only as a treatment complication and not as an ethical dilemma for the profession. Although Stone argues that "psychiatrists have an ethical obligation to expose colleagues who sexually abuse their patients," he rightly points out that this is complicated by the psychiatrist's obligation to protect the patient's confidentiality. To avoid the "moral inertia" that comes from the dilemma of conflicting ethical responsibilities, Stone proposes a method by which the psychiatrist who hears of the abuse and the abused patient can review the clinical, ethical, and legal remedies that are available.

Both authors agree that therapist–patient sex, regardless of how it is labeled, is an abuse of power and authority and a profound betrayal of trust, not unlike incest. To prevent such destructive practices, trainees must be taught to differentiate erotic and other countertransference feelings from sexual practices. One appropriate place for such clarification is within the supervisory relationship. In our experience, however, countertransference is seldom emphasized in supervision, and the sexual feelings of the therapist are often considered a taboo topic. While not a replacement for discussions in supervision, gender courses can reinforce the necessity and value of having these discussions. In our teaching about gender values, for example, we have found it useful to focus discussion on the question of how enduring are psychotherapists' ethical and moral obligations to their patients after termination. Through course work and a more open supervisory dialogue, clinicians learn to identify and cope with the wide range of affects and impulses that are an inevitable part of therapists' experiences. At the same time, they can begin the necessary process of establishing an ethical code of professional behaviors.

Teaching Value Clarification   22

The Example of Gender and Psychotherapy

Patricia Perri Rieker
and Elaine (Hilberman) Carmen

Teaching residents in psychiatry to be aware of sexist attitudes in psychiatric theory, training, and practice is difficult for both the instructors and the trainees. When residents are confronted with the extent to which sex-role socialization has shaped not only their own values but also the values and behaviors of their mentors, patients, and intimates, they respond with intense anxiety. The instructors, as the messengers who bring the "bad" news, become the objects of their hostility and frustration. Thus, an important aspect of the instructor role is the ability to remain empathic (and nonviolent) when confronted with the most creative forms of resistance to learning. Until recently, there has been little reinforcement for residents to explore gender attitudes and few rewards for instructors' efforts to teach in this affect-laden and value-conflicted area.[1] In this paper we describe an effective model for teaching and evaluating a one-semester course on gender and psychotherapy, in which a central feature is team teaching by a psychiatrist and a sociologist.

The most prevalent teaching formats in psychiatric education are seminars, case conferences, and individual psychotherapy supervision. Seminars generally focus on knowledge or skill development, and case conferences emphasize identification of intrapsychic processes. Although individual supervision explores transference phenomena, countertransferences that might illuminate the basic attitudes and intellectual orientation of the therapist are usually not explored, especially when the resident and supervisor share similar values and explanatory frameworks. Thus, the usual teaching formats have been limited in their ability to develop residents' awareness of the ways in which clinicians'

Reprinted from *American Journal of Psychiatry* 140(4):410–415, 1983. Copyright © 1983 by the American Psychiatric Association. Reprinted by permission. This is a revised version of a paper presented at the 25th annual meeting of the American Academy of Psychoanalysis, Houston, May 7–10, 1981. The authors thank the course participants, whose experiences and insights furthered the authors' understanding of the process of value change, and Drs. Teresa Bernardez and Elissa Benedek for their critical review.

attitudes and values, embedded as they are in explanatory frameworks, can alter diagnostic and treatment processes.

As a result, conventional psychiatric training programs seldom include teaching formats that systematically examine how social, political, and economic conditions, or the very structure of society, shape the life and the intrapsychic experiences of the patient.[2] Perhaps most important, residents are not taught that there are alternative models for explaining the same behaviors or that all conceptual models contain implicit value assumptions, both epistemological and political, which affect the entire therapeutic process (references 3 and 4 and "Sociological Imagination in Psychiatric Training" by P. P. Rieker, presented at the 132nd annual meeting of the American Psychiatric Association, Chicago, May 12–18, 1979).

GENDER COURSE OBJECTIVES AND FORMAT

The gender course focuses on the identification of residents' underlying conceptual models and the way in which they influence thinking and practice. In any teaching in which clarification of values is central, as in teaching about gender, the course design must facilitate an awareness of both personal attitudes and intellectual values in addition to the presentation of new knowledge. In our course, cognitive and affective learning objectives were made explicit: (1) to understand the psychological and behavioral consequences of sexual inequality; (2) to become aware of gender attitudes in psychiatric theory, training, and practice; (3) to introduce the new knowledge about the psychology of women, men, and sex roles; (4) to identify one's own attitudes/biases about women and men; and (5) to explore the impact of one's gender values on the treatment of patients.

The elective course was six months in duration and met every two weeks for three hours. Each seminar was structured around a series of specific content areas. These content areas included social science and values in psychiatry, the psychological consequences of gender inequality, psychology of men and women, sexuality, anger and aggression, victimization, family and professional roles, and implications for psychiatric practice. The wide spectrum of written materials consisted of books, research and journal articles, ideological statements, and fiction.

Participants took turns bringing refreshments during the last hour of each session. In contrast to the structure imposed by the readings in the first part of the class, the "social hour" was more informal and residents reflected on the learning process as they experienced it in and out of class. First-year residents were not eligible to elect the course because of the confusion associated with acquiring new professional identities and their inexperience as psychotherapists. Course enrollment was limited to 10. We attempted a balance of men and women, which we have learned over the five years of teaching this course is essential to effective teaching about gender.

In our roles as coinstructors, we shared personal and professional experiences to illustrate the readings and were active in the identification of underlying values, relevant attitudes, affects, and group processes. As a psychiatrist/sociologist team, we were able both to clarify the distinction between psychological and social explanations of behavior and to demonstrate the value of combining the two perspectives in clinical practice.[5] Instructors and participants maintained confidentiality concerning all patient and personal material discussed in the class. However, participants gave permission for us to use their written evaluation material for publication.

We accomplished the course evaluation using a variety of qualitative methods. A structured questionnaire, completed anonymously by all participants, invited comments about what new knowledge, attitudes/values, and skills were acquired; effects, if any, on personal and professional roles and relations; stresses and learning problems encountered; and an assessment of the coinstructors. Additional data were obtained from process summary notes maintained by the instructors and from summaries of participants' personal journals, which included their responses, over time, to the course content and process. The journal not only represented the natural history of individual experiences in the course but also facilitated personal learning and reflection.

Interestingly, it was not always possible to predict from behavior in class either the extent or nature of the learning; for example, some people who had been relatively quiet in class demonstrated considerable learning in their evaluations. Clearly, an inner dialogue both accompanies and takes the place of active class participation. As one male resident stated in his evaluation,

> Most significant was learning at an emotional level that the effects of sexual inequality are powerful, pervasive impediments to emotional closeness, creativity, personal power and independence and other essentials of good mental and physical health.

TEACHING AND LEARNING ABOUT VALUE CHANGE

Changing values and attitudes about gender and understanding the implications for clinical practice involve learning at both intellectual and emotional levels. The required readings imposed the intellectual framework for transmitting the new thinking and research about gender. It is in this context, however, that traditional sex-role behaviors and conflicts are enacted. The powerful affective responses of both male and female residents to two women in positions of authority[6] provided the experiential data through which each participant came to confront deeply embedded sex-role stereotypes and behavioral norms. This ongoing confrontation with the taken-for-granted self and the defensive anxiety and anger it generated together accounted for both the successful learning and, paradoxically, the difficulty in teaching the course.

Uniformly, the participants wished that the material would "go away," and this led to tension within the group and between participants and instructors. This tension took different forms for different people and also fluctuated with the topics for discussion. The forms of resistance included distancing, feelings of wanting to drop the course, anger at instructors, and questioning the accuracy of the content. As one resident wrote,

> It seemed that the acquisition of this new body of knowledge invariably set in motion an emotional shift in my perspective which led to discovery and clarification of my own personal biases. This emotional shift was initially experienced as a vacillation between believing the data, and trying to dismiss its validity and relevance.

The experience of teaching this course over time was both gratifying and frustrating. Inevitably, we would spend several hours alone after each class unwinding and venting our anger in response to the complex forms of resistance and to the unending challenges to our authority. Preparation for each subsequent class took into account the ongoing group dynamics, which were sometimes difficult to understand. This understanding was helpful in assessing when interpretations of the process could be used effectively to address conflict, reduce anxiety, and enhance learning. In this way, new topics could be introduced without increasing the resistance or generating unnecessary conflict with the participants.

STAGES IN VALUE CHANGE AND PROFESSIONAL RESOCIALIZATION

To demonstrate the interplay between the intellectual and affective aspects of learning and growth, we have reconceptualized Light's five-stage analysis of the intense socialization experience of becoming a psychiatrist.[7,8] The following stages summarize the process of value change as understood through our observations and residents' evaluations over the years of our teaching this course.

Stage 1: Feeling Different and Being Discredited

Clearly, the process began before the first class met. Residents who elected the course identified themselves as different from those who did not in that they were aware of and sensitive to sex-role socialization and gender issues. Nevertheless, the decision about whether or not to elect this course was accompanied by considerable ambivalence and anxiety. One resident stated, "I was initially rather anxious. . . I had some concern that I would change my views and values drastically and was fearful to some extent about what effect that might have on my outside life, my work, my relationships, etc." Another resident expressed his concern over being discredited this way: "Before the initial meeting I noticed considerable anxiety which I believed was related to not wanting to discover that I had sexually biased attitudes."

By the time of the first class, the participants had already read *The Longest War*,[9] which focuses on alternative perspectives for explaining gender differences, experiences, and behaviors. In addition, the primary readings for the first seminar discussed the implications of these alternative explanations for psychiatric practice. Participants came to class believing that they were "neutral" in their roles as therapists. They were prepared to find out that they had gender values and stereotypes, but they were completely unaware that there was any connection between these biases and their clinical perspectives or behaviors. This lack of awareness was reflected in early discussions, in which the residents rarely talked about the readings in terms of perspective.

Thus, the instructors' task was to help them understand that they all had perspectives and to explore the constraints and limitations imposed by these intellectual frameworks. However, in accomplishing this the residents felt discredited. As one resident described it,

> I started the course feeling fearful and attacked. I felt that though the initial material was very well done, the initial discussion was biased and narrow-minded. But I was also sincere in my belief that men and women are equal and very much wanted to discover my own semi and unconscious biases. After the first session, I wasn't sure of anything.

Stage 2: Moral and Intellectual Confusion

The first major conflict between the participants and the instructors arose when residents began to make a connection between their personal values and clinical perspectives. This awareness was prompted by readings that described the structure of inequality and its psychological implications for women and men.[10-12] Class discussions at that point remained highly intellectualized and covertly hostile and were reflected in strenuous denials of the validity and/or the relevance of the data as a way of making the confusion disappear.

As the data became more compelling and the validity and relevance could no longer be denied, participants attempted a "truce" with the instructors in which they acknowledged the existence of inequality but insisted that it had the same impact on the lives of women and men. The readings about men's restricted roles contributed to the idea that women and men are equally oppressed. Explaining that the inequality is qualitatively and quantitatively different for men and women provoked overt anger, and both the group process and evaluation confirmed the strong feelings. This was usually projected so that it was the instructors, rather than the participants, who were accused of being rigid, indoctrinating, intolerant, and indicting.

The women residents initially expressed relief at having their experiences validated by the readings and became angry as they cited examples of the previous lack of validation. Subsequently, they formed an ambivalent alliance with the men to avoid open conflict and alienation from peers. The men had considerable difficulty empathizing with women's anger at their subordination until they developed a sense of what men had lost as a result of sex-role restrictions. The papers that conveyed this focused on homophobia and intimacy among men. From these readings, the male participants came to understand the lack of intimacy, fathering, and emotional support from other men that derive from the traditional male sex role.[13] This was a point at which the men felt intense grief and guilt, especially about conflicts with parents. Initially much anger was directed at mothers for overly controlling behaviors, and it took longer for them to understand the sins of omission, namely, the absence of nurturance and support from their fathers: "The realization of the male role restrictions on parenting time and nurturance gave me a broader perspective to my father's own career-drivenness and emotional unavailability. Unfortunately, the perspective doesn't fill the loss."

In this stage, all participants found their professional values challenged and their identities threatened. They were fearful of what they might learn about themselves as individuals and as professionals. Concerns about self-worth and competence were prominent and took the form of feeling attacked, coerced, controlled, and/or rejected by the instructors. None of the old values felt very comfortable, and the new ones had too many implications for personal lives and professional practice. Participants thought they were alone in not being able to distinguish the right way to do therapy or to understand the material.

Despite the confusion, residents attempted to apply the new knowledge in their clinical work. They appeared to be motivated both by compelling insights and by the need to engage in "good" behaviors that would please the "dangerous" instructors. These attempts at implementation were often premature, as the following example illustrates. A resident shared a vignette about a woman patient described as being in an "oppressive marriage." During the therapy hour he made a speech about her unfulfilling role, gave a short discourse on sex-role socialization, and felt heroic as the patient seemed in complete agreement. Unfortunately, this interesting interpretation took place during the patient's first visit.

Stage 3: Numbness and Exhaustion

The lack of immediate success in integrating the new way of thinking about gender with current therapeutic and personal relationships created a temporary emotional withdrawal. Participants appeared tired and disheartened and felt the problems were so pervasive that nothing could change. Many of the male participants were ambivalent and fearful about changing the existing arrangements or simply felt no pressure or responsibility to change. The ambivalence and indifference were reinforced by existing norms and a lack of male role models with whom they could identify in the training program. Although female participants were less ambivalent about the necessity for change because of their own experiences with inequality, they were afraid of the personal and institutional isolation that might result from directly confronting sexism. Thus, for both women and men, ambivalence, conflict, and demoralization resulted as the participants tried to maintain a familiar sense of self along with an altered reality.

Over the span of the course, however, we were quite impressed with the ability of the participants to tolerate considerable tension, personal pain, and disorientation. We use the term "disorientation" to refer to the impact on the participants of having their values clarified and challenged. They were courageous in pursuing the very learning goals that increased their sense of vulnerability. There were periodic "tune-outs," but people invariably came back. Ultimately, one of the important course experiences was that of learning how to confront conflict openly both within the group and within themselves.

As a male resident and a female resident commented,

> I found that after many of the sessions, I came out feeling surrounded by women and wishing they would all go away and leave me alone. Sometimes I felt overwhelmed, trapped and pushed by all "these women" and the dread and scare that I felt had to do with the fact that I had let myself listen to what it was like to be unequal and I knew that I couldn't make that knowledge go away. I couldn't not change myself.

> I still feel very discouraged and overwhelmed when I realize the enormous impact of sex roles and feel angry but without any clear target for the anger. At times in the classes I would just sort of tune out rather than try to deal with all of these feelings.

Stage 4: The Moment of Truth

In the context of working through the risks and benefits of changing, residents began to experience, in a more affective way, gender conflicts and values that were previously inaccessible. This "moment of truth" or insight for each participant came in a highly individualized way as the result of the interaction beween the course content and process, personal life issues, and an ongoing inner dialogue. Some examples of the personal learning that preceded the awareness of professional implications follow:

> By this time (fourth session), I could listen to women being angry without running or trying to talk them out of their feelings and around the time of the readings about motherhood, I started talking to my mother about her trouble giving up her kids. . . . I gave up my anger at her for having trouble in letting me grow up.

> Arrived late—realized I was *very* anxious . . . couldn't remember a thing about the article on female anger, even though as I was reading it I felt it was great and true—became impressive demonstration of my own internal prohibitions.

> I had recently ended a four-year love relationship with a woman who was struggling with these very issues . . . and to hear it in a more neutral atmosphere was helpful, precipitating considerable grief in me upon recognizing the personal consequences of what until then I had considered her problem.

The reading materials that most commonly evoked these insights were those that focused on anger and sexuality. Lerner's papers on prohibitions against anger in women and on men's envy and fear of women as a basis for sexual inequality were pivotal content areas (reference 14 and paper presented at the 131st annual meeting of the American Psychiatric Association, Atlanta, May 8–12, 1978). Somewhat later in the course the participants were able to reconsider the paper on envy and devaluation of women to understand that the fear and anger they experienced in relation to the instructors was an excellent example of Lerner's thesis. These changes in perception were described well by a female resident:

> I do feel it would be useful learning to look at the reactions of the group members to the leaders in light of the material at hand, because it would be *in vivo* a demonstration of our biases and reactions . . . For the first part of the course I perceived the leaders as quite powerful and I wanted to please them. . . . This feeling was heightened when the topic of anger came up, and I felt controlled by them. As I began to realize that this was a reflection of

the subject matter, and of my own shit, my perceptions of the leaders changed; they seemed more real, and less powerful.

Another example was provided in graphic terms by a male resident, who wrote, "Both became more real, whole people to me . . . which paralleled my decreasing need to please, be dependent on, or rebel against 'big momma.'"

These personal insights led to a considerable drop in defensiveness and increased ability to "see" the consequences of gender bias in their personal lives and relationships. As participants began to exchange concrete examples of these insights in class, they became aware of the benefits of being in a group of their peers with whom they shared experiences and from whom they learned. Everyone in class, at one time or another, was an instructor to everyone else. Feedback from peers was considerably more effective than that from the instructors, who were still "suspect": "I felt the book [*Toward a New Psychology of Women*][10] was tremendously biased and attacking of men. The women thought it was great; it really hit home for them, and that reality hit me."

Stage 5: Redefining Professional and Personal Identities

As the participants recovered from their earlier disorientation, they attempted to integrate the new material into their personal and professional roles. However, as they looked to the institution for support for these new roles and perspectives, they found themselves in the older structure of values, where there was little support for making such changes in their clinical work. The lack of reinforcement by many of their teachers left them disappointed and angry:

> With my supervisors I am raising questions about subordination and role restriction as a way of formulating the case. . . . Some try to minimize the importance. The biggest change for me is that I am more confident about the importance and their minimizations don't affect my perception.

Anger toward their supervisors did not diminish the grandiose expectations they still had of the instructors. Participants' anger toward the instructors resurfaced toward the end of the course because we were not powerful enough to create a structure in which the new perspective could work without conflict. They were unable to erase or undo their new learning, which they were already integrating into their clinical work. However, the most disquieting effect of the new perspective was to increase their degree of conflict and discomfort with the old world: "I became angry at the instructors/role models for what they'd shown me . . . to have images of rape, to feel oppressed. . . . I wanted to be naive again."

Concerns about the quality of supervision and other professional relationships were prevalent during this stage and were made concrete through a group of readings about erotic countertransference and sex between therapist and patient.[15,16] Participants were uniform in their reports that supervisors rarely addressed erotic or other countertransference feelings. These reports are consistent with resident feedback over the last five years of teaching this course and with recent literature on countertransference.[15,17] Residents described receiving both overt and covert messages from supervisors that this material was "taboo." For example, a male resident who attempted to discuss his sexual feelings toward a male patient was told by his supervisor that this was irrelevant and he should get on with the work of treating the patient. The more covert message was that this material was inappropriate for supervision and belonged in personal psychotherapy.[17] Participants wondered whether there might be a connection between inadequate models for identifying and working through countertransference feelings and the sexual abuse of psychotherapy patients. Invariably, the class in which this was discussed ran late and participants were intensely involved and self-revealing. They were relieved to have finally had an opportunity to openly explore these issues and to develop models for contracting with supervisors and patients.

CONCLUSIONS

Because redefinition of self is a slow process, the reintegrated professional and personal identity comes in waves over time. The new perspective may provoke a recasting of one's entire life history or may be limited to one's professional socialization. Thus, the emergent self goes through alternating periods of resistance, anger, grief, reflection, and acceptance. Despite the disorienting aspects of this process of value clarification and professional resocialization, participants were able to translate the new knowledge into their personal and professional lives. Personal knowledge focused on increased awareness of gender values and the pervasiveness of sex-role socialization. In this light, participants reevaluated their personal, family, and professional relationships. Some of their conclusions follow:

> The course was a continual unfolding of the deep, pervasive ways in which sex-role socialization and gender values affected and are expressed in my life—e.g., my total professional deference to male co-therapists, my handicapping myself to avoid competing with men and being successful, my psychic blinders to men being attracted to me in professional settings (peers and advisors), my passivity, my self-denigrating cuteness.

> What began as a hope that I was immune to role restriction and sexual bias has given way to beginning grief over the impact of these issues on me, my relationships, and my family of origin.

In terms of clinical knowledge, participants now take histories that include experiences of physical and sexual victimization, powerlessness, family roles, and sexuality. This additional information has resulted in more effective therapeutic relationships with their patients and access to previously undisclosed information. Within the therapeutic process itself, participants are better able to identify indirect expressions of anger and to understand its social origins and political implications:

> I have become much more alert to the symptoms of subordination and unequal power ... I have seen much improvement in the individuals' self-esteem when they can begin identifying others' power manipulations (including the therapist) rather than feeling personally responsible for things going badly.

> With women's accounts of sexual harassment and the understanding of the male's devaluation of the powerful woman imago, I became much more aware of the hostile content in my own seductive fantasies and behavior.

Although the question of the permanence of the observed changes cannot be answered at this time, we do know that one of the conditions necessary for maintaining and building on the new knowledge is a work environment in which value clarification efforts are reinforced. Nevertheless, we believe that the participants acquired a perspective on their own perspective that will give them a way to continue to monitor their own work. They came to understand that there is a social context for viewing both patient dilemmas and the therapist–patient interaction. We have concluded that a requirement for effective therapeutic role performance is the ability to stand outside the self, to observe the cognitive-value interaction, and to question one's own values and intellectual framework without paralyzing fear of personal or professional annihilation. In this sense, the course produces better clinicians.

REFERENCES

1. Carmen E. (H.), Driver F.: Teaching women's studies: values in conflict. *Psychology of Women Quarterly* 7(1):81–95, 1982
2. Carmen E. (H.), Russo N. F., Miller J. B.: Inequality and women's mental health: an overview. *Am J Psychiatry* 138:1319–1330, 1981
3. Stone A. A.: Presidential address: conceptual ambiguity and morality in modern psychiatry. *Am J Psychiatry* 137:887–891, 1980
4. Rawlings E. I., Carter D. K.: Values and value change in psychotherapy, in *Psychotherapy for Women*. Edited by Rawlings E. I., Carter D. K., Springfield, Ill., Charles C. Thomas, 1977
5. Rieker P., Begun J.: Translating social science concepts into medical education: a model and a curriculum. *Soc Sci Med* [A] 14:601–612, 1980
6. Mayes S. S.: Women in positions of authority: a case study of changing sex roles. *Signs* 4:556–568, 1979

7. Light D.: *Becoming Psychiatrists: The Professional Transformation of Self*. New York, W. W. Norton & Co., 1981

8. Goffman E.: *Asylums*, New York, Doubleday, 1961

9. Tavris C., Offir C.: *The Longest War—Sex Differences in Perspective*. New York, Harcourt Brace Jovanovich, 1977

10. Miller J. B.: *Toward a New Psychology of Women*. Boston, Beacon Press, 1976

11. Morin S. F., Garfinkle E. M.: Male homophobia. *Journal of Social Issues*. 34(1)29–47, 1978)

12. Lewis R. A.: Emotional intimacy among men. *Journal of Social Issues* 34(1):108–121, 1978

13. Pleck J. H.: Men's family work: three perspectives and some new data. *The Family Coordinator* 28:481–488, 1979

14. Lerner H. E.: Early origins of envy and devaluation of women: implications for sex role stereotypes. *Bull Menninger Clin* 38:538–553, 1974

15 Bieniek C., Barton G. M., Benedek E.: Training female mental health professionals: sexual countertransference issues. *J Am Med Wom Assoc* 36(4):131–139, 1981

16. Davidson V.: Psychiatry's problem with no name: therapist-patient sex. *Am J Psychoanal* 37:43–50, 1977

17. Goin M. K., Kline F. Countertransference: a neglected subject in clinical supervision. *Am Psychiatry* 133:41–44, 1976

Toward an Analysis of Sex-Role-Related Issues in the Therapeutic Relationship

23

Alexandra G. Kaplan

In the extensive literature on transference and countertransference, there is a notable absence of any discussion related to the impact of the sex of patient and therapist on the clinical process (Berman, 1972; Berzins, Welling, and Wetter, 1978). The implicit assumption is that clinical dynamics transcend such reality components as the sex of patient or therapist, especially in the more analytically oriented therapies (Seiden, 1976). But this assumption should be open to serious reexamination. Freud (1931) suggested that there may be certain content areas that would be differentially revealed by the patient depending upon the sex of the therapist. In acknowledging his difficulty in grasping the nature of the preoedipal relationships between his female patients and their mothers, Freud concluded, "It does indeed appear that women analysts—as, for instance, Jeanne Lampl-de Groot and Helene Deutsch—have been able to perceive these facts more easily and clearly because they were helped in dealing with those under their treatment by the transference to a suitable mother-substitute" (pp. 226–227).

Freud's notion, limited in scope though it may be, is consistent with the emphasis placed by sex-role researchers on the extent to which women and men are perceived as having different personality characteristics (Rosenkrantz, Vogel, Bee, Broverman, and Broverman, 1968; Spence, Helmreich, and Stapp, 1975). These differential perceptions are reflective of a culture in which, according to Bem (1972), "Learning to be a 'psychological' male or female is one of the earliest and most pervasive tasks imposed upon the individual by his culture." Our culture makes clear distinctions between the feelings, behaviors, and role expectations that are assumed to be associated with each sex. These sex-role stereotypes pervade the structure of our families (Bernard, 1974), our educa-

Reprinted from *Psychiatry* 42(5):112–120, 1979. Copyright © 1979 by the William Alanson White Psychiatric Foundation, Inc. Reprinted by permission. This article is a revision of a talk delivered in the Grand Rounds Lecture Series, Downstate Medical College, Brooklyn, New York, November 1976.

tional systems (Frazier and Sadker, 1973), media communications (Sternglanz and Serbin, 1974), and work roles (O'Leary, 1974). They are internalized by us as children, and remain with us as adults as conscious or unconscious components of our personalities, whether or not our political beliefs support the efficacy of differential traits for males and females. If we accept that the therapeutic process is reflective of the broader social context in which it is embedded (Berger and Luckman, 1966; Szasz, 1963), then it is reasonable to assume that the reactions of both patients and therapists will, in part, be influenced by their internalized concepts of sex-appropriate behaviors.

I wish to explore here the influence of sex of patient and therapist on the dynamics of the therapeutic relationship, in order to provide a framework within which components of transferential and countertransferential dynamics can be examined. This paper is not a predictive statement of the behaviors of women and men in therapy, nor is it an argument in support of the existence of distinct differences between the sexes within a therapeutic setting. The remarks which follow, however, are predicated on the assumption that the failure to explore the potential impact of sex-related dynamics can obscure certain aspects of the therapeutic relationship. While this analysis could appropriately be applied to all four sex dyads, it will be limited to women in therapy with male and female therapists, given that the majority of patients in therapy are women (Chesler, 1972).

SEX-ROLE SOCIALIZATION AND STRUCTURAL AND FUNCTIONAL COMPONENTS OF THE THERAPIST'S ROLE

The process of socialization includes strong pressures to develop feelings, behaviors, and a sense of self that are considered appropriate for one's sex (Kagan, 1964; Mussen, 1969; Williams, 1977). Kagan provides a succinct and useful summary of the directions of this differential socialization:

> In sum, females are supposed to inhibit aggression and open display of sexual urges, to be passive with men, to be nurturant with others, to cultivate attractiveness, and to maintain an affective, socially poised and friendly posture with others. Males are urged to be aggressive in face of attack, independent in problem situations, sexually aggressive, in control of regressive urges, and suppressive of strong emotions, especially anxiety. (p. 143)

Bakan (1966) seeks to understand the perceived differences between women and men in terms of two fundamental modalities which he terms *agency* and *communion*. Agency, according to Bakan, is characterized by self-protection, self-assertion, isolation, the urge to master, and the

repression of thought, feelings, and impulses. Communion is characterized by a sense of being at one with other organisms, openness, contact,
noncontractual cooperation, and the lack and removal of repressions.
While individuals of both sexes contain aspects of both of these modes,
Bakan argues, "What we have been referring to as agency is more characteristically masculine, and what we have been referring to as communion is more characteristically feminine" (p. 110).

From these two rather different approaches, a pattern of expectations
related to each sex emerges. Females are seen as having an emotionally
open, nurturant, and affiliative stance, while males are seen as having an
emotionally inhibited, self-assertive, and interpersonally distant stance.
These dimensions are directly related to *structural* and *functional* components of the therapist's role. The therapist assumes the responsibility for
establishing and monitoring the *structural* components of the therapy
hour. As such, she or he defines the rules of conduct for the relationship,
including when and where to meet, what is appropriate for discussion,
and what is expected of each participant. The therapist also utilizes her
or his expertise to shape the basic nature of the material brought forth
for discussion. While the patient may attempt to influence this structure,
it is the therapist who determines the ultimate success of these attempts.
The patient's only source of independent power lies with noncoopera-
tion within the structure or termination of the relationship, both of
which defeat the very pupose for which the relationship was established.
These characteristics represent the *authority* dimension of the therapist's
role (Langs, 1973). The personality traits most conducive to an effective
handling of a position of authority—independence, assertiveness, and
emotional distance—are those most consistent with masculine rather
than feminine patterns of sex-role socialization. Thus, it seems reasonable to expect that the stances of male and female therapists will differentially reflect their greater or lesser preparation for the authority component of their role.

The reverse situation exists regarding the *functional* components of
the therapist's role. While one's particular stance varies according to
one's theoretical orientation, certain commonalities emerge across
approaches. Clinicians are expected to be empathic, intuitive, interpersonally astute, sensitive to intrapsychic dynamics, capable of showing
compassion for others, good listeners, and able to postpone gratification
of their needs in favor of those of the patient. These traits, which represent the *empathic* dimension of the therapist's role (Little, 1951), are all
consistent with the nurturant and socially competent traits that are
emphasized in the feminine but not the masculine socialization process.
This differential socialization should be reflected in how male and
female therapists handle the empathic component of their role.

Consider the task facing the female therapist. Her challenge is to accept the legitimate authority of her role as therapist in the face of cultural pressures to be deferential, and to integrate that stance with expressions of warmth and empathy without letting the latter feelings predominate as she generally has been encouraged to do. For the male therapist, the situation is reversed. Whether or not the individual male therapist is comfortable with the authority of his position, this aspect is consistent with the masculine model within which he has been socialized. His challenge is to temper this with the empathy which is appropriate for his role, but for which his upbringing has not especially trained him.

For clinicians of both sexes, the possession of both of these qualities—authority and empathy—would be most desirable in virtually all modes of therapy. The viability of such a coexistence of masculine and feminine characteristics has been documented by researchers involved in the study of androgyny (Bem, 1976; Spence, Helmreich, and Stapp, 1975). An androgynous person, as defined by these writers, can embody both stereotypic masculine and feminine characteristics so as to be able to respond in the most situationally appropriate, adaptive, and effective manner. In addition, the androgynous individual would exhibit an integration of feminine and masculine characteristics so that she or he could be assertive but in a manner that would demonstrate compassion for others, or independent without threatening the links that she or he has to significant others. If one were to argue that all therapists are successfully able to integrate authority and empathy in their clinical work, then it would have to be said that all therapists are androgynous. While we may wish to believe this, given the demands put upon us by virtue of the nature of our profession, it does not seem to be the case. In a study of the sex-role orientations of 76 therapists, Berzins (1975) found that 18% of the males and 28% of the females were androgynous, with the rest distributed among the other sex-role orientations. Much as therapists may wish to be equally adept at all aspects of their clinical work, it seems necessary to consider the ways in which, as men or women, they may be predisposed to some basic types of reactions rather than to others.

The barriers to the successful blending of stereotypic traits are somewhat different for male and female clinicians. For the latter, the temptations are strong to emphasize traits in both directions. There is, on the one hand, the stance that Menninger (1936) describes, in which women therapists "Strive to imitate men, to imitate their male colleagues and follow them even in their errors." On the other hand are the women clinicians who, seeking to develop alternative models of therapy outside of a "patriarchal" structure, argue for the redefinition of therapy as an arena for intimate sharing by both participants and the building of a totally egalitarian relationship. This position represents an extreme reliance on empathy as a therapeutic tool, but ignores the component of authority which seems essential for effective clinical functioning.

While male therapists could also theoretically be pulled to either end of this dichotomy, rarely do they seem to revert to a monolithic application of the empathy dimension. It is a common observation among students of sex roles that it is far easier for women to adapt culturally valued masculine traits than it is for men to adapt culturally disdained feminine traits (Kenworthy, 1979). Also, women have the political support of the feminist movement to reject what is seen as an "authoritarian" model of therapy, while men have no such backing. Women therapists have much to gain by accepting the legitimate authority inherent in their role: an enhanced sense of competence, a lessened vulnerability to patients' manipulations, a greater feeling of control over their clinical work. The advantages to men of adapting a more empathic stance are far more ambiguous. There is a large measure of comfort (protection) in the diffidence and nonrelatedness that characterize a position of excessive authority. For women, the integration of feminine and masculine characteristics feels typically like growth; for men, it may feel compromising or threatening.

SEX-ROLE-RELATED ASPECTS OF THE PATIENT-THERAPIST RELATIONSHIP

Female Therapists and Authority

The female therapist working with a female client brings to her role an upbringing which has not especially prepared her for the aspect that is rooted in a position of authority. Similarly, her female client has not been encouraged to recognize women as authority figures. This aspect of the patient's reaction is suggested by the fact that most women, when asked, indicate a preference for a male rather than a female therapist (Lewis, 1976). Lewis proposes that this preference is directly related to their seeing the male therapist as more qualified, and placing a greater trust in the male therapist's wisdom. Confronted with a female therapist, the female patient is likely to translate these initial doubts into subtle challenges to the therapist's competence. The female therapist seems regularly to be questioned as to whether her age, her theoretical orientation, her marital status, or her level of training renders her the most suitable therapist for that patient's particular problems. More often than her male counterpart, she is addressed by her first name, rather than as "Doctor." Frequently, especially in the early stages of therapy, her interventions are ignored or evaded, and she is faced with indirect attempts to manipulate the scheduling or direction of the therapy hour.

This subtle pattern of evasive, tentative forms of resistance can be difficult to understand without a recognition of its potential roots in the patient's doubts about the legitimate authority of her therapist. Such a recognition is not easily achieved, partly because our therapy training does not encourage us to examine the possible impact of sex-related factors on our clinical work, and partly because the therapist's sex is the latent rather than the manifest content of the patient's response. Resistance, after all, is a common component of initial stages of therapy, regardless of the sex of the patient and/or therapist. However, viewing this reaction from a sex-role perspective can add to our interpretation of relevant dynamics the possibility that the patient is using a culturally validated image of women to shape the particular nature of her resistant stance.

The task of the female therapist is to understand the interrelationship between her own behaviors and the patient's reactions to those behaviors in influencing the patient's response. Given her lack of preparation for a position of authority, she should be especially attentive to ways in which she might be undermining or belittling her own position. Indecisiveness, a tendency to smile too frequently or to giggle, a ready willingness to relax the boundaries of the therapeutic hour, all might communicate to the patient a position of less than sufficient authority. At the same time, the therapist should consider that these behaviors might have stronger implications than if coming from a male therapist. Nunberg (1965) reminds us that patients come to therapy with a readiness for certain forms of transferential relationships. To the extent that this readiness is influenced by the sex of the therapist, it could predispose the patient to exaggerate the implications of certain of the therapist's reactions, while minimizing the implications of others. It is even possible that female therapists would have to convey a greater measure of authority than their male counterparts in order to command respect. Bloom, Weigel, and Truatt (1977) found that when subjects were shown what they believed to be therapists' offices, greater credibility was accorded the female therapist with a traditional rather than a humanistic office, while the reverse was true for male therapists. While the decor of one's office is but a small portion of one's posture of authority, this study supports the importance for female therapists of giving close attention to the ways in which they are communicating their authority to their patients, and the ways in which these communications are received.

Female Therapists and Empathy

While female patients may not be initially prone to recognizing the authority of their female therapists, they would probably be likely to expect and acknowledge the empathic quality of their therapists' reactions. However, even mild empathic responses are in danger of being translated by the patient into indications of much more pervasive nurturant or protective dimensions of a maternal role. If the therapist is thereby seen as mother, then the patient becomes daughter, an ambivalent paradigm (Balint, 1973). Fundamentally, the mother-therapist becomes perceived as giver, and the daughter-patient as receiver. But the therapist cannot avoid her own accompanying wish to receive (therapists, of course, have also been daughters). If the female therapist senses and responds to her patient's wish for nurturance, a wish that plays upon a basic element of her own upbringing, then her own need to receive becomes especially acute. I will comfort you, the therapist's unconscious trade-off may read, but in return I seek loyalty, acceptance, and personal validation. This stance taps into the patient's ambivalence between her wish for maternal comfort and her fear that the acknowledgment of her own neediness could inhibit her anger, create too great a dependency on the therapist, or diminish that side of her which is strong, independent, and capable. This ambivalence is not infrequently acted out in the early sessions of therapy, especially with high-achieving, nontraditional women. For such women, the very act of seeking therapy, of recognizing that side of them which feels helpless and afraid, threatens their budding sense of self as competent and self-sufficient. As a result, they may evidence subtle plays for distance and control of the therapy hour, intermingled with requests that the therapist be more caring. Ideally, a sex-role analysis of this pattern of relatedness could prevent the therapist from becoming unwittingly pulled in by the patient's seeming neediness, and then puzzled by the disconfirmation of her interventions as the patient rejects her offerings. But this is the ideal. In the too frequent reality, these women patients have struck the very Achilles heel of their female therapists. "Look how much I have to offer you," the therapist seems to be saying: "How can you continue to refuse me?" The pain is especially acute because these female clinicians, themselves undoubtedly high achievers and bearing a strong measure of independence, feel a kinship with these women that magnifies their wish to help them. It is this wish that can blind their sensitivity to the dynamics at hand. Thus, rather than finding an adequate means for supporting both the neediness and the independence, the therapist's response becomes: "If only I give a little more, then they will see the value I hold for them." As the client becomes increasingly distant, the therapist reaches even further out, responding to the fear of loss by an attempt to enmesh. This stance by the therapist can seriously impair the therapeutic relationship, and at worst can lead to a premature termination.

Male Therapists and Authority

For women in therapy with male therapists, the kernel of their initial reaction is an augmentation, rather than a diminution, of therapeutic authority. The salience which the therapist's authority comes to have can elicit several patterns of responding. Some female patients readily assume the role of subordinate in the face of a dominant male (Miller, 1976). These women may be especially prone to entering readily into a dependent relationship with their therapist, accepting without due reflection the content of clinical interventions, or withholding felt criticisms of their therapist. Other female patients demonstrate their implicit recognition of their male therapist's authority by their flagrant, overt rejection of it. The therapist may find himself the recipient of his patient's generalized hostility to men (Rice and Rice, 1973). He may sense that he can do no right, that his interventions are invariably rejected, that his patient is making increasing demands on him to better meet her needs.

Like the female therapist, the male therapist can benefit from a sex-role analysis of the therapeutic relationship under both of these conditions. His first task would be to scrutinize his own behavior for evidence that he is unwittingly assuming an overly authoritarian stance to which the patient is either acquiescing or rebelling. Similarly, the patient's reactions should be examined for the extent to which they are reflective of a generalized attitude toward men. It is likely that both of these elements are playing some role in shaping the clinical dynamic, and that both need to be addressed in the therapy. As Rice and Rice point out:

> Since it is likely that male therapists (as products of our society) share certain chauvinistic attitudes at present, part of a woman's greater feelings of hostility toward men, including her therapist, seem appropriate and justified. Such feelings should be honestly acknowledged and dealt with in the therapeutic relationship. In fact it is in the therapy situation that a woman's generalized feelings of hostility toward men might most appropriately be expressed, accepted, and worked through. (1973, p.192)

Certain factors might militate against male therapists' identifying their reactions to overly dependent or strident women patients. Dependency in women is more likely to be seen as an appropriate than a problematic trait, hence more likely to be accepted than worked on (Miller, 1976). Such dependency also facilitates the ease with which patients enter into therapy, and is therefore less prone to becoming subject to clinical examination. A sex-role perspective on therapy, however, could serve to alert male clinicians to the possible existence of this dynamic.

Male therapists may also confront certain difficulties in accepting and working through the various manifestations of their female patients' anger. Anger is not a feeling which our culture typically validates in women (Lerner, 1977). For many women, the direct expression of anger may be a new experience, and as with any newly acquired trait, its application may be less than fully rational or coherent. It may also seem overblown, out of context, and inappropriate. The task of the male therapist is to differentiate between the legitimacy of the woman's *feelings* of anger and the problematic aspects of its particular form of expression. Clinical observations, however, suggest that male therapists may have some difficulty accepting the legitimacy of this anger. In some cases, women's anger is perceived as a direct but inappropriate reaction to the therapist. This can prompt a confrontative, self-protective reaction, characterized at its worst by a clear disconfirmation of the validity of the patient's feeling. In other cases, the angry woman patient may be responded to in a distant, withholding manner, which becomes noticeably more supportive when the patient's anger is reduced to tears and self-blame. The countertherapeutic elements in these responses should be obvious.

Male Therapists and Empathy

Males bring to their role as therapist a cultural heritage which has not encouraged the open expression of feelings, intimate sharing between peers, or a sensitivity to the emotional states of others. While men differ in the extent to which they have internalized these cultural prescriptions, their relative lack of training in interpersonal skills and their knowledge that such behaviors are generally accorded an "unmanly" status may inhibit their capacity for clinical empathy. This difficulty may be especially acute with female patients, considering Kernberg's (1965) position that empathy is dependent upon a therapist's trial identification with the patient, and the possibility that such identification is rendered more difficult in opposite-sex therapy dyads.

Empathy requires, first of all, an accurate assessment of the patient's emotional state. Clinical experience has revealed certain situations in which male therapists rather poignantly misperceive even overt manifestations of their patient's emotional reactions. In one instance, a male supervisee reported at length on a patient whom he had seen as distressed and overwrought during the hour, evidenced by frequent crying spells. Upon listening to a tape of the session, however, it was revealed that such crying spells had in fact been limited to a periodic shaky quality to her voice, accompanied by a welling of tears in her eyes. In this case, the therapist's own tendency to cry only when extremely overwrought had led to his exaggeration of the patient's emotional reaction. In another instance, with an experienced therapist, a patient reported growing discomfort with the basic direction of the therapist's work. The therapist, in a supportive tone, reflected upon the patient's feelings of being lost and overwhelmed, while ignoring her stated expression of dissatisfaction. When the patient pointed this out to the therapist, he abruptly changed the subject and did not return to it for the remainder of the hour. The impact this had on the patient soon led to a termination of their work.

Empathy also requires the ability to respond nonjudgmentally to the material the client brings forth. If male therapists feel uncertain about their capacity for relating to women, or insecure in the face of women's strengths, this nonjudgmental quality may become impaired. The work of one male therapist most clearly illustrates this point. In working with a couple, this young therapist consistently supported the husband rather than the wife. He associated this reaction to his dislike of the woman because she was overweight. This was dealt with in supervision and seemed to be resolved. However, several sessions later, the therapist reported that his work was made difficult by the woman patient's frequent use of verbal tics, such as "You know what I mean," or "Isn't that right?" Again, the tape-recording of the session revealed no such expressions from the woman, but an intermittent use of these very terms by her husband. The woman in this couple, more academically successful and articulate than her husband, had threatened the therapist's sense of his own competence, to which he responded by demeaning her posture and elevating that of her husband. A direct discussion of the therapist's affective reactions to women was necessary to alleviate this countertransferential pattern.

CONCLUSIONS

This paper has argued that both patients and therapists bring to the therapy hour remnants of their upbringing within a culture that values differential characteristics for women and men. This upbringing can influence both the stance taken by each member of the therapy dyad and the ways in which each perceives and interprets the behaviors of the other. A knowledge of basic patterns of sex-role socialization can attune the clinician to pertinent clinical dynamics that might otherwise go unrecognized or be misperceived. It is suggested that such a sex-role analysis be added to the framework with which we attempt to understand the nature of the therapeutic relationship.

The difficulties of attuning ourselves to the sex-related aspects of our work should not be underestimated. There is a noticeable wish in contemporary society to transcend sex-role stereotypes, to minimize the extent to which our own behaviors might be reflective of sex-related traits whose values we as individuals no longer espouse. This is exacerbated by the absence in the literature and in clinical training of consideration of sex-related aspects of the therapeutic relationship. However, working within a tradition that emphasizes the therapist's continuous self-examination, it seems fruitful to add a sex-role perspective to the content of this inquiry. Such an exploration is difficult to initiate by oneself, or even in supervisory dyads, where the distinction between idiosyncratic and sex-related factors can too easily be obscured. I have found great utility, however, in the use of same- or mixed-sex supervisory groups for this purpose. Within such groups, sex-related dynamics begin to emerge if one is attuned to listening for them, and a greater clarity in therapeutic work can then be achieved.

REFERENCES

Bakan, D. *The Duality of Human Existence;* Beacon Press, 1966.

Balint, E. "Technical Problems Found in the Analysis of Women by a Woman Analyst: A Contribution to the Question "What Does a Woman Want? " *Internat. J. Psycho-Anal.* (1973) 54:195—201.

Bem, S. L. "Psychology Looks at Sex Roles: Where Have All the Androgynous People Gone?," presented at U.C.L.A. Symposium on Women, May 1972.

Bem, S. L. "Probing the Promise of Androgyny," in A. G. Kaplan and J. P. Bean (Eds.), *Beyond Sex-Role Stereotypes: Readings Toward a Psychology of Androgyny;* Little, Brown, 1976.

Berger, P. L., and Luckman, T. *The Social Construction of Reality;* Doubleday, 1966.

Berman, E. "The Woman Psychiatrist as Therapist and Academician," *J. Med. Educ.* (1972) 47:890—893.

Bernard, J. *The Future of Motherhood;* Dial Press, 1974.

Berzins, J. I. "Sex Roles and Psychotherapy: New Directions for Theory and Research," presented at 6th Annual Meeting, Society for Psychotherapy Research, Boston, June 1975.

Berzins, J. I., Welling, M. A., and Wetter, R. E. "A New Measure of Psychological Androgyny Based on the Personality Research Form," *J. Consult. and Clin. Psychol.* (1978) 46:126–138.

Bloom, L. J., Weigel, R. G., and Truatt, G. M. "Therapeugenic Factors in Psychotherapy: Effects of Office Decor and Subject–Therapist Sex Pairing on the Perception of Credibility," *J. Consult. and Clin. Psychol.* (1977) 45:867–873.

Chesler, P. *Women and Madness;* Doubleday, 1972.

Frazier, N., and Sadker, M. *Sexism in Schools and Society;* Harper & Row, 1973.

Freud, S. "Female Sexuality" (1931), *Standard Ed. Complete Psychol. Works,* Vol. 21; Hogarth, 1961.

Kagan, J. "Acquisition and Significance of Sex-Typing and Sex-Role Identity," in M. L. Hoffman and L. W. Hoffman (Eds.), *Review of Child Development Research,* Vol. 1; Russell Sage Foundation, 1964.

Kenworthy, J. A. "Androgyny in Psychotherapy: But Will It Sell in Peoria?," *Psychol. of Women Quart.,* (1979) 3:231–240.

Kernberg, O. "Notes on Countertransferences," *J. Amer. Psychoanal. Assn.* (1965) 13:38–56.

Langs, R. *The Technique of Psychoanalytic Psychotherapy,* Vol. 1; Jason Aronson, 1973.

Lerner, H. "The Taboos Against Female Anger," *Menninger Perspective*, Winter 1977, pp. 5–11.

Lewis, H. B. *Psychic War in Men and Women;* New York Univ. Press, 1976.

Little, M. "Countertransference and the Patient's Response to It," *Internat. J. Psycho-Anal.* (1951) 32:32–40.

Menninger, K. "The Psychological Advantages of the Woman Clinician," presented at Amer. Med. Women's Assn., Kansas City, Mo., May 13, 1936.

Miller, J. B. *Toward a New Psychology of Women;* Beacon Press, 1976.

Mussen, P. H. "Some Antecedents and Consequents of Masculine Sex-Typing in Adolescent Boys," *Psychol. Monogr.* (1961) 75, No. 506.

Nunberg, H. "Transference and Reality," *Internat. J. Psycho-Anal.* (1965) 32:1–9.

O'Leary, V. E. "Some Attitudinal Barriers to Occupational Aspirations in Women," *Psychol. Bull.* (1974) 81:809–826.

Rice, J. K., and Rice, D. G. "Implications of the Women's Liberation Movement for Psychotherapy," *Amer. J. Psychiatry* (1973) 130:191–196.

Rosenkrantz, P. S., Vogel, S. R., Bee, H., Broverman, I. K., and Broverman, D. M. "Sex-Role Stereotypes and Self-Concepts in College Students," *J. Consult. and Clin. Psychol.* (1968) 32:287–295.

Seiden, A. M. "Overview: Research on the Psychology of Women. II. Women in Families, Work, and Psychotherapy," *Amer. J. Psychiatry* (1976) 133:1111–1123.

Spence, J. T., Helmreich, R., and Stapp, J. "Ratings of Self and Peers on Sex-Role Attributes and Their Relation to Self-Esteem and Conceptions of Masculinity and Femininity," *J. Personality and Soc. Psychol.* (1975) 32:29–39.

Sternglanz, S. H., and Serbin, L. A. "Sex Role Stereotyping in Children's Television Programs," *Developmental Psychol.* (1974) 10:710–715.

Szasz, T. S. *Law, Liberty, and Psychiatry,* Macmillan, 1963.

Williams, J. *Psychology of Women;* Norton, 1977.

Psychiatry's Problem with No Name

24

Therapist–Patient Sex

VIRGINIA DAVIDSON

The inclusion in the Hippocratic oath of a specific injunction against a physician's having sexual relationships with patients indicates that this concern has a venerable history among physicians. Elaboration of these same ethical proscriptions in the current annotated version of medical ethics applicable to psychiatrists confirms that this concern exists into the present.[1] Moral outrage is regularly expressed by physicians toward those physicians who, in spite of the ethical restraints imposed by the above-mentioned codes, nonetheless indulge themselves sexually with their patients. Yet the force and sincerity of the call for integrity among physicians[2-4] does not appear to have much deterrent effect on that segment of the profession that chooses to have sex with their patients.

How can this ethical stance be reconciled with the increasing evidence that indicates therapist–patient sex may be far more prevalent than previously thought? Writers who have dealt with this topic have comforted themselves and their audiences with the hopeful observation that serious forms of unethical behavior—such as having sex with one's patients—exists only among a few practitioners.[5-7] One writer, finding the idea "absurd" that any well-qualified analyst could not refrain from being carried away by physical contact with an attractive patient, commented that such an impulse-ridden person would scarcely be safe on a dance floor.[8] The more serious question is whether there are a considerable number of male therapists who are not safe, with women patients, in the consulting room.

The idea that women patients may develop intense sexual feelings toward their male therapists during treatment for psychological illness did not originate with psychoanalysis, although it has been during the past 75 years that this relationship, in the metaphor of transference-countertransference, has been extensively studied. Before that, the magnet-

Reprinted from *American Journal of Psychoanalysis* 37:43–50, 1977. Copyright © by the Agathon Press, Inc. Reprinted by permission. Paper presented at the annual meeting of the American Psychiatric Association, 1976.

izers of the 18th century were well aware of the erotic component in the therapeutic encounter; the possibility that sexual seduction might occur between male magnetizer and female magnetized was recognized; the fact that the female patient was "passive," and that the male magnetizer was "active," was considered likely to increase the possibility that seduction might occur. An 18th century Viennese physician and magnetist, Anton Mesmer, introduced the term "rapport" into our psychological language. He was well aware of the importance of his own charisma in the therapeutic relationship and of its importance in treatment outcome. Mesmer's most famous patient was a blind woman pianist who developed a strong attraction to him during the course of treatment, and he similarly to her. During the period in which she was his patient, Mesmer became permanently estranged from his wife.[9]

Approximately 100 years later another Viennese physician, Josef Breuer, came into difficulty in his marriage because of the erotic attachment an attractive female patient had toward him. The importance of this relationship in the history of psychoanalysis is well known; alongside many other hysterical women patients, Breuer's Anna O. took her place in psychotherapeutic history. Little attention has been paid to the role women patients have played in the development of dynamic psychiatry, although their names, when paired with their famous male physicians, are familiar: Mesmer's Maria Paradis, Janet's Leonie and Madeleine, Charcot's Blanche Wittman, and Freud's Elizabeth von R. Still less attention has been paid to the effects these therapeutic relationships have had on the marriages of the physicians themselves; for example, during the treatment of Anna O., Mrs. Breuer became jealous and finally, morose. When Mrs. Freud heard about the situation, she immediately identified with Mrs. Breuer and required reassurance from Dr. Freud that their marriage would not be complicated by therapeutic relationships of that sort.[10] So wives of psychiatrists have had a long history of concern and understandable interest in the animal magnetism, rapport, and erotic transferences and countertransferences that characterize a part of their husband's working role. For the most part, these women have formed a silent population, yet we know that the effects these therapeutic relationships have on marriages of psychiatrists are considerable.

Within psychoanalysis the development of therapist–patient sexual relationships inside or outside the therapeutic hour has always posed a problem for discipline. Freud's position on therapist–patient sex was clear,[11,12] yet his warnings that therapists should never gratify their patients' erotic demands did not prevent some of his followers from marrying their patients.[13,14] Analysts maintain that therapy must always be carried out for the best interests of the patient (as opposed to the analyst) and that an atmosphere of basic trust is crucial for treatment, yet they have demonstrated little interest in reconciling lapses in the conduct of their practitioners with the basic rules of analytic practice. Even when presenting the case histories which document the existence of the problem within psychoanalysis, the issue is not raised as an ethical dilemma for the profession but tends to be seen as a complicating feature of treatment.[15] Emphasis on the transference is probably related to the greater degree of comfort that is maintained when the "problem" of therapist–patient sex is seen as a manifestation of the patient's—rather than the analyst's—illness. Marmor[14] is one of the few writers who has seriously suggested that the therapist could be seductive and could exhibit "countertransference acting-out" within the context of therapist–patient sex. While this is a refreshing departure from the time-worn saw of "transference acting-out," Marmor comes to a disappointing conclusion. For therapists who cannot master their countertransference feelings, he recommends termination of therapy; then, marriage to a patient under these circumstances is seen as an "honorable end-point" of the seductive therapeutic relationship. Several interesting questions come to mind about this approach.

What is to be done with the therapist's current wife?

What is to be done when the therapist enters into the same situation with another patient in the future? For if the same rules of human conduct apply to therapists as to patients, we can assume that this particular kind of acting-out in the service of the repetition compulsion will recur in time.

Are male therapists licensed to choose from their female patients which ones they prefer as marital partners, so long as they verbally terminate the doctor–patient relationship before marriage?

Is it possible for the psychiatrist ever to terminate his moral and ethical obligations to the patient or do these endure for an indefinite amount of time after the termination of the fee-for-service relationship? There is some legal precedent for believing that duties of a physician toward a patient continue after termination of the contractual agreement.[16] Aside from the legal question, it seems unlikely that the patient can ever erase the import of the therapist–patient relationship.[17]

That the doctor–patient relationship (male doctor–female patient) is a subject of much attention in the popular press, the cinema, and medical advertising need hardly be called to attention—everyone knows that already. Yet when note is taken of this fact, it is more often discounted than investigated.[18] Rather than discount these sources of popular culture which reveal much about how the male doctor–female patient relationship is seen in larger society (as well as within the medical community), it might be well to examine the portrayal of this relationship. One recent example (October 1975) is a cover from *Esquire* magazine which is an excerpt from a short story about a woman whose relationship with her analyst included sex on the couch. Although written by Truman Capote, the vignette has much in common with the clinical histories reported by Chesler, Belote, and Dahlberg.[19-21] From the cinema is a scene from Ingmar Bergman's *Scenes from a Marriage*, shown at the 1975 annual meeting of the American Psychiatric Association; in it the estranged husband asks his wife if she is having sex with her psychiatrist. She matter of factly replies that they have gone to bed a couple of times, but that it was a dead loss.[22] In that, too, there is a parallel with the clinical literature. Seductive male therapists have unenviable track records as lovers, suffering frequently from impotence and premature ejaculation.[20-23] Finally, the view of women patients that is afforded us from the cartoons and advertising printed in our medical journals suggests that the idea of women's sexual availability is closely intertwined with the male physician's image of himself with female patients. Young, attractive women are frequently pictured in various stages of undress to draw attention to ad copy designed with the male physician in mind. One recently published survey of medical journals found that obstetrical and gynecological journals contained the highest percentage of advertising that was unflattering and degrading to women.[24]

Before the 1970s, there were few published series of cases describing therapist–patient sex, although the history of dynamic psychiatry has been punctuated with famous therapist–patient marriages and love affairs. Not much has been written about them for obvious reasons, and they belong more to the oral history of psychiatry then to the published accounts of relationships. Masters and Johnson noted in 1970[2] that an "unfortunately large" number of their patients had had sex with prior therapists. This was the first time to my knowledge that any data had been published which suggested that therapist–patient sex was not limited to a small number of ill-trained quasiprofessionals. Dahlberg's article, also published in 1970, reported on nine patients who had had sex with their therapists. Dahlberg had collected the data over a 20 year period, and he noted the difficulty he had getting his paper accepted among organizations since it was "too controversial." It is possible that there have been other such case reports over the years which have been collected but suppressed at publication because of the nature of the material. Chesler[19] reports on 11 women who had sex with their therapists. Belote[20] advertised in a San Francisco newspaper and obtained 25 cases of women who had had sex with their male therapists during treatment.

The Kardener et al. study[25] revealed that 10 of the psychiatrists in the sample acknowledged that they engaged in erotic activities with their patients; 5% acknowledged that they engaged in sexual intercourse. The most interesting aspect of this study is that Kardener clearly implies that there are kinds of kissing, touching, and affectionate hugging between patient and psychiatrist that are *non*erotic. More than 50% of the psychiatrists in the sample acknowledge that they engaged in such nonerotic behavior with patients. How kissing, hugging, and touching (however affectionately labeled) within the context of the psychiatrist–patient relationship can be considered nonerotic requires a certain amount of imagination—or a determined lack of it.

In a recent article, Michael Stone[5] reported on unethical behavior among psychiatric residents, including two examples of sexual affairs with female patients. He describes the sloth with which the senior psychiatrists responded administratively, when they responded at all, to the residents' behavior. In one case, the errant resident was referred for psychoanalysis; in the other, the resident was dismissed. But it seems that he was dismissed only from that training program; presumably he continued training elsewhere. In all cases that have been reported in the literature, not one raises the question of what to do with the psychiatrist who seduces patients in the course of therapy—whether it is called transference or countertransference, love or acting-out (or up), incest, or rape. Whether some therapists involve themselves in serial affairs with patients is suggested by some of the case reports, but even the question of how to deal with this phenomenon is not raised. No one asks whether such a therapist is fit to continue the practice of psychotherapy, for example, while he is being treated for professional misconduct.

Other more difficult data sources to tap include the inevitable knowledge that every practicing psychiatrist has about the community in which he/she practices. The fact that the history of the community most likely includes a certain number of therapist–patient marriages is an indicator of the extent to which the practice of marrying patients is accepted by one's peers. Conversations with colleagues may reveal that certain psychiatrists (sometimes with their patients) are in treatment for the complications related to therapist–patient sex. Treatment, then, may be little more than a convenient way for the seductive psychiatrist to escape censure. By becoming a patient himself, he binds the treating psychiatrist to all the rules of confidentiality and ethical practice and at the same time secures for himself a certain protection and immunity. I have no solution to offer to this practice; I mention it only to indicate the enormity of the ethical question involved.

The available evidence indicates that erotic practices with patients may be quite widespread and that they involve practitioners at all levels of training, from psychiatric resident to training analyst. The therapist who engages in sex with patients or who marries patients may be quite acceptable in his community. If he is to marry a patient, it is hoped that proper—even if somewhat hasty—termination of the therapist–patient relationship precedes the assumption of the therapist–wife one. But even in cases where the niceties of conventional practice are not observed (the "honorable end-points" of relationships) no real risks are run by the psychiatrist who engages in such practices. If he is an academician, he will lose no rank; if he is in analytic training or aspires to enter it, such behavior will not prejudice his candidacy, for he will himself be in treatment with a competent analyst whose training has prepared him for dealing with such difficult cases; he risks little censure from his community peers and no risk of unfavorable action from the local ethics or grievance committees—composed as they are likely to be of men more like himself than otherwise.

While these studies do not discuss the existence of female therapist–male patient sex, it is likely that this phenomenon exists as well, although certainly to a much lesser degree.[26] Whether women therapists are less involved on account of their fewer numbers in the profession, or because of the greater societal barriers which operate against a woman's expressing her sexual feelings, or because of different cultural expectations that define the sexual role of the woman therapist cannot be said at this time.

In attempting to understand the phenomenon of therapist–patient sex, several important questions beg for answers:

Is this particular form of patient exploitation related to sexism within the profession? Does it represent the covert sanctioning by male practitioners of behavior which degrades all women? The image of women patients as available sex objects for their male physicians pervades our popular culture and is rampant in our medical advertising.

Do male therapists, who themselves do not engage in sexual activity with patients, lend subtle support to the practice by protecting their errant male colleagues with silence or with treatment? Do they allow facile notions to go unchallenged which place the blame for seductive psychotherapy on the woman patient?

Is therapist–patient sex a form of rape? Do women victims of seductive therapy need special forms of therapeutic intervention when they decide to reveal to friend, family, or another therapist that prior therapy has included sex? Women victims in both instances experience considerable guilt, risk loss of love and self-esteem, and often feel that they may have done something to "cause" the seduction. As with rape victims, women patients can expect to be blamed for the event and will have difficulty finding a sympathetic audience for their complaint. Added to these difficulties is the reality that each woman has consulted a therapist, thereby giving some evidence of psychological disequilibrium prior to the seduction. How the therapist may use this information after the woman decides to discuss the situation with someone else can surely dissuade many women from revealing these experiences.

Do women patients need women advocates within the profession, especially on the ethics and grievance committees to ensure that their complaints are not dismissed out of hand, much as rape victims have needed advocates within the health care system to obtain proper medical and psychiatric attention?

Women therapists are increasingly interested in the phenomenon of therapist–patient sex,[27,28] and in the questions it poses for the ethical practice of psychiatry. They readily identify with women patients and with wives of psychiatrists as well—the two groups of women most affected by this practice. Since it is generally agreed that therapist–patient sex is psychologically deleterious for the involved woman patient and is unethical practice for the male practitioner, it remains to be explained why such an unhealthful practice continues to flourish within the profession.

REFERENCES

1. Official Actions of the American Psychiatric Association. The principles of medical ethics with annotations especially applicable to psychiatry. *Am. J. Psychiatry* 130:1061, 1973.
2. Masters, W. H., and Johnson, V. E. *Human Sexual Inadequacy*. Boston: Little, Brown, 1970, pp. 388–391.
3. Demac, D. Masters blasts innumerable patient rapes. *Hosp. Trib.* 9(13):1, 1975.
4. Macklin, R. Ethics, sex research and sex therapy. *The Hastings Center Report* 6:5–7, 1976.
5. Stone, M. Management of unethical behavior in a psychiatric hospital staff. *Am. J. Psychother.* 29:391–401, 1975.
6. Braceland, F. Historical perspectives of the ethical practice of psychiatry. *Am. J. Psychiatry* 126:230–237, 1969.
7. West, L. J. Ethical psychiatry and biosocial humanism. *Am. J. Psychiatry* 126:226–230 1969.
8. Mintz, E. Touch and psychoanalytic tradition. *Psychoanal. Rev.* 56:365–376 1969.
9. Ellenberger, H. *The Discovery of the Unconscious*. New York: Basic Books, 1970, pp. 891–893.
10. Jones, E. *The Life and Work of Sigmund Freud*, vol. 1. New York: Basic Books, 1953, pp. 224–225.
11. Freud, S. Observations on Transference-Love. *The Complete Psychological Works of Sigmund Freud*, Tr. by James Stachey, vol. XII. London: Hogarth Press, 1958, pp. 159–171.
12. Jones, E. *The Life and Work of Sigmund Freud*. vol. 3. New York: Basic Books, 1953, pp. 163–165.
13. Roazen, P. *Brother Animal*. New York: Alfred A. Knopf, 1969.
14. Marmor, J. Sexual acting-out in psychotherapy. *Am. J. Psychoanal.* 32:3–8, 1972.
15. Voth, H. M. Love affair between doctor and patient. *Am. J. Psychother.* 26:394–400, 1972.
16. Dawidoff, D. J. *The Malpractice of Psychiatrists*. Springfield: Charles C. Thomas, 1973.
17. Finney, J. C. Therapist and patient after hours. *Am. J. Psychother.* 29:593–602, 1975.
18. Siassi, I., and Thomas, M. Physicians and the new sexual freedom. *Am. J. Psychiatry* 130:1256–1257, 1973.
19. Chesler P. *Women and Madness*. Garden City, N.Y.: Doubleday, 1972.

20. Belote, B. Sexual intimacy between female clients and male psychotherapists: Masochistic sabotage. Unpublished Ph.D. dissertation, California School of Professional Psychology, 1974.
21. Dahlberg, C. Sexual contact between patient and therapist. *Contemp. Psychoanal.* 6:107–124, 1970.
22. Bergman, I. *Scenes From a Marriage.* Tr. by A. Blair. New York: Pantheon Books, 1974.
23. Boas, C. V. E. The doctor–patient relationship. *J. Sex Res.* 2:215–218, 1966.
24. Moyer, L. What obstetrical journal advertising tells about doctors and women. *Birth Family J.* 2:111–116, 1975.
25. Kardener, S., Fuller, M., and Mensh, I. A survey of physician's attitudes and practices regarding erotic and non-erotic contact with patients. *Am. J. Psychiatry* 130:1077–1081, 1973.
26. Perry, J. A. Physicians' erotic and nonerotic physical involvement with patients. *Am. J. Psychiatry* 133:838–840, 1976.
27. Minutes of Northern California Psychiatric Society Committee on Women, 1975–1976.
28. Report of the Task Force on Sex Bias and Sex-role Stereotyping in Psychotherapeutic Practice. American Psychological Association, April 1975.

Sexual Misconduct by Psychiatrists

The Ethical and Clinical Dilemma of Confidentiality

25

ALAN A. STONE

During the past decade there has been an increase in malpractice suits, ethical complaints, and even criminal charges against psychiatrists for sexual abuse of patients.[1] When a psychiatrist is publicly exposed because of such abusive conduct, it often turns out that a substantial number of his or her colleagues acknowledge (usually in confidence) that they had long known of this unethical conduct. Rarely do these colleagues recognize that they may have failed in their own ethical responsibilities. Section 2 of APA's annotated *Principles of Medical Ethics*[2] directs us to "strive to expose those physicians deficient in character or competence." The sexual abuse of patients is an egregious manifestation of deficiencies in character and competence.[2] Yet standing in the way of this affirmative ethical duty to expose such physicians is the equally important obligation to protect the confidentiality of patients.

The psychiatrist has usually heard about his or her colleagues' sexual misconduct from patients in the course of therapy, during consultations, and, perhaps even more often, from other psychiatrists who share such information with the expectation of collegial confidentiality. Often this information is in the form of vague rumors or even gossip. Rarely is there what could be considered well-documented evidence. Thus on the one hand the psychiatrist typically has only hearsay knowledge and on the other hand he or she is bound by section 4 of the *Principles*,[2] which requires us to "safeguard patient confidences within the constraints of the law." Given these limitations, it is easier to do nothing. Even when one does recognize the often ignored affirmative duty to "expose" such a colleague, one often feels helpless to do anything about it. Doing nothing, then, can become the accepted norm of professional behavior, while taking action to expose a colleague can become the deviant exception to

Reprinted from *American Journal of Psychiatry* 140(2):195–197, 1982. Copyright© 1982 by the American Psychiatric Association. Reprinted by permission.

this norm. Whatever the reasons for this collective failure to act, in retrospect it creates the appearance of a "conspiracy of silence." Critics, for instance, charge that the ethical duty of confidentiality to the patient is used hypocritically to cloak the offending therapist, that psychiatrists are more responsive to the requirements of professional etiquette and to each other than to their professional responsibility to patients, and that the canons of ethics protect the profession and not the patient.[3]

Whether or not such criticisms are deserved, it is clear that physicians place a high value on confidentiality, a value which is not limited to patients. Confidentiality is traditional during the investigation of ethical complaints of doctors.[2] Even after an offending physician has been given a fair hearing, exhausted all appeals, and been sanctioned, that result customarily has remained confidential.[2] Although the impulse to protect a colleague's career and sympathetically encourage a rehabilitative process is laudable, the possibility of continued abuse of unsuspecting patients is the potential cost of this customary practice. Nowhere in the canons of ethics is this potential cost confronted, and nowhere is the psychiatrist given guidance as to how to reconcile the conflicting duties of confidentiality and of exposing unethical colleagues.

CONFIDENTIALITY IN PSYCHIATRY

Confidentiality has merited special consideration in psychiatry, not only because it is necessary to protect the privacy of patients but also because an expectation of privacy is essential to protect the process of psychotherapy itself, particularly the intimate process of psychoanalytic therapy. This professional interest has led some psychiatrists to oppose their patients' waivers of confidentiality.[4] Although this opposition has emphasized the patient's interests in confidentiality and the complexities attendant on a fully informed waiver, there is also a professional interest in protecting the therapeutic zone of privacy.[5]

The canons of ethics address these legitimate professional concerns, but when confidentiality becomes an absolute value—a trump that wins out over all other clinical and ethical considerations—we drastically limit our ability to take responsibility for policing our own profession. We fall into a pattern of moral inertia. The annotated *Principles*,[2] of course, are not absolute about confidentiality; they make it clear that a psychiatrist may release confidential information with the patient's authorization after "apprising him/her of the connotations of waiving the privilege of privacy."

The American Psychoanalytic Association's *Principles of Ethics for Psychoanalysts*,[6] in contrast, makes no mention of this alternative. Section

6 states, "Except as required by law, a psychoanalyst may not reveal the confidences entrusted to him." Although section 12 urges the psychoanalyst to "expose without hesitation, in an ethical fashion and through appropriate channels, illegal or unethical conduct of fellow members of the profession," no guidance is given about such a waiver of confidentiality. How does the psychoanalyst resolve the conflict between section 12 and section 6? If we assume that a psychoanalyst has become convinced that a patient has been sexually abused by a colleague, the ethical dilemma is how then to proceed "in an ethical fashion" to expose that colleague's misconduct when that misconduct has become known in a context of confidentiality.

This dilemma is perhaps more common than we generally acknowledge, and it is not just an abstract conflict of two ethical principles. The ethical dilemma is grounded in real clinical problems, which the public and our critics may not fully appreciate. If we examine the ethical dilemma in more detail, the clinical problems will emerge.

The Ethical and Clinical Dilemma

It should be clear to the psychiatrist, if not the psychoanalyst, that the patient can resolve the physician's conflicting ethical duties by waiving confidentiality. At once, however, clinical questions arise. First, whether the psychiatrist should put this burden on the patient is problematic. What is often at issue here is the conviction of the psychoanalytically oriented psychiatrist that to focus on his or her own ethical dilemma with a patient will disrupt the transference-countertransference, distort the therapeutic process, and give the therapist's concerns priority over the patient's treatment. All of this runs counter to traditional psychoanalytically oriented training. Thus, for understandable and professionally legitimate reasons, psychoanalytically oriented psychiatrists treating a patient who has been sexually abused by a previous therapist may put off raising the ethical problem. In that delay the decision to do nothing may become the inevitable result.

More is at stake, however, than technical considerations. In the example of the patient who is believed to have had sex with her previous therapist, the ethically responsible psychiatrist cannot go forward in any useful way without the patient's becoming involved in substantiating the ethical complaint. Such patients in my experience often feel guilty, humiliated, and ashamed. Their feelings are not unlike those of a woman who has been subjected to an incestuous relationship with her father. The sexual activity has taken place in the context of a "father transference," and the woman may not have worked through those transference feelings and what they mean to her. She may be bewildered and uncertain, still in a sense loving the therapist and clinging to the notion that the therapist really loved her. These are not easy feelings to sort out. Just as with incest, once the line of taboo has been crossed the ordinary categories of human emotion seem blurred and confused. Even if the patient now condemns her therapist-seducer, there is the problem of what kind of and how much punishment she wants to exact and how she feels about making this private matter—including her own sexual activities—public.

Those of us who, on the one hand, have traditional training in psychoanalytic therapy and, on the other hand, are trying to help a patient cope with all of these conflicting emotions are understandably hesitant to push the ethical problem. Furthermore, there can be no doubt that pursuing any kind of ethical or legal complaint will involve the patient in a major real-life commitment. Her credibility may be challenged, and she must endure in the face of adversarial confrontation and procedural delay in order to accomplish anything. All this must be clearly explained to the patient if she is to make a knowing waiver of confidentiality. Clearly much more is at stake for the patient than for the psychiatrist who is impelled to make an ethical complaint. Even the psychiatrist runs the risk of being labeled "judgmental" or a "troublemaker" by some colleagues.

Some patients, of course, will refuse to waive confidentiality even when the psychiatrist does present the ethical issue. How much then should the therapist press the patient and try to convince her that she should waive confidentiality and join the psychiatrist in taking this burdensome step? Some psychiatrists, including even some psychoanalysts, now believe that it is therapeutically important for sexually abused women to act. The real-world confrontation is considered a crucial therapeutic parameter for such a woman to work through and master the trauma of this sort of experience. These therapists see no conflict between clinical and ethical objectives. Rather, they would claim it is central to the therapeutic alliance and to a beneficial outcome. They would minimize all of the therapeutic reasons for caution and neutrality described above. Of course, they also recognize that the patient will need considerable emotional support and are prepared to supply it, just as they would with a rape victim.[7] They would argue that the failure to take such action limits the value of any insight therapy, including psychoanalysis.

A POSSIBLE SOLUTION

There is insufficient evidence to choose between these two clinical approaches on empirical grounds. But it is quite clear that traditional approaches may lead to an aggregate failure of ethical responsibility. Ingenious psychoanalytically oriented clinicians have devised sensible procedures to balance these seemingly contradictory approaches. The therapist–administrator split,[8] whatever its limitations, may be a technical procedure particularly applicable in these situations. The therapist who is convinced that a patient has been victimized can suggest to the patient that they both discuss the situation with a consultant (the administrator). If the patient agrees, thereafter the consultant would assume responsibility for ensuring a knowing waiver of confidentiality. The patient and consultant can press appropriate ethical and legal remedies, while the therapist and patient can remain in a traditional therapeutic relationship if that seems desirable. This step of consultation will not guarantee that an ethical complaint is made; the patient may still decide in favor of privacy and confidentiality. Even more commonly in my experience, the patient may remain ambivalent, hurt, and angry but may not want to harm the career or the marriage of the unethical psychiatrist. The consultation may serve only as an abreaction to an authority figure.

Nonetheless, enlisting a consultant removes some of the traditional inertia. It allows someone who is selected as a consultant because he or she is knowledgeable and skilled about legal and ethical procedures to discuss the matter realistically with the patient. Such consultants could be designated by local psychoanalytic societies and by APA district branches. To use such consultants is an ethically responsible step for the therapist to take that violates no ethical principle. Indeed, section 9 of the American Psychoanalytic Association's *Principles*[6] and section 5 of APA's annotated *Principles*[2] encourage consultation, although neither explicitly recognizes that consultation should be used for ethical problems of this nature. Unless convinced that it is contrary to the patient's best interest, the consultant, in my personal opinion, should feel free to encourage the patient to participate in some real-world action (ethical, disciplinary, or legal) against the unethical psychiatrist and offer to assist in that action.

There are also several less drastic measures a consultant might take. For example, with the patient's consent he or she might notify the offending psychiatrist that a consultation has taken place, urge the psychiatrist to seek treatment if that seems appropriate, and warn him or her about the possible consequences of continued sexual abuses. The offending psychiatrist will at least be on notice that a consultation has taken place and that a concerned and knowledgeable colleague has become involved. This procedure by no means resolves all problems, but it is preferable to the present appearance of moral inertia. The use of a consultant in this role will not be achieved without complications. The problem of split transference, with the patient playing off one psychiatrist against the other, may occur. The pursuit of ethical or legal redress may undermine the significance of therapy and the therapeutic alliance. If the patient is married or has close relatives, either the consultant or the therapist will have to deal with their involvement. If legal redress is sought, the lawyer–client relationship may add further complications; in my experience, however, a sensitive lawyer rapidly takes over the responsibilities of the consultant and encourages the patient's therapeutic relationship with her psychiatrist.

The vast majority of psychiatrists are ethical and competent. They are deeply troubled by the unethical conduct of the very few who sexually abuse and mistreat patients and discredit the profession. We may feel that these offending colleagues need treatment rather than punishment, but all too often we take no action at all because of our conflicting ethical responsibilities. We owe it to ourselves and our patients to confront publicly the conflicting ethical responsibilities we experience privately. Like our patients, once we openly identify our problems, perhaps we can begin to find more effective ways to deal with them responsibly.

REFERENCES

1. Trent C. L., Muhl W. P.: Professional liability insurance and the American psychiatrist. *Am. J. Psychiatry* 132:1312–1314, 1975.
2. American Psychiatric Association: *The Principles of Medical Ethics with Annotations Especially Applicable to Psychiatry.* Washington, D.C., APA, 1981.
3. Norton M. L.: Ethics in medicine and law—standards and conflicts. *Medical Trial Technique Quarterly,* Spring 1980, p. 377.
4. *Caesar v. Mountanos,* 542 F 2d 1064 (9th Cir. 1976).
5. Appelbaum P.: Confidentiality in psychiatric treatment, in *Psychiatry 1982: The American Psychiatric Association Annual Review.* Edited by Grinspoon L. Washington, D.C., American Psychiatric Press, 1982.
6. *Principles of Ethics for Psychoanalysts and Provisions for Implementation of the Principles of Ethics for Psychoanalysts.* New York, American Psychoanalytic Association, 1975.
7. Hilberman E. C.: *The Rape Victim.* New York, Basic Books, 1976.
8. Stanton A., Schwartz M.: *The Mental Hospital.* New York, Basic Books, 1954.